Jene Halsey

AS I KNEW THEM

"THE DREAMLAND OF OTHER DAYS"

AS I KNEW THEM

PRESIDENTS AND POLITICS
FROM GRANT TO COOLIDGE

BY

HENRY L. STODDARD

*"Great men have been among us; hands that penned
And tongues that uttered wisdom; better none."*
—WORDSWORTH

HARPER & BROTHERS PUBLISHERS
NEW YORK AND LONDON
1927

TO THOSE
IN EVERY DEPARTMENT
OF NEWSPAPER-MAKING WITH WHOM,
THROUGH HALF A CENTURY, I HAVE
HAD THE PRIVILEGE OF SHARING
THE TRIALS AND TRIUMPHS OF A
GREAT CALLING, THIS BOOK
IS DEDICATED
IN THE SPIRIT OF CORDIAL
FELLOWSHIP

CONTENTS

Contents

Contents

Contents

Contents

Contents

Contents

Contents

Contents

Contents

Contents

Contents

ILLUSTRATIONS

Illustrations

FOREWORD

THESE reminiscences are not an attempt to write history or to make revelations. History is for other pens than mine, and revelations for those who may feel justified in making them. The confidences reposed in me remain confidences despite the lapse of time, and the passing on of the men chiefly concerned. Those that possess lasting value will find their way into the political annals of the country through other persons authorized and competent to present them. The rest will be no loss except to the curious.

The reader is on notice, therefore, that *As I Knew Them* is just a review of the period from Grant to Coolidge based upon the writer's impressions as he has moved along with the years. It has the limits of one man's observations and the fault of human prejudices.

At least twice during the writing I would have abandoned the task were I not held to it by my belief that we should not live wholly in the present, that we should not drop out of mind the men who in other years played an important part in the development of our nation, each according to his light. I have endeavored to recall and interpret some of those men.

Half a century is a long span,—too long to do more in one volume than touch the "high spots" and give them your individual interpretation for whatever it may be worth.

I have found that memory plays queer pranks. Men and events familiar to me in my early newspaper career, then seemingly destined to endure as important and historic figures, now come to mind in dim, shadowy outline.

Age-yellowed newspaper files, old pictorial weeklies with their savage cartoons, back-shelf books with their half-forgotten stories of other days have acted like great sounding-boards hurling back at me voices long silent—the well-remembered tones, the dramatic gestures, the fervor of men whose sturdy partisanship excited multitudes.

"Swinging 'round the circle" with candidates for President or Governor, studying the tumult of conventions for the one

Foreword

real note, trailing political "spellbinders" to estimate their influence on voters of different localities, listening to the ambitions of the "ins" and the pleas of the "outs"—what a picture is recalled as your mind turns toward such a panorama of the past! It would be a masterpiece if one could paint it on canvas or put it in words that would adequately describe it.

Many of the men of whom I write lived in a period of tense feeling and strenuous pioneer effort, and their judgments took on the deep color of their time. We must keep that fact in mind as we consider their careers and their utterances. Until Roosevelt entered the White House, every President since Lincoln, except Cleveland, had served in the Civil War. Almost down to Roosevelt's day, also, most of the leaders in one or the other House of Congress, if not in both Houses, had worn the Blue or the Gray in the fierce struggle of the two sections.

Their places in the councils of the nation are now held by their sons and grandsons, and the gracious hand of Time, smoothing out the passionate lines of civil war, long ago extended its beneficent influence over a north, south, east and west that rejoice in one loyalty to our common country, in one hope for a common destiny.

Only to those who, like myself, have lived through that era can the reality of a nation unified by the blood of its men and the silent heroism of its women appear so truly like a glorious vision of triumphant sacrifice.

My newspaper career kept me in the thick of events, among those who had much to do with this achievement, and I am led to the opinions I express and to the picture I have in mind of the future of our country by all I have seen and heard.

As quickly as stage hands shift the scenery for another act, and with the same definite result, the World War made our own conflict and its fading prejudices seem as remote as though a century had elapsed. The curtain rose on a new scene— with its own problems, its own perils, and its own commanding figures. Those new figures are to play rôles as decisive in

Foreword

our nation's destiny as were the rôles played so well by others in days gone by—but henceforth the world is the stage on which they must appear.

Our isolation in the Western Hemisphere has made it possible for us to build a nation in our own way; we have needed no alliances, and our spirit has been against bargainings and intrigue. Our motives have always been written on open pages for the whole world to read. We must not abandon that wise policy, but that does not mean that we should go through this world heedless of other peoples. I see no peril more dangerous to us than the delusion that there is greatness in loneliness. No nation, no individual, standing alone is great, or remains powerful for long. It can satisfy only its own selfishness, and selfishness breeds its own inescapable penalties.

America can no longer live within its continental boundaries, or merely pick and choose when, where and how it shall go outside of them.

Now and hereafter we must think and act in world terms. New tests as a nation are ahead of us. Strive as we may to turn back the currents now flowing so swiftly and persistently across the Atlantic and the Pacific, carrying problems of other peoples to our shores, we shall not be able to prevail against them more than we prevail against the tides of the two oceans.

The America of today has responsibilities that if met with proper spirit will be the glory of the America of to-morrow.

We face an era in which example and intimacy are to be the potent influences for better understanding. A more candid, more dependable force than statesmanship is bringing the nations of the world into relations more secure than written treaties—the force of the airplane, the wireless, the radio and travel. The great beacon lights that now illumine the path to safety on landing fields are destined to displace the camp-fires of contending armies and the cheers of welcoming multitudes everywhere give more promise of peace everlasting than any roar of cannon the world has ever heard.

Foreword

Commander Richard E. Byrd's flight across the Atlantic in June, 1927, had, I firmly believe, no incident more significant than the reply of the lighthouse keeper on the coast of France when thanked for having sheltered the wrecked crew until dawn. He said he desired no thanks; he did it because of his affection for America!

Wealth and power have come to us in appalling and perilous abundance. Their safety to us, their real value, lies in the use we make of them. How are we to use them?

To make America envied? Feared?

I hope not.

The America that I have known for more than threescore years, if it is to be true to the conception of its founders, must be zealous for a kindlier, more lasting place in the world than riches can purchase or power command. Other nations, once wealthy and powerful, have been envied and feared—and have perished. No nation of all the past down to our own times has put righteousness above covetousness in dealing with others less strong. America, giant America, must do that.

Two years ago I toured the world. Everywhere—in Europe, Japan, China, India, Africa—I met the inquiry, What is it about America that makes it possible for so many of its people to be happy and prosperous? Who rules so wisely and so kindly?

My answer was, just the people themselves.

In every country I visited there were emperor's palaces and castles, as well as forts, soldiers and battleships as symbols of might and of the right of might to decide the fate of peoples. It was impossible to make others understand why it was different with us—why the calm and simplicity of a log cabin in Kentucky and of a modest country house among the oaks and poplars of Mount Vernon inspired and held the loyalty of more than a hundred million people.

When men and women told me of the America they had in mind and of their intense desire to see it and become part

Foreword

of it, their faces glowed as though thrilled by the thought that there really is a land where opportunity awaits effort, and content is possible to every man.

"Show us the way!" is the world-wide appeal. "Show us the way!"

We *must* respond. America must not become merely another nation patterned after so many that have been deaf to that human cry, and whose power has served only the vanity and greed of ambitious rulers. We have not yet responded. Unfortunately, today the voice of America is regarded by the world as the voice of a critic, not of a friend, as the voice of a nation made pretentious and superior by sudden wealth.

I could not reply to the charge frequently made in my hearing in Europe last summer that in the past seven years our country had contributed too little to those finer sentiments that must prevail among nations if peace on earth is to abide.

Our gold is all we have offered other peoples burdened with war's terrific sacrifices. Gold has its necessary uses, but our failure to offer with it that "one touch of nature that makes the whole world kin" seems to be putting us in the attitude of a nation having all the callousness of great wealth to the fate of others. That, of course, is not the real America— the America that Americans know. It must not be the America that the world knows.

In our day of strength, America needs, above all, to be humble. I cannot help recalling the prayer uttered by McKinley's mother the night he left his home in Canton, Ohio, for Washington to be inaugurated President: "I prayed God to keep my boy humble!" That should be the prayer and the hope of every American—keep us as a nation humble, keep us in sympathy with every effort, wherever made, however feeble, to put into every life the inspiration of opportunity, the hope of a better day.

I would have America, my America, endure by right rather than perish, as other nations have perished, by reliance upon might.

Foreword

I would have "the light that never was on land or sea" shine round the world from our shores like a blazing beacon from a mountain top.

I would have America neither feared nor envied for its power or its wealth, but loved because its power is the moral power of fine purpose, because its wealth is the wealth of a helpful, understanding bond underwriting the brotherhood of man, because its example is the example of a nation dedicated with genuine, passionate devotion to those principles that place the welfare of the many above privilege for the few, thus providing a firm foundation upon which to rest human hopes.

Who cannot look with pride and hope to such a future for our America when a great military commander like Grant could write as President in his last message to Congress:

> "Rather do I believe that our Great Maker is preparing the world in His own good time to become one nation, speaking one language and when armies and navies will no longer be required."

Or, when we read Roosevelt's words:

> "We here in America hold in our hands the hope of the world, the fate of the coming years."

Or these words from Woodrow Wilson:

> "We are done with provincialism and we have got to have a view now and a horizon as wide as the world itself. America has a great cause which is not confined to the American continent. It is the cause of humanity itself."

Or, finally, these words from Calvin Coolidge:

> "We are not going to be able to avoid meeting the world and bearing our part of the burdens of the world. I desire my country to meet them without evasion and without fear, in an upright, downright, square American way."

Our past justifies such a future; more, it demands it. It is a trust bequeathed us by the men who founded as well as by those who developed the nation now become so great. Their

Foreword

careers and their sacrifices reveal their determination to build an America that would seek its strength in the welfare of its people, demanding nothing from other nations but respect and nothing from its citizens but loyalty.

That was the moving spirit back of the men of '76, when they pledged "to each other our lives, our fortunes and our sacred honor"—of the men of '61, and finally of the men of the marvellous period since '65 about whom I write.

With weaknesses and mistakes that prejudice may exaggerate or favor modify, the leaders whose achievements are the nation's history gave their best to public service. They led no armies in a tyrant's cause, they sought no victories but those of peace and justice; though their opinions differed widely and intensely, they struck a common chord and found common ground in their patriotic endeavor to further the aspirations of their country.

The story of their careers is inspiring—not the less so because you may have only condemnation for the policies, methods and personality of one or the other. A study of both sides—particularly of the side with which you have less sympathy—always leads to better understanding. It is the whole, and not a part, that counts.

I realize that these pages are a too brief summary of a half century that has no equal in world history, but if they should persuade the reader to seek to know more intimately the men who have shaped, as well as some who are still shaping, our nation's destinies, I shall feel repaid for my effort.

In confirming my recollections, and particularly in the interpretation of recent events, I have had the generous aid of many associates in my newspaper work of earlier days. Friends in public life have also cooperated. To each and all of them I herewith make grateful acknowledgment. Sherwin Lawrence Cook, of Boston, and George L. Edmunds gave me the benefit of research, for which I am thankful. The staffs of the New York Public Library and the New York Society Library, have also been invaluable aids, particularly Mr.

Foreword

Frank Weitenkampf. My secretary through thirty years, Mrs. S. C. Rosensweig, has as always loyally carried the burden of detail.

The standard reference books and histories covering the period have been freely consulted too. Even those silent repositories of fact, however, cannot deprive memory of its license to wander far afield now and then. I ask the reader, therefore, to accept these pages not as an authenticated record of the times, but merely as the impressions of an observer travelling the great highway.

Henry L. Stoddard.

Mayfair House
New York City, 1927.

AS I KNEW THEM

AS I KNEW THEM

CHAPTER I

THE DREAMLAND OF OTHER DAYS

"You Have Been Coming Here Longer Than Any Man I Know"—A Boy's Vision of His Future—Printer, Proof-reader and Reporter— The Country Weekly and Its Place of Confidence—Chance Makes Opportunity to Cover Half a Century of Politics.

"MR. STODDARD," said Irwin Hood Hoover, Chief Usher at the White House, as I entered it one afternoon in response to President Coolidge's invitation to luncheon, "you have been coming here longer than any man I know, and I have been here since Harrison's inauguration."

Hoover's words startled me.

"Is it as bad as that?" I asked.

"Yes," he replied, "that's about right."

. . . . . how noiseless falls the foot of Time!

A few hours later, on the Congressional Limited out of Washington, a former United States Senator, a Congressman and I drifted into discussion of the Presidents since Lincoln each of us had personally known; we endeavored to agree on which of them had grown while in office and which had not. We differed widely in opinion at the outset, but before the journey to New York City was over we found ourselves not far apart; partisan and personal prejudice gave way, slowly but steadily.

That train talk, and Hoover's reminder of the flight of years, are responsible for this book.

My mind thus started on its wandering went back to the time almost half a century ago when, as political correspondent of the Philadelphia Press, in the field and also at Washington, I had my earliest contact with national party leaders.

I

This intimacy, begun in 1884, has never ceased. In the presidential campaign of that year I had my first political assignments of importance. I was sent to Buffalo to look into Grover Cleveland's early career; that task accomplished I was assigned to travel with James G. Blaine, and the closing weeks of the campaign I spent at Republican national headquarters in New York City.

In the years from that day to the present, I have met either casually or on closer terms every President since Lincoln except Garfield, as well as most of the national leaders of both political parties, especially those in the East.

THE COUNTRY PRINT SHOP

It may not be out of place here at the outset to write briefly of myself and to say that I began my career, if such it may be called, as a typesetter on the New York Tribune. I have no recollection of any other desire than to be a printer, reporter and editor. It was the one ambition of my boyhood and it has remained my one ambition through life. No public office has ever held the fascination for me that an editor's desk possesses, no work has had the thrill of a newspaper correspondent's duties "covering" a great event.

In boyhood, my vacations from the public schools of New York City were often spent in Hudson, Columbia County, New York, where my grandfather's little printing shop on the main street was to me the most interesting place in the world. In 1778, now 150 years ago, my grandfather, four generations back, had trekked over the Connecticut border and had started the Hudson Register, continuously published since then, and now a prosperous daily. The newspaper was transferred to other ownership years ago, but the printing shop was retained.

In that family printing shop, as a boy, I learned the boxes of the printer's case—that is, the divisions out of which each letter of the alphabet is picked by the typesetter. All the men of four generations of my family had stood in their youth in front of the same dust-covered cases, setting type for, and publishing, a monthly magazine called the Rural Repository, one of the earliest publications in the country to be illustrated.

Later, in the office of the Eastern State Journal, at White Plains, New York, a weekly newspaper then owned by an uncle, I undertook during school vacations to gather and write village news paragraphs, to set type, and to "feed" a Washington hand-press.

Best of all, I learned there the place of confidence and power held by the country weekly. May it never decrease! I gained a respect for and interest in those modest publications that increases with every year of my life.

DREAMING OF LIFE'S WORK

My keenest delight was to read thoroughly all the "exchanges"—that is, the weekly newspapers published in other villages and county seats, near and remote. When other persons were too busy with their own work to be concerned about my doings, I would often sneak into the partitioned corner of the composing room set aside as the editor's sanctum.

Seated in the editor's cane-bottomed swivel chair, tilting it far back, and with my feet on the desk, assuming as closely as I could his pose of serene and lordly ease, with country weeklies scattered thickly on the floor about me, I would dream dreams of editorial triumphs that could not have been dreamier or more alluring had they been wreathed in the smoke of a favorite cigar spiralling above one's head. Horace Greeley was not my goal. The man who in my mind had the world at his feet was the editor of a country weekly!

Restless to get really into newspaper work, I had no sooner been graduated from Public School 49 in New York City, thus gaining the right to enter the College of the City of New York, than I found a position as a beginner in the composing room of the New York Tribune. Diploma from my school in hand, I was now eager to get to the types (not linotypes in those days). I reported for work at six o'clock that night, thrilled with ambition to win my way some day to the editorship of a county-seat newspaper.

Here those imperceptible currents that affect one's life seem to have changed mine. On the Tribune I was soon made a proof-reader, and "teamed-up" with dear kindly "Old Man" Barlow of Horace Greeley vintage and resemblance. I attribute my keen desire to know public men and to study public affairs largely to the fact that, night after night, I read with Barlow the proofs of Whitelaw Reid's editorial leader, Z. K. White's Washington dispatches, and George W. Smalley's letters or cables from London. Cables, in those days, came across the Atlantic as mere skeletons on which the flesh of language was hung in the Tribune office by a jovial and talented Irishman named O'Dwyer.

I was impressed and inspired in those proof-reading days by the evidences of all that those great writers seemed to know of conditions and events, and the important personages, high in position, they discussed with such intimate knowledge. Could I ever get to know even a single one of the great men they knew so well?

I made up my mind to try—just how to try I did not know.

CHANCE, AS USUAL, MAKES OPPORTUNITY

Chance solved the problem for me as it has solved it for so many. Ordinarily one would regard New York City as the place of opportunity. In a small way, I happened to be of service to Charles Emory Smith, then the famous editor of the Philadelphia Press. That led to my joining the staff of that newspaper, and a year or so later I was able to satisfy my longing to write politics and mix with politicians.

The "Press" was then known for its brilliant editorial staff, among whom were Dr. Talcott Williams, beloved as "T. W." by all who know him, and Bradford Merrill, in recent years the able editorial director of the Hearst news-papers.

Do not think that I achieved the distinction of writing politics, as I then regarded it and still regard it, without months of "watchful waiting." I did not. The details of that wait for the great event are of no interest to others; sufficient that at last, when least expected, the day dawned when I was the proud and happy correspondent of the Phila-delphia Press "in the field." I was assigned to interview Congressman Samuel J. Randall, then the Democratic Speaker of the House of Representatives!

Randall was reluctant to talk, but I kept at him, finally telling him it was my first political assignment and I did not want to fail. Randall was a high tariff Democrat, and it was important to get his opinion on pending legislation. My recollection is that I got enough from him to have it regarded in the office as a "beat."

"And so far—far into the night," as the talented Briggs puts it with such intimate truth in his understanding cartoons.

CHAPTER II

POLITICS AND POLITICIANS

Companionships and Friendships That Are Fine Examples of Loyalty—No University So Trains You To Know Your Own Levels—How Lincoln Was Nominated—All Presidents Represent The Conflict Of Politicians—Clay, Blaine, Bryan—The Stump-Speaker's Silent Foe —Women And The Radio In Politics.

IT has always seemed to me the duty of newspaper writers, whether correspondents or editors, to seek the men in control of government, or of large enterprises, and to talk with them, when possible, more or less intimately—"off the record," as lawyers say—the better to understand and appraise their purposes. In such discussions you come to know the real man, who is not always so accurately reflected in what you read and hear of him.

In my own case I know that meeting the responsible leaders of the two political parties through so many years has been a helpful experience and a privilege for which I am grateful. From them I got a broad and ever new outlook on the country as a whole, on the interplay of contending forces in it,—the forces of business, of sentiment and of prejudice that merge into the composite life of the nation.

The companionships too have been most enjoyable; many of them ripened into friendships which have shown me inspiring examples of loyalty, courage and honor among rivals. Out of the passion and tumult of conventions, Legislatures and Congress I have learned to respect the opinions and motives of others, and to withhold judgment until certain, very certain, that prejudice is out of mind, so far as it may be possible to exclude it.

6

As I Knew Them

What a schooling there is in such an experience! It carries on the lessons of the little red schoolhouse now disappearing much too rapidly from our countryside,—lessons in those realities and simplicities of life that give solid backing to those who will learn them. No university so trains you in understanding the bigness and the littleness of others or so holds you at your own proper level.

Every human instinct—whether good or evil, courageous or cowardly, fair or false, selfish or unselfish—is in action when the men of politics gather to make party platforms and to achieve individual ambitions. The struggle to hold or to secure a hold on the largest body of public opinion, to find and nominate the candidate who best expresses and typifies the mind of the people, requires the same resourceful genius, if it is to succeed, as does the conduct of a great industrial enterprise—or even war.

From that fierce crucible flows ultimately the nation's leadership in men and policies. Its results are the best evidence we have of the progress of the world, for if government does not advance nothing does.

Disappointment with some result in legislation or in candidates leads us at times to denounce those in responsible position and irritably to question the wisdom and ultimate success of our experiment in government. Later, how frequently we see with clearer vision and realize that, when measures are undertaken on the scale of a continent, the meeting of many minds is a more dependable guide to the country's needs than the judgment of one mind, however wise that mind may be.

HOW LINCOLN WAS NOMINATED

Take for illustration that outstanding example of the work of politicians—the nomination in 1860 of the crude and little-

7

known Abraham Lincoln over the polished and widely-known statesman, William H. Seward. At the moment, the country was staggered by the news from the Republican national convention. Seward rejected! Salmon P. Chase rejected! Lincoln nominated! It seemed incredible.

Yet who today would reverse the unexpected verdict of that gathering of politicians?

Picture that historic convention assembled out in Chicago in the flimsy frame building called "The Wigwam."

One name easily led all others as the man to nominate— William H. Seward, former Governor of New York, twice-chosen Senator, the national leader, if such there was at the time, of the Republican party. Talented, distinguished, experienced in statesmanship, he loomed a towering figure among the candidates. Two-thirds of the delegates were claimed for him in advance.

Who will attempt to fathom the influence that led those politicians to turn from wealth, prestige, and experience and nominate a Lincoln over a Seward? As though inspired much as the founders of our Republic seem to have been, the delegates sensed in the nation's plight the need of a candidate who, to use an expression then common, "belonged" to the people.

Has monarchy ever scored such a triumph for mankind as democracy then scored—as politicians scored?

WE SHOULD BE PROUD OF OUR PRESIDENTS

Washington is the one man ever chosen as our nation's chief Executive by unanimous consent. All of our other twenty-eight Presidents through a century-and-a-half have come to us out of the same conflict of politicians in caucus or convention as did Lincoln.

They represented different types of citizens, and came from different stations in life, each reflecting at the moment the keenness of the politician searching for the man who meant

"THE WIGWAM"—WHERE LINCOLN WAS NOMINATED IN 1860

THE THINNING LINE OF ZOUAVES, IN THEIR "WOOLEN TOGS"—SEE PAGE 51

to the people just what they had in mind. If a mistake was made it took only four years to correct it—a brief time in the life of a nation. This fluidity at the head of our nation, this changing point of view with each succeeding President, gives every element in our national life opportunity to express itself. On the other hand, it is an influence tending to keep the President's thought directed toward public opinion.

Though not all the men who have occupied the White House have been of strong character and purpose, it is an inspiring tribute to representative government that as a people we are able to say that the highest ambition of every President has been to leave the country better off because he had served it. Even James Buchanan may be so classed, though his timid attitude during the last year of his term amounted almost to surrender of national sovereignty.

Surely we have reason to be grateful when we contrast the course of our Presidents with the experience other nations have had with their rulers. Not one of the twenty-nine we have had in 150 years exercised the great power of his office with thought of a personal dynasty or indulged in sighs for new worlds to conquer.

The nation made up of thirteen "original" States has been extended from the Alleghenies to the Pacific coast, and then beyond. In every instance, beginning with Jefferson, this has been done at the urging of a President. Though each expansion meant the addition of an empire, territorially, it was his country's greatness, not his own, that moved the man at the head to action. Thomas Jefferson, faced as President with the responsibility of decision, put aside his earlier antagonism to expansion and negotiated the "Louisiana Purchase." The territory embraced in the transfer was larger than that of any of the Empires of Europe, except Russia, and more remote at the time than any of our ocean possessions today; yet Jefferson, rather than see it forever under foreign sovereignty, did not hesitate to abandon his former opinions.

As I Knew Them

Only one President has ever stood against expansion. Grover Cleveland refused to permit Hawaii, at its own request, to come under our flag; the islands would not be ours today if his will had prevailed. Even Woodrow Wilson bought the Virgin Islands in 1917.

CLAY, BLAINE, BRYAN

While we have had no imperialists in the White House, it is equally true that none of the men who finally became President have represented only the hurrahs of the roadside.

Alluring and deceptive as those hurrahs always are to ambitious men, they have seldom melded down as majority votes in our Presidential ballot-box. The careers of Henry Clay, James G. Blaine and William J. Bryan are outstanding demonstrations that the path of popularity, when travelled too rapidly, does not always lead to the presidential chair.

In his day, each of those men had a following so loyal and so enthusiastic that it seemed to represent a majority of the people. Clay was the "Mill-boy of the Slashes," Blaine was the "Plumed Knight"; to his supporters Bryan was "The Peerless One," while his opponents called him "The Boy Orator of the Platte." Those three men, or their supporters, struggled through three or four national campaigns for nomination or election as President; Bryan was the most successful in achieving the indorsement of his party.

Accepting as valid Bryan's statement that he did not seek to be named in 1912, the record stands that he was nominated on the three occasions when he desired to be. Clay and Blaine, each denied nomination in two or three conventions, succeeded in being nominated only to be defeated in the election.

Yet no candidates ever had more enthusiastic supporters than had Clay, Blaine and Bryan; no candidates ever seemed to develop in their campaigns greater evidences of popularity. Bryan of course would have been a tragedy in the White House. He came perilously near being one as Secretary of

State. Clay and Blaine, however, were statesmen well qualified to be at the head of the nation.

THE WARWICKS OF OUR POLITICS

Nevertheless the Presidency was not for any of them. The fate that denied it to them gave them the consolation of decisive power with their party to nominate others; in recognition of that power each served as Secretary of State in the Cabinet of the President he had named. Henry Clay's support made John Quincy Adams President in 1825; the Blaine influence nominated Garfield in 1880 and Harrison in 1888; Bryan forced Wilson's nomination in 1912. President-makers they could be but not Presidents.

YEP, BRYAN'S GOING TO SAN FRANCISCO!

Clay is the only man of the three who continued through an entire term with his President; also the only one who did not oppose his chief's policies in the subsequent convention. Blaine contested Harrison's nomination in 1892; Bryan was elected delegate from Nebraska in 1920 on a platform opposed to Wilson's League of Nations.

BOURKE COCKRAN'S WRONG ESTIMATE

Before leaving the subject of "hurrah" candidates, let me recall to many readers the Bourke Cockran speech in the

1892 Democratic convention. I listened to Cockran when, as spokesman for Tammany Hall, he declared that if Cleveland were made the Democratic candidate he could not be elected, adding "He is popular every day in the year but election day."

That sentence, in a hectic speech, brought great applause, but it was not true. It should have been reversed.

Cleveland never excited the emotional support that characterizes a hurrah campaign. His popularity was expressed silently in votes on election day. In that respect it was in extreme contrast with the kind of popularity enjoyed by the three men I have just discussed. In his three campaigns, Cleveland led each time in the popular vote, and twice had an electoral college majority.

THE STUMP-SPEAKER'S SILENT FOE

Year after year, as I study election returns, I am impressed more and more by the number of citizens who do a lot of uninfluenced home-thinking before voting for President or even for candidates seeking far less important offices. Such voters are not so numerous as they should be, but my observation leads me to believe that their number is increasing—and it should.

The impassioned rhetoric of the stump-speaker loses much of its persuasive power crossing the threshold of the home. There it faces the higher test of calm analysis and second thought; there it has to battle on higher levels than the blare of bands and the emotions of the crowd; there in the future, in my opinion, it will have to meet a foe of increasing potentiality—the motives of the family as voiced in the quiet of the fireside by wife, mother or daughter.

Women are individual; they have little of the crowd-mind such as controls most men; at least in public affairs. The ballot is yet too new to women for this independent thought to be shown, but it seems to me certain to come. Probably no other agency is hastening it so much as the radio. That marvel of the age has taken the place of the saloon and the corner soap-box as the new centre of political influence—the radio, in the home, with the entire family "listening in." It is the keen rival of the newspaper and the stump-speaker.

TWO CONTRASTS BY RADIO IN 1924

In the years ahead of us there is going to be developed in this way a "silent" vote much more numerous than heretofore and more difficult to analyze in advance; more remote from corruption, from demagogy and partisan control. Two examples may be cited to substantiate this prophecy. In both instances a definite influence was exerted that would have been impossible by any other means.

The first was the radio report of the Democratic national convention in Madison Square Garden in 1924. More than a million people "listened in" on those proceedings day after day. No newspaper could have reported them, no orator could have reviewed them, in the realistic way the radio carried them into so many homes.

It is not necessary for me to dwell upon the effect on the Democratic party. Its disastrous consequences are conceded. Had John W. Davis possessed the popularity of a Wilson and a Roosevelt combined he could not have overcome the blighting effects of that convention; his election was never a possibility.

In contrast was the influence of the radio report of President Coolidge's address the night before election in that same 1924 campaign. The "hook-up" carried his voice to every voter who had a radio receiver. It is impossible to estimate how many hundreds of thousands of people heard him as he dwelt on the patriotism of voting, never once referring to his own candidacy, finally bidding the folks good night, "including my father, up on the Vermont farm, 'listening in'."

That radio speech made votes for Coolidge, everywhere. In one campaign, therefore, we have two instances of decisive radio influence that nothing else could have equalled. The people heard for themselves and acted on their own impressions.

Often enough to be accepted as a factor this "silent" vote emerges from the ballot-box as the surprising feature of the election. It rarely goes to the seemingly "popular man." I regard it even now as a stabilizing influence in our politics. It is a menace to every party machine that becomes defiant with power and also a challenge to too hasty progress with new policies even in the right direction. It wants no short-cut to the millennium. It prefers time to think while on the way.

FASSETT THOUGHT HE COULD DEFY IT

Many a candidate has missed nomination in convention because party leaders were fearful that by reason of his extreme views he could not command that "silent" vote; often candidates have been amazed when receiving election returns, to discover that the voice unheard in the campaign speaks loudest on election day. It is the voice of those who have thought things out with their own best selves.

I remember when in 1891, J. Sloat Fassett, of Elmira, New York, a State Senator and Congressman several terms, demanded of Boss Thomas C. Platt that he be nominated for Governor. Fassett would have made an excellent Governor. He was eloquent, able, and experienced in public affairs, but he was known as a Platt lieutenant; indeed, the personal relations between the two men were almost as close as father and son. Platt demurred. He said to Fassett in my presence at Rochester as the convention assembled: "You're too close to me, Sloat. They call me a boss and the people opposed to me as a party boss would be opposed to you. There are too many voters of that kind for you to risk it this year. Better wait for an issue."

The ambitious Fassett, however, remained unconvinced, so Platt let him have his way. He ran against Roswell P. Flower and was beaten by the "silent" vote from the homes in the rural districts.

CHAPTER III

THE "SWINGS" OF A CAMPAIGN

Fortune Moves Backward And Forward Before Election—Candidates Deluded by Hurrahs—Blaming Others For Their Defeat—The Sherman-Alger Rivalry To "Persuade" Southern Delegates—Many Primaries Are A Contest Of Pocket Books—Every Nominee In A Primary Feels He Is His Own Party Platform.

I ALWAYS study with keen interest the "swings" of a campaign. In almost every contest there are currents of opinion that can be definitely charted as they flow to and from a candidate several times before merging into the mighty stream of settled public opinion. Matthew Stanley Quay, so long the controlling power in Pennsylvania politics, always urged his lieutenants to hold the high waves back until near election day, so as to be able to coast their candidate in on the crest. But such strategy is only for masterful campaigners, as Quay, of course, was.

I have known only a few candidates for public office who were not persuaded as they listened to the final hurrahs of the campaign, that they would win—and the greatest delusion is usually among those having least chance. Candidates for nomination are equally blind to their own fortunes.

I have sat in convention by the side of men who, despite the plain evidence that they were not in the running, confidently believed as the roll-call progressed that the next county or district called—always the next—would turn the tide in their favor. Disappointment as the roll-call proceeds seems only to encourage new hope until the last vote is polled. Never will candidates see defeat so long as it is possible to see anything else. In business and in the professions men usually know their possibilities—seldom in politics.

16

As I Knew Them

John W. Mackay, father of Clarence H. Mackay, was one of the few men I ever met who, while deeply interested in politics, kept a common-sense view of his own relation to it. He was one of the "Bonanza" Kings of the sparsely settled State of Nevada. He spent a great deal of his time around the Hoffman House in New York City.

Of course, this was many years ago. His influence made State officials and national legislators, but he could not be induced himself to accept office. When the Legislature wanted to make him Senator he refused and said: "I would rather be at home in a silver mine in Nevada than out of place in the United States Senate!"

Some degree of courage is required to make such a statement—and to mean it.

THE LOSER OFTEN SCENTS BETRAYAL

More than once I have met men in conventions convinced that the people eagerly demanded their nomination, and who, when not named, blamed their defeat on the disloyalty of party leaders, asserting they had reason to rely upon them for support. Whether that reliance should in fact be called a hope rather than a settled matter is a question; usually it is a hope, for as a rule politicians keep their word. You must have it definitely, however, for "I'll do what I can," means nothing.

I had one example some years ago when a candidate for nomination for the Presidency, smarting under a defeat that came when he seemed close to victory—seemed so to others as well as to himself—told me several weeks after the convention had adjourned that his long friendship with the presiding officer was ended. He said:

"We have been friends for years, but in the chair he proved untrue. He promised our people to recognize us for a motion to recess, provided we showed certain strength on the first two ballots that final day; we showed that strength and more. If we could have forced a recess before another ballot, we

17

had enough help promised to nominate me. The chairman, however, despite his agreement would not see our man when he rose to make the motion. Instead of recognizing him, he hurriedly announced another ballot and directed the Secretary to call the roll. Of course, no motion was in order during roll-call. That cost me the Presidency."

I did not intend to reveal the identity of the candidate and the presiding officer referred to above; but since writing it death has removed the impropriety of doing so—perhaps it has made it a duty. The candidate was General Leonard Wood and the presiding officer was Senator Henry Cabot Lodge. The Harding "drive" was set for the Saturday morning session of the 1920 Republican convention; Wood did not believe there was "staying" strength behind Harding; he was convinced that, if after one or two test ballots that morning he was still holding his column intact, he could arrange to take over a considerable block of Lowden votes. A recess would be necessary to negotiate this transfer, and Wood believed he had Lodge's word to aid him secure the recess.

Later, in Manila, I talked over the convention with General Wood, recalling incidents familiar to both of us. Despite an heroic effort to conceal his disappointment and to make the best of life as he found it, the General carried to his grave the deep wounds of two poignant regrets—Wilson's refusal to permit him to go with our army to France, and Lodge's refusal to allow the motion to recess the Chicago convention.

THE SHERMAN-ALGER RIVALRY

Senator John Sherman, of Ohio, in two conventions a candidate for the Presidency, died believing that in 1888 he was defeated by the loss of Southern colored delegates pledged to him but "persuaded" by the money of Governor Russell A. Alger, of Michigan, to support Alger. He publicly upbraided and never forgave the Michigan man, who really had as

18

much right to Southern delegates, if he could get them, as had Sherman.

In that convention as in many other conventions it was simply a question of who bought Southern delegates best—that is, who bought them last,—the last being the buyer just as the roll-call starts.

No charge of disloyalty was ever made by Sherman against James A. Garfield, however, who was nominated in 1880 by the convention he had addressed in Sherman's behalf. While Sherman acquitted Garfield, as he should have done, he did not acquit half the delegates from his home State of Ohio.

The Buckeye delegates were an unstable lot then, as always. Ohio delegates seldom "stay put"—and they did not with Sherman.

"The only shade that rests on my feeling about Garfield," wrote Sherman, "is that he went to the convention by my selection and comes away with the honor I sought." Thus, Senator Sherman always felt that his Presidential fortunes were unkindly dealt with in two conventions by those upon whom he had relied.

A CONTEST OF POCKET-BOOKS

Twin with campaign hurrahs in furnishing candidates false foundation for hope is the extravagant use of money—probably it is responsible for more disappointments on election day than is so-called popularity. Besides, it is a vicious and demoralizing influence, now extending, I regret to say, to State-wide primaries as well. The theory back of primaries, that if the people are wise enough to elect their public officials they are wise enough to select them as candidates, is not working out as anticipated.

I was an early advocate of primaries; I am not yet ready to abandon them—certainly not if the old convention ways are to be restored; but I am ready to concede that in the populous States primaries have degenerated into a rich man's sport. Unless he is backed by the wealth of others, which in its implications is worse than spending one's own money, a poor man now has only the remotest chance in a primary in any large state.

The term of Senator Frank Flint of California, ended when the election of Senators by State Legislatures was abandoned for election by popular vote. His colleagues were surprised when he announced that he would not enter the primaries. "It is purely a business problem for me," said Flint when asked his reason. "The unavoidable personal cost of my candidacy in a State-wide primary will exceed the total of my six years' salary as a Senator."

Senator Flint does not stand alone in his reluctance to impoverish himself by remaining a Senator.

It is no longer debatable that in many States, primaries are a debauching contest of pocket-books instead of a contest of men or of principles. At most not one-third of the money contributed is put to any legitimate or effective use.

EVERY PRIMARY NOMINEE HIS OWN PARTY

Another disturbing development of the primary is the loss of the strength and unity of organization. The nominee assumes to be superior to the platform of the party under whose emblem he sought nomination in the primary and election by the people. Authority is gone, for every nominee of a primary, unlike a convention nominee, deludes himself that he and not his party won the day.

That feeling of superiority to party control finds its reflection in many State Legislatures and particularly in the unstable party majorities in both houses of Congress; it kills party responsibility.

Those of us who have vivid recollections of "King Caucus" and of steam-roller conventions cannot, however, accept the old conditions, even though we realize the weakness of the new ones. We cannot go back, for in America we never go back, but some method must be found for rigidly limiting expenditures in primaries and for asserting the authority of party control over those who enter them as candidates for party favor.

CHAPTER IV

THE GENERALS IN PRESIDENTIAL BATTLES

Bliss, Cortelyou, Willcox, Hays and Butler—Millions Spent In A National Campaign—The "Cash And Carry" Army—Hays Would Not Have "Politics Adjourned," For He "Had Counted The Steps"— The Republican Slogan "Win The War Now!"—Bliss Ended Discussion, "T. R." Did Not And Became President.

IN ELECTION campaigns, even more than in primaries, money melts like snow in a spring freshet. Successive national chairmen of both political parties while talking with me have fixed their estimate of the working "efficiency" of a campaign dollar between 25 and 33 per cent. I have never heard any experienced politician rate it higher; I have heard many rate it lower. Yet I have never known any politician who did not seek more and more of it for campaign use, despite this knowledge.

It is impossible to estimate the total expenditures of a Presidential campaign. Each of two national committees now confesses to over three million dollars, but the State and local committees spend as much more. Certainly not less than fifteen millions, in one way or another, are expended every four years by the two great parties in a Presidential campaign—much of it as useless in effecting results as water over the dam.

And the most wasteful expenditure is the last ditch "drive" for which the campaign committee always goes heavily in debt. Every doubtful State makes such an appeal to the national committee and every doubtful County to its State Committee. If the party loses, the banks from which the Committee borrows must wait until the next campaign to be repaid. If the party wins the obligations are met in a year or two.

But how? From those who expect Administration favors in Washington and in State Capitals and who are willing to pay in advance for them!

THE "CASH AND CARRY" ARMY

Far too many persons desire to be known as "friends of the Administration" at any cost to themselves—whether the Administration is city, state or national. I am glad to be able to say, however, from my observation that the "cash and carry" friends of an Administration rarely realize on their investment. Nevertheless there is always an embarrassing number of them. They do not have to be sought. They stand around during and after the campaign check book in hand, with some office or honor in mind.

This does not apply to all campaign contributors, or even to a majority, and seldom to the largest contributors. Men of fortune are usually men who believe strongly, wholeheartedly, no less in their politics than in their own affairs. The late Cleveland H. Dodge, for example, was probably by far the heaviest contributor to Woodrow Wilson's political fortunes. Yet I never heard of his wanting anything for himself; he was interested in the success of Wilson's Administration. Both George Perkins and Frank Munsey frequently declared to Roosevelt and to other friends in 1912 that if he were elected President they would not accept any office in his Administration.

CHAIRMEN WHO WANTED TO KNOW

Cornelius N. Bliss, of New York city, several times Republican national treasurer, George B. Cortelyou in the Roosevelt campaign, Willcox in the Hughes campaign, and William M. Butler, Chairman of the 1924 Coolidge campaign, are, so far as I know, the only political generals who would not allow expenditure without money in hand to meet it. That policy is always bitterly opposed by party leaders who declare it cramps the campaign. I think it makes organizations more careful of their money and thereby helps the campaign; whether it does or not, its result after election is to save Presidents and Congress from unpleasant decisions.

I am told that Cortelyou and Butler had the best budgeted national campaigns ever made, and personally scrutinized more closely than any other chairmen the use made of the money furnished by them to each State.

The national campaign work that most interested and aroused the energies of party workers, however, was that of Will Hays.

HAYS UNADJOURNS POLITICS

Hays in 1918 succeeded William R. Willcox as chairman of the Republican national committee. He had the enthusiasm of a new mind for a campaign on new lines. He wanted something different from the old conventional way of waiting until the ticket is in the field before beginning to fight. He believed in organizing at once. He called it, in Hoosier language, "getting the jump" on the other fellow.

As we were then at war with Germany President Wilson had said that "politics is adjourned." Hays wanted politics unadjourned. He believed that a Republican majority elected to Senate and House in 1918 would aid in the conduct of the war at least as effectively as would a Democratic majority— perhaps more so. Some Republican leaders hesitated to "unadjourn" politics; they thought it would seem unpatriotic. Colonel Roosevelt and others, however, backed the Hays plan to win Congress if possible, and to begin a two years' continuous battle for the Presidency.

HE HAD "COUNTED THE STEPS"

An interesting story was told at the time illustrative of the acquiescent mood of the Senators that for a brief period held the Hays plan in check. Hays went to Washington to persuade them that a fight should be made. That was then an unfamiliar city to him; as a stranger he was deeply interested in all he saw. One thing he did with Hoosier-like curiosity was to walk up the Capitol steps, and to count them. That done, he proceeded to the conference.

When he found himself confronted by the Senatorial attitude of indifference, he remarked that he did not believe the particular Senator most opposed to his plan realized what was going on in the country. Sitting day after day in the Senate Chamber he had not been out among the people.

"Senator," he said, "do you know how many steps there are on the front of this building?"

"No—never counted them," came the quick reply. "What have they got to do with it?"

"Well, I have counted them," replied Hays. "I counted them this morning. You have been looking at them every day for years. You have thought you knew all about them, but you don't even know how many there are. They were new to me, and I was interested enough to want to know how many there are. It's the same with conditions through the country. You have sat here and assumed that you know them; I have been out among the people and I have asked them what they thought. I know what they think because I have counted the steps. I know we can win."

The Senator agreed to let Hays have his way.

"WIN THE WAR NOW!"

The night after that climb of the Capitol steps, Hays was the recipient of a unique honor at the hands of a group of Washington correspondents of Republican newspapers and themselves Republicans. It was their wish to know this gritty little son of Indiana who had jumped into political eminence "over night" as it were. The war had hardly begun so far as America was concerned and the proposed "adjournment of politics" had not appealed strongly to these writers. They wanted Hays to indicate a line of political activity that was partisan yet patriotic.

In his address to the diners Hays said, "the first duty of every Republican in the United States is to help win the war."

"Let me amend that, Mr. Hays," said a voice at his elbow, "why not include the word 'now' in the slogan?"

"You're right!" cried Hays. "Win the war *now!* We'll make that the battle cry of the Republican party."

The Hays argument prevailed with Republican leaders. Promptly Hays undertook a canvass of every State. He got to know the men on whom he could depend. Party enthusiasm grew; everybody went to work, and a Republican majority was elected in both Houses of Congress.

Later, in preparing for the presidential campaign, Congressman Ogden L. Mills, of New York city, joined Hays in an effort to ascertain the sentiment in every State on different issues. Thus the National Chairman was able to present the convention in Chicago, in 1920, with an outlined platform as well as an organization mobilized for battle. It was one of those things "never done before."

Its result was that the Harding and Coolidge ticket entered the campaign an assured winner. From the moment of the nomination, its election was a certainty. The "tides" and "swings" were absent from the campaign of 1920 and the night of November 2—Harding's birthday by the way—was a night of complete triumph. Even the Solid South yielded to the onslaught of the busy little chairman of the G. O. P.

It was a campaign of big expenditures; it also was a campaign of big results. Hays had "the jump."

ELUDING THE VICE PRESIDENCY

I have spoken of Cornelius N. Bliss, treasurer of the Republican National Committee. I would like to divert here to tell the story of how he missed becoming McKinley's successor as President by refusing to allow his name to be used for Vice President in the 1900 convention. It is well to know something of Bliss, whose son is now worthily bearing his name. He was one of New York city's "merchant princes" in days of old as the head of Bliss, Fabyan & Co. He had a distinct aversion to holding public office but he liked the game of politics—he thoroughly enjoyed a seat at the table. He was among the earliest and most influential of McKinley's supporters. He declined to be McKinley's Secretary of the Treasury,—only at the last moment to consent good-naturedly to be his Secretary of the Interior. Before the first term had expired Bliss had resigned and was back at his old desk in Worth Street, New York city.

While I sat talking with him there about two weeks before the national convention a telegram was handed him. He read it, then handed it to me. It was signed Hanna (Mark Hanna). In effect it said that some friends expected him to come over to Washington on the Congressional Limited and meet with them that evening in Hanna's house.

"I know what that means. They want me to go on the ticket," he said, "and I'll be d—d if I will. I've had enough of Washington."

"But this is the Vice Presidency—quite different from a Cabinet job," I urged.

"Yes—that's the argument I'll hear if I go over to Hanna's tonight and I'll hear it so much that I may believe it. So I am not going."

Bliss' secretary entered to say that the telegraph boy wanted to know if there was any answer.

"No answer," replied Bliss.

That response gave me hope for an instant that perhaps he was thinking it over. But not so.

"If I reply now," he said to me, "they'll have another telegram on the heels of this one. The best way is to let my telegram start as the Congressional Limited starts this afternoon—then it will be too late for further discussion."

As I Knew Them

And he laughed a good hearty laugh at the way he would elude Hanna.

BLISS ENDED IT: T. R. DID NOT

In truth Bliss then eluded the Presidency as well as Hanna. President McKinley had refused to have anything to do with the choice for Vice President, but his esteem for Bliss would have made it impossible for him to refuse to support him had he been favorably inclined. Hanna had failed with other names, and had taken up Bliss because he knew he was the one man for whom McKinley would exert his influence.

The next week in Washington I asked Senator Hanna about Bliss. "There would be no fight over him if he would say the word," he replied. "We can get support (meaning McKinley) for him that we cannot get for any other man."

On the convention train from New York city to Philadelphia some days later, I asked Bliss if he had noticed how strongly Gov. Roosevelt was resisting Tom Platt's purpose to name him for Vice President. "Yes, I have," he said with a good-natured laugh. "There's this difference between us in that matter—I resisted it and ended it; Teddy is resisting it but not ending it!"

And a Presidency was in the offing!

CHAPTER V

BAD CITIZENS, BAD POLITICIANS

The Disloyalty Of Non-Voters—Absentees From The Polls Are Chiefly Those With Most At Stake—The Politician Is Individual, Ambitious And Alert—Senses What We Want Before We Know It— Compare The List Of Good Laws With Bad Ones—We Can Be Proud Of Our Men In Public Service—Some Who Left Their Impression On Their Party And The Nation—They Spell America.

LET me say here that no justification of or apology for our government by politicians is offered by me to the too-many citizens who neglect to vote. I class such citizens with Edward Everett Hale's "Man Without a Country." It is regrettable that in State elections nearly 40 per cent of quali-fied voters do not go to the ballot-box; in Presidential elec-tions fully 30 per cent neglect to exercise their privilege,— much more than that percentage when you include many women who still refuse to vote.

When we think of the hardships that have been endured, the sacrifices that have been made, to give to every man the title of "freeman," to insure him a voice in the government under which he lives, the refusal of so many citizens to appre-ciate their heritage and accept its responsibilities is beyond my comprehension.

Everyone must pay in some way for things worth while, and the price asked of each individual in return for the high privilege of citizenship is participation on election day in the choice of officials who under the law are to protect and promote his welfare. It is as small a contribution as could be asked of anyone; the amazing feature is that the persons with most at stake are the most numerous on the list of those missing at the ballot-box! They are also the loudest in criti-

29

cism of those who give their time and who at least are making an effort.

To my mind the disloyalty of such non-voters to their citizenship bars them, and their opinions, from the right to consideration. They are defaulters on their membership in the body politic. Until they reinstate themselves by the exercise of the franchise they are not in position to challenge the verdict of the ballot-box. Those who perform their duty as citizens clearly have that right, but when on occasion their confidence in the wisdom of our voters lags, I ask them to find any form of government that has provided a nation with a line of rulers comparable to our Presidents.

Politicians are responsible for their selection; many of them were politicians. In the cases of Lincoln and Roosevelt the better the politician the better the statesman; just as the opposite is true, for example, of Woodrow Wilson.

ALL KINDS IN POLITICS

When you meet the men who hold public office or who sit as delegates in our national and State conventions, you often find an unusual type of citizen—individual, ambitious, alert,—close students of their country and the world. Many of them see a career in politics and diligently try to make a record; some are in office or public affairs at the sacrifice of their personal interests; others there are—as Richard Croker, one-time Tammany boss, candidly conceded as to himself—"working for their pockets all the time."

Men in politics do not represent a cross-section of virtue or of vice, but of humanity at its average.

I know how the term "politician" grates on the ears of men and women in private life; I know the impression created by newspaper and partisan denunciation of our "do-nothing Congress," our "corporation-owned" Governors and Mayors, and our "bolshevik" legislators. These are largely the commonplace accusations of the "outs" against the "ins," sometimes justified but always exaggerated.

THE STRUGGLE FOR NEW LAW

We have only to consider present laws regulating our railroads, our corporations, our food, and for that matter ourselves, to realize that we accept and indorse today what yesterday we denounced as radical and destructive measures devised by political demagogues. Often those political demagogues sense what we want long before we know we want it. At the first suggestion of getting out of old ruts to face new responsibilities or restraints, we make wry faces, utter outcries of protest and publish shrieking editorials. Suddenly faces relax, cries soften into silence, editorial tone changes—and the so-called demagogy becomes the welcomed law of the land.

Such is the history of two-thirds of the legislation of the past thirty years affecting national and State policies.

Undeniably, much bad legislation—such as measures called "strike" bills and others against public and private interest—is attempted in Congress and in State legislatures. Bills are introduced, committee hearings are held, fiery speeches are made, and newspaper articles prophesy fierce struggles. But how many of those measures really become law?

GOOD LAW OUTWEIGHS BAD

After adjournment let any citizen take the list of laws enacted at any session, put the good laws in one column and the questionable laws in another. He will find the column of helpful and needed legislation quite lengthy and the other column close to the vanishing point.

Another way to get an accurate reflection of the purposes of the majority of men in public life is to consider all our national and State laws. Despite the weaknesses and contradictions, where will you find a better framework of government? Yet it is wholly the work of politicians, and it is steadily reaching high levels.

MEN WHOSE CAREERS SPELL AMERICA

Taking them by and large, our country can be proud of the men who give their lives to public service. I certainly feel so whenever I recall the Republican and Democratic leaders I have known. What a list of names could be taken from the not-too-distant past and posted in a deserved "hall of fame!"

I shall not here name all, who, dead and gone, are entitled to a place in the kindly memory of those who remain, but I am sure that many readers will share the pleasure I always have in recalling them. They were politicians as the term is used; some dominated their State organizations; some were interested solely in policies and not at all in party machinery; some were passionate, fiery, and, let us say, from our point of view, reader, vicious and wrong; yet all left their impress on the policies of their party and the laws of the nation. Here is a list worth looking over:

Take Henry Cabot Lodge, Henry L. Dawes, George F. Hoar, John W. Weeks and Murray Crane, of Massachusetts; Orville H. Platt, of Connecticut; Eugene Hale, Nelson Dingley and Thomas B. Reed, of Maine; Arthur Pue Gorman, of Maryland; Redfield Proctor and George F. Edmunds, of Vermont; Allan G. Thurman, the Red Bandana statesman, of Ohio; Jonathan Dolliver, of Iowa; Dan Voorhees, the Tall Sycamore of the Wabash; Albert J. Beveridge, of Indiana; John C. Spooner, of Wisconsin; Roscoe Conkling, Thomas C. Platt, Warner Miller, Frank Hiscock, William M. Evarts, Sereno E. Payne and David B. Hill, of New York; John G. Carlisle, of Kentucky; John Sherman, "Calico" Charles Foster and "Fire-Alarm" Joseph B. Foraker, of Ohio; Governor "Dick" Oglesby and Shelby M. Cullom, of Illinois; Cushman K. Davis, of Minnesota; L. Q. C. Lamar, of Mississippi; Samuel J. Randall and "Pig Iron" W. D. Kelley, of Pennsylvania; John B. Gordon, of Georgia; John M. Daniel, of Virginia;

As I Knew Them

Wade Hampton, of South Carolina; Henry M. Teller, of Colorado; Roger Q. Mills, of Texas; John T. Morgan, of Alabama; William B. Allison, of Iowa; Stephen B. Elkins and William L. Wilson, of West Virginia; Thomas F. Bayard, of Delaware; "Joe" Blackburn, of Kentucky; Zach Chandler, of Michigan; "Silver Dollar" Richard Bland and George G. Vest, of Missouri; Preston B. Plumb and John J. Ingalls, of Kansas; Zebulon B. Vance, of North Carolina; "Pitchfork" Benjamin R. Tillman, of South Carolina; Charles Culberson, of Texas; "Fighting Bob" La Follette, of Wisconsin; and Albert Baird Cummins, of Iowa.

—Oh, like the brook I could go on forever!

I am not going to say that these men—some only recently dead—who were controlling figures in their time, were superior to the leaders in public life today, but I do say that they were strong, purposeful men who believed powerfully in the measures they advocated, and whose careers at Washington meant more to the country than perfunctory responses to roll-calls. Their clashings, their strivings, their wisdom and unwisdom, taken together, spell America; what more could be asked of them?

BAD MEN AND GOOD MEN IN POLITICS

Of course, there are bad men in politics—too many of them. We owe their presence largely to the neglect of so many "good" citizens to vote. So, too, there are "bad" lawyers, "bad" bankers, "bad" doctors, "bad" business men. They, also, are too often on the front pages of newspapers to the exclusion of their betters, but the same rule applies to them as to "bad" politicians. Like the frogs in the pond, a few are responsible for a lot of noise.

Office-holding, like every other calling, has its human weaknesses. Men vested with power often yield to temptation for the sake of their purse, their party, or their desire for greater power. You find them here in America; you find them the world over. No governing class has yet been developed in any nation that is standardized on one level of unswerving integrity and unselfishness. Until such a class is developed in this world or the next—probably in the next—I shall hold to the high estimate I have of the responsible men of both parties in our public service, and the motives that actuate them.

CHAPTER VI

THE PRESIDENTS OF HALF A CENTURY

From Lincoln To Coolidge Some of Our Ablest Chief Executives—Cleveland, Roosevelt and Wilson, Our Outstanding Presidents, But Harrison Ablest of All—Inaugurating Cleveland as President—Reporting Grant's Struggle With Death—Travelling With Jefferson Davis—"Great Lives Never Go Out—They Go On!" Declared Harrison.

S INCE my first experience in political reporting in the Blaine-Cleveland campaign, a definite opinion has slowly formed in my mind of the men I have met while they served as Chief Executive of the nation. The quick, sharp and often partisan judgment of the day has not always withstood the modifying influence of time, of better information or of mind broadened by events.

Casting up their weaknesses and their strength and striking a balance, I believe that from Lincoln to Coolidge inclusive, we have had in the White House some of our ablest Presidents, and certainly more Presidents of ability than during the years from Lincoln back to John Quincy Adams.

Presidents grow in office as men in other places of responsibility grow,—if it is in them to grow,—by their opportunities. Crises bring out character and test judgment. Our earlier Presidents—Washington, Adams, Jefferson, Madison, Monroe—whom we properly rank so high, were among the founders of our Republic; as such they had opportunity to impress themselves upon our history not open to their successors except to Lincoln with the struggle to save the Union and to Woodrow Wilson with the World War.

How well the Presidents since the Civil War would have

handled the problems of our earliest Presidents it is mere speculation to say; how well they would have met Lincoln's problems or what course from 1914 to 1920 any one of them would have pursued had he been in Woodrow Wilson's place, is speculation also. What we do know is, that taken collectively they did mighty well as trustees of a limitless inheritance during half a century of national development more marvelous than Emperors of old times or new ever dreamt of.

It is one task to create a nation, another to unify it, still another to hold its restless spirit from excesses that lead inescapably to destruction.

This last task has been the task of our Presidents since Lincoln. Each has had his own way and each has sought his own results; all differed in personality, method and policies.

CLEVELAND, ROOSEVELT AND WILSON

If I were asked to pick the three outstanding Presidents of that period, I would say as most men would say—Grover Cleveland, Theodore Roosevelt and Woodrow Wilson. I feel as though I were doing an injustice to Benjamin Harrison not to crowd him into the three, for, intellectually, he outranked them. He was the ablest of all. During Harrison's one term we were at peace with the world, prosperity made new high record-marks, and a calm, reasoned policy prevailed in all matters, so far as the President's influence extended. History, like news, is made up of the unusual, and no important events of unusual character occurred during Harrison's term to bring out the sterling qualities of the man.

Whether to your liking or not, it must be conceded that Roosevelt, Cleveland and Wilson gave their respective administrations definite significance in American history. They were not mere patronage dispensers for their party (although in patronage they abided largely by their party demands); they were more concerned with measures than with offices. For example, one rarely heard any contention in the White House over patronage while Roosevelt was there; there was a constant struggle over "My Policies."

Cleveland's serious troubles also were over policies, not patronage. Cleveland did his work laboriously as it came along, day by day; he did not reach for more; he was content to deal with that which came before him as before a Judge on the bench. Cleveland found so much in his todays that he had no time left for tomorrows.

Roosevelt and Wilson, on the other hand, centred on tomorrow. Wilson admitted frankly that he was "playing for the judgment of tomorrow." Both he and Roosevelt worked and thought in terms of the future—one with the quick vision, determination and energy of warm blood; the other with the cold analysis of the cloister.

In my study of the two men Wilson stands out, clear cut and rigid, in the sharp definite lines of a steel engraving; when I turn to Roosevelt he is revealed in strong human tints, the warm flesh tones of a Rembrandt or a Franz Hals.

FROM UNION CHIEF TO CONFEDERATE LEADER

It was my fortune in the period between January 1885 and May 1886 to be assigned by the Philadelphia Press to "cover" three men who figure largely in American history, though in very different ways. Early in 1885 I was sent to Albany to remain with Grover Cleveland until he left for Washington in March to be inaugurated President. I then returned to New York city to report General Grant's gallant fight against the inevitable there and at Mt. McGregor, where he died. Less than a year later I was travelling with Jefferson Davis on his farewell tour of the South.

Few newspaper correspondents have had such an experience in the brief space of sixteen months,—Cleveland, Grant and Davis! Of course, no one could study such men, day after day, without benefiting. The thing that most deeply impressed me was their unaffected simplicity. They corrected a youthful impression that greatness had to be linked up with the manner of a grand seignior.

The vigil almost at Grant's bedside in particular gave me many opportunities to study him at close range, especially toward the last on Mt. McGregor—under conditions that tested the fibre of the man and bared it to the world as only intense suffering can do.

I had seen him frequently in the summer of 1882 and 1883 as he drove along the ocean drive at Long Branch, New Jersey, and once I had interviewed him in his home there, but it was a different Grant that I looked upon in New York city in 1885 suffering from cancer.

GRANT'S LAST BATTLE

In the early period of his illness he was frequently able to leave his bed for an hour or so. He would sit in an arm-chair in front of the second story window of his house, 3 East 66th Street. At times he would stand for a few moments looking out. Always there was a group of three or four correspondents gathered on the opposite sidewalk. We had established a patrol and took turns on duty night and day.

There were many times when I wondered whether the General did not regard us as a sort of death-watch—whether whenever his gaze fell upon us the thought did not come to his mind—"Well, here I am—still in the flesh—still cheating you out of that big piece of news you are waiting for."

When not too depressed Grant would recognize some of the newspaper men he knew and smile pleasantly—pleasantly, but sadly, very sadly. He was then struggling to complete his "Memoirs" in the hope that their sale would furnish financial provision for his family. It was a race with death for a fortune. On Mt. McGregor he won it by a few days. With the task done, collapse quickly followed.

38

As I Knew Them

"GREAT LIVES NEVER GO OUT—THEY GO ON!"

Some years later, standing on the porch of that cottage, while delivering an anniversary address commemorating Grant's death there, ex-President Harrison used this memorable sentence:

"It is said that a great life went out here. Great lives such as General Grant's never go out. They go on!"

CHAPTER VII

JEFFERSON DAVIS' FAREWELL TO THE SOUTH

A Tour From Beauvoir, Mississippi, to Savannah—Davis Stands On The Spot On Which He Had Been Inaugurated President—The Old Gray Uniforms Of The "Lost Cause"—Davis Says "Your Common Country"—Women Shower Him With Flowers—A Question I Never Asked—Davis Would Not Go To Richmond.

SUPPOSE we leave Grant and other leaders of the North for a moment to record some memories of Jefferson Davis, whom I accompanied as correspondent, in May, 1886, when he made the unveiling of a statue to Senator Ben Hill at Atlanta the occasion for what was in fact a farewell tour of the South.

The former President of the Southern Confederacy travelled in a special train from his home, Beauvoir, Mississippi, to Savannah, stopping at several cities to be greeted by old comrades. Nearly all the chieftains of the army boarded that train at different stations, and remained for a time.

I doubt whether there ever was such a meeting of men who had fought and lost together—certainly not with so many mothers, wives and daughters of intense memory present. It was a reunion as well as a farewell. Two beautiful daughters of the South—Miss Winnie Davis and Miss Fannie Gordon —were of the immediate party.

How vividly I can remember Davis standing on the portico of the State Capitol in Montgomery, Alabama, that portico on which he had stood twenty-five years before when inaugurated President of the Confederate States of America. I have witnessed many stirring scenes since then, but none that moved me more deeply. Tear-drenched recollections came to thousands that thronged the Capitol steps and the

40

wide Avenue extending far away,—much as Pennsylvania Avenue at Washington leads from the national Capitol.

Old gray uniforms had been taken from trunk and garret, tattered with wear, stained with the grime of battle and bivouac, to cover once more the waning forms of veterans of that "lost cause." It was the last occasion so many were to be seen upon those who had worn them in battle. And then we were not so far from war's passions as to be beyond their thrilling influence. The sight of their old President opened floodgates of precious memories.

"YOUR" NOT "OUR" COUNTRY

Davis spoke at Montgomery with great feeling. Here are some extracts from his speech:

"I am standing now very nearly on the spot where I stood when I took the oath of office in 1861. Your demonstration now exceeds that which welcomed me then. I felt as I came here that I was coming to my home—coming to a land where liberty dies not and serious sentiments will live forever.

"Associated here with so many memories—thrilling and tender —I have felt that it were dangerous for me to attempt to speak to you as my heart would prompt me. Not that I am always treasuring up bitterness against any one, but I am overflowing with love and admiration for our people!

"We have no desire to feed the fires of sectional hate, while we do not seek to avoid whatever responsibility attaches to our belief in the righteousness of our cause and the virtue of those who risked their lives to defend it.

"Alabama having resumed her place in the Union, be it yours to fulfill all obligations devolving upon all good citizens, seeking to restore the general government to its pristine purity, and, as best you may, to promote the welfare and happiness of your common country."

I was not the only one who heard and noticed that Davis said "your" common country, not "our" common country.

As I Knew Them

At the old Exchange Hotel, Davis was given the rooms he had occupied as President before going to Richmond. When he entered them the evening of his arrival the women not only of Montgomery but of all Alabama gathered on the balcony outside and showered him with flowers, until his rooms were literally carpeted with roses. I never saw so many, or so much real feeling accompanying them.

The same scene was repeated wherever we stopped. At Atlanta, everyone of importance in the State greeted him. When the crowd saw Generals James Longstreet and John B. Gordon, in their gray uniforms, on horseback, escorting Jefferson Davis to the Ben Hill statue, it went wild. They were led by Captain Evan Howell, father of my friend Clark Howell, editor of the Atlanta Constitution. Henry W. Grady, who was the South's eloquent orator of the day, made the most of that stirring spectacle. Davis spoke briefly, closing with these words:

"My friends, these are the days of peace; let us not be less faithful in peace than we were in war."

At Savannah, the Savannah Light Artillery laid down a heavy barrage of Southern hospitality which instantly put the organization in sharp competition with the Ancients and Honorables of Boston, so famous as genial hosts until the Volstead law dimmed the lustre of their renown.

A QUESTION NEVER ASKED

Davis, at that time in the eighties, was a feeble man. On the train between stops he would rest on a couch, in what was then called a drawing room. In turn one after another would sit beside the couch and talk with the old man. This gave me an opportunity to speak with him several times.

With the eagerness and indiscretion of a youthful correspondent I longed to ask him the great question, whether he would not like to say something that would bridge the last gap between North and South and tend to restore him as well as others to the citizenship they had abandoned.

Twelve years later, Congress unanimously passed a bill doing that very thing and President McKinley signed it. Of course I had no such ambitious plan in mind, but it seemed to me that some well-considered word from Davis while on that farewell tour might have advanced the unifying spirit.

It seemed to me unfortunate that any former citizen, particularly one born on our soil, should be nearing his grave as a man without a country. I racked my brain to find some discreet way of approach to the subject, but there was none less obvious than the frank and pointed question. It was never asked.

AN EXILE IN HIS OWN LAND

Nevertheless, I was sure that a man who in younger years had made a good record in Mexico as a soldier for his country, who had been Secretary of War in his nation's government, Congressman and United States Senator, must have something deep in his heart that he would like to say to a reunited nation; must feel that he would like to die a citizen of it;—must feel that a word from him, twenty years after the event, might, by revealing the convictions that stirred him to the course he pursued, modify the tone of history and possibly the opinion of his time.

If only a way could be found for such a word without misunderstanding!

More than once I sat by his side hoping to find that way. The desire for "news" was strong in me but there was something, I do not know what, stronger still, that silenced me as I looked upon the frail and fading figure that was all that remained unconquered of a great conflict. He died, five years later, as he had lived.

In spite of his years there was something statesman-like

about Davis. He still showed the manner, ways and mind of a man talented for government. All the South turned out to greet him. The cordiality of his old comrades cheered him, but he seemed to feel that he was a man apart, even from them, and to hold himself as one from the outside looking in. He asked about many men and sections of the South; it may be that he inquired about men and affairs north of Mason and Dixon's line; if he did I never heard of it.

Evidently he had blotted that section of our country out of mind—at least in conversation.

While he denied that he was embittered, he surely had unpleasant recollections that still controlled him. The world of his activities was a closed book; he wanted none of its pages opened for discussion or revision; he had written "finis" to it as it was.

Every persuasion was used to have Davis extend his trip to Richmond. He refused. He had no desire to revisit the old Capital of the Confederacy. Yet in Richmond his body has its last resting place; there the silence of the tomb is the only answer to the question I could not bring myself to ask the Chieftain of the Lost Cause.

CHAPTER VIII

ALONG THE HIGHWAY OF TIME

A Marvellous Nation-Building Period—No Two Persons Get The Same Impression Though They Travel The Same Road—The Years Mellow Opinion—Youth And Later On—Gaynor Says "How Petty They All Seem As The Great Moment Approaches!"

THE years that have elapsed since the activities of General Grant and Jefferson Davis cover a marvellous nation-building period. To have lived through such years, to have witnessed your country moving steadily on and on, despite baffling world currents, some within, some beyond, its control;—its people wandering almost to destruction's brink and then finding anew the road that leads to national strength and unity and fine purpose;—is like the gradual realization of a dream whose grandeur and glory even those who have dreamt it can only dimly visualize.

It would require someone more certain of himself than I to offer his recollections of its men and events, and his estimate of them, in any other form than as the contribution of a single individual, to be given place with similar contributions in the sifting mind of the historian, there to be checked off against other impressions and other facts as well worthy of consideration.

Just as no two persons see precisely the same rainbow though they scan the horizon at the same instant and from the same spot, and as no two travellers on the highway get precisely the same lights and shades upon the same mountains and valleys, so those of us who are fortunate enough to have continued the journey through life to the allotted span do not get the same impression of all we have seen, heard and lived through.

As I Knew Them

We must differ, often widely, in opinion, when we undertake to assay the ability, the purpose and the character of our fellow-men—particularly those upon whom great responsibilities have rested.

And the years have their influence on one's judgments, too. Opinions mellow like good wine. I am not sure that Balzac was wholly right when he said that you do not begin to live until you have recollections. The thought has its consoling side, and some measure of truth. Nevertheless there's a great deal worth while, vital and inspiring in the years of youth. Then, for you, the world is in springtime and budding blossom; you are at the beginning; you are living in a world of imagination; the real one lies unrevealed just ahead of you— always just ahead of you, and, finally, in the lengthening and baffling shadows. You do not begin to plumb the depths of life, you do not get beyond the shallows or reach that level where "deep calleth unto deep" until you near the tapering end of the pyramid of years and look down upon the turbulences below of which you were once a part.

Glorious were those strenuous days of youth with their triumphs and their defeats, their stirring dreams and their cruel awakenings, their resolves and their fears. As Father Time leads you not always gently out of them, steadily on towards the inescapable goal, you see the true character of much that is behind you—how selfish, how misery-breeding, how needless and how futile!

Yet it is life!

I recall that when Judge William J. Gaynor was Mayor of New York city, the Democratic State leaders seriously considered nominating him for Governor. Gaynor was dangerously ill at his Long Island home. James Creelman, still well-remembered as a newspaper correspondent, was an intimate friend of the Mayor, and was sent to learn his attitude.

46

As I Knew Them

Ordinarily, Gaynor would, no doubt, have been favorably disposed. But when Creelman brought up the subject, he replied wearily:

"Creelman, I'm not interested in Governorships. When a fellow lies in the Valley of the Shadow of Death he is not thinking of vanities or ambitions. How petty they all seem as the Great Moment approaches!"

CHAPTER IX

"HURRAH FOR LITTLE MAC"

A Memory Picture Of A McClellan Parade—New York City's Mayor Who Sympathized With Rebellion And Jesse Seligman Who Bought Bonds To Save The Union—"Vote As You Shot"—The Stirring Marching War Songs And The Picturesque Zouaves—Heroes? Of Course! They Could Do No Wrong—My Enthusiasm In 1880; My Revulsion in 1884—But For James G. Blaine I Would Have Voted In Defiance Of All I Had Been Seeing, Hearing And Believing—The Personality Of Blaine—"Trusts Are Largely Private Affairs"—Blaine And Some Other Political Leaders Who Were Open To Suggestion; Also Others Who Were Not—Roosevelt And "Unpleasant Truths"—Alton B. Parker's One Big Move.

LET me illustrate this changing judgment that comes with the years by giving a picture of the 20-year period following 1865, the tense passion of the people then, and the impressions made upon youthful minds, my own among the number.

That period covered my boyhood and young manhood. Throughout those years, it was definitely settled and accepted by the older folk to whom I listened with unquestioning faith that everything done, or sought to be done, by a Republican was by the grace of God; while everything done or sought to be done by a Democrat was with the connivance of the devil.

This belief was strengthened in my mind by a picture that even now, so many, many years later, is with me vividly of a parade that passed in front of my home on Franklin Street in lower New York City late in the Presidential campaign of 1864.

That afternoon I was wearing my first trousers—velveteen, with a little Eton jacket; my mother had allowed me to stand on our stone steps and watch the paraders. They were wildly shouting "Hurrah for Little Mac."

One of the enthusiastic paraders ran up the steps and en-

48

deavored to make me repeat "Hurrah for Little Mac." Frightened I beat a frantic retreat into the house.

THE BIGGER MEANINGS

I do not know why those hurrahs lasted through my child-mind as something to be remembered, but they did. Some years later, when I came to understand the meaning of the McClellan candidacy against Lincoln, I kept the sight of that parade, and the sound of its hurrahs, before me as final and convincing evidence that the devil was surely the guide, philosopher and friend of the Democratic party. What other influence, I asked, could or would oppose Abraham Lincoln?

During these years of youthful, patriotic fervor, I hated New York city, my birthplace, for its support of McClellan in 1864, for its Copperhead rioting against drafting soldiers to serve in Uncle Abe's army fighting the Johnny Rebs, for its eagerness to displace Webster's inspiring line, "The Union— One and Inseparable" with that sordid trade symbol "Business as Usual."

I had contempt for Fernando Wood, mayor of the city in 1861, who openly sympathized with the South; and intense admiration for Jesse Seligman, the New York banker, who, though born in another land, had patriotically led the bond-buying in support of our government when it sorely needed such support.

"VOTE AS YOU SHOT"

I was by no means alone among young men of my day in that feeling. For years after the war, every boy just coming of voting age was harangued from Republican platforms to vote as his father or uncle or elder brother had shot; he obeyed as loyally as though he were on the battle line back in the '60's and had had the command to fire.

Under the conditions how could it have been otherwise?

"VOTE AS YOU SHOT!"

As I Knew Them

Grant, Sherman, Sheridan, Meade, Logan, McCook, and other Union Generals were the inspiring figures in our national life.

No gathering was of importance without one or more of them present; no marching band or banquet orchestra ever omitted "The Battle Hymn of the Republic," or "We're Coming Father Abraham, 300,000 More," or "Marching Through Georgia." Ellsworth's and Duryea's fierce-looking "Zouaves" in their picturesque woolen "togs," as they were called, marched in our Decoration Day parades headed by a fife and drum corps playing, shrilly but oh so gloriously, "Rally 'Round the Flag, Boys, Rally Once Again."

Who now recalls those Zouave uniforms—loose, short jacket of blue trmmed with red; and waistcoat, red with Turkish trousers, red fez and sash, and yellow leather leggings? What boy could resist the tune and the sight!

When the bullet-shattered flags of the Grand Army of the Republic were carried along Broadway and lower Fifth Avenue there was no timid, abashed lifting of our hats as we notice today when the flag goes by; our hearts beat faster, our eyes filled with tears, our thoughts instantly went back to the awful conflict, then so tragically close to every home.

Heroes? Of course; to us, they were heroes—every one of them! They could do no wrong—certainly none we would not promptly forget and forgive. Down in Congress the persistent cry was "For the old flag—and an appropriation." The old crowd of war days stood solidly together with equal enthusiasm for both; every protesting voice was challenged and condemned as from traitorous quarters.

REPUBLICANS OVER-PLAYED THE WAR

With such sentiments controlling my youthful spirit I could not conceive how Winfield Scott Hancock, a worthy Union General, could accept the nomination of the Democratic party for President; particularly against James Abram Garfield,

another Union General. Fortunately, in 1880, I was not
eligible by a year to vote so I did not have to settle in my
mind just how the devil had managed to lure General Hancock
away from the Lord's cause.

The national election of 1884 seemed a long while for me
to wait. I was convinced that my vote must forever be dedicated to keeping the Democratic party idle on the mourners'
benches. Impatiently I awaited the hour when the ballot-box
would reflect my super-heated patriotism. When finally the
hour came, the heat was gone, and a chilly, reluctant vote was
cast by me for James G. Blaine—cast for Blaine's sake—not
for the party.

As a correspondent I had accompanied Blaine on part of
his campaign tour. I had seen much of him on that trip; I
certainly felt that I was in the presence of a man of real
ability. To me, he towered high above the unknown and unapproachable Cleveland. Had I not in this way met Blaine
I am sure I would have found courage to vote, as I really
wanted to vote, in defiance of all I had been seeing, hearing
and believing since the "Hurrah for Little Mac" episode.

THE PERSONALITY OF BLAINE

For me the Republican party had overplayed the war; reaction had set in. I had no desire to vote as others had shot.
The thought had become revolting to me. If I were to remain
a Republican, the party would have to make some other appeal
than to the passion and prejudice of a war twenty years past.

It did just that in the personality of Blaine. It was
not possible for an unprejudiced person to meet the man
from Maine without being attracted to him. As correspondent of the Philadelphia "Press" I had unusual access to
Blaine. That newspaper was one of the leading supporters
of the "Plumed Knight"; Blaine was in constant communica-
tion with Charles Emory Smith, my editor. Now and then,
I was the channel used.

As I Knew Them

Thus Blaine's mind was revealed to me in a most intimate way, and I was impressed by his readiness, after discussion, to adjust his course to the suggestion of others, or give sufficient reason for not doing so.

"TRUSTS ARE LARGELY PRIVATE AFFAIRS"

I recall one incident of that character that brought a storm of criticism down upon Blaine. He returned from a long vacation in Europe in 1888 while the Harrison campaign was getting under way, and was urged to make a "keynote" speech. He finally agreed to speak at Portland, Maine. On the train from his home in Augusta, Joe Manley, Blaine's chief lieutenant, gave the correspondents printed proofs of the speech. While we were reading them Blaine came over and said, "Gentlemen, I have been urged to add something about trusts, and I may do so." Thus warned we waited for the interpolated sentence.

"Trusts are largely private affairs!" declared Blaine in the middle of his speech with great emphasis.

Instantly every correspondent lost interest in the printed copy. Telegraph service was not efficient in those days, and the telephone was still merely hoped for. The Blaine declaration had to be on the wires promptly, if it was to appear in the morning papers. The newspaper section of Blaine's audience therefore disappeared with a rush,—much to his amazement, he told me later.

That one sentence, however, was the first sensation of the Harrison campaign and, of course, got the ticket no votes. Blaine, like other leaders in politics, was alert to public opinion, but in that case he had no thought that his utterance would arouse such widespread condemnation. Harrison had to repudiate it.

Later Blaine came to New York city and made a speech from the Fifth Avenue Hotel balcony modifying his "trust" sentence. He never referred to the fact, however, that it was not in his Portland speech as originally planned, and that it had been incorporated because of the persistent urging of a friend upon whose judgment he relied.

PRESIDENTS WHO WOULD LISTEN

Of all the Presidential candidates since that day (and I have known all the Republican candidates and most of the Democratic)—Theodore Roosevelt was the only one as receptive to the counsel of others as Blaine. However, there was this difference between the two men: Blaine had the tact to listen long to poorly considered and often selfish suggestions, getting rid of his visitor without hurting his feelings; Roosevelt, on the other hand, often became irritated in such circumstances and did not always try to conceal his restlessness or even his resentment. He had contempt for time-wasters. The man with real purpose, however, always found Roosevelt willing to listen and to heed.

I can imagine that many readers will question this statement about Roosevelt. All his critics and some supporters regarded him as self-willed; intolerant of the ideas of others. Those who really knew the Colonel know how untrue that was. His weakness was in listening too often and acquiescing too readily. It was the source of many of his troubles. But the Colonel always shouldered responsibility for his course, once taken, and stood silently and uncomplainingly for mistakes due to friendship.

ROOSEVELT AND UNPLEASANT TRUTHS

An incident in my own contact with Roosevelt is illustrative. In 1903, my newspaper, the New York Evening Mail, was not in accord with some of his policies. Believing that no good would come of argument, and having no reason for taking up a busy President's time, I did not call at the White House on several visits to Washington. Discussing the situation frankly with George B. Cortelyou, then Secretary of Commerce and Labor, he asked, "Have you talked this way to the President?"

"No," I answered. "I doubt whether he's a man who likes to hear unpleasant truths."

"Oh, yes he is," said Cortelyou. "He's a good sport. Better see him."

Nevertheless, I still thought it of no consequence; there were more than enough people pressing their views upon the President. My paper was expressing my opinions—why bother him with them?

FRONTING UNPLEASANT TRUTH

That afternoon, I found a note in my box at the Arlington Hotel asking that I telephone Mr. Loeb, the President's secretary. I did so, and was told the President would like to see me about five o'clock.

"Hello," exclaimed the President as we met. "I hear you think I cannot stand unpleasant truths."

"Well, Mr. President," I replied in some confusion at such a sudden attack, "I doubt whether many men care to."

"I don't," he snapped. "I don't—when they come from people whose judgment I don't respect. But I'm always ready to listen to a sound argument against any policy I'm pursuing, and by George! I'll switch if I'm convinced."

And Theodore Roosevelt, to my personal knowledge, lived up to that assertion much too generously many times.

MCKINLEY, HARRISON AND CLEVELAND

McKinley was a patient listener, but McKinley's long experience as a Congressman had made him shy of visitors with "views"; he did not encourage them and he had the art of making their visits pleasant but brief. If you knew your subject, however, McKinley gave you time, and he was not afraid to agree, even when it involved modifying his own views.

Cleveland and Harrison looked upon counsel with that apprehension one might feel in handling dynamite. Bryan and Wilson were still worse—they simply accepted no suggestions from any source. Their policies and acts were based on *"principle"* or they believed they were, and both took refuge from suggested change by declaring they could not yield because *principle* was involved.

Probably no two men in our public life were so hostile—no other word is adequate—to counsel as Wilson and Bryan. They could not conceive that there was wisdom in any mind but their own. The one exception with Wilson was Colonel House, and he did not last to the end. At the very moment when Wilson most needed his counsel and his information, he dropped House and, when House went, the Wilson policies dwindled into gestures, phrases and futile defiance.

PARKER'S ONE BIG MOVE

Alton B. Parker, of course, does not count, except that for a few months he was the chosen leader of his party. He hailed from the historic Esopus Creek in the lower Catskills and owed much of his prominence to David B. Hill. During his meteoric national career as a Presidential candidate in 1904, he acted like one who did not comprehend just what had happened to him. Only on one policy did he know whether he was going or coming. No one else could tell, either. His famous "Gold" telegram to the Democratic national convention at Kansas City, stands out like a lone pine on a mountain top above the timber line.

Everyone was so amazed by that masterful seizure of a rare opportunity—and none more amazed than his own party leaders—that the inspiration if not the actual authorship of the telegram was generally attributed to helpful friends. But Parker wrote and sent that telegram without consulting anyone except a World reporter named William McMurtrie Speer, then acting as his secretary. Speer urged him to send it. No candidate ever did a more courageous act. If Parker had maintained throughout the campaign the pace he set that first day he might have given Roosevelt a closer finish. As it was, he merely "also ran." I deal more fully with the Parker telegram incident in the chapter on Cleveland's second term.

CHAPTER X

GRANT—SOLDIER, NOT POLITICIAN

He Frankly Acknowledged His Mistakes—What A Tempter Is Power!—Misfortunes Followed The "306" Convention—What The Civil War Meant To Us—His Battle Against Disease—W. C. T. U. Protests Brandy-Injections—The Reporters' Struggle For News— "Whom Do You Represent?"—The Fifty Million Club—"On The Beach At Long Branch"—Grant Vetoed Inflation And Led The First Battle For Sound Money—Silencing The Noisy "Rag-Baby" Green-back—Grant The First Over-Seas Expansionist—The World One Nation, Using One Language—Grant's Determination Never To Turn Back.

WE covered quite a span of years in the last few pages discussing the responsiveness to suggestion of different Presidents and candidates. It brought us further from Grant and closer to the present than I had intended, but having started on the way I had to go through the list. Now let us turn the clock back.

No one could watch General Grant as I did for weeks, while he was under the strain of full knowledge of his approaching death, without getting an insight into the real man. Patient, burden-bearing and trustful he surely was,—too much so for his own good. Appomattox, not Washington, is his monument.

Grant was President long before my newspaper activities began, but it was not difficult for me to see, as I studied him in later years, that down deep in his heart he must have known when he entered the White House in 1869 that politics was not his field of endeavor, though he never knew, until too late, that politicians can be trusted not to intrigue about as much as you trust a mule not to kick.

58

As I Knew Them

What was said of Taft while President by the memorable Senator Dolliver, of Iowa, might have been said forty years earlier with even greater truth of Grant in the White House: "an amiable man, completely surrounded by men who know exactly what they want."

Grant knew war; he did not know politics, and politics you *must* know if you are to be a success in the White House.

Whenever I recall Grant as I saw him, day after day, awaiting death with stoic calmness, I can vision such a man as a great leader in a mighty effort of desperate chances such as war. It leads me to wonder why in so many instances, the alert reasoning mind essential in a victorious warrior fails of high accomplishment in civil administration.

Grant knew it,—acknowledged it with praiseworthy candor at the close of his second term in 1877. What I could never reconcile with his frank statement of his mistakes is the fact that when in 1880 the same influences and the same men responsible for the numerous shortcomings of his Administration needed his name again as a means to control the Republican party, Grant permitted them to make him their candidate.

THE PASSION FOR POWER

What a tempter is power! Men risk as much to attain it as they do to acquire wealth—perhaps they risk more. Apparently the desire for gold takes hold of you no more intensely than does the desire for power, particularly if you have once exercised such great power as the ruler of a nation possesses. Evidently, the call in 1880 to a new exercise of power found a response in this man who had been three years at the head of a victorious army and eight years at the head of a nation.

Travelling around the world, after giving way as President to Hayes, Grant was fêted everywhere as no other American had ever been. He landed at San Francisco with the

human weakness, after such an experience, to believe almost any exaggeration about himself, even that the people, marshalled by the Republican party, were eager to return him to the Presidency for another term.

The deep interest and pride shown at home in Grant's reception abroad; the unquestioned esteem in which he was held as victorious commander in a terrific struggle, lured him to neglect precautions he would have taken before engaging in battle—the precaution to look beyond the assurances and flatteries of a group led by Roscoe Conkling, seeking to recover the control they had held over the party organization while he was President.

MISFORTUNES FOLLOW THE "306" CONVENTION

The memorable struggle of the "306" Stalwarts in a vain effort to secure his nomination was the result of this yielding by the great Union soldier to men who would use him. The Garfield assassination and the exile of Conkling from politics were other results. A sadder fact, so far as Grant is concerned, is that one misfortune after another followed him from that day until he died five years later, cancer-stricken, bankrupt, humiliated, but grimly struggling to finish his last job "if it takes all summer."

Remembering well the temper of the people of those days I have always felt that the refusal to nominate Grant was to him a blessing in disguise. To be rejected by a convention of his own party was, of course, humiliating, but how much harder to bear would have been his humiliation had he been nominated and then rejected by the people. The country was in no mood to return Grant to the Presidency. For many reasons, in addition to the third term outcry, his candidacy would have shattered his party as badly as did Taft's renomination in 1912. It might even have destroyed his good name beyond the power of his military fame to redeem it.

Later, when the wounds of defeat had almost healed—they

CONKLING, THE TEMPTER. "OH, LET HIM HAVE PEACE," SAID PUCK

Reprinted from U. S. Grant's "Personal Memoirs," Permission of Century Company.

A GRANT MEMO—FORCED BY PAIN TO CONVERSATION BY WRITING

never heal completely with any man when the Presidency is involved—the abundant evidences that he held the affection of his countrymen, despite his mistakes, had a sustaining influence on the dying Grant.

WHAT THE CIVIL WAR MEANT TO US

Often I recall the days and nights when as a reporter I patrolled in front of the house in which he lay incurably ill, and I am thrilled when I read in his "Memoirs" the thoughts he was recording for his countrymen as the darkness of eternity was settling upon him. He must have felt that almost every word he wrote might be his last. Here are a few paragraphs from his last chapter—as worthy of reading today as when he penned them:

"The cause of the great war of the rebellion against the United States will have to be attributed to slavery.

"It is probably well that we had the war when we did. . . . We are better off now than we would have been without it . . . Our republican institutions were regarded as experiments up to the breaking out of the Rebellion and monarchical Europe generally believed that our republic was a rope of sand that would part the moment the slightest strain was put upon it. Now it has shown itself capable of dealing with one of the greatest wars ever made, and our people have proven themselves to be the most formidable in war of any nationality.

"But in this war was a fearful lesson and should teach us the necessity of avoiding war in the future.

"The war has made us a nation of great power and intelligence. We have but little to do to preserve peace, happiness and prosperity at home and the respect of other nations. Our experience ought to teach us the necessity of the first; our power secures the latter.

"I feel that we are on the eve of a new era, when there is to be harmony between the Federal and the Confederate. I cannot stay to be a living witness to the correctness of this prophecy but I feel it within me that it is to be so."

61

As I Knew Them

From the first definite symptoms of his illness it was known that Grant could not live many months. The seat of trouble was at the base of his tongue. There were times when the pain caused by speaking was so great that the General resorted to conversation by "memos" written on a small pad. On at least two occasions, before he was moved to Mt. McGregor, it seemed as though Grant could battle no longer. From one of those sinking spells the doctors revived him by injecting brandy into his arm. Grant could not swallow. He was too weak to withstand the pain and racking cough that would follow; therefore, an arm injection was resorted to.

The Woman's Christian Temperance Union made a great furore over this news when we printed it next day. I do not recall whether it was in one of their national conventions, or at some less formal gathering, that the temperance women adopted resolutions indignantly denouncing the doctors for giving the General intoxicating liquor!

From every nation, from every State and city, came messages of sympathy. His long illness thus gave him opportunity to know the kindly attitude of the world. Congress by unanimous vote empowered President Arthur to restore him to his old rank as General, thus insuring a needed pension for his widow.

DOCTORS VS. PUBLIC INTEREST

The demand for news from his sick room was keen and sincere. It put a heavy strain upon the newspaper men "covering" the case, for the early attitude of both doctors and family made it difficult for us to ascertain the facts. Doctors and family did not realize at first the pressure from the public for news, nor the wrong impression created by secrecy.

Doctors, as all newspaper reporters have reason to know,

have not much regard for public interest in their patients; they are reluctant to make known the events of the sick room. In their eyes the only news is that the patient dies or gets well —meanwhile, silence. Their bulletins, when issued, are technical, and usually not easy of interpretation by the ordinary person. This was much truer in the days of Grant than it is today.

An incident following one of the General's sinking spells clarified the situation then, and gave Grant's medical advisors a realizing light on the duty a physician owes to the public when a man whose career is history lies stricken on a sick bed—perhaps a death bed. The interest of the people is much more than mere curiosity; it is the companion piece of patriotism. Partisan differences disappear, unkind judgments are set aside; the deeper instincts of man have full play.

DR. SANDS AND HIS LITTLE BLACK BAG

Grant's doctors did not appreciate this fact. When entering or leaving the General's house they turned from reporters, darting to and from their hansom-cabs as though escaping from hold-up men. They simply could not comprehend that the public had any right to know more than their brief bulletins revealed—or concealed—with the result that a battle for news developed between the doctors and the newspaper men.

Dr. Henry B. Sands, the surgeon in the case, always carried a little black leather case of surgical instruments. He did not attend the daily conferences with the physicians, but whenever he came along, two or three times a week, carrying his black case, we correspondents were all set for an operation.

We knew that the condition was so serious that an operation would have been performed in the early stages of the disease if the patient had not been General Grant. We did not know, nor did the doctors know, at what moment an operation might become unavoidable, despite the probability that it would result in the famous commander's collapse under the knife. That the doctors dreaded. It is a result people do not always accept without question when a great man's life is at stake. So the doctors fought against an operation.

Early one April morning, about three o'clock, as I remember, our sentries patrolling in front of Grant's house, noticed the gas lights in the General's room suddenly turned on; a moment later the colored butler raced out of the front door and through the street to Madison Avenue. There he jumped on a Madison Avenue horse car. There were no residential telephones in those days. The newspaper sentries knew that that meant a call for the doctors; they sounded the alarm for all of us. They broke up at least two poker games in a basement we had hired around the corner as a rendezvous. Soon we gathered in front of the house; soon also the physicians came; also Dr. Sands with his case of instruments.

"Here's where that operation is done," we all agreed.

But it wasn't.

"WHOM DO YOU REPRESENT?"

In time Dr. Sands came out of the house. He undertook to make his way to a waiting hansom-cab. The newspaper men formed a "blockading" line in front of him. The situation was too important for us to permit the ordinary turn aside.

"Why do you fellows bother me?" shouted the doctor, quite angrily when he found his way barred. "I don't know any of you men, and I don't want to. Why do you question me? Whom do you represent?"

Up spoke "Deacon" Ransome, of the New York Tribune— a serious, quiet-mannered, positive character. He would readily have been accepted in clericals. That is why we called him Deacon.

The Deacon saw his opportunity.

"Dr. Sands," he said, advancing close to the famous surgeon and looking him straight in the eye, "We represent fifty million people, comprising the entire population of these United States, and every man, woman and child of them is deeply interested in this dying man who saved a nation for them. We are here to get the news and give it to those fifty million people. It is for you to say whether they are to have it."

Dr. Sands seemed stunned. He looked back into Ransome's quiet strong features, saw how earnest the man was, and then gave way completely.

"Perhaps you're right," he said, and a kindlier expression swept away his frown. "Perhaps you're right," he repeated. "But I am not in charge. I'll go back and see Dr. Douglass. Between us we may be able to satisfy you."

Dr. Sands was as good as his word and the full story of General Grant's terrific struggle for life that April morning was promptly made known. The facts, serious as they were, were less distressing to the country than if the policy of secrecy had been maintained.

THE FIFTY MILLION CLUB

That same night the correspondents organized the "Fifty Million Club." We held our organizing dinner in the back room of a German combination restaurant and saloon, at Third Avenue and 67th Street. For many years our annual reunions were kept up. Death steadily thinned the Club membership, however. William O. Inglis, Stephen Bonsal and myself are the only members now living, so far as I know.

The Fifty Million Club reported every incident of Grant's illness and death. It also gave to the world the story of his burial on Riverside Drive, New York city, that August day with North and South bowed in his honor, through their leading men gathered at his grave. The club membership included many newspaper writers who afterward achieved world-wide reputation—Julian Ralph, James Creelman, Wm. McMurtrie Speer, Edward G. Riggs, and others.

"ON THE BEACH AT LONG BRANCH"

I first saw General Grant when I called at his cottage at Elberon, near Long Branch, on the Jersey coast, in the summer of 1882—the year after Garfield had passed away in the Francklyn Cottage, half a mile distant. Grant was seated alone in a little summer house on the bluff overlooking the ocean. It was a rule of the Grant family that no one was to disturb him at such times, but as I had not been informed of it I ignorantly broke in on the General's meditation.

Whatever his first impulse may have been, he smiled when I stated my purpose—and thereafter became more interested in the ocean than in my presence. Later I was told that he liked to go down there by himself, and for an hour or so smoke cigars and look out silently upon the ocean. After such a career, what thoughts he must have had!

The Grant cottage is still an object of keen interest; it has not been changed materially since the General occupied it. He had used it also while President. In those days Long Branch was the summer Capital of the nation. "On the Beach at Long Branch" was the popular ballad of the time. There notables in social, business and political life gathered in holiday mood; there the roads were thronged with family "barouches" behind high-stepping steeds and the winding horn of the four-in-hand was heard with delight where now we are distracted with the nerve-racking warning of the auto.

DRIVING ON THE OCEAN BOULEVARD

Grant enjoyed his afternoon drives on the ocean boulevard; stopping at Hildreth's West End Hotel for a chat with friends on those big wide hospitable verandahs. No one could be more modest and affable. He was a good mixer in company he liked. Nor did he seldom miss a talk with his friend, P. J. Casey, manager of the Western Union down there, who held the confidences of more important men than any other person

From Harper's Weekly.

AND THEY SAY HE WANTS A THIRD TERM!

I ever knew. Casey went to Long Branch for his health in the eighteen-sixties after his doctors had condemned him. He is still there, though his medical advisers long since passed away.

The results of every conference Grant, as President, held went through Casey's hands. So with other important men like George Pullman, John Hoey, and Thomas T. Eckert, who made Long Branch their summer home. Casey kept them in touch with their city affairs. Every New York city newspaper seeking to verify news from the coast or to locate leading men, wired to Casey. Not many persons, not even many in high position, are, like Casey, made the confidant of every one.

Of course Grant never was part of the social life of the Jersey shore. He disliked society, but he liked to meet the men to be found down there, and he loved to hit up a stiff pace behind a pair of lively horses.

I was too young to be deeply impressed by faces, but in later years as I recalled my impression of Grant's face—I saw the face of a man with many unexpressed thoughts, not all of them pleasant. It was then that he lent his name to the unfortunate Grant & Ward brokerage firm.

GRANT'S FIGHT FOR SOUND MONEY

No one who knew Grant well, no one who knew him even as slightly as I knew him, could regard him in any light other than as an unwitting agent in the scandals of his two terms as President. And they would be right in that judgment. In the army, he could pick aides of fighting qualities, but in the White House, surrounded by politicians, whom previously he had always avoided, he proved himself an amazingly poor judge of character.

Only a guileless man would have failed to realize what was going on all around him, as Grant failed to realize it. When in 1872 he was reelected by a heavier vote than in 1868 he assumed that he was right, that the people had approved him and his weaknesses. Thereupon Grant followed his characteristic of sticking to his course.

But if Grant went wrong in his choice of men, he was right,

sure and firm in many of his policies, particularly in his determination to have the government meet its obligations at face value, and also put its currency on a sound basis. During the Civil War, the London Times had said:

"No pressure that ever threatened is equal to that which now hangs over the United States.

"If in future generations the United States faithfully meet their liabilities they will fairly earn a fame which will shine throughout the world."

In his inaugural in 1869, Grant urged Congress to commit the government to do this very thing and Congress responded with one of the most remarkable after-war declarations ever made by any government. It resolved:

> "In order to remove any doubt as to the purpose of the government to discharge all just obligations to the public creditors. . . . it is hereby declared that the faith of the United States is solemnly pledged to the payment in coin or the equivalent of all obligations of the United States."

Senator Joseph R. Hawley, of Connecticut, during the debate voiced the dominant feeling when he declared, "For every dollar of the national debt the blood of a soldier is pledged. Every bond in letter and spirit must be as sacred as a soldier's grave."

Though this committal was only a promise without date of performance it is something that Americans can look back upon with pride in view of the course adopted by all the countries engaged in the World War except England. A substantial minority of Republicans was against the pledge; the Democratic party urged a pledge in "lawful money" which meant any kind of money decreed by Congress; in essence, the Democrats did not differ from the advocates of greenbacks carrying no promise of redemption except in other greenbacks.

The "ragbaby," as greenbacks were called, seemed the most popular infant ever born, and certainly it was the noisiest. A compromiser in the White House would surely have heeded the clamor for "cheap money," but Grant was not a man of compromise. In his stand against inflation in 1872 his veto went to Congress against the protest of many Republicans close to him.

Nor was he content with an undated greenback redemption pledge. When the 1874 elections deprived the Republicans of control of Congress, Grant insisted that before the session ended the party should fix a date. He knew he could not force immediate resumption, so he agreed to January 1, 1879 —four years ahead. Many Republicans supported the bill because they believed that it would be repealed before it became effective, but Grant had faith that Congress, having pledged itself, would keep the pledge. And his faith was justified. Had he not forced action at that time, the fate of the greenback would have been uncertain until after 1881, for the Democrats remained in control of the House until that year.

Put all the Grant weaknesses in the scale on one side, and exaggerate their harm beyond reasonable estimate; then put in the scales on the other side the benefit accruing to this country from the pledge to pay its bonded obligations in full and to make the greenback worth one hundred cents in gold anywhere, any time. The balance would have to weigh heavily as a credit to Grant. It is beyond the power of figures to state it. At the close of the world war in 1918 we saw the currencies of Europe depreciate almost to the vanishing point and government obligations shrink to worthless paper; millions of people, impoverished by that wild orgie in printing-press money, demanded more of such money because they saw no hope for them in "dear" money. Following our Civil War our own country was in identically the same mood. The clamoring was for cheap money—and plenty of it.

If there is one man to whom the nation is indebted more than it is to Grant for "holding the fort" against inflation, against repudiation of our bonded obligations and against the "ragbaby," I have not found his name in the history of time.

I have never seen the statement in any publication, but I

have authority for saying that every feature of the resumption act was written in the White House under Grant's supervision. John Sherman, then chairman of the Senate Finance Committee, and a vigorous advocate of early resumption, was put in charge of the bill. The history of our present Federal Reserve law is much the same. It, too, has White House origin, with Robert L. Owen, of Oklahoma, as its champion in the Senate, and Carter Glass, of Virginia, in the House. Its essential features were worked out, however, by President Wilson in conference with Bryan, McAdoo and Col. E. M. House.

John Sherman's success with the resumption bill led to his selection by President Hayes as Secretary of the Treasury, and, therefore, as the official to put the act into effect in January, 1879. By these two steps Sherman made himself the leading influence in Washington in financial legislation, and on them he based his candidacy for the nomination for the Presidency in 1880 and 1888.

GRANT THE FIRST OVER-SEAS EXPANSIONIST

Another problem that became quite acute during Grant's administration has peculiar interest today because of our present sovereignty over the Philippines, Hawaii and Porto Rico. Surely, at that time we had enough to do to knit together the two sections of our country without going beyond our shores for more problems and more territory; but beginning in 1867 the question of possible outlying possessions came in for vigorous debate in Congress, with the usual charges by the opposition that those favoring expansion were corruptly influenced.

Russia wanted to sell us Alaska; Denmark wanted to sell the Virgin Islands, and Santo Domingo formally asked to be annexed. In Congress there was serious talk of urging our State Department to negotiate with Great Britain for the cession of Canada! Alaska we fortunately secured, thanks to

Secretary of State Seward; we refused to pay less than three
million dollars for the Virgin Islands only to pay $25,000,000
for them in 1917; and the annexation treaty with Santo Domingo was defeated in the Senate Foreign Relations Committee largely through the opposition of Senator Charles Sumner,
its chairman.

I do not suppose that many people are aware that Grant
was the first of our Presidents to advocate the extension of
our sovereignty beyond our ocean shores. We have heard
much about "imperialism" since Dewey sailed into Manila
Bay in 1898; McKinley and all of his successors except Wilson have been assailed as "imperialists." Grant, however,
led the way in 1870 by urging the Senate to ratify a tentative
annexation treaty he had made with Santo Domingo. The
government of that island strongly desired to come under our
flag; Secretary of the Navy George M. Robeson and later a
commission headed by Andrew D. White, were sent to study
the problem, and, if it seemed best, to negotiate annexation.

With characteristic persistence, Grant urged the Senate
to act favorably on the report made. It might have done so
but for the hostility of Senator Sumner. The gossip of the
day attributed Sumner's opposition to the fact that he and
Grant were far apart on all questions.

However that may be Sumner fought as desperately against
the acquisition of the West Indies islands as an earlier
Massachusetts Senator—Daniel Webster—in 1846 fought
against the effort to fix our northwest boundary north of the
present States of Washington and Oregon. Webster insisted
that it was best to let England own territory that was a
pathless wilderness destined forever to burden humanity with
Indian warfares. Fortunately, Webster did not succeed in
keeping our flag from the territory we now possess; unfortunately Sumner won his fight to keep us out of Santo
Domingo. The treaty had a majority but not a two-thirds
vote.

As I Knew Them

Though checkmated, Grant believed to the last in the wisdom of annexation, and said so emphatically in his second inaugural. Although Santo Domingo has never come under the American flag, Grant's vision has been justified by our possession of the Hawaiian Islands, the Philippines, Porto Rico, Guam and the Virgin Islands, not to mention our control over Cuba and Samoa.

Surely the stars in their courses have fought for the destiny of which Grant had a vision. Did he see still further down the vista? Who knows? At least I cannot leave the subject without remembering these words from his second inaugural address, March 4, 1873:

> "In the future while I hold my present office the subject of acquiring territory must have the support of the people before I will recommend any proposition looking to such acquisition.
>
> "I say here, however, that I do not share in the apprehension held by many as to the danger of governments becoming weakened and destroyed by reason of their extension of territory. Commerce, education and rapid transit of thought and matter by telegraph and steam have changed all this.
>
> "Rather do I believe that our Great Maker is preparing the world, in His own good time, to become one nation, speaking one language, and when armies and navies will no longer be required."

GRANT FRANKLY ACKNOWLEDGES HIS MISTAKES

In view of the quotations so often made from the utterances of those who assailed Grant's administration, it would be unjust to omit Grant's own words in defense. They have the strength of simplicity. Most men retiring from high positions speak only of their achievements, if they speak at all, and are silent regarding their mistakes. Grant dwelt upon his mistakes. No one can question the sincerity of one who writes:

73

As I Knew Them

"In submitting my eighth and last annual message to Congress it seems proper that I should refer to, and in some degree, recapitulate the events and official acts of the last eight years.

"It was my fortune or misfortune to be called to the office of Chief Executive without any previous political training. From the age of seventeen I had never even witnessed the excitement attending a Presidential campaign but twice antecedent to my own candidacy and at but one of them was I eligible to vote.

"Under such circumstances it is but reasonable to suppose that errors of judgment must have occurred. Even had they not, differences of opinion between the Executive, bound by an oath to the strict performance of his duties, and writers and debaters must have arisen. It is not necessarily evidence of blunder on the part of the Executive because there are differences of views.

"Mistakes have been made as all can see and I admit. But it seems to me oftener in the selections made of assistants appointed to aid in carrying out the various duties of administering the government—in nearly every case selected without a personal acquaintance with the appointee, but upon recommendations of the representatives chosen directly by the people. It is impossible where so many trusts are to be allotted, that the right parties should be chosen in every instance.

"History shows that no administration from the time of Washington has been free from these mistakes. But I leave comparisons to history, claiming only that I have acted in every instance from a conscientious desire to do what was right, constitutional, within the law, and for the very best interests of the whole people. Failures have been errors of judgment and not of intent."

SUPERSTITION NEVER TO TURN BACK

Let me quote from Grant's "Memoirs" a story he tells of an incident in his early life that gives you the keynote to his success. In 1844, returning from furlough to Jefferson Barracks, Missouri, he found his regiment had been transferred elsewhere. He set out on horseback to join it. By the most direct route he would have to ford a creek. He chose that way instead of the longer one. Here is his own story:

74

As I Knew Them

"There is not water enough in the creek at ordinary stages to run a coffee mill and at low water there is none running whatever. On this occasion it had been raining heavily and when the creek was reached I found its banks full to overflowing and the current rapid. I looked at it a moment to wonder what to do.

"One of my superstitions had always been, when I started to go anywhere or to do anything not to turn back or stop until the thing intended was accomplished. So I struck into the creek. I headed the horse for the other side and soon reached it, wet through. I went on, however, to my destination."

Had Pemberton, the Confederate Commander who surrendered Vicksburg to Grant, or had Lee, in the battles of the Wilderness, known what Grant called his "superstition" they might have realized earlier than they did in those historic engagements that the Union Commander had begun something he was going to stick to, at all costs, until finished.

CHAPTER XI

HAYES—A PRESIDENT OF FINE PURPOSE

Not Too Late To Do Him Justice—The Same Title To Office As Every Other President, Backed Also By Decisions On Which Existing Law Is Based—A Boy's Impression Of Tilden, "The Sage Of Gramercy Park"—Hayes' Splendid Background In Ohio—No Challenges But Firm Purpose—Justice To The South, Even Though It Meant Political Hostility—Prophecy As To Silver Coinage—A Telegram That Became Historic—Removing Chester A. Arthur From Office—Hayes Restores The Republican Party To National Control.

NO MATTER how many years may have elapsed, it should never be too late for Americans to do justice to every man who has ever occupied the White House and it certainly is not too late to do justice now to Rutherford B. Hayes. He belongs among our Presidents of ranking ability. If you are disposed to deny him this foremost place, read his public papers, and you will concede that no President excels his clear style, his convincing reasoning, his broad, earnest purpose.

Hayes and Benjamin Harrison are not as fully credited as they should be for their wholesome, patriotic and courageous endeavors while at the head of government. I knew Harrison fairly well, but only twice, long after his Presidency, did I meet Hayes, who so far as his Administration from 1877 to 1881 is concerned still lives in the person of his son, Col. Webb C. Hayes. Col. Hayes aided his father at the White House, and, of course, was his confidant. As such he is identified with the events of the period. He now resides at Fremont, Ohio, where at Spiegel Grove State Park he and Mrs. Hayes have erected and endowed the Hayes Memorial Library and the Hayes Historical Association.

I group Hayes and Harrison together for the moment because they were of much the same stock and temperament. Both men, in their calm, unpretentious adherence to their convictions reflected, as in a mirror, the spirit and meaning of American institutions as they have come down to us through the generations of which their forefathers were a part. If we cannot find that spirit in the careers of such men it is not to be found anywhere.

No citizens of better aims have ever been born on American soil than those two men, and none ever brought into the nation's service, whether on battlefield or in civil life, higher ideals of duty or greater courage to uphold them.

HAYES' TITLE THE SAME AS THAT OF OTHER PRESIDENTS

The circumstances surrounding Gov. Hayes' election as President affected for many years and in some minds still affect proper appreciation of his Administration. A phrase or expression that appeals to public fancy more often distorts or ignores the truth than states it. This was the case with the cry of "counted out!" raised when the electoral commission rulings denied Tilden's claims to the Presidency. Under cover of that cry Tilden has escaped the condemnation he justly deserves for directing a conspiracy to buy the electoral votes needed to give him a majority.

I cannot here go into the details leading to the Electoral Commission decision. In 1876 we were only eleven years from civil war; the clear minds of both political parties dreaded another serious clash; our weakness, not our strength, led to the belief that it was more important to declare somebody elected President than who that somebody might be. The Democrats in Congress voted to create the Electoral Commission; a majority of Republicans opposed it. Both political parties agreed in advance to accept its decision. When the time came to make good on this pledge of their own seeking, the Democrats refused to do so.

Yet Congressman Abram S. Hewitt, chairman of Tilden's

national campaign committee, had said on Jan. 25 while urging the measure in the House:

> "Partisan, as from my position I· am supposed to be, but patriotic as I hope henceforth to be regarded, I have deemed it my plain duty to labor zealously toward the attainment of some just and constitutional plan whereby but one President should be declared, and by a title which all citizens would respect. It was essential to the formation of such a plan that it should be fair between the two political parties, that the scales of judgment should be so evenly poised that the dust in the balance would incline the beam. Such a plan in my judgment the committee were able to agree upon and have presented to Congress.
>
> "No man can predict who will become President by virtue of its operation, but all men can predict that it will be the man who is lawfully entitled to be President. If the law should violate the equity of the case, it is ground for the amendment of the law, but not for rebellion against its decrees. It substitutes law and order and right for strife, anarchy and wrong."

An 8 to 7 decision, like many of our 5 to 4 Supreme Court decisions, was too close to convince the losers, and the Democrats claimed that their man had been defrauded. Yet the decision was made by the machinery they had created, and ten years later they united with Republicans in Congress in enacting a law governing the counting of the electoral vote on precisely the same lines upon which the Electoral Commission had acted. The bill was passed by more than a two-thirds vote of each House, and Grover Cleveland signed it. His attesting signature validated and perpetuated the rulings made in 1877. Thus, in addition to the title to office under the forms of law held by all Presidents, Hayes had the confirmation of a commission whose rulings are now law.

"THE SAGE OF GRAMERCY PARK"

I got into active newspaper political writing in what might be called the aftermath of the Hayes-Tilden controversy.

TILDEN AND HIS BAR'L

That is to say, for some years after 1876, every partisan discussion, wherever held or however begun, finally ended in
charges of "fraud" and "counted out" by Democrats with a
sharp retort by Republicans; in Congress "the stolen Presidency" was a favorite Democratic topic.

I listened attentively to it all, and at first with some sympathy for Tilden. That sympathy might have been stronger
had I not seen Tilden reviewing a night parade from the
balcony of the Everett House, Union Square, New York City.
With several school chums I had gone "uptown," as Union
Square then was, to catch a glimpse, if we could, of the "Sage
of Gramercy Park," as his followers hailed him or "Whispering Sammy" as others called him.

"Little old New York" was not then so large that a parade
could be lost in its engulfing crowds, and the Tilden parade
that night made it seem as though the entire population was
on the march. Calcium lights of intense brightness were then
used to "spot" people, and as that light centred on Tilden
it revealed to us a sallow-faced, dried-up old man. A Dick-
ens could have used those features for one of his malevolent
characters. Certainly he was not an inspiring spectacle for
school-boys to look upon, and we walked back home wondering
how such a man could expect to be elected by the people to any
office.

Nevertheless, youth leans toward the under dog and I had
that kind of boyish sympathy for Tilden's cause until, as a
proof-reader in The New York Tribune, I read and revised
before publication many columns of that newspaper's exposure
of the cipher dispatches sent from Tilden's home by his
nephew who was also his secretary. Those dispatches were
crude efforts to bribe any and all of the election officials having control of the disputed electoral votes.

That experience brought back to me the Tilden face I had
seen on the reviewing stand during the campaign; all over
those pinched, bloodless features I saw written the story I
was now revising—the only story in American history of an

attempted purchase of the Presidency by one who was seeking it.

WHAT HAYES DID NOT LACK

It was said of Hayes in the Presidency that he lacked what politicians called "magnetism"; just as Harrison lacked it, just as Cleveland abhorred it,—that quality which Harding's able Secretary of State, Charles Evans Hughes, is supposed also to lack.

But Hayes was not lacking in purpose or ability to give the country his best. And he had much to give that the country then needed. He had no alliances to compromise him. He was the nominee of a convention of which Blaine had been the anticipated choice. But anticipation was not realization, as so often happens, particularly in conventions. The Conkling-Cameron vindictiveness toward Blaine had been so deep that to defeat the nomination of the Maine man they turned to Hayes. They took a chance that he might prove amenable—and lost.

A WINNING CAMPAIGNER AND TRIED EXECUTIVE

Often I have been surprised when discussing Hayes to find how little is known of the splendid background he had as an executive and legislator when he entered the White House. It would seem that, in many minds, his career began with the challenge of his title to the Presidency. In fact, he was elected to Congress in 1864 while with his command on the battlefield. He served two terms and was then nominated as the one man likely to beat Allan G. Thurman, "the noblest Roman of them all" as the latter was called, for Governor of Ohio. He did beat Thurman.

When up for reelection Hayes was called upon to defeat George H. Pendleton—"Gentleman George." Pendleton had run for Vice President with McClellan in 1864 and he also had a substantial following for President in the convention of 1868 when Horatio Seymour was nominated. Pendleton was a hard man to defeat, but Hayes defeated him.

In 1872 Hayes failed of reelection to Congress because of the Liberal Republican split occasioned by Horace Greeley's candidacy for President. Two years later, the Democrats had "Old Bill" Allen in the field for reelection as Governor; the Republicans realized they had to nominate a vote-getter and they turned to Hayes. Though 1874 was a year of Republican defeats, Hayes again vanquished a strong opponent.

On this winning record Ohio Republicans offered Hayes to the 1876 presidential convention. They had a candidate who had proved that he knew how to win, and one against whose record not a word of scandal could be uttered,—a necessary qualification in view of conditions than prevailing in Washington. He was a partisan but not a politician. The men responsible for nominating him knew he was not of their type; they also knew that even if they had the votes to nominate one of their type he would not be elected President.

In such a situation Hayes became the nominee of his party without an entangling alliance, without a pledge.

NO CHALLENGES, BUT FIRM PURPOSE

The newly-elected President faced a condition almost impossible to overcome except for a man conscious of his own rectitude and firmly resolved to follow the path that seemed to him best. He issued no challenges except the calm recital of facts, uttered no defiances to those who yelled "Fraud!" to those who criticised and denounced his policies. The temptation was great but achievement, not retort, was Hayes' objective.

He left to others the responsibility for prolonging chaos. If the Democrats wanted to test his title in court, as they declared they would, (though they never did) he had nothing

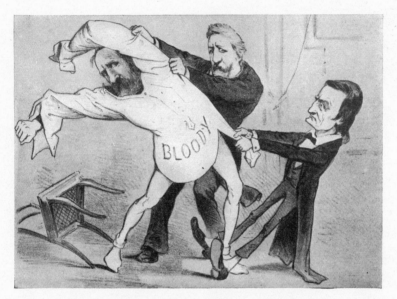

BLAINE AND EVARTS FIND THAT HAYES DOES NOT LIKE THE SHIRT

to say in advance of the test; if the spoilsmen of his party were determined to "ditch" his Administration he had nothing to say in advance of that test; if the paper money advocates in Congress were going to fight to repeal the specie resumption law before it became effective, he was ready also for that battle.

In the North because of Republican dissensions many of the large States were under Democratic control; in the South the last of the Republican Governors, Senators and Congressmen were on their way out.

All this must have had its depressing influence on Hayes in his own counsels, but no evidence of it ever came into public view.

THREE FINE POLICIES

Hayes had three policies definitely in mind when he entered the White House—first, to free the South of Federal soldiers sent there to maintain "carpet-bag" Governors, then in office only in South Carolina and Louisiana, also to bring about a gentler, kindlier attitude, in the hope of a real reunion of the States; second, in his appointments "to abide by the true rule that honesty, capacity and fidelity constitute the only real qualifications for office"; third, to make good his own insistence that "The resumption act can be, ought to be and will be executed" on Jan. 1, 1879; finally, to resist the efforts of silver producers to force the government to coin and circulate silver dollars at par despite the steadily downward trend in the price of silver.

It was a splendid programme for the nation, particularly for the South. The Republican Federal machine vindictively opposed the first two policies, and a minority of Republican legislators united with the Democrats in favor of silver.

Nevertheless Hayes persisted. He emphasized his purpose to redeem greenbacks by selecting as his Secretary of the Treasury the man in charge of the specie resumption bill in Congress when it was enacted—John Sherman.

His second purpose he hoped to accomplish and, so far as was then possible, did accomplish by selecting David M. Key, of Tennessee, to be his Postmaster General. Key had been a Brigadier General in the Confederate Army. Let us not in these days minimize the broad sympathy and firmness necessary for such a step.

Hayes had to meet the charge from Republican leaders that his Southern policy meant a "Solid South" politically hostile to every Republican Administration beginning with his own; also, that a Republican majority in the Senate or the House of Representatives would in future have to be elected from Northern States, for no Republican could be elected in the South.

Nevertheless, he believed that prejudice born of war, the partisanship of politics, should give way to the higher obligation to unite the country. Within three months South Carolina and Louisiana had Governors chosen in their own way. The immediate political consequences were precisely as anticipated—and they have remained so substantially ever since.

HAYES' STRONG CABINET

But the deepest impression made by Hayes at the beginning was in his selection of his Cabinet. It was not a council of politicians that he gathered around his table. For individual ability and for unity of purpose, the Hayes Cabinet was one of the strongest ever assembled; its solidarity stood the test of time as have few others. George McCrary retired in a year to enter the United States Senate, but, broadly speaking, the Hayes Cabinet stood with its chief from beginning to end.

The Secretary of State was William M. Evarts; Secretary of the Treasury, John Sherman; Attorney General, Charles Devens; Secretary of War, George W. McCrary; Secretary of the Navy, Richard W. Thompson; Postmaster General, David M. Key; Secretary of the Interior, Carl Schurz.

Not only did a Democratic House embarrass Hayes when he began his Administration; he had also the opposition of the Senate, under control of the hostile Conkling-Cameron faction. It was arrogant and contemptuous. Conkling loudly declared in his imperious way that he would never enter the White House while Hayes was there. As fate ordained, he actually never did enter it again at any time. Other political leaders, both Republican and Democratic, at odds with other Presidents before and since Hayes, have exiled themselves from the Executive Mansion in the same spirit of disdain for the chief Magistrate of the nation, but always with the same unfortunate result to themselves as in Conkling's case. In such matters the people stand by their President.

MAKING THE GREENBACK GOOD

Hayes made no rejoinders. He had larger tasks than factional politics. His first big task was to see to it that the pledge to redeem the greenback on Jan. 1, 1879, was kept. A majority in both branches of Congress was opposed to the effort, but they knew that any tampering legislation would be met with a veto. Thus they willingly awaited the event confident that the Treasury would be swamped by the demand for coin in place of greenbacks. The President would then have to turn to Congress for help; that would be the day of opportunity for the "more money" theorists.

The day never came. Few greenbacks were presented for redemption. People wanted confidence in the greenback, not gold in exchange for it. Once that confidence in it was established, it became good enough for them to keep. Grant in urging the resumption law had said "it would secure a currency good wherever civilization reigns—a currency which has as its basis the labor necessary to produce it and which will give to it its value."

As I Knew Them

A TELEGRAM THAT BECAME HISTORIC

No date in our financial history means more to America than Jan. 1, 1879. Many persons regard the telegram announcing the result of the Treasury's experience that day as evidence of one of the greatest triumphs ever scored by our government. Everyone was anxious to know how heavy the drain of gold from the Treasury would be and how the Treasury had stood it. The Sub-treasury in New York City amazed the world by announcing at the close of the day's business that it had gained not lost gold, and that only $40,000 of greenbacks had been presented. Here is that historic telegram, reproduced from Andrew's "Last Quarter of a Century," published in 1896:

The Telegram Announcing the Result of the First Day's "Resumption" at the New York Sub-Treasury

Half a century later, our nation's promise to pay, though still printed on paper, is accepted the world over at face value. Americans thrill with proper pride that everywhere a dollar bill is as good as gold. Little is it realized, however, that Grant, our soldier President, made the first battle to have it so accepted, and that Hayes finished the fight.

INGERSOLL SAYS: "I KNOW THAT MY REDEEMER LIVETH"

When Secretary of the Treasury Sherman announced that the Government had that day redeemed and would continue to redeem all its paper in coin, upon demand, Robert G. Ingersoll, the great agnostic of his time, convulsed the country by declaring in a speech from the sub-Treasury steps to a thronged Wall Street: "I am thankful to have lived to see the day when the greenback can raise its right hand and declare 'I know that my Redeemer Liveth.'"

A KINDLY ATTITUDE TOWARD THE SOUTH

No President has ever approached the South in kindlier spirit than did Hayes. The man who had been a brave soldier in the Union cause now wanted a union of sympathies and peaceful purposes. In his inaugural he said the Southern people were "still impoverished" and "the inestimable blessing of wise, honest and peaceful self-government is not yet fully enjoyed." He added: "The time has come when such government is the imperative necessity required by all the demands, public and private, of the States."

But Hayes did not mean that the South could nullify the Constitution as to the negro vote. "Only a local government that recognizes the right of all is true self-government," he wrote, "a government that submits heartily and loyally to the Constitution and the laws. They must obey the whole Constitution as it is."

That was precisely what the South was determined not to do. All else done for it counted for nothing. Its response to Hayes' withdrawal of troops maintaining "carpet-bag" State governments was a demand through the Democratic

87

Congress for the withdrawal of United States Marshals protecting the negro vote for President and Congressmen.

A FIRM BUT NOT DEFIANT PRESIDENT

"Riders" were attached to departmental appropriation bills, —the army and navy, for instance, left without pay—in the hope of driving Hayes into acquiescence. Veto after veto from the White House met this persistent effort to break down the national election law. It could not be done. Hayes sent the bills back with messages placing responsibility on Congress for failure to meet the ordinary expenses of government. Congress adjourned; he called it back.

Never in angry denunciatory tone, never arraigning those who, led by a "Solid South," were trying to break down his Administration, he replied in language that is a model of sound reasoning. "Only the shadow of the authority of the United States at national elections will remain," he wrote, "the substance will be gone." Here is a trenchant paragraph from another of his series of vetoes:

> "Elections should be free from all apprehensions of interference. No soldiers, either of the Union or of the State militia, should be present at the polls to take the place or to perform the duties of the ordinary civil police force. There has been and will be no violation of the rule under orders from me during the Administration; but there should be no denial of the right of the National Government to employ its military force on any day and at any place in case such employment is necessary to enforce the Constitution and laws of the United States."

There was the strength of honorable purpose as well as of frankness in these words. In 1894, President Cleveland sent Federal troops into Chicago during the Debs strike on the same interpretation of duty. The north rallied to Hayes' support—so much so that Southern leaders in Congress recognized the unwisdom of continuing the battle. They abandoned it until Grover Cleveland became President in 1885. Then they had their way, and have had it ever since.

TWO HISTORIC AND CONTRASTING UTTERANCES

Two utterances early in Hayes' term measure the wide gulf between Hayes and the Conkling-Cameron-Logan group of Republicans in control of the party organization:

"He serves his party best who serves his country best," wrote Hayes in a message to Congress.

"When Dr. Johnson called patriotism the last refuge of a scoundrel," declared Roscoe Conkling while denouncing Hayes' civil service reform as "snivel service," "he forgot the possibilities contained in the word Reform."

Hayes listened to such denunciations, but kept right on. Removals from office were made "for cause" only. Fewer men were dropped than under any previous administration. It was the first effort since John Quincy Adams' day to put merit ahead of "pull" in government service. The anger of party politicians was not concealed. They wanted a quarrel with Hayes, but it takes two to make a quarrel and Hayes would not quarrel. He stuck to his policy, repeatedly in his messages to Congress summarized its good results, and let it go at that.

OUSTING CHESTER A. ARTHUR FROM OFFICE

His one conspicuous move, and one that had fateful consequences, was his removal from office of Chester A. Arthur and Alonzo B. Cornell. Arthur was Collector of the Port of New York; Cornell was Surveyor. They ignored Hayes' order to keep their offices out of politics; finally their defiance became intolerable and he demanded their resignations. Within a year Cornell was elected Governor of New York and Arthur elected Vice President.

Later on I deal with that subsequent phase, but it is interesting to record now that Hayes nominated as Arthur's successor the father of Theodore Roosevelt. Conkling blocked his confirmation by the Senate; Hayes' only reply was to send another name, which Conkling had to accept.

HOW WE GOT THE CART-WHEEL DOLLAR

Unfortunately, winning the battle for the greenback did not win another of the same type—the battle to prevent the coining of silver dollars at a fixed ratio regardless of the price of silver bullion. Hayes was firm, clear and persistent in that struggle; his messages to Congress have the force of accurate analysis and prophetic warning of the inevitable consequence of attempting to circulate a coin dollar not worth its bullion value; but Congress had a listening ear only for the plea of the silver men to "do something for silver."

Richard P. Bland, a Democrat, of Missouri, led the do-something-for-silver forces in Congress. He sponsored a bill providing for the compulsory coining monthly of not less than $2,000,000 nor more than $4,000,000 silver dollars. (In the west these coins still circulate, but how many Eastern people today recall those big cart-wheel Bland dollars?) "If Wall Street won't take silver dollars," yelled Bland in debate, "we'll stuff greenbacks down its throat until it chokes." Extreme as that statement is in the light of today it nevertheless accurately voiced the intensity of feeling in 1878—and for that matter in the struggle Cleveland made fifteen years later to repeal what was really a modification of the same law.

Bland came to be known as "Silver Dollar Dick"; his loyalty and his service to the silver cause compared with Bryan's were as 16 to 1. Before Bryan raided the Democratic convention in 1896 the Missourian was the indicated nominee; he held a long lead over Bryan with 235 votes on the first ballot, and his column of devoted supporters was all that stood solidly when on the fifth roll call the Bryan tornado gathered up two-thirds of the delegates. With Bland, silver was a cause; win or lose it had his whole heart. With Bryan, silver was merely a means to an end.

HAYES PROPHESIES THE RESULT THAT CAME

Bland's triumph in 1878 over Hayes was complete. In the Senate he had such an able man as William B. Allison, a Republican, of Iowa, as an ally—one who was to become a strong contender for his party's nomination for President in 1888, and who twice refused to be Secretary of the Treasury. Hayes met the Silverites with a veto. Two-thirds of each House then voted to enact the law despite a veto message so sound, so prophetic that Cleveland's later words seem only confirmation.

The law had scarcely become operative before gold began to flow from the Treasury like an ebbing tide. Everyone wanted gold coin; few would accept silver. Three out of every four silver dollars that were coined were unsought. They remained in government vaults. Hayes urged relief by an amendment authorizing the coining of silver dollars at bullion value—but Congress would not yield.

Helpless against a two-thirds vote, Hayes finally warned that the government could not continue losing its gold; nor could it force a depreciated silver dollar into circulation. Sooner or later a crisis must come. Congress ignored his appeal, whereupon Hayes left it to the event to justify him. And it did.

In 1893, Cleveland facing the crisis Hayes had foreseen took up the battle and repealed the law; in 1896 the issue was taken to the nation's ballot box where McKinley's triumph over Bryan gave the approving seal of the people to all that Hayes had urged upon Congress, nearly twenty years before.

In the light of the events between 1878 and 1896 the following prophecy from Hayes' pen is of highest interest:

"Any expectation of ease from an issue of silver coining to pass as a legal tender at a rate materially above its commercial value is, I am persuaded, a delusion.

"National promises should be kept with unflinching fidelity. There is no power to make a nation pay its just debts. Its credit depends on its honor."

Of course, it is only a matter of individual opinion to speak of Hayes' Administration as among the best in purpose and achievement we have ever had,—unless you have the attesting authority of the people of his time. Fortunately, that authority is to be found in the election results.

When Hayes entered the White House, the Republicans had lost control of the House of Representatives and of New York, Indiana and several New England States. Two years later those States were back in the Republican fold; four years later, as he retired from office, he installed a Republican as his successor in the White House, and a Republican majority was elected to both branches of Congress, despite an increasing number of Democrats from the South, then become "Solid."

Arthur failed to elect a successor of his own faith, Cleveland failed twice, Harrison failed, Taft failed; Wilson, after two terms, failed. Roosevelt alone shares with Hayes the distinction of being followed by a President of his own party. Despite the attack upon his title to office, despite the cynical attitude of the party "organization" leaders in Congress, the Hayes Administration demonstrated that it had won the confidence and support of the people when in the 1880 elections the Republican party was restored to complete control of the national government for the first time since 1874.

CHAPTER XII

"BLAINE! BLAINE!—JAMES G. BLAINE!"

A Popular Cry For Nearly Twenty Years—The "Plumed Knight" Of Politics—Conkling's Silence Cost Defeat—Conkling's Home County Turned New York Against Blaine—A Feud That Lasted Unto Death —"His Turkey Gobbler Strut"—Blaine's Fight Put Hayes And Garfield In The White House—The "Bloody Shirt" Era—Three Incidents That Defeated Blaine In 1876—Abolishing The United Rule In Republican Conventions.

THERE ought to be some way other than the dry annals of history to keep such a man as James Gillespie Blaine in the minds of people for so brief a period as has elapsed since his death in 1893. I saw so much of him during his later years, knew so well his purposes and recall so distinctly the spirit with which the country debated every move he made and every word he uttered that to me it is amazing that reference to him is so often met with silence or with queries that suggest that "Rum, Romanism and Rebellion" is the one remembered incident of his career.

No title of President attaches to his name, nor is he conspicuously identified with any historic policy as, for instance, Henry Clay is identified with the protective tariff policy; but Blaine's activities, lasting through the quarter century following the Civil War, influenced an era in our nation's life when leadership was held only by men of strong convictions.

The test of Blaine's place in the politics of his day is that he outlasted all his rivals, that his struggle for the Presidency forced Roscoe Conkling to accept Hayes and Garfield, that his own direct word to his followers nominated Harrison, and that, though defeated in 1884 in his candidacy for President, he polled more votes than would have been polled by any other Republican that year.

I base this last statement on the opinion of many Republican leaders at the time. In the pivotal State of New York, Judge Charles J. Folger in 1882 had polled only 342,464 votes as the Republican candidate for Governor; Cleveland then polled 535,318. Two years later, the Blaine vote for President was 562,005—a substantial increase. Cleveland polled 563,154. Cleveland's first plurality of 192,854 was reduced to 1,047. Certainly on such figures Blaine, though defeated, carried the Republican flag near to victory.

I do not like the word "magnetic" applied to individuals; it has too often proven merely another term for shallow and insincere. Something broader and deeper attracted you to Blaine. He held the people to him because he was kindly, and considerate—a sharp contrast to the lordly, autocratic Roscoe Conkling, Senator from New York, whose vindictive, relentless antagonism cost Blaine the Presidential nomination in two conventions and the election in 1884.

CONKLING'S SILENCE MEANT DEFEAT

Of course, I do not mean that Conkling alone caused Blaine's defeat. There were several factors adversely affecting the Blaine vote, the most damaging being Burchard's "Rum, Romanism and Rebellion" speech, but the loss of enough votes to have elected Blaine, despite all other weaknesses, can be definitely traced to Conkling's silence in the face of persistent newspaper rumors that he preferred to see the Republican party defeated rather than see Blaine in the White House.

"I am not practicing criminal law," is the caustic reply he was reported to have made when urged to speak for Blaine.

Conkling's attitude led his home county—Oneida County, New York—for once in its history, to return a Democratic plurality. Had that county given Blaine the Republican plurality it gave Garfield in 1880 or Harrison in 1888 he would have overcome the 1,047 plurality accorded Cleveland in the total vote of New York State. The harmful influence of Conkling's silence extended, however, far beyond one county or one state. It was an example for many of the old "306" Stalwarts in several States, and cost the Republican national ticket many votes.

Thus, the last influence in politics of this forceful figure was withheld when needed to save his party from defeat. The rôle of sulker was neither heroic nor consistent for a man whose claims to leadership had been advanced, and whose every appeal for support had been based, on the theory that loyalty to the organization was the highest test of honorable obligation and fidelity to party. But Conkling knew no law save his own desires.

A FEUD THAT LASTED UNTO DEATH

No feud between two men with such numerous followers ever lasted so many years, or proved so disastrous to their party, as that between Blaine and Conkling. Its roots were deeper than differences over policies; they were personal, and, on Conkling's side, had the vindictiveness of affronted dignity and of thwarting of his plans in two conventions. It began in 1866—before either man had become a national figure. Probably both of them sensed a personal antipathy when in 1863 they met as strangers on the floor of the House, Blaine having just been elected.

Life-long antagonisms, like life-long friendships, sometimes have their beginning in an instinctive feeling that comes, we know not why or how, almost at the first glance of the eye, the first hand clasp, or the first word of conversation.

Looking back upon those first impulses, or impressions, you find that they usually have controlled a subsequent course. That is why I believe that even had Blaine never declared in Congress his disregard for Conkling's scorn, nor referred to his "over-powering turkey-gobbler strut,"—the two men would have been out of sympathy from their earliest contact, and sooner or later would have found themselves in rivalry over Republican policy.

"HIS TURKEY-GOBBLER STRUT"

That Blaine rejoinder to Conkling became an historic episode. It occurred in 1866. Conkling was opposing an appropriation bill that Blaine sought to have passed. The New York Congressman had referred to Blaine with the sarcasm he knew so well how to use. The Maine man took the floor at once. Turning directly toward Conkling he said:

> "As for the gentleman's cruel sarcasm, I hope he will not be too severe. The contempt of that large minded gentleman is so wilting, his haughty disdain, his grandiloquent swell, his majestic, supereminent, overpowering turkey-gobbler strut has been so crushing to myself and others that I know it was an act of the greatest temerity for me to venture upon a controversy with him."

The "turkey-gobbler strut" sank unforgivably deep; it clung to Conkling in cartoon and satire throughout his career. Even in those early days, before Conkling's disdain for others had reached its ultimate toploftiness, there was a dread in Congress of crossing swords with him; his irony, his tempestuous outbreaks, were avoided by debaters whenever possible. And for this young member from Maine,—of his own party,—to enter into oral combat with the Utica statesman was deemed an undertaking that meant annihilation in Republican councils at Washington. It did not prove quite so deadly for Blaine, for at the next session he was chosen Speaker, but it did keep him out of the White House.

BLAINE'S FIGHT MADE HAYES AND GARFIELD PRESIDENT

Blaine entered Congress from the Augusta district. Conkling was then in his second term. Blaine, born in Penn-

ROSCOE CONKLING'S "TURKEY GOBBLER STRUT"

sylvania, had been a school-teacher and a newspaper reporter; next he bought the Kennebec Journal, and settled down in Maine. Several terms in the Legislature were followed by election to Congress;—then he became Senator, then Secretary of State for Garfield, next for Harrison. He was a presidential candidate in four national conventions—assuming that he was not even a "receptive" candidate in 1888.

I think it an accurate estimate of Blaine that he commanded the enthusiasm of as many voters, in and out of his party, as any man in our public life, even including Theodore Roosevelt and William J. Bryan. Such a career, of course, is political history. Some day an historian's pen will describe it adequately, when much now forgotten about Blaine—and the good about our public men is too often forgotten—will be accorded the attention and significance it deserves.

THE "BLOODY SHIRT" ERA

Nor is it my province to deal at length with that period following the war called the "Bloody Shirt" era of our politics. Its intense phase lasted until after the defeat of Grant for nomination in 1880 as "the soldier candidate," "the man who put down the Rebellion." Had Grant then been nominated for President his candidacy would surely have revived the dying war passion; the country would have been taken back to 1869 when Charles Sumner announced that he was seeking re-election as Senator from Massachusetts on the one plank: "Shall the men who saved the Republic continue to rule it, or shall it be handed over to rebels and their allies?"

The Bay State answered with a Republican majority elected to the Legislature instructed to send Sumner back to Washington.

Blaine shared these sentiments, prejudices or war passions, call them what you will. New England was the heart of them. It had sacrificed heroically to save the Union, and it forgot slowly. Blaine probably could not have survived politically had he not flaunted the "Bloody Shirt," for "old soldier" votes were too numerous to be ignored. He, too, called upon the North to keep the war won by keeping in control the party that had won it.

When a general amnesty bill was under consideration by Congress, Blaine led in urging an amendment excepting Jefferson Davis. The South hotly denounced this amendment as an affront; it insisted upon exempting all or none; Blaine as strongly stood for all but one. Almost thirty years later, with Davis dead, such a measure as the South desired passed Congress and William McKinley, himself a Union soldier, signed it; but in 1873 it had not a chance of passage.

"ANYBODY TO BEAT BLAINE"

Came 1876 with the Democrats controlling New York and other large States; the House of Representatives Democratic and the Senate in peril; Grant with a discredited administration. Not a hopeful outlook. Roscoe Conkling in New York, Don Cameron, in Pennsylvania, Zach Chandler in Michigan, Oliver P. Morton in Indiana, "Black Jack" Logan, a fine Union General in Illinois—these were the controlling figures in the Republican national organization.

They had but one opponent strong enough to challenge them—Blaine, now an avowed candidate for President. Conkling would tolerate no compromise with Blaine. He must be beaten. But how and with whom? Grant? He seemed to be the only man who could defeat Blaine in Convention. Dare they risk their fortunes on Grant—a soldier seeking three consecutive elections to the Presidency? Some favored going ahead, others thought the country should first be sounded. This was done.

There is no evidence that Grant was a party to these activities except that he did not stop them; also, he wrote two or three letters that certainly did not place him definitely in opposition. He said he had not wanted a first term, and did

not want a third term, but there was no law against his seek‑
ing one if he desired. However, the Grant talk subsided
even before the House of Representatives passed an anti-
third term resolution, with all Democrats and all but twelve
Republicans voting for it. Blaine was among the twelve non-
voters.

Deprived of their candidate, the Conkling-Cameron-Logan
forces could unite only on a programme of anybody-to-beat
Blaine. The nominating convention met in Cincinnati, June
14. There was every indication as it convened that it would
be a Blaine convention. Oliver P. Morton, the silver-tongued
orator from Indiana who was Grant's spokesman in the Senate, Governor Hartranft, of Pennsylvania, a product of the
Cameron dynasty, and Conkling himself were candidates "to
beat Blaine." Benjamin F. Bristow of Kentucky, who while
Grant's Secretary of the Treasury had defied the spoilsmen
of his party and had resigned rather than acquiesce in their
supremacy, was also a candidate with a substantial following.
In a smaller way, Marshall Jewell, of Connecticut, once
Grant's Postmaster General, was another.

Lastly there was one other candidate—Rutherford B.
Hayes, then Governor of Ohio, a candidate on his own record
and without alliance with anyone. He got the nomination.

"LIKE AN ARMED WARRIOR, LIKE A PLUMED KNIGHT"

I have heard those who participated in the convention tell
of the impressive scene when Robert G. Ingersoll made his
historic plea for Blaine. Here is the memorable sentence of
that speech:

> "Like an armed warrior, like a plumed knight, James G. Blaine
> marched down the aisles of the American Congress and threw his
> shining lance full and fair against the brazen foreheads of the
> defamers of his country, and the maligners of his honor. For
> this convention to desert such a man would be like an army desert-
> ing a general on the eve of battle."

As I Knew Them

From the moment of that utterance, Blaine became the Plumed Knight, the "Henry of Navarre" of American politics.

THREE UNUSUAL INCIDENTS LED TO DEFEAT

Once again, cheers did not nominate—the leader of a great enthusiasm went down in defeat. These three incidents, each unforeseen, combined to thwart Blaine's ambition:

First, he had a sun-stroke the Sunday before the convention, while walking to church in Washington. He fell unconscious on the church steps. His opponents made the most of that temporary illness.

Second, a roll-call on which it was firmly believed Blaine would poll a majority vote should have followed the Ingersoll speech. The darkness of early evening had come, however, the gas fixtures were out of repair and there was fear of gas-lights in a crowded convention hall; adjournment until morning was therefore ordered. Night gave opportunity to strengthen the anti-Blaine forces.

Third, Benjamin F. Bristow, of Kentucky, who had more than enough votes to nominate, was opposed to Blaine as well as to Conkling-Cameron supremacy. In Washington, when he learned of Blaine's illness, he called at the Blaine home to express his sympathies; it is said that he asked to see him. As Bristow was also a candidate, he was "on suspicion" and was curtly told at the door by someone—not with Blaine's knowledge—that neither Blaine nor the family was at home. Bristow's anger had not cooled when the convention began balloting three days later; he turned his delegates to Hayes.

Senator Hoar, of Massachusetts, a man extremely careful of his utterances, was a delegate to the convention. He was never a Blaine man. In his Autobiography he wrote "if Bristow had not visited Blaine's house that Sunday morning, Blaine would, in my opinion, have been the nominee for the Presidency."

As I Knew Them

BREAKING THE UNIT RULE IN REPUBLICAN CONVENTIONS

Though Blaine did not win his first battle for the Presidency, a great cause that he advocated did win.   That cause was the right of every delegate in a national convention to vote according to his individual will.   Since 1876 every Republican convention has honored that right, though few persons keep it in mind that Blaine was the man who made the battle to establish it.   He chose as his battle ground the very citadel of bossism—the Cameron-controlled delegation from Pennsylvania.

When Don Cameron as chairman cast the vote of his delegation solidly for Governor Hartranft, four delegates challenged Cameron's right to cast their votes under the unit rule. They asked to be recorded for Blaine.   Edward McDowell, a Pennsylvania delegate, was presiding.   Though he voted for Hartranft, he ruled that the vote of each delegate should be recorded as announced by the delegate.   On a division the convention sustained him—395 to 353.

The majority, though slender, was broad enough as a precedent to insure every delegate in subsequent Republican conventions the right to his own vote; it was the first triumph of liberalism in the party—and to Blaine is due the credit.

CHAPTER XIII

THE "STALWART" CONVENTION OF 1880

The Last Ditch Stand Of The Conkling-Logan-Cameron Forces—Four Days Before The Convention Could Organize—Grant Really Beaten When Unable To Revive Unit Rule—Conkling's Inspiring Struggle—The Example of A. Barton Hepburn—Conkling's Resolve Not To Enter The White House—"If Asked What State He Hails From"—Garfield Undertakes A Contrast—"Not The Billows But The Calm Levels Are The True Measure"—The "306" And Those Who Stood Resolutely Against Them—Conkling Not a Good Loser.

INTENSE as were the incidents of the 1876 convention, and historic as was its abolition of the unit rule, it had more than its equal in both respects four years later in Chicago. In strategy, in bitterness, in dramatic oratory and in its surprising result, no convention of any party ever exceeded the Republican convention of 1880.

It was the last-ditch stand of those Republicans made powerful by patronage during the eight years of Grant. Though under Hayes they had largely lost their influence, they were now determined to nominate a President upon whom they could depend. Again Blaine was their one towering obstacle; again Blaine was the man they had to beat.

This time, however, unlike 1876, they had a candidate to match against him—Grant. He was a name, and their greatest need was a name the country knew. On a platform declaring him to be the soldiers' candidate, they planned to raise the old "Union Forever" issue. It was a cruel effort to intensify war passions—to prolong the "Bloody Shirt" era—and only men blinded by a desperate determination would have resorted to it. The battle of the "Stalwarts" was not a battle for patriotism but for sordid politics, and the tragic results that flowed from it are not its only condemnation.

The convention lasted six days, but less than two days were required for those thirty-seven ballots in which the "306" became famous. History gives scant attention to the real battle of the convention. That took place in the committee on credentials and the committee on rules. There the Grant forces struggled night and day for control. They lost—and that early defeat definitely forecast their inability to nominate their candidate. Grant was no longer a possible nominee.

WAR TO THE KNIFE

Though the Convention Sessions began Tuesday noon it was late Saturday afternoon before it received and adopted its committee reports. Think of 700 delegates waiting four days to organize! Every moment of that unprecedented delay had been a moment of desperate struggle in committee. The Grant men fought to secure a report seating their contesting delegates; they fought harder still to defeat an addition to the rules based on the action of the 1876 convention insuring to each delegate the right to declare his own vote. A majority of the rules committee finally adopted it; a minority brought the fight against it into the convention. Result: 479 votes in favor of the 1876 ruling; 276 against.

Thus the unit rule was buried beyond hope of resurrection; by the same token, that vote settled Grant's fate despite the power of oratory, despite the solid phalanx of "Stalwarts." The one substantial hope of his nomination had rested on securing power to silence on roll-call the anti-Grant minorities in State delegations controlled by Grant majorities. New York, for example, had 22 anti-Grant delegates who under a unit rule would have been voted by the chairman for Grant. Thus, when that rule was voted down, the candidate went with it.

As I Knew Them

Conkling, however, saw only victory ahead. His courage, his spirit, his faith in himself made him a leader who always won until defeated, and he had the rare talent of imbuing his followers with the same confidence. He was just such a commander as men loyally follow even unto death. His memorable speech nominating Grant had the inspiring qualities needed to enthuse men in a desperately hard battle. No other convention speech, not even Bryan's "Cross of Gold" speech, has been more often quoted. It would have been impressive even had it been delivered by a less-gifted orator, but, spoken by the tall and stately Conkling, its dramatic effects were emphasized.

In the years just following the convention I listened to many discussions of the speech. There were two opinions. As oratory, it was unchallenged; as a vote-getting, persuasive influence it was questioned. I agreed with many who heard it,—that it had the weakness of the speaker's intolerance of opposing views. There is no evidence that it added a single vote to those already committed to Grant; its strength was that it created an atmosphere of heroic endeavor around the "306" delegates battling through thirty-six strenuous ballots until they went down together to defeat. In the political literature of the day they were acclaimed as the possessors of a loyalty equalling that of the gallant "Six Hundred" of Tennyson's Light Brigade: "Theirs not to reason why, theirs but to do and die."

Such was in truth the creed of the "Stalwarts"—"theirs not to reason why." Conkling did the reasoning and the commanding. His word was law. His rule was guided by an iron hand that wore no velvet glove. Extreme in his friendships, he was equally so in his enmities. He never forgot a favor nor forgave a slight. He demanded from all the homage due to great ability; in return he gave a fine loyalty and sympathy.

THE EXAMPLE OF A. BARTON HEPBURN

I have always kept in mind one example of Conkling's recognition of loyalty among his supporters. It concerns the late A. Barton Hepburn, for many years President of the Chase National Bank of New York City and a man of great wealth. Hepburn himself is my authority, though so many years have elapsed since he told me the story that its detail may not be wholly accurate. Substantially, it is this:

Hepburn was a village school teacher in St. Lawrence County, Northern New York. Because he was not in politics, the warring Conkling and Anti-Conkling factions in Hepburn's village compromised by selecting him as a delegate to the Republican State Convention. In the county convention, however, the Conkling forces passed resolutions instructing all St. Lawrence delegates to vote with Conkling.

When the issue came in the State Convention, many of them ignored their instructions. Hepburn insisted that inasmuch as he had come pledged he would remain pledged to the end. That night he was aroused from sleep by a message that Senator Conkling desired to see him. Amazed that such a great man should send for a poor school-master, he hastened over to Conkling's room. Conkling told him he had heard of his decision to stand by his instructions. He said to him: "This is your first convention, but I hope it won't be your last. Every man who stands by his word succeeds." He then told Hepburn to be sure to call upon him if he could ever be of help to him.

A year or so later, a National bank examiner was to be appointed. Conkling sent for Hepburn; offered him the position. He accepted and thus began a career that brought Hepburn into national esteem as a student of finance, a banker of great ability and, finally, a man worth many millions. The experience of his first convention remained with him as a guide through life.

CONKLING THE MAN

Conkling could do such things as the favor to Hepburn graciously but always there was in addition an attitude that an emperor might have envied. Upon a body of commanding stature, his fine head was carried in every sense above his fellows; his high forehead was only partly concealed by an Hyperion curl of silvery white hair; he stood so erect that he seemed taller than six feet, though he was not; his stride had the majesty of a consciously superior person.

Conkling had the virtue of frankness and of personal integrity; he also had the deplorable vice of a temper not always controlled and of a tongue distinguished because it spoke too frequently in scorn and contempt.

For example, Conkling never doubted that his flamboyant declaration that he would not enter the White House while Hayes was President—his contemptuous reference to Hayes' "Snivel Service" policy—belittled Hayes in the eyes of the people. In fact, they helped Hayes, for they emphasized the absence from his Administration of those influences which for eight years had brought the Republican party close to defeat.

"IF ASKED WHAT STATE HE HAILS FROM"

You can imagine the tense scene in that 1880 convention when such a man as I have described strode down the centre aisle toward the platform. Instead of taking the usual place on the platform by the chairman, he climbed upon a newspaper correspondent's table. There he stood facing an applauding multitude. This was the moment of test for his leadership; he knew it; so did the delegates. Almost fifteen minutes elapsed before Conkling could get silence. Then, in a deep tone that sounded through that meeting hall like a great cathedral organ, he began his memorable speech for Grant—

> "If asked what State he hails from
> Our sole response shall be,
> 'He hails from Appomattox
> And its famous apple tree.'"

Then came that powerful close in answer to the cry against a third term:

> "Having tried Grant twice and found him faithful we are told that we must not even after an interval of years, trust him again. My countrymen! my countrymen! Why? Why? What stultification does not such a fallacy involve? Is this an electioneering juggle or is it hypocrisy's masquerade?
>
> "There is no field of human activity, responsibility or reason in which rational beings object to an agent because he has been weighed in the balance and not found wanting. There is, I say no department of human reason in which sane men reject an agent because he has had experience making him exceptionally fit and competent.
>
> "From the man who shoes your horse to the lawyer who tries your cause, the officer who manages your railway or your mill, the doctor into whose hands you give your life or the minister who seeks to save your soul—what man do you reject because by his works you have known him and found him faithful and fit?
>
> "What makes the presidential office an exception to all things else in the common sense to be applied to selecting its incumbent?
>
> "Who dares to put fetters on that free choice and judgment which is the birth-right of the American people?"

In those days reporters did not use stop-watches,—as they have done since the Bryan chaos,—to time the period of enthusiasm following nominating speeches. Otherwise when Conkling concluded they might have recorded a full half hour of tumult.

GARFIELD UNDERTAKES A CONTRAST

Soon came James A. Garfield, Senator-Elect, himself an orator of power. His speech had none of Conkling's dramatic intensity. He knew he could not equal Conkling in that respect; it was his hope to make a contrast. And he did. Garfield's speech, though now forgotten, was the greatest factor in making him the candidate of his party for the Presidency. Conkling's speech, though still quoted in every collection of convention oratory as a model, did not add a vote or save his candidate from defeat.

Picture the great convention slowly settling down to order after the tumult over the Conkling address; picture Garfield, as spokesman for the John Sherman candidacy, standing on the same reporter's table on which Conkling had stood, waiting as he had waited for a listening audience; picture Senator George Frisbie Hoar, the chairman, almost breaking the gavel while pounding for order. Then read this masterly opening, this strategic oratory. It united audience and speaker. No voice that would reach that vast audience could have been more placid, more quieting, more disarming of opposition, than was Garfield's as he began:

"Mr. President: I have witnessed the extraordinary scenes of this Convention with deep solicitude. Nothing touches my heart more quickly than a tribute of honor to a great and noble character; but as I sat in my seat and witnessed this demonstration, this assemblage seemed to me a human ocean in tempest. I have seen the sea lashed into fury and tossed into spray, and its grandeur moves the soul of the dullest man; but I remember that it is not the billows but the calm level of the sea from which all heights and depths are measured.

"When the storm is past and the hour of calm settles on the ocean, when the sunlight bathes its peaceful surface, then the astronomer and surveyor take the level from which they measure all terrestrial heights and depths.

"Gentlemen of the Convention, your present temper may not mark the healthful pulse of our people. When your enthusiasm has passed, when the emotions of this hour have subsided, we shall find below the storm and passion that calm level of public opinion from which the thoughts of a mighty people are to be measured, and by which their final action will be determined.

As I Knew Them

"Not here, in this brilliant circle, where 15,000 men and women are gathered, is the destiny of the Republic to be decreed for the next four years. Not here, where I see the enthusiastic faces of 756 delegates, waiting to cast their lots into the urn and determine the choice of the Republic; but by 4,000,000 of Republican firesides, where the thoughtful voters, with wives and children about them, with the calm thoughts inspired by love of home and country, with the history of the past, the hopes of the future, and reverence for the great men who have adorned and blessed our nation in the days gone by, burning in their hearts—*there* God prepares the verdict which will determine the wisdom of our work tonight."

A SPEECH THAT MADE A PRESIDENT

The speech was Garfield's triumph. His tone, his manner, his words were suited to the deeper purpose of the delegates. He was the man of the hour—the whispered beneficiary of a deadlock. No one had brought it about, no one could have brought it about; it seems to have come into the minds of many delegates at the same moment that here was the man to bring peace and success to the party. The feeling spread like a tidal wave.

SOME CONVENTION FIGURES OF INTEREST

Some figures about that convention will be interesting. There were 756 delegates, making 379 votes necessary to nominate. Grant always led on roll-call through the 36 ballots until the last, when Garfield had a majority. In fact, it was on the next to the last ballot that Grant scored his highest vote—313. Beginning with 304, he kept within 304 and 313 until the break to Garfield, when 306 delegates stood by him. Hence the famous "306" battalion of Stalwarts so much talked of in politics.

Solidarity always is an inspiring spectacle; it denotes conviction, earnestness and loyalty—qualities that every robust person applauds. In that convention, however, solidarity was not the exclusive possession of the Grant men. It has always seemed to me that the delegates who withstood the force of such a name as Grant are at least as worthy of praise for their courage and loyalty as the 306 who rallied unitedly around the standard of his renown.

There were 450 delegates who resisted on every ballot the Grant candidacy.

The struggle was a clean-cut battle between two factions—with Blaine as the leader of the 450 delegates (though not the candidate of all), and Conkling the leader of the "306," for the real leader was Conkling, not Grant. It was a Blaine and Conkling struggle for mastery of the party, its candidates and its policies. Again, as in 1876, Blaine triumphed over him. True, the Maine man did not secure the nomination for himself; but his struggle forced the selection of a candidate beyond Conkling's control.

CONKLING NOT A GOOD LOSER

But Conkling could never tolerate defeat. With Garfield nominated he sulked and sneered. He even neglected to call upon the nominee at his hotel. "No friend of mine will go on this ticket," he is reported to have declared when reports reached him that the Vice Presidency was to be offered. For a month he allowed politicians to guess whether he was for the ticket.

Grant took a broader view. Promptly and manfully he declared for Garfield. His attitude forced Conkling and other Stalwarts into line. They bargained with Garfield, or claimed to have bargained, their influence in return for control over patronage, but they never contributed much enthusiasm to the campaign.

There were times when Garfield's election seemed only a possibility. He was a Congressman, a Senator-elect and a Presidential candidate at the same time. Often such immaterial things affect public sentiment. They did, for a time, in Garfield's case. Despite many adversities, however, such as the forged Morey letter against organized labor, and a charge involving his Credit Mobilier connections, Garfield won. But his path of glory led shortly to the grave.

CHAPTER XIV

GARFIELD TO HIS GRAVE, CONKLING INTO EXILE

A Tragic Era In American Politics—The New York Collectorship A Storm Centre That Leads Conkling To Resign His Senatorship— Thomas C. Platt, Also a Senator, Says "Me Too"—Arthur, Though Vice President, Joins The Fight On Garfield—Assassin Guiteau Shouts "I Am A Stalwart Of The Stalwarts!"—Conkling Asks "How Can I Battle With A Shroud?"—The Victim Of A New York City Blizzard.

MARCH 4, 1881, saw the inauguration of a second Republican administration with which Conkling shortly, with characteristic haughtiness, declared he would have nothing to do.

The appointment of Blaine, the man he literally hated, as Secretary of State was sufficient to convince Conkling that a conspiracy was planned against his political interests. His opposition to Hayes had not gone beyond ignoring him—of assuming that for four years the White House was vacant, pending the installation of a tenant whom he would name. Garfield, however, had scarcely crossed its threshold before Conkling denounced him as a man of broken promises. In his own mind he saw Blaine controlling the President's course, and the vision frenzied him. It was intensified by the nomination of William H. Robertson as Collector of the Port of New York.

Conkling's rage knew no limits. The patronage-centre of New York politics, the office from which Hayes had removed Chester A. Arthur, now Vice President, because he had made it a political headquarters, was the one place that Conkling was determined must be restored to his political assets.

Garfield held a different view. Probably, had the Collectorship been held by a Conkling adherent, Garfield would have continued him rather than offend the New York Senator; but Hayes had cleansed the office of factional politics, and Garfield was resolved not to undo Hayes' good work. Without consulting Conkling he selected Robertson.

Then came a most sensational incident and the most tragic chapter in American politics. Conkling resigned his Senatorship and sought to have the New York Legislature re-elect him as a protest against Garfield. Thomas C. Platt, then newly-elected to the Senate, joined with Conkling. The newspapers called him "Me Too" Platt.

CONKLING'S GAUNTLET

In a century of contention between Congress and the President, some of it vindictive, no Senator had ever issued such a challenge. Only men carried away by a false sense of their own importance, and an equally poor appreciation of the high office of President, would have risked their careers in an effort so unlikely of success. It is conceivable that a Legislature would oppose a President of its own party on a matter of policy—such, for example, as the League of Nations—but it would never do so on such an issue as the resignation of Conkling and "Me Too" raised.

Conkling's control in New York was so absolute, however, that he never doubted his triumphant re-entry into the Senate with his defiance of Garfield indorsed by a Republican Legislature. Cornell, then Governor of New York, had also been removed from the customs service by Hayes; his influence was openly with Conkling. Arthur, though Vice President, went to Albany to aid in humiliating the President he was so soon to succeed.

"HOW CAN I BATTLE WITH A SHROUD?"

Fate had in store a destiny merciless for Garfield and only less tragic for his bitter opponent. While Conkling and

Platt were still struggling to have the Legislature reelect them, Charles Guiteau's bullet shocked the country. It ended two careers—Garfield's by death and Conkling's by exile from politics.

Without a word of warning Guiteau fired two shots at the President at a range of less than a dozen feet. Then brandishing his weapon high as Patrolman Kearney and a colored porter grabbed him he shrieked in a maniacal voice, "I am a Stalwart of the Stalwarts!"

Naturally such a cry created the suspicion that Guiteau must be the direct agent of a plot, but there was no evidence to support that theory.

Once more the New York leader's power to destroy was demonstrated. This time, however, Conkling had pulled the pillars down upon himself, too. In the calm of reflection, it became evident that Guiteau had planned assassination before the Conkling resignation, but at the moment that was the one tangible motive the people saw, and the Conkling régime collapsed like a house of cards. The Legislature promptly elected Warner Miller and Silas Lapham as Senators.

Conkling never again held public office, attended a convention or participated in politics. After Garfield's death he was asked whether he would continue his fight. Dramatically he replied:

"How can I speak into a grave? How can I battle with a shroud? Silence is a duty and a doom."

CONKLING'S TABLE OF STORY-TELLERS

For the seven remaining years of his life the former Senator made his evening headquarters at the Hoffman House, then owned by Ed. Stokes, the slayer of Jim Fisk, of Erie Railroad fame. There I met Conkling. There, night after night, in Stokes' café, famous for its costly paintings, Conkling gathered about him noted story-tellers like John Chamberlain of Washington and Tom Ochiltree of Texas, and doubtless found refuge in such company from thoughts of a career brilliant, disappointing and ended.

Conkling's ability might easily have taken him to the White House had the kindly qualities of his personal relations governed him in politics. But Conkling loved to use words as a prize-fighter loves to use his fists—and, similarly, he sought to land hard on his opponent. His career illustrates that nothing is more perilous in politics than the quick, sharp retort. The power of oratory, fascinating and pleasing as it is, leads you to extremes that later embarrass.

To a young man it seemed an honor to sit, when invited, at Conkling's table of famous raconteurs. I found, however, that it meant drinking not once but often through the evening. While no teetotaler, I had no desire to acquire the opposite habit. I made up my mind to give up the brilliant company. Several weeks later, as I was passing through the café, I saw Conkling seated alone at the table. I walked over to greet him.

"Young man," he said, "I observe that we have not had the pleasure of your company lately."

In later years, with more experience, I probably would have given some more polite answer than to tell him the decision I had made; instead, I told it.

"Well," said he, "that isn't very complimentary to the rest of us, but you are right. Yes, young man, you are right. We are old hands at it, and know how to take care of ourselves in all situations, but it is different at your years. Be your own master—don't let drink master you."

At another time, when a certain public man was under discussion, Conkling said to me, "Never trust a man whose eyes come close together. I have done so—only to regret it."

DIES DEFYING A BLIZZARD

A man of Conkling's temper had to die as he had lived—in defiance of opposing forces. His life was ended as his political career had ended—by his supreme confidence that he was superior to opposition. The great blizzard of 1888 buried New York city deep in snow. Transportation ceased; few people tempted the storm's fury. Conkling was one of the few. He walked from the City Hall to Madison Square—less than two miles—battling for two or three hours through the storm and paid the penalty with his life. He who had made so many others the victim of his wrath became himself the victim of the Storm King's wrath.

CHAPTER XV

ARTHUR, POLITICIAN, MAKES GOOD

The Country Wonders About Its New President—Levi P. Morton's Story Of How He Lost The Vice Presidency And Arthur Won It—Hayes' Letter To The Senate Giving His Reasons For Removing Arthur From New York Collectorship—Cornell, Also Ousted, Becomes New York's Governor—In The White House No Longer "Chet" But "Mr. President"—Arthur Remained A Stalwart, But Not A Conkling Lieutenant—How Arthur Cleared Cleveland's Path To Fame—Why Vice Presidents Are Seldom Nominated For First Place.

"'CHET' ARTHUR in the White House!"

The country staggered that September morning in 1881 as it read that Garfield was dead at the Long Branch cottage and that at midnight Chester Alan Arthur had been sworn in as President in his home on Lexington Avenue, New York City. Arthur—the Conkling lieutenant in New York politics, the ousted Collector of Customs, the Vice President who only a few months before had gone to Albany to urge the Republican Legislature to return Conkling and Platt to the Senate as a rebuke to the President with whom he had been elected. He had not hesitated to refer to Garfield as a man of broken promises just as he had not hesitated, after Hayes had removed him from office, to echo Conkling's belittling sarcasm when speaking of Hayes. In the campaign, as "the tail of the ticket," he had been characterized as a "pot-house" politician. Republican papers, not holding Arthur politically in high esteem, did not take the trouble to defend him.

Here he was in the White House, however—the head of the nation; with nearly a full term of four years to serve. Would he remain a ward politician or would he seek higher levels? Would Conkling control him?

These were the questions of the day. They prompted another inquiry to which people had theretofore given little heed—what led a Republican national convention to select as its candidate for Vice President—the successor to the President—a man whose career was that of a machine politician?

HOW MORTON LOST THE VICE PRESIDENCY

Many stories were told. I was still hoping and working for my opportunity to become a political reporter when that convention was held, so I cannot speak of it from personal knowledge. My convention work began four years later. I can only repeat the interesting story told me by Levi P. Morton, Vice President with Harrison, and later Governor of New York, as to how he lost his chance to be named on the ticket with Garfield and how Arthur snapped it up.

Morton was a delegate to the convention and one of the "306." He was also a Congressman, and the head of the New York banking house of Morton, Bliss & Company. In 1894, I was crossing the Atlantic on the old *Normandie* of the French Line. On deck one afternoon Morton remarked that he might have been President had he not allowed an opportunity to slip by him. He then told Senator "Ed" Wolcott, of Colorado, and myself this story:

Having nominated Garfield, the convention recessed for a three-hour breathing-spell before deciding whom to name for Vice President. Though Garfield was not a "Half Breed," as the Blaine men from New York were called, he was nominated by their influence; his supporters thought it good strategy, therefore, to have a pronounced "Stalwart" on the ticket. A committee with authority decided upon Morton, and sought him at his hotel. They told him their purpose, explaining also that because of the brief recess an immediate "yes" or "no" was necessary.

As I Knew Them

Morton, being more of a banker than a politician, felt he should not make such an important decision without consulting Conkling, his chief, who had openly urged all Stalwarts to keep off the ticket. He told the committee he would be glad to accept if Conkling would give his consent. He undertook to find Conkling and then give his reply.

The committeemen evidently regarded Morton as too timid. They wanted a Stalwart but they wanted one who would act first and talk about it afterward with his chief. Conkling might say "Amen" when he would not say "go ahead." So they began canvassing other names—"Chet" Arthur, for one. Arthur was an active Conkling lieutenant in the convention; he was well known to the delegates, and some of his New York colleagues had already started a complimentary boom for him.

Moreover, he was thoroughly "organization,"—just such a man as the New York machine would pull straight for. That was the real test of availability in the minds of the Garfield men, and they decided to ask Arthur if he would accept without waiting permission from anyone. They called him out of a group of delegates in the hotel corridor, and made their offer. There was no hesitation about his "yes." Furthermore, he stated that the New York delegates were to hold a meeting in the convention hall just before the session began and declared that he would then get the formal support of a large majority of them.

MORTON HEARS ARTHUR NAMED

Meanwhile, Morton had had difficulty in locating Conkling. "Sulking in his tent," the newspaper men said of him. When finally Conkling was found, he told his too loyal lieutenant to do as he pleased—that he was not interested. Morton, ignorant of the Arthur incident, hurried to find the Garfield committee. That, too, took time. He was ready to say "yes" but had no one to whom to say it! Finally, he went to the convention hall. There in an ante-room he found the New York delegates in meeting. As he entered he was amazed to hear Stewart L. Woodford announcing that a formal offer of the Vice Presidency had been made and accepted by Arthur. Morton promptly gave up his search for the Garfield men.

Such was the story Morton told us of his lost opportunity to become President. Eight years later, Morton was named and elected Vice President with Harrison,—but Harrison lived out his term.

There were stories that Conkling upbraided Arthur, that Arthur replied that it was an honor greater than he had ever anticipated, and that he should not be expected to put it aside. The only story I have ever heard or read, however, having the authority of one of the participants is the story told by Morton.

HAYES' PLAIN DUTY AS TO ARTHUR

Of course, the Democratic press pounded hard at Arthur during the campaign. They dwelt in detail upon his removal by President Hayes as Collector of Customs at New York less than two years before. He was then serving his second term by appointment from President Grant. He had also been ward leader, county chairman and local spokesman for Conkling. The message Hayes wrote the Senate was extensively used throughout the campaign. In view of subsequent developments this extract from it, dated Jan. 31, 1879, is of interest:

> "For a long period of time it (the Custom House at New York) has been used to manage and control political affairs. The officers suspended by me are and have been engaged in the active personal management of the party politics of New York city and State. The duties of the offices held by them have been regarded as of subordinate importance to their partisan work. Their offices have

been conducted as part of the political machinery under their control. I regard it as my plain duty to remove the officers in question."

Two years later Cornell was Governor of New York and "Chet" Arthur, the removed Collector, was the elected Vice President on the Republican national ticket.

Less than three years later he occupied the White House as President!

So runs the world!

ARTHUR REMAINS A STALWART

It was another Arthur, however, who sat in the White House as President. No longer "Chet" but Chester Alan Arthur, he responded quickly to the responsibilities and dignity of his high office. True as he had been to Conkling until Guiteau's bullet had done its deadly work, Arthur, thus tragically thrust into the Presidency, realized that he and Conkling must thereafter travel separate paths. The man whom he had recognized as his political chief and guide so many years was now his peril.

Conkling could not see this—he could not realize that, with Garfield just laid in his grave, any recognition of him by Garfield's successor was impossible. It was in Conkling's mind that he should have Blaine's place as Secretary of State. He never asked for the appointment but he never forgave Arthur for not tendering it to him.

But Arthur did not abandon those with whom he had been aligned in Republican politics. He replaced Blaine with Frelinghuysen, of New Jersey, William Windom in the Treasury with Charles J. Folger, Chief Justice of the New York Court of Appeals; Wayne MacVeagh with Benjamin H. Brewster as Attorney General; he kept Robert Todd Lincoln as Secretary of War. The new men were all of the "Stalwart" type—but they were men of ability and the country at once placed a higher estimate on Arthur.

As I Knew Them

It was a strange turning of the tide that Arthur should not only uphold the civil service rules established by Hayes but should as President sign the first effective civil service law; also that he should be the first President to veto a river and harbor appropriation bill as excessive—the bill that had come to be known as the "pork barrel" bill into which politicians of both parties dug deep.

HOW ARTHUR CLEARED CLEVELAND'S PATH TO FAME

But Arthur could not bring peace to the Republican party, particularly in his own State of New York he failed. Like many men who suddenly acquire great power, he wielded it like a club instead of using it to cement. New York was the centre of the faction storm area. There Arthur abandoned conciliation and sought to dominate. He forced the nomination for Governor of his Secretary of the Treasury Charles J. Folger. Personally, Folger was a man of character and ability—much too fine in all qualities to be made the certain victim of the Stalwart and Half-Breed factional strife.

In such circumstances any Democratic nominee was certain of election, and what was later called "Cleveland luck" came to the Mayor of Buffalo, scarcely known beyond Erie County. Thousands of Half-Breeds refused to vote for Folger. The latter's overwhelming defeat made Grover Cleveland a national figure and the indicated candidate of the Democratic Party for President two years later.

It exerted still another influence—it impaired Arthur's standing with Republicans at Washington and throughout the country. Obviously, leadership was lacking. Arthur as President won commendation from many who were frankly critical when he entered the White House, but he never made the deep impression on his party essential for a nomination for President on his own account. He was never a probable nominee. The votes he received in the convention merely reflected the patronage power of the man at the head of government.

As I Knew Them

After leaving the White House, Arthur mingled with old and new friends in New York City. As ex-President he was no longer a news centre, but some passing matters of public concern, now forgotten, brought me to his home on Lexington Avenue, on two occasions. I recall his dignity, his kindness and his determined purpose to keep out of controversies.

Chagrined by the refusal to make him the party candidate for President, he never sought political influence again.

PARTIES SELDOM FOLLOW VICE PRESIDENTS

Yet Arthur should not have been surprised by that refusal. Up to that time no Vice President, succeeding to the Presidency by death, had been nominated subsequently for a full term.

Of Tyler, who became President following Harrison's death in 1841, the Whigs in Congress formally declared one year later "Those who brought him into power can no longer be held responsible." He was not even mentioned in their convention as a possible nominee.

Andrew Johnson, who was Lincoln's running mate and successor, barely escaped conviction on impeachment charges made by Republicans, and in 1868 vainly turned for nomination to the Democratic convention—that of the party that had opposed him in 1864.

Millard Fillmore, who succeeded "Old Zach" Taylor in 1850, alone was able to maintain a strong hold on his party. He was defeated by General Winfield Scott for nomination only after 50 ballots—the longest convention struggle up to that time.

These refusals of a political party to follow a Vice President are the inevitable consequence of the tendency in conventions then and now to "balance" national tickets by selecting as Vice Presidential candidate a representative of the defeated minority. Such men are nominated for a purpose, not for their fitness. The two Vice Presidents who have succeeded to the Presidency since Arthur's day have been elected to succeed themselves. Unlike Arthur, neither Roosevelt nor Coolidge was nominated as consolation to a minority. They were named as individuals for their worth, and not as members of defeated factions. That is true also of Charles G. Dawes, nominated for Vice President with Coolidge in 1924. Thomas R. Marshall was of this class, too; but Charles P. Bryan, Adlai Stevenson and Arthur Sewall were named solely to satisfy the disappointed.

CHAPTER XVI

BLAINE WINS AND LOSES

*His Superstition That He Would Never Be President—"That Hoss'
Eyes Is Sot"—Prefers Circus To Nomination Talk—My First Con-
vention Experience—The "Mugwumps" Make Their Initial Bow In
Politics—A Most Unsavory National Campaign—Both Cleveland And
Blaine Had To Endure A "Whispering" Campaign—"Tell The
Truth!" Said Cleveland And Silence Followed—All Correspondents
Listened To Rev. Dr. Burchard's Address But None Heard "Rum,
Romanism And Rebellion"—Blaine Would Not Repudiate Until Too
Late—The "Belshazzar Feast" Also Cost Him Many Votes—All The
"Breaks" Against Blaine—How New York Went For Cleveland—
Watterson Gets Excited And The Crowd Yells "Hang, Hang, Hang
Jay Gould"—Blaine Stops The Agitation.*

B LAINE in retirement, Conkling practicing law—how the
mighty had fallen! Scarcely more than a year since the
intense struggle in the Chicago convention of 1880, yet those
two mighty captains of warring factions had been swept
out of office. Conkling had been twenty years in continuous
public service at Washington, Blaine eighteen.

Though Conkling lived for seven years after his Senate
resignation he never regained political prestige or power—
never sought to do so. Blaine had twelve more years to live,
which meant the same thing as twelve years of keen interest
in politics, for politics was the elixir of life for the Maine man.
He loved the game, but after his brief term as Garfield's
Secretary of State he seems to have centred in that office
the deep ambition of his later years. There he believed his
lasting reputation could be made. The only occasion upon
which he ever frankly confessed a desire to return to public
office was after Harrison's election in 1888, and the State Department was the place he sought. Harrison named him.

As I Knew Them

BLAINE PREFERS CIRCUS TO TALK

It is difficult to believe that Blaine was not eager for the 1884 nomination for President; but if he was, he kept his desire well concealed. After his failure in 1876 and 1880 he had a presentiment, really a superstition, that no turn of the political tide would ever carry him into the White House. He frequently used a homely New England phrase to speak of things settled and gone by—"that hoss' eyes is sot." He quoted that phrase whenever his friends spoke to him of the Presidency, and seemed uninterested.

In Paris, while Richard C. Kerens, of Missouri, and Stephen B. Elkins, of West Virginia, were visiting him in his hotel, they began talking of the approaching presidential nomination. Blaine suddenly left the room. Soon returning, he held in his hand high above his head tickets for the circus that evening, exclaiming in joyous tones: "Now here is something that means more fun than nominations. Let us have dinner and go."

Nevertheless, when the hour struck for the election of delegates there was a flare-up of the old ambition, though he insisted that it was merely the flickering embers of a fire almost burnt out. Protesting his indifference, declaring his preference to complete his half-finished "Twenty Years of Congress," he saw the column of Blaine delegates steadily growing taller; with its increase there developed in him that desire that in politics so often controls men against their better judgment. It controlled Blaine. Despite his acquiescence, the feeling that the Presidency was not for him clung to him like fate, and was never stronger than while the 1884 convention was making him its candidate.

THE "MUGWUMP" APPEARS IN POLITICS

My first convention—1884! Four years earlier in that same city, in that same hall, stirring scenes had been enacted,

A HISTORIC CARTOON: CLEVELAND AND ROOSEVELT IN 1885

strong men had battled. My mind was full of stories of dramatic incidents that then and there had taken place. My ear anticipated debate and oratory as memorable. I was eager to witness just such a struggle as had kept the 1880 convention in tense session six days; I pictured in my mind the great men, the stirring speeches, the sharp thrusts and retorts, the riotous gallery demonstrations I was to see and hear.

It did not occur to me that such a convention as that of 1880 is not often assembled—that a Conkling, a Garfield, and a great issue over which men differ fiercely are its essentials. They were absent in 1884. Of course, there were clashes, there were denunciations of Blaine, there were threats of bolting the ticket, but there was none of that spirited, inspiring leadership on one side and challenging determination on the other that four years before had held nearly 800 delegates at grips, roll-call after roll-call.

It was a contrast, not a repetition; it was a field of battle from which the gladiators had disappeared and only less commanding men remained. On one side was the candidacy of President Arthur with an indifferent following; on the other side the candidacy of Blaine, the "Plumed Knight" of a vast army of voters. Between, stood men of the type never so much at home as when in a protesting minority, never so happy as when assailing someone with suspicion and innuendo. Later, they were characterized as "Mugwumps" in politics. Blaine was their *bête noire*.

As a group in the convention they were unable to agree to support any candidate. Many of them including Theodore Roosevelt wanted to name Senator George F. Edmunds, of Vermont—a fine constitutional lawyer, who, if made the party candidate, would have lasted in the campaign about as long as an icicle under a noontime summer sun. Throughout the sessions there was not a speech that enthused nor a ballot whose close result thrilled more than did the fog-horn voice of the clerk who called the roll.

One man had all the enthusiasm—Blaine; one man got all

the shafts of malice and slander—Blaine; and one man, from
start to finish, was the obvious choice and nominee—Blaine.
I did not then personally know Blaine. Moreover it was then
doubtful whether my first vote would be cast for any man
nominated by the convention I was attending.

Nevertheless I could not reconcile the attacks upon Blaine
with the cheers with which his name was always greeted—the
kind of cheers that meant sincere feeling. One or the other
of the two extremes was wrong in its estimate of the man—
there was no middle ground.

The intense feeling for Blaine was significantly disclosed
by the great Blaine delegations that crowded Chicago during
the convention. A notable expression was that conveyed in a
giant transparency carried by a delegation of cheering torch-
waving Kansans; it read:

"25,000 for the Republican Nominee, but
75,000 for B L A I N E!"

A MOST UNSAVORY NATIONAL CAMPAIGN

With Blaine nominated the Democrats sought a candidate
whom the country could discuss without linking him to the past
of that party. Grover Cleveland met that requirement. He
had no political past. A most unsavory national campaign
followed. The private lives of both men were assailed. I
remember hearing Henry Ward Beecher, the famous Brooklyn clergyman, in Cooper Union, New York city, open the
attack upon Blaine's integrity. George William Curtis, whom
Conkling scornfully dubbed "the Man Milliner" because his
publishing firm owned the woman's magazine called "Harper's
Bazaar," wrote and talked and worked furiously. So did
Carl Schurz.

In that year Theodore Roosevelt and Henry Cabot Lodge
began their long political friendship. Both opposed Blaine
in the convention, but both had decided in advance to stand

with their party. The New York *Times* bolted Blaine; the New York *Sun* bolted Cleveland and supported Ben Butler; many Republicans announced themselves for Cleveland; as many Democrats declared for Blaine.

Blaine had to meet the charge that the correspondence known as the Mulligan letters, written while he was Speaker of the House of Representatives, disclosed a corrupt relation. The attack on Cleveland had to do with his early life in Buffalo and his alleged remissness in war. "Tell the truth" was Cleveland's answer when his supporters asked what should be said. That reply silenced both truth and untruth in newspaper publication.

A WHISPERING CAMPAIGN

But it was a whispering campaign,—the whispering of scandals about both candidates too malicious to be uttered aloud.

Enough was insinuated if not actually charged publicly to sink the campaign to the lowest levels. Many of the Mulligan letters had been read by Blaine in Congress, eight years before, challenging their false interpretation. Since then, he had been a candidate in two conventions, had been re-elected Senator from his State, and had been Garfield's Secretary of State. He had survived all these tests of faith in his integrity; indeed he had grown in popular favor.

In 1884, however, the battle was for the Presidency itself, not for a nomination, and the old interpretations were revived. The opposition left no sentence or word in the correspondence unblurred by malice. I never thought the charges cost Blaine many votes, though they undoubtedly influenced conservative opinion to the belief that he was at least careless in his letter-writing. Though Blaine was Speaker of the House at a time when stories of corrupt influence in Congress and in the national Administration were the gossip of the day, not a word

"THE PLUMED KNIGHT" AS PUCK SAW HIM

involving him was ever uttered until the letters were produced just before the 1876 convention.

Cleveland, on the other hand, was called a "hangman" because it was asserted that while Sheriff of Erie County, New York, he had personally supervised two executions. That was the mildest of the reports of his Buffalo life, as boy and man—some true, many untrue.

"RUM, ROMANISM AND REBELLION"

I could cite half a dozen incidents of that campaign, any one of which adversely influenced enough votes to have carried New York for Blaine, and New York would have elected him. I have already quoted Conkling's silence as one factor. The historic incident, of course, and the one that cost Blaine most votes, was the Rev. Dr. Burchard's "Rum, Romanism and Rebellion" sentence in an address of welcome to Blaine in the old Fifth Avenue Hotel in New York city. I heard that speech. It had been crowded into a forenoon reception because Blaine was to review a Business Men's parade in the afternoon and the night had been set aside for a banquet tendered by the "captains of industry" destined to become known as "Belshazzar's Feast."

I do not know whether Presidential candidates were "trailed" earlier than 1884 by agents of their rivals, instructed to watch for "breaks," but a Democratic sleuth followed Blaine in that campaign, took stenographic notes of all he said and reported every incident to William C. Whitney and Senator Arthur Pue Gorman. This trailer was present at the Burchard meeting with eyes and ears alert. He heard the alliterative phrase and realized its damaging possibilities. He hastened to the Cleveland headquarters just one block away—and by late afternoon the city was flooded with sensational circulars intended to arouse Catholic voters.

Following the meeting a dozen or more newspaper correspondents sat on the famous "Amen Corner" benches in the old Fifth Avenue Hotel discussing its news features. Not one of us gave heed to the utterance that was soon to become a national sensation. Our group included Cleveland men, Blaine men and Butler men but regardless of our politics we were presumed to be wide-awake news-gatherers. Imagine the shock to our pride a few hours later when the deluge of circulars came, sensationalizing a story that every one of us had seen, heard and *missed!*

WE SAW, BUT DID NOT HEAR

I say that we had seen and heard. That is only half true— actually we saw, but did not hear Dr. Burchard. I doubt whether many persons heard him. He stood atop the corridor stairway leading from the street level to the first floor. A noisy crowd filled the place. The clergyman's voice was poor, his delivery uninspiring. Thoughts and eyes were centered on Blaine, who faced him listening indifferently.

Blaine, I am sure, was correct in his subsequent statement that he did not hear the damaging words. But neither Blaine nor the correspondents, inasmuch as we had responsibilities in the matter, can be excused on that plea. It was our duty to know what he said. A clergyman's speech however, seemed to us the last thing to be followed closely for a sensation; it was assumed to be non-explosive. Yet dynamite was there! —dynamite that cost a Presidency!

In all my subsequent campaign experiences, I have not heard such an uproar as that which broke out everywhere as the Burchard sentence became known. Instantly appeals were made to Blaine to repudiate the utterance. But Blaine never liked to answer attacks; he was not a man to take the defensive, preferring always to battle on ground of his own choosing. All that he would say was the brief truth that he had not heard much of Burchard's address and in particular had not heard the unfortunate expression. Next day he continued on his way home to Maine, speaking at different cities accord-

The World.

VOL. XXV., NO. 8,672.　　NEW YORK, THURSDAY, OCTOBER 30, 1884.—WITH SUPPLEMENT.　　PRICE TWO CENTS.

THE ROYAL FEAST OF BELSHAZZAR BLAINE AND THE MONEY KINGS.

MAMMON'S HOMAGE.

Blaine Hobnobbing With the Mighty Money Kings.

The Banquet in His Honor at Delmonico's Last Night.

Millionaires and Monopolists Seal Their Allegiance.

ing to schedule; but until Saturday night he gave no further heed to Burchard. Then he learned that Catholic churches were to be flooded with circulars on Sunday. This information led him to act—too late, unfortunately, to repair the damage done.

Indisputably, Blaine would have been elected President by a heavy popular vote had there been no Burchard speech. It was estimated then that in New York alone he lost 50,000 votes. My estimate in the Philadelphia Press fixed the loss at more than 50,000, but whatever the actual figure may have been it was large enough to have insured the State and the Presidency to Blaine by a substantial plurality.

"BELSHAZZAR'S FEAST"

However, Burchard's speech was not the only vote-losing incident of that fateful last week of the campaign. Some "captains of industry," as they were called, with unwisdom characteristic of business men when they mix in politics, had persuaded Blaine to accept a banquet at Delmonico's, then New York City's most famous restaurant. Cyrus Field, Jay Gould, Andrew Carnegie and men of their type were the sponsors. The dinner was fixed for the same date as the Burchard meeting. It was served on the finest dinner plate Delmonico possessed; the quality of guests and service made it truly "a swagger affair." The only banquet rivalling it that I ever attended was James Hazen Hyde's anniversary of the Equitable Life Assurance Society at the Waldorf about 20 years ago. The Democrats promptly characterized it as "Belshazzar's Feast"—pictured it with all-gold dinner plate, waiters in livery and knee breeches, the banqueters with be-diamonded shirt-fronts.

The New York *World's* headlines next day were:

MAMMON'S HOMAGE
Blaine Hobnobbing With the
Mighty Money Kings

As I Knew Them

The Banquet in His Honor at
Delmonico's Last Night

Millionaires and Monopolists Seal
Their Allegiance.

Blaine had questioned the wisdom of the dinner. His secretary, Thomas H. Sherman, still living in Gorham, Maine, confirms my recollection that Blaine had written and telegraphed objections, but at last good naturedly had set aside his own reaction to it. Next day, even before criticism had reached its volume, he declared the dinner would cost him votes. He seemed more concerned about its effect than about Burchard's "Rum, Romanism and Rebellion"—both appearing in the same day's papers.

ALL THE "BREAKS" AGAINST BLAINE

In a close contest the mistakes of management made by the defeated side become conspicuous and as you look back upon them you challenge the wisdom of those responsible. All the "breaks" of the Blaine-Cleveland campaign were against Blaine. Looking them over afterward, realizing how easily *all* except a terrific rain-storm on election day could have been avoided—and realizing also that avoiding any one of them would have saved the day—the list of errors seems a pathetic array of "might have beens." Blaine himself never displayed interest in discussing them. Frequently he said he always knew it would not be, and was not particularly disturbed when his superstition proved to be a reality. He resumed work on his "Twenty Years of Congress."

HOW NEW YORK WENT FOR CLEVELAND

The Republicans conceded Blaine's defeat slowly. They might not have done so without demanding some kind of official enquiry into the New York State vote had they not realized the futility of such a proceeding. Cleveland himself was the Democratic Governor of the State and the City of New York was Tammany. Republicans had no alternative but to accept the vote as returned, however false. And it was false.

Another obstacle in the Republican path was the recollection of the Hayes-Tilden controversy, then only eight years past. No one wanted another such struggle for the Presidency.

The loss of New York meant to Blaine what the loss of California in 1916 meant to Hughes—the loss of the Presidency. The thirty-six Electoral votes of the Empire State made a total of 219 Electoral votes for Cleveland against 182 for Blaine. Transfer New York's 36 votes to the Blaine column and the result would be 218 for Blaine to 183 for Cleveland.

Those who recall the tense situation while the California vote was being slowly counted and re-counted in 1916 to determine whether Hughes or Wilson had been elected will realize the depth of feeling for two days while the Democrats figured a slender 1047 plurality for Cleveland in New York State. Notoriously, most of the votes cast for Governor Benjamin F. Butler, of Massachusetts, Greenback candidate, supported vigorously by the New York Sun, were counted for Cleveland. That counting was done in Long Island City and Gravesend Bay, by "Battle Ax" Paddy Gleason and John Y. McKane, two local Democratic bosses. Later McKane went to Sing Sing Prison for similar election practices.

"NO MORE '76!"

In 1876-77, while the Hayes-Tilden result was still undetermined, one Democratic Southern editor wrote fiercely; "The Solid South has gone for Tilden and Hendricks and by the God of Battles they shall be inaugurated!"

Henry Watterson, editor of the Louisville Courier-Journal,

and then also a member of Congress, frantically urged Democratic leaders to mobilize 100,000 Democrats to march, unarmed, to Washington and camp there until Tilden was installed in the White House as President.

In 1884, while the final returns were being gathered from close States, (New York in particular) Watterson did not renew his demand for an army, unarmed, to seat Cleveland in the White House, but he was the first to rage against another Democratic President being "counted out."

"No more '76" was the cry raised by Democrats throughout the country.

Everywhere crowds gathered in front of newspaper bulletin boards for the latest returns. In New York city a mob marched up and down outside the Western Union office, at Broadway and Dey Street, demanding that "held back" returns should be made known. They threatened Jay Gould, then chief owner of the Telegraph Company. "Hang, hang, hang Jay Gould," was their marching chorus along lower Broadway and on Union and Madison Squares.

They wanted the Paddy Gleason returns from Long Island City and Gravesend accepted as the true returns, but the telegraph company would not carry them until they were returned as official.

BLAINE STOPS THE AGITATION

Partisan contentions lasted night and day. The newspapers contributed their share of intemperate talk. Blaine himself finally put an end to the agitation. I was in Republican campaign headquarters in New York city about eleven o'clock Thursday night, talking with Stephen B. Elkins and National Chairman B. F. Jones (of the Jones & Laughlin Steel Company) when the telegraph operator handed Mr. Jones a message he had just taken over the special wire from Augusta, Maine:

As I Knew Them

"I concede election of Mr. Cleveland. Good-night, Blaine."
He wanted no more discussion, even with his managers.

Democrats rejoiced that they had at last won the Presidency. The House of Representatives was also theirs. But the jubilation of the "Mugwumps" was characteristic of all balance-of-power groups when they succeed in making their influence felt. It exceeded all other demonstrations. "Mugwumps" was the name given bolting Republicans. Each believed himself to be responsible for defeating Blaine and acted accordingly. Their feeling is well illustrated by these lines on a banner displayed in Morristown, New Jersey, (reproduced from Albert Bigelow Paine's "Th Nast," published by the Macmillan Co., in 1904):

> The World says the Independents did it.
> The Tribune says the Stalwarts did it.
> The Sun says Burchard did it.
> Blaine says St. John did it.
> Roosevelt says the soft soap dinner did it.
> We say Blaine's character did it.
>
> BUT WE DON'T CARE WHO DID IT—
> IT'S DONE.

CHAPTER XVII

"THE SOUTH'S IN THE SADDLE"

A President Elected By The "Solid South" Stirs The Old War Spirit—Hard To Realize In These Days The Feeling Then Prevailing—New Influences, New Policies, New Men In Control—Cleveland, Stranger, And Strange To All—My Winter's Study Of Him In Albany—"He Got A Hammer And Joined The Anvil Chorus"—Cleveland Trusted Timidly Throughout His Career—Always Perplexed, Always Burdened, By "The Damned Clamor For Office."

THE jubilant faction feeling had full swing for a few days. Later, as the country realized that the line of Republican Presidents since Lincoln had been broken, there was a period of wondering what the consequence would be to the nation.

Men and women of today cannot appreciate the concern manifested as to how the first Democratic President since the war would organize his Cabinet and shape his policies.

"The South's in the saddle" was the cry from radical Republican papers. They did not hesitate to assert that a man who had hired a substitute to fight for him when drafted in the Civil War would yield weakly to the South. This charge was unfair, but so were most of the charges in that campaign.

The truth about Cleveland's war record is that he was one of three brothers. By lot two enlisted, and Grover stayed at home as the family's support. This was common practise and did not reflect on the patriotism of the one who remained behind. Nevertheless, the charge had its weight.

There were also many people morally certain that a raid on the national treasury by "Southern Brigadiers" for Southern war claims and pensions would follow the presence in the White House of a Democrat whose support in Congress as in the Electoral College was largely from a "Solid South," still regarded as unrepentant and unreconciled.

If the Senate had not remained Republican, thus acting as a brake against complete Democratic domination, feeling in the North would have been far more tense. As it was, there was renewed waving of the "Bloody Shirt," and gloomy prediction was made, some of it sincerely, of what was to happen to our Government with the South to the fore.

SEEMS LIKE A NIGHTMARE NOW

Today, in the full consciousness of our unquestioned solidarity as a nation, such anxieties seem like a nightmare. We cannot accept them as real and it is just as well that they do seem unreal.

This generation has to turn to history to learn the meaning of Mason and Dixon's line. In 1885, however, every boy and girl heard of it and knew it from father or brother who had stood four years on the brink of that deep and broad gap separating and devastating two sections of our country, overflowing with the blood of two valiant armies—a sacrifice then too recent not to stir to passion on both sides when brought into discussion.

Many of the captured flags of Southern regiments are now back in the States whose soldiers carried them in battle, granite monuments on Gettysburg and other battlefields mark with equal and enduring glory the valor of grey as well as of blue. These tributes of a united country are the triumphs of time, the conquering spirit of the brotherhood of men.

WAITING FOR THE CURTAIN TO RISE

But it was not so when Cleveland's election was flashed across the country. The North still visioned the smoke of battle, still heard the echoes of the clash of arms, as it looked southward. Leading newspapers eagerly sought every piece of news that gave color to the new "crisis." They hurried their political correspondents to Albany for the winter to report Cleveland's progress in arranging to take over the national government, after a quarter of a century of continuous Republican administration.

New influences, new policies, new men were in control. It was like waiting for the curtain to rise on a play which many believed would be a tragedy; others looked to it hopefully; all were uncertain, anxious.

Would this unknown man, snatched from the Buffalo Mayoralty to be Governor of New York, then from the Governorship to be President (all in two years) play his rôle well or poorly? Even his own party associates wondered; is it strange, then, that others doubted?

Representing the Philadelphia Press, I was one of the group of newspaper men stationed at Albany. We saw Cleveland every day by appointment. He was not an overflowing source of news. Daniel S. Lamont, then his secretary, and in his second term Secretary of War, was more helpful though almost as cautious.

As I Knew Them

Many times over our nightly poker table in the old Delavan House, (now gone), we discussed the new chief executive of our nation with the brutally frank cynicism of newspaper correspondents when in their own company; no surgeon's scalpel is keener or more revealing. Stranger to all of us, and strange in his ways, he puzzled us. Frankly, we couldn't "get him." To some he seemed like one lost in a wilderness, but the prevalent opinion among us was that he acted as though controlled by a belief that suddenly he had been called to shoulder the crushing burdens of the whole world. That Cleveland had real character deep down in him, we were sure; but how and when would it get to the surface? What clash would bring it there? It got there.

Of another thing we were more certain—there would always be a wide gulf between this unusual man and every news-gathering corps. We agreed that no matter how long he remained in public life no bridge would ever span it. No bridge ever did.

Nor was Cleveland stranger only to the correspondents. His party leaders, some summoned to meet him, and many who had volunteered, had not much better luck in getting his mind. Influential as many of these leaders had been and would be in shaping Democratic policies, few could say with certainty after their first interview with Cleveland just how closely they and the President-elect were in agreement. Cleveland absorbed greedily, but yielded scantily. He was candid enough to say that he had not studied national questions deeply, but he also seemed careful not to ask many of his visitors to enlighten him. He listened to their suggestions—and said little. There was no great gain on either side.

Of course, correspondents knew nothing of the note of despair and of distrust of others that Cleveland was even then sounding in letters to such intimate friends as his law partner,

143

Wilson S. Bissell. We had sensed it, though, from our daily interviews with him and also from our talks with his visitors.

In our own way, each of us formed our impressions; they varied, but finally we dug under the thick covering of restraint and reluctance which he made no effort to conceal. He always had the manner of a man oppressed. Any one of us could have written of him as he wrote of himself at the time to Bissell:

"I am sick at heart and perplexed in brain. I almost think the professions of my friends are but the means they employ to accomplish personal selfish ends. Henceforth I must have no friends."

THE FATE OF BUFFALO MEN

In Buffalo, many who had been on close terms with Cleveland in his earlier years believed that their time, too, had come. They looked to him to appoint them to important places. All through Cleveland's first term there were loud wails from Buffalo that he was overlooking his old friends. The story is told of one eager Buffalonian who after waiting vainly to hear from the White House, decided to go down personally and "get something." Charles W. Goodyear, then close to Cleveland, advised him not to go. He went—and returned.

Later a friend said to Goodyear:

"What did ———— get?"

"He got a brand new hammer," replied Goodyear, "and promptly joined the anvil chorus!"

Never throughout his entire career did Cleveland lose his strange feeling that everyone approached him with a sinister purpose—that he should trust others timidly, if at all. With personal friends not concerned in public affairs, particularly in later years, while on fishing or duck-shooting trips, he was a congenial companion. Such intimate friends found him ready to hear a good story and now and then to tell one himself; but he retired into a shell, tortoise-like, when outside of that environment. He was determined to isolate and to burden himself, and then to lament his condition.

Nearly ten years later—during his second term—he wrote Everett P. Wheeler of New York: "There never was a man in high office so surrounded with difficulties, and so perplexed and so treacherously treated and so abandoned, by those whose aid he deserves, as the present incumbent."

FACSIMILE OF CLEVELAND'S LETTER TO "DEAR CHARLEY"

This extract is reproduced from Charles H. Armitage's book "Cleveland As Buffalo Knew Him," published by the Buffalo Evening News. The quotation reads:

145

As I Knew Them

Sept. 14, 1884.

"Dear Charley: Since you left me last night, I have been thinking and much of the time feeling very blue, and wishing that the Presidential nomination were in—or on some other shoulders than mine."

CLEVELAND "PERPLEXED"—AND SO WERE OTHERS

But Cleveland was not the only person perplexed. During those weeks at Albany as President-elect, the newspaper correspondents had a baffling time in their daily effort to reveal such a man and his purposes to a nation that had taken him "on faith."

Had the "official spokesman" idea then been developed to its present efficient state in Washington, the correspondents might have written the real Cleveland into the news of the hour with the accuracy and timeliness with which President Coolidge is revealed from day to day. I doubt, however, whether Cleveland could have played the rôle of "official spokesman" or if he would have undertaken it. Had he done so the possible irritations of such meetings would have made that particular "official spokesman" usually a deaf and dumb man.

Even as things were, so far as newspaper correspondents were concerned, Cleveland was a close approach to one. All interviews with us were coldly polite, but brief and rarely enlightening. Sometimes he was brusque, sometimes sullenly silent, occasionally he smiled. He never stooped to pettiness; he was never unpleasant, but he made no effort to conceal that newspaper correspondents were merely tolerated callers. Confidences such as many public men repose in correspondents were out of the question; light remarks were taboo. The business of our once-a-day call was quickly dispatched, and many of us were confident that we heard a deep sigh of relief as we left his presence.

146

As I Knew Them

So passed the winter of 1885. Finally, on March 1, the newspaper writers travelled from Albany to Washington the same night as Cleveland, though not on the "Cleveland Special," for interesting reasons that belong in another chapter.

CHAPTER XVIII

NO FAREWELLS FOR CLEVELAND

The Country Woke Up To Learn That He Had Travelled Through The Night To Washington—Gossip That He Never Set Foot On The Streets Of The Capital—Party Leaders Established Relations Slowly And Some Not At All—A Story About Salt—Refining The Crudities Out Of Cleveland—"If Every Other Man Abandons This Issue I Shall Stick To It"—Blaine Promptly Cables A Challenge And Republicans Enthuse—Ordering The Return Of Captured Battle Flags—Pension Vetoes Anger G. A. R.—"There's One More President For Us In Protection."

I DO not know how many of our presidents-elect, if any, left their homes for the White House without a word of farewell to neighbors, or public announcement of their departure. Grover Cleveland did. Cleveland was then a bachelor. While Governor, the Executive Mansion at Albany was his home. When he resigned to prepare for the Presidency, he rented a house in Albany, instead of returning to Buffalo.

As the first Democrat elected to the Presidency since Buchanan, and conscious of the still bitter war-time prejudice I have described, Cleveland was convinced that his way to the White House would be blocked by some light-headed Republican. He anticipated assassination. His elected predecessor had thus met death.

It was determined, therefore, to keep secret the hour of his departure from Albany. Even as late as the forenoon of March 1—three days before inauguration—the correspondents were still without information. Thus, we were forced to guard the New York Central and West Shore railroad stations, prepared to board any train Cleveland might take.

Late that afternoon, just in time for the last train connecting at Jersey City with the Washington midnight, we were notified that the Cleveland party had driven in sleighs to a siding at Kenwood, several miles south of Albany, on the West Shore road, where a special train awaited them. Silently, Arab-like, he had stolen away.

The country awoke next morning to learn that the President-elect had travelled over night and was safe in the national capital.

He had never been there before. It was his first glimpse of it. Nor did he ever learn much of the city itself. After his first term it was said that as President he had never set foot on its pavements. This was probably an exaggeration of the gossip arising from the great precautions always taken for his safety; but those who were then in Washington knew that Cleveland was never seen on its streets—as Harrison, his successor, was seen, as Wilson was seen, as Coolidge is often seen.

When Harrison succeeded Cleveland in 1889 he was surprised to find a night and day corps of secret service detectives guarding the White House, in addition to the ordinary watchmen. He promptly assigned the detectives elsewhere.

"I'd rather have a bullet inside of me," he said, "than to be living in constant dread of one."

LISTENING TO THE MUGWUMPS

Cleveland made his way toward national policies and toward Democratic leaders from the different States in the same over-cautious mind that controlled him in all else. Though the influences and leading figures of the national capital were new to him, he was distrustful of proffered help, even from the responsible men of his own party in Congress. He preferred to grope in the dark, with no guide, lest a guide mislead him. Confidential relations were established slowly, if at all.

Partisan though he was—no President, not even Andrew

Jackson, was more intensely partisan—he had a strange conviction that he could serve his party best by listening more favorably to Carl Schurz, Everett P. Wheeler and George William Curtis than to most of his Democratic associates. Neither time nor the spectacle of a divided party ever dispelled that feeling. Few men conspicuous in Democratic councils ever became Cleveland's confidants.

Democratic Senators and Congressmen knew him only by name before he occupied the White House, and many of them never got to know him more intimately. Samuel J. Tilden, for example, living only a hundred miles from Cleveland while he was President-elect, was never asked into conference, which might have been done even for appearance' sake. Tilden's few letters of compliment had polite but uninviting response. Others who had long borne the party burdens had similar experiences.

Another day had dawned!

Quickly, Democrats at Washington realized that they had a difficult man to deal with. His adherence to his own conception of party policies quickly put Democratic leaders on notice as to the character of the man at their head.

The first to feel that a new power controlled the party's fortunes was Thomas A. Hendricks, elected Vice President with Cleveland. "The Democratic party isn't in power," he said after a few interviews at the White House. "Grover Cleveland is making a party of his own." So far as the Hendricks type of politician was concerned, that statement was true. The President's aversion to Hendricks and Voorhees, who controlled the Indiana Democrats, was so great that when he wanted information about men and conditions in the Hoosier State he sent for Benjamin Harrison, then Senator, and destined to be his successor.

"WE LIKE SALT!"

The late Andrew D. White, in his Autobiography, repeated a story told in Washington illustrative of the way Cleveland impressed most of his own party associates. Several Congressmen who had never met him were leaving the Capitol to pay him a call. Philetus Sawyer, a Republican Senator from Wisconsin, happened to meet them.

"How do you like your new President?" asked Sawyer.

"Oh he is a good man, a very good man," they replied.

"Yes, but how do you *like* him?"

"Oh we like him."

"Well," persisted Sawyer, "I'll tell you a story before you go to the White House if you will promise me Honest Injun to tell me when you come back whether it fits your case."

They agreed.

"Up in Wisconsin, some years ago, in a wood-choppers' camp, they drew by lot to determine who should be the first cook, with the understanding that anyone who complained of the cooking would at once become cook. While the beans were boiling in the pot on the fire the cook started to salt them but the box of salt slipped from his hand and into the pot.

"The choppers had the beans for dinner.

" 'Thunder and lightning,' exclaimed one of the diners as he tasted them, 'these beans are all salt!' Then, quickly remembering what would happen to him if he complained, he looked over smilingly at the cook and added, 'but I like salt.' "

Sawyer was waiting for the Democrats when they returned from the White House.

"Honest Injun," he said, "how was it?"

They laughed and then one said: "Sawyer, we like salt!"

REFINING THE CRUDITIES OUT OF CLEVELAND

It is always a temptation for writers and orators to refine the crudities out of historic figures until they cease to be life-like or even human. Some are thus spoiling many men whom Americans love to honor, despite their known weaknesses. They are distorting the real Cleveland. Those in active political life in Cleveland's day would not recognize the real Cleveland in the man now portrayed in anniversary addresses and fulsome biographies. Idolaters speak of him, for example, as a most affable man. That may be said with Cleveland dead, but it was not said of Cleveland living. Probably his greatest weakness was his inability to meet men agreeably —particularly those who differed in opinion with him. He was always suspicious of them, and was too easily moved to denounce them personally. What is now called "Cleveland courage" was in his day known in Washington in most instances as obstinacy.

Before inauguration in 1885, Cleveland did not pretend familiarity with national questions. He had voted for every Democratic candidate for President since 1860 with the consistency of a New Jersey-born Democrat, and gave no serious thought to policies. To Carl Schurz, he wrote: "I am ashamed to say it but the truth is I know nothing about the tariff. Will you tell me how to go about it to learn?"

He also gave a long interview to T. C. Crawford, a foremost newspaper correspondent, representing the New York World. In that interview he declared that the tariff was a new subject to him—that he would have to study it.

THE ISSUE THAT BROUGHT BLAINE'S CHALLENGE

Yet, in December, 1887, only two years later, he excluded every other topic from his annual message to Congress. He had reached certain conclusions; to him they had the appeal of the discovery of a new doctrine, though in fact they were only new to him; the results of reading the kind of tariff literature that Carl Schurz would recommend. He wanted wool put on the free list, and a "tariff for revenue only" substituted for a tariff for protection. The zeal of a new advocate led him to adopt the unprecedented course of confining his entire message to that single issue.

The Mills "tariff-for-revenue-only" bill was the outcome.

It was in that "free wool" message that Cleveland used the memorable phrase "A condition, not a theory, confronts us."

As I Knew Them

The condition was a national treasury with a surplus, due largely to customs tariff revenue; he wanted less revenue and less surplus.

He did not dream then that, after 1893, during his second term, he was to realize keenly the embarrassment of a continuing deficit as against the comforts of a surplus.

Few Democrats in Congress were consulted in advance. Those who knew of it promptly advised against a "one-issue" message, with a fight for the Presidency and Congress only seven months ahead. Particularly were they against centering the fight on free wool, thus arousing the farmers of the country. It was not "good politics"; party solidarity would be sacrificed. But Cleveland was adamant.

"If every other man in the country abandons this issue," he declared to Speaker Carlisle, "I shall stick to it."

This utterance—seemingly reflecting courage but actually reflecting unwisdom—brought the criticism that it was a stand much too extreme for a President with other responsibilities and policies of equal importance; and one that would not be made by a party leader desiring to keep his party united and effective.

Still, Cleveland remained unmoved. He was going to be bigger than his party. The message went to Congress.

By cable there promptly flashed a challenge from his old opponent, James G. Blaine, then in Europe, rallying the Republican party to the old issue of protection. At once, you could see Republicans everywhere, unifying, enthusing, because of their brightened prospects.

"ONE MORE PRESIDENT IN PROTECTION"

In a personal letter Blaine wrote a Republican friend privately "There's one more President for us in Protection."

Blaine was right; the Democrats who protested were right. Cleveland and his party went down in defeat. The government was turned back wholly to Republican keeping.

His tariff message, however, was not tne only cause of
Cleveland's defeat. His record for vetoing pension bills con-
solidated the G. A. R. vote of the country against him, and
kept alive the old stories of his alleged remissness in war.
There were rumors (absurd as they now seem) that the
President was to recommend pensions for Southern soldiers.
The Cleveland vetoes were the result of thorough investigation in each case made by himself; most of them were justified.
The country, however, still susceptible to war prejudice, was
shocked by the succession of pension vetoes, whether just or
not.

THE RETURN OF CAPTURED BATTLE FLAGS

Worse still, in view of this aroused sentiment, was an order
in 1887 from the War Department by Adjutant General
Drum, directing the return of captured battle flags—return of
those held by the South, as well as those held by the North.
Here was confirmation, said radical Republicans, that the
"South is in the saddle," as they had charged it would be when
Cleveland went to Washington.

"No rebel flags will be surrendered while I am Governor,"
telegraphed Fire-Alarm Foraker from the Ohio State Capitol.

Even General Sherman was so aroused that he wrote:

"Of course I know Drum, the Adjutant General. He has
no sympathy with the army that fought. He never captured
a flag and values it only at its commercial value. He did not
think of the blood and torture of battle. Nor can Endicott,
the Secretary of War, nor Mr. Cleveland."

The North responded to the Foraker outcry. While the
agitation was at fever heat, it was found that the War Department had no jurisdiction over the flags, that Congress
alone had absolute power of disposal.

Cleveland promptly withdrew the order, but politically the
damage had been done. Foraker was reelected Governor of

NO RETURN OF SOUTHERN FLAGS

Ohio by a tremendous vote, and the Republican struggle to retrieve the Presidency gained new impetus and hope.

Less than 20 years later without a word of protest—instead, with many words of praise—Congress unanimously passed, and President Roosevelt signed, a bill to do the very thing so hotly resented in Cleveland's day. Once more it was demonstrated that 1887 was part of another era in our history, another temper of the people. Though the flag order may have been the right thing to do, 1887 was not the right year in which to attempt it, nor was the first Democratic Administration since the war the right Administration to undertake it.

Cleveland resented defeat. Of course no man accepts it joyously, but it was the first reverse in Cleveland's public career, and his dissatisfaction with the result had lost little of its keenness as he watched the inauguration of Harrison as his successor. Usually the retiring Chief Magistrate conceals his feelings behind a smiling countenance, and tries to show some interest in the proceedings. Cleveland made no such pretence. I have seen several Presidents accompanying their successor to the Capitol, and participating in the ceremonies there, but I have never seen one who frankly showed that he was at odds with all that was going on as Cleveland did in 1889. Later, in 1893, he may have looked upon a second term, as he wrote that he did, as an "infliction," but in 1889 his countenance and his manner told a different story most emphatically to those who looked upon him, as I did, during the formal transfer of title.

CHAPTER XIX

BLAINE GIVES WAY TO HARRISON

"My Heart's In The Highlands, My Heart's Not Here" Enthused The 1888 Convention, While The Plumed Knight Was In Scotland—"Blaine Or Bust" Was The Spirit Of The Delegates, And California Aided With A Carload Of Champagne—Blaine Thought That Only a United Party Could Win And Knew He Could Not Unite It—Discussion Of A Father's Son Ticket, Lincoln And Grant—Blaine Urged Harrison And Phelps, But Phelps' Bang Disqualified Him—Why John Spooner Lacked Faith in Harrison—"Bob" Ingersoll Makes A Slip And Is Hissed Into Silence—Tom Platt's Sunday Afternoon Carriage Ride And Its Result—A Colored Delegate Who Wanted Whitewash And Plenty Of It.

BLAINE would have been the leader in the second battle against his former antagonist had he not taken himself out of consideration. For nearly a year he had been travelling Europe; from Italy he wrote two open letters strongly insisting that he must not be nominated. He took the stand that a defeated candidate could only be a burden to his party in a second effort.

When the convention met in Chicago, in June, 1888, Blaine was coaching with Andrew Carnegie in Scotland. Anyone who doubted the loyalty of the party to its "Plumed Knight" would have learned the truth in the tumult when the band struck up that Scotch ballad: "My Heart's in The Highlands, My Heart's Not Here." That was the truth. The heart of the convention was with Blaine.

No one then in Chicago will ever forget—I certainly shall not—the demonstrations for Blaine in the convention, in the hotels, on the streets. "Blaine or Bust" flags and banners were everywhere. What a time there was in the old Leland hotel, where "Mike" De Young, the San Francisco publisher,

and other "Blaine or Busters" from the Pacific coast made
their headquarters! They were for Blaine and Blaine only.
They had brought a car-load of native champagne from California with them—and not a drop was wasted!

Bitterly they arraigned the old Blaine leaders who, under
orders, were keeping his name out of the convention. Never
have I seen men so intense, so determined to name the man
of their choice with or without his consent. The days and
nights were sweltering hot, but not too hot for De Young and
his followers to gather Stephen B. Elkins, Joseph H. Manley,
Charles A. Boutelle and Richard C. Kerens in their rooms
and upbraid them time and time again for deserting their
chief. A cable from Blaine, read to the convention by Boutelle, finally cooled the ardor of the "Blaine or Bust"
contingent.

LINCOLN AND GRANT—A FATHER'S SON TICKET

Not many men could have resisted the temptation for another "go" at the man from whom they had suffered defeat;
most candidates would have demanded such an opportunity
from their party as Cleveland demanded it in 1892. Blaine,
however, never sought it; he was so emphatic more than a year
in advance that party leaders then began to look around for
another candidate.

One ticket they considered had great possibilities if it should
hit the people right; it was also fraught with the peril of making a wrong impression. That was a "father's son" ticket, as
it was called—made up of Robert T. Lincoln and Frederick
D. Grant. Lincoln and Grant! What names to conjure with!
In 1880, such a ticket might have been an ideal, victory-win-
ning outcome of that convention struggle; but eight years later
it would have been an experiment. While the national leaders
were debating it, Fred Grant was defeated for election as Secretary of State of New York. That sealed the fate of the
Lincoln and Grant ticket.

157

What Debs said of injunctions—that they "don't go here" —applies in conventions often to refusals of nominations. I saw David B. Hill in 1894, then Senator, nominated for Governor by a New York Democratic convention over which he had asked to preside so as to be in a position to stop any effort to name him. He couldn't stop it. In 1914 I saw Oscar S. Straus nominated for Governor while presiding over a state convention that, despite his protests, insisted that refusals to run for Governor "don't go."

BLAINE URGES HARRISON AND PHELPS

When the 1888 convention met, Blaine was in that same plight—he had to have a candidate or he would himself be made the nominee. He had written favoring Benjamin Harrison, but a more recent expression was needed. He, therefore, cabled Stephen B. Elkins urging a ticket of Harrison and Phelps—William Walter Phelps, Congressman from Englewood, New Jersey. In addition to my newspaper work I was acting as secretary for Elkins, and the Blaine cable came into my possession.

The Blaine leaders finally lined up for Harrison, but they could not pull Phelps through. Phelps parted his hair in the middle and wore a bang down his forehead—slightly more of a bang than Elihu Root's. Had Phelps not been present personally in the convention, the question of his bang might never have come up; but with Phelps and his bang day after day in plain sight of the western delegates there was no hope that he could win their favor. Had they known Phelps better, they would have known an able, manly colleague.

A REAL CONVENTION IN 1888

That 1888 convention was unusual. It is truer of that convention than of any I ever attended that the prevailing desire was to nominate the man most certain to win. Defeat had brought unity. Senator John Sherman, of Ohio, was the only candidate who had been conspicuous in the great convention battles of the past. Newer names were pressing to the front. Nineteen men were balloted for in the eight ballots—the longest list ever. Judge Walter Q. Gresham, then of Illinois, although Hoosier born, had pressed Harrison for the Indiana delegates, but had failed to get them. Illinois, however, favored him. He had been Arthur's Secretary of the Treasury and, in 1893, became Cleveland's Secretary of State. That brilliant Senator from Kansas, John J. Ingalls, destined later to become a Bryan man, figured in the contest; so did Chauncey Depew. Despite the fact that he was President of the New York Central railroad, Depew had all but one vote from New York and thirty more from other States.

The chief contenders, however, were Senator Sherman, Senator William B. Allison of Iowa, Governor Russell A. Alger of Michigan, ex-Senator Benjamin Harrison of Indiana and Judge Gresham. The Allison crowd eliminated Depew by crying "Railroad!" Depew eliminated Allison by responding "Granger!" So those two candidates forced each other out.

Senator John C. Spooner, then the leading corporation lawyer of Wisconsin, wanted Gresham nominated. Wisconsin was voting solidly for Harrison under the influence of "Uncle" Jerry Rusk, then Governor. Spooner stood with his State. Nevertheless, he insisted that Harrison was not big enough to be President.

"Why," said he, "only a few months ago we waited and waited to get a bill from him for some law work he had done for us down in Indianapolis. Finally we sent him a check for $1,000. His bill crossed our check in the mails. When we opened his letter we found he had charged only $400. No man who under-estimates the value of his services is a big man."

This from the man who was accepted as the best legal mind of the Senate!

As I Knew Them

Robert G. Ingersoll, who had called Blaine the "Plumed Knight" when nominating him in 1876, favored Gresham. Popular as Ingersoll was, he had an unfortunate experience.

An evening "get-together" meeting was held while the convention was in recess. Party orators were invited to speak with the understanding that no names of candidates would be used, and no reference made to them. Everybody was eager to hear Ingersoll. Though he was late on the list, scarcely a person left the Auditorium until Ingersoll appeared. He had not spoken long, however, before by some misunderstanding he mentioned his candidate, Gresham. Instantly, hisses from the audience forced him to stop. It was probably the only time in his career that Bob Ingersoll had to leave the platform!

PLATT'S SUNDAY CARRIAGE RIDE AND ITS RESULT

There are always "ifs" to a convention—at least to the candidates' rivalries. John Sherman believed that despite Alger's raid on his Southern delegates he would have been nominated if the convention had remained in session Saturday afternoon for another ballot or two, while he was scoring his high mark. It adjourned over Sunday—to meet Monday morning. Sherman had hopes of the New York delegation largely controlled by Tom Platt. And on Saturday he had substantial basis for his hopes.

Sunday afternoon, however, Platt went carriage riding along Michigan Boulevard with Stephen B. Elkins. Elkins had the Blaine cable; he was also known to be one of Harrison's confidants. Moreover he was a persuasive man. When they returned to the hotel, Elkins had Platt's pledge of the New York delegates for Harrison. On Monday they so voted and Sherman thus met defeat a second time—in no kindly mood.

As I Knew Them

Before I leave the 1888 convention, let me record two incidents—McKinley's first appearance as an influential figure, and his speech refusing to allow delegates to vote for him. Second, the open matching of plethoric pocket books by Russell A. Alger (former Governor of Michigan and later McKinley's Secretary of War) and by bankers backing John Sherman.

Ever since Sherman in 1875 put through Congress the specie resumption act, and particularly since as Secretary of the Treasury he actually resumed payment, the banking interests had backed his candidacy for President. His relations with the First National Bank in New York city were so close during the resumption crisis that that institution was popularly called "Fort Sherman."

"LOOKING AFTER MY FENCES"

There never was any question of Sherman's ability; he ranked among the strongest men in Washington during his thirty years there. But Sherman was not a good mixer. Republicans respected him, but never wanted to nominate him for President. He inspired no enthusiasm and his delegates lacked the loyalty that only enthusiasm commands. He had none of the resourceful ways of the politician, yet he is responsible for a term that is almost a commonplace in politics—"looking after his fences."

The Ohio Senator was not conscious that he was uttering words that would be caught up by the country. He was a candidate for the Presidency and there were many contests in Ohio over delegates to the convention. Sherman returned from Washington to his home in Mansfield to look after some personal matters but particularly to talk with a tenant on his farm who had been bothering him about the poor condition of the fences. A crowd greeted Sherman at the railway station, demanding a speech. The Senator thanked them for their welcome but said that he had not come home to talk politics but "to look after my fences." At once the newspapers took up the phrase and "looking after my fences" found a place in political literature.

A large proportion of Sherman's delegates in national conventions came from down South, and nine-tenths of them were colored. The story is told elsewhere, so far as Sherman is concerned, but of General Alger, who also depended upon the colored brethren, it was reported that his managers had run a railroad pay car over from Detroit to the Chicago stockyards. Colored "statesmen" were said to be in continuous line there like a box office queue. Negro delegates look so much alike that they ran no risk when, after selling out to Sherman, they would drift over to the Alger car one by one and sell out once more. They wore a path from one headquarters to the other.

THE NEGRO DELEGATE WHO WANTED WHITEWASH

Tom Donaldson, a rare character from Philadelphia, was handling some of the Sherman funds. He had a room on the top floor of the old Grand Pacific Hotel. Tom had just paid off one Southern darkey when a tall, dusky son of the South entered.

"Is dis yere de place where de whitewash am?" he asked.

"The very spot," said Donaldson.

"And is you de man wid de brush?"

"I'm the fellow."

"Well, suh, I'm from ole Mississipp', and all I've got ter say to you, suh, is ter get out yo' brush, sir, and splatter me until I'se whiter'n a ghost. Splatter and splash dat whitewash, suh, on dis black skin o' mine."

And so it has been in every Republican convention to this day, whenever there has been a close contest.

To make a showing on the roll-calls, zealous managers of ambitious candidates for President offer Southern delegates either office, or money, or both; though where those delegates will go from one ballot to another is as uncertain as the direction of a grasshopper's next jump. I do not know of any candidate ever nominated by such votes; nearly all candidates who have sought them have by that very act lessened their support from Republican States. When a convention makes up its mind to nominate, it seeks the man who has greatest backing in States likely to cast their electoral votes for him.

In 1888, both Sherman and Alger with their whitewashed colored delegates were put aside and Harrison came through a winner in that Monday morning finish.

CHAPTER XX

HARRISON—ABLE, WISE AND COLD

The Profoundest Lawyer Ever In The White House, According To Depew—An Earnest President, But He Never "Played To The Galleries"—General New Said "Ben, Be A Human Being" And Later Ben Said "I Tried It, John, But I Failed"—"Lige" Halford's Suit Of English Plaids And Harrison's Comment—Two Occasions When Harrison Swore—A Fine Teller Of Hoosier Stories—Tom Platt Knew His Bible And Matt Quay The Classics—Harrison Said He Had No Desire To Follow A Hearse Into The White House—Candidates Who Prefer Sleep To Election Returns.

CHAUNCEY M. DEPEW, in his "80 Years of Public Life," states that Benjamin Harrison was the profoundest lawyer ever at the head of our government. I must leave it to lawyers to settle that point with Depew, who at 94, as I write this, is still competent for an argument; but I do not believe that anyone will dispute that Harrison ranks among our ablest Presidents.

Earnest, thorough and prudent, he lived up to the great responsibilities of his office; he gave a conservative, constructive administration. Under him, the country made a new high record of prosperity. Politics, friendships, or antagonisms did not enter his decisions when a vital issue was at stake. He was never moved to do anything for effect; he had an extreme distaste for what is called "playing to the galleries."

I recall how Harrison while listening to you would fold his arms across his chest and look searchingly at you. He never realized that it made you feel as if you were before an inquisitor. It really meant that he was giving you his thoughtful attention. Such traits made it difficult for him to hold those who did not know the man well nor understand his ways. Some said his "yes" was as uninspiring as another man's "no."

164

That may have been true; it is also true, however, that it was genuine.

Indictments of such wholesale character are always unjust. They were unjust to Harrison. Frequently he proved himself a sympathetic, cordial friend, though he could not make an outward show of his feelings. Restraint was natural with him; he could not honestly be effusive, and pretence he detested. What he said he meant, and what he meant he said.

In these days of a freer, less restrained life, we are apt to characterize such personal traits as "narrowness." With Harrison they were in keeping with their time. He was a product of that austere period in our nation's history when it was wrong to dance, wrong to use Sunday except in religious duty, wrong to look upon life except as serious business. His character developed in that atmosphere and it was not made less rigid by his four years in the Union army. He had to be what he was. And when you sum it up, he was a splendid type of American citizen.

"BEN, BE A HUMAN BEING"

Several years before Harrison became President, he was leaving Indianapolis one afternoon to make a campaign speech in another Indiana city. His friend and neighbor, General John C. New, accompanied him to the railway station.

"Now, Ben," said New as they parted, "I know you'll capture them with your speech, but for God's sake be a human being down there. Mix around a little with the boys after the meeting."

When he met New two or three days later Harrison said: "John, I tried it, but I failed. I'll never try it again. I must be myself."

It was said in those days that General New was the only man who ever called Harrison "Ben" and that New was the only man Harrison ever called by his first name. Even his law partner W. H. H. Miller, who became Attorney General in his administration, was always addressed as "Mr." Miller and he, in turn, addressed his senior partner as "General Harrison."

On occasions, Harrison might drop the "Mr." while talking with friends, but he never got close enough with anyone to use first names.

HALFORD'S SUIT OF ENGLISH PLAIDS

Major Elijah W. Halford, "Lige" as everyone in Washington called him while he was there as Harrison's secretary, is now living in Leonia, New Jersey. He was once asked by one of his old Indianapolis newspaper colleagues, how he was getting on with the President.

"Oh, very well," he replied. "I think I have him sized up. When I see him in the morning and he greets me with 'Halford, how are you today?' I sit down by his desk for a pleasant talk about matters. When he greets me with 'Good morning, Mr. Halford,' I bolt for the door and wait until after lunch for the talk."

Despite these traits there was an abundance of Hoosier humor in Harrison. Not many men could better tell a witty story, or so much enjoyed doing so. When the Indiana delegates were leaving Indianapolis for the Chicago convention of 1888, at which Harrison was nominated, Halford, who even then was more or less Harrison's personal representative, turned up at the station in a suit of loud plaids, distinctly foreign in pattern and cut. He had just returned from his first trip to London, where he had bought it.

Harrison looked at the clothes curiously, and then asked Halford where he got them. He was told. You will remember that the cornerstone of the Harrison candidacy was Protection and the purchase of American-made goods.

"Halford," he said laughingly, "those plaids may be all right down here where there's no convention, but if you wear them in Chicago they'll beat me on the first ballot."

From "Judge"

YES GRANDFATHER'S HAT FITS BEN—FITS BEN. HE WEARS IT WITH DIGNIFIED GRACE,
OH YES! SO RALLY AGAIN AND WE'LL PUT UNCLE BEN RIGHT BACK IN HIS GRAND-
FATHER'S PLACE—CAMPAIGN SONG IN 1888.

As I Knew Them

Of course, many stories of Harrison were told while he was in the White House. Here is one that I heard then. There were many occasions when he did not conceal his anger, but only two on which his anger was expressed by profanity. One was when in Cincinnati he entered the Ohio Medical University in search of his father's body, stolen from the grave. When he found it in the dissecting room he used language that is not printable here.

The second occasion was at the battle of Resaca, in Georgia, in 1864. Harrison was at the head of his regiment charging the enemy. He had captured the Confederate battery. One lone Confederate was left by his comrades on a horse he couldn't manage. Harrison grabbed the dismayed gunner by his coat collar, dragged him from his mount and with intense but also unprintable words ordered him back into the lines of captured men. "Fighting Joe" Hooker rode up while Harrison and his men were "brushing up" the captured position.

"By God," he exclaimed as he saw what had been accomplished, "Harrison, I'll make you a Brigadier General for this day's work." And Harrison won promotion on the field.

The better people knew Harrison the better they realized that his strong character was not to be underestimated. How could he have been other than a man of purpose and integrity —great grand-son as he was of a signer of the Declaration of Independence, grand-son of "Old Tippecanoe" who defeated Henry Clay for the Presidential nomination and Martin Van Buren for reelection, and himself a gallant soldier in the Civil War!

Harrison's State papers and his subsequent lectures are an interpretation of national problems and purposes unsurpassed for sturdy patriotism, clear, vigorous language and sound thinking.

167

As I Know Them

There were two principal causes for Harrison's unpleasant experience in being defeated for reelection in 1892 by Grover Cleveland, whom he had defeated four years before. One was the McKinley tariff law, enacted in 1890 and extremely unpopular in the early period of its operation; the second was Harrison's refusal to permit the Quay-Platt national committee machine to dictate his Cabinet members or his lesser office appointments.

Matthew Stanley Quay was the master strategist in the politics of that day. His only rival for that distinction was Thomas Collier Platt, of New York, but Platt was not his equal. Those two men who for more than a decade controlled their State organizations and linked its policies and its candidates to interests that were not public interests, were men of education—Platt, a graduate of Yale, Quay of Jefferson College, Pa. Platt was not such a student of literature as Quay, but he knew his Bible as few men do, while Quay was devoted to the classics. The Pennsylvania boss was a persistent reader of the best literature.

Seated in the fine library that reflected his culture, Quay would turn from books of the most elevating influence to discuss with his lieutenants the distribution on election day of funds collected from corporations and others seeking privileges to which they were not entitled; or he would plan in the calm atmosphere of the classics the slaughter of his political enemies.

PLATT'S "SUNDAY SCHOOL" AND QUAY'S ADDITION, DIVISION AND SILENCE LETTER

Platt in New York had what he called his "Sunday School" every Sabbath morning, frequently adjourning it to attend church. His "Sunday School" was made up of politicians

168

from different sections of the State as well as of legislators gathered to discuss pending measures. Platt was also President of The United States Express Company, and a successful business man. It was never charged of either man that he made money out of politics.

Strange perversity of nature, was it not, that with such background Platt and Quay should have had no more laudable ambition in politics than the possession of power—power to reward, power to crush, power to say "do it" and it is done, or "don't do it" and it is not done.

Quay was chief lieutenant and finally the successor to the Cameron dynasty—Simon and Don, father and son,—in Pennsylvania politics. To Quay, politics was the breath of life— to win his only purpose. The end always justified the means. The one big indiscreet move he ever made was when he wrote a letter recommending a local Republican worker for a job in the State Treasurer's office at Harrisburg, with these words: "He understands addition, division and silence."

The letter was too good to escape eventual publicity. A few years earlier Quay nominated General James A. Beaver for Governor. His one letter of advice to his candidate read: "Dear Beaver: Don't talk. M. S. Quay."

When Quay was asked to manage Harrison's first campaign, he agreed to do so provided Harrison would agree not to make speeches. "I don't like 'spouting' candidates," he said. Finally it was understood that Harrison would stop speech-making whenever Quay objected.

Harrison made his first speech at his home to visiting Republicans. No protest came from Quay. A second speech was made shortly afterward to another delegation. Next day this telegram from Quay: "Keep at it. You're making votes."

HARRISON GETS A RURAL RESPONSE

The Quay telegram brings to mind an experience General Harrison had just after his election as Senator. It was Harrison's habit, when possible, to "try" his speeches on a back country audience before using them before larger audiences. He went down to Hendricks County, Indiana, once for that purpose. When the meeting was over, and while he was wondering how his speech had gone, a typical Hoosier farmer asked him to step over in the corner of the room. He did so.

"That's a fine speech you made," said the farmer.

"Thank you for the compliment," replied Harrison.

"As I listened to your way of talking I made up my mind that you're a first class talker. Now, I have spent five years inventing something that will go like wild fire with a good talker back of it. While you're not busy down there in that Senate why can't you talk up my machine? It's a big chance for a first class talker and I hadn't heard you ten minutes tonight before I knew you'd fill the bill for me. It's a big chance for both of us—what do you say?"

Harrison "regretted" that he would be otherwise engaged.

"Jest my luck," said the farmer, "jest my luck. I suppose some other fellow has heard your talk and got in ahead of me."

NO BARGAINS FOR THE PRESIDENCY

While Quay was managing the campaign,—and winning it against heavy odds,—he sent word to Indianapolis that James J. Hill, then building his railroad empire in our Northwest would contribute heavily ($50,000 as I recall it) to the campaign fund. But Harrison must agree, to appoint as Secretary of the Interior one of three men whose names would be submitted by Hill after election. Harrison not only refused, but directed that a contribution should not be accepted from Hill, even without conditions.

This incident is now related because it is typical of Harrison's course as President. The influence of his administration could not be bargained for. He fought without flinching against those who would have it otherwise—unfortunately too many having such tendencies were powerful leaders of his party. He did not hesitate to recognize campaign services freely given. In his inaugural he said he believed in honoring party service. But he denied every appointment urged upon him as fulfilment of a promise made to secure campaign services or contributions. Party service for the sake of the party was recognized but party service for a position was not.

"Remember," he had said to the managers of his convention battle for nomination in 1888, "no bargains, no alliances, no trades. I may like to be President, but if I am to go to the White House I don't propose to go shackled."

NO DESIRE TO FOLLOW A HEARSE INTO THE WHITE HOUSE

In the 1880 convention Harrison might have made a bargain for the Vice Presidency when the Conkling-Cameron forces were trying to break into different State delegations to capture votes for Grant. He was chairman of the Indiana delegation, supporting Blaine. During the balloting he was handed a card that is still in existence reading, "General Logan and Mr. Cameron will call upon General Harrison at his hotel tonight at nine o'clock."

The two chieftains of the Stalwart forces called promptly at the hour stated. They had authority to say that Harrison would be nominated for Vice President if he would throw the Indiana delegates to Grant. During the interview they temptingly called attention to Grant's age, his strenuous career in war, and his eight tiring years as President, leaving Harrison to infer that a Vice President elected with Grant probably would find himself President before the term ended.

"Gentlemen," said Harrison, "I am not ambitious to enter the White House following a hearse."

That ended the interview—and Harrison continued to vote for Blaine until the latter released his supporters in favor of Garfield. Eight years later Blaine showed his appreciation by urging Harrison's nomination.

As I Knew Them

The only man who ever claimed to have a pre-convention bargain with Harrison, was Senator Platt, of New York. That year the "Big Four"—Platt, Warner Miller, Chauncey Depew and Frank Hiscock—controlled the New York organization. Platt, however, was the potential figure. He delivered most of the New York delegates to Harrison on the nominating ballot, claiming afterward an understanding with Senator Stephen B. Elkins, supposedly speaking with Harrison's consent, that he would be made Secretary of the Treasury. That Sunday afternoon carriage ride was the basis of Platt's claim.

Harrison denied knowledge of the Elkins promise and, later, Platt absolved Harrison from responsibility. In the chapter on McKinley the reader will see how Platt eight years later sought to bargain with McKinley for a promise of the same office—only to find another man who would not pay *that* price even for the Presidency.

CANDIDATES WHO PREFER SLEEP TO ELECTION RETURNS

One would suppose with such a prize as the Presidency at stake, every contender in the race would sit up through election night eagerly studying the returns from different States to learn his fate. It would seem that sleep would be impossible. Yet Tom Sherman, who was Blaine's Secretary for a quarter of a century, tells me that at about eleven o'clock election night, before New York, Indiana and other large States had been definitely heard from, Blaine said that he was sleepy, and was going to bed. Turning to Sherman he added, "Let me know all about it in the morning, Tom."

In the same way in 1888 General Harrison turned from the election returns at about the same hour and went to bed. All evening he sat in his library with the family and some

172

friends. Early returns from New York were not encouraging. Gloom settled on the visitors. About nine o'clock noticing the unsmiling faces, Harrison said:

"Cheer up, everybody. This is no life and death affair. I am very happy here in Indianapolis and will continue to be if I'm not elected. Home is a pretty good place."

The detailed figures from only one State—Indiana—interested him keenly. He wanted to know as soon as possible the returns from every Hoosier county. His son-in-law, James R. McKee, now living in Greenwich, Conn., was tabulating the Indiana figures. Toward 11 o'clock he finally said, "This last bulletin settles it. We've got Indiana."

Harrison listened to McKee's summary.

"That's enough for me tonight then," he said. "My own State is for me. I'm going to bed."

Next morning a friend who had called at midnight to congratulate him asked Harrison why he had retired so early.

"Well," he replied, " I knew that my staying up would not change the result if I were defeated, while if elected I had a hard day ahead of me. So I thought a night's rest was best in any event."

WHY HARRISON DELAYED NAMING BLAINE

Perhaps an extreme illustration but as good as any I can give of Harrison's legalistic way of doing things—a way that was largely responsible for the charge of coldness—was his refusal to announce any definite commitments between election day and the meeting of the Presidential electors of all States, as required by law, on the second Monday of January following election. It is then that they formally cast their votes for President and Vice President. Harrison held that he had no right to assume his election as President until after that formality.

Of course, every aspirant for office, particularly Cabinet portfolios, was pressing for word from Indianapolis, but none came. Nor was the reason stated, though it should have been. Chief among the restless ones were the Blaine followers, with Whitelaw Reid and Charles Emory Smith in the lead. They demanded action—insisting that 80 per cent of Republican voters resented Harrison's tardy recognition of Blaine's qualities for Secretary of State. At Reid's request, in December, I personally mailed a round-robin letter to Harrison with twenty important signatures to that effect. But Harrison, though he knew he was going to offer Blaine the post, remained uncommitted until the electors had acted. Then he promptly invited Blaine into his Cabinet.

"WE'D BETTER TAKE BLAINE IN"

There are always protests against the leader in the race for high position, and there were protests against Blaine as head of the Cabinet. Many Republicans foresaw friction. Harrison, however, said to one man who was to be with him in official capacity and who thought John Sherman should be Secretary of State: "You and I want to be happy in Washington. It will not be as pleasant for us with Blaine out as with Blaine in. So we had better take him in."

That same argument, advanced by Col. Edward M. House in 1913 to Woodrow Wilson, led the latter to make Bryan his Secretary of State. Indeed, that highest and most dignified of national positions has been accorded men for that reason more frequently than has any other Cabinet portfolio. But even Blaine's enemies knew that he was by far the best-equipped man for the place. Harrison believed so, too. He once told me that he looked upon Blaine as the ablest statesman of his party. That, in truth, can be said of the whole line of Secretaries of State from John Jay to date. They have been men of broader experience and proven ability than our Presidents.

The prophecy of trouble between Harrison and Blaine was verified when Harrison refused to appoint Walker Blaine as first assistant Secretary of State. Reluctantly Harrison made him solicitor of the Department rather than offend Blaine; but he did not believe that a Secretary of State should have his son in the Department.

The next break came two years later when Harrison refused to make a Brigadier General of Colonel Coppinger, Blaine's son-in-law. Harrison would not jump Coppinger over the heads of his seniors in service.

"You had it in your power to please us in one matter two years ago," said Mrs. Blaine to the President, "and it is now in your power to please us a second time. Yet you don't do it. I cannot understand it."

In both instances Harrison regretted that he could not acquiesce in Blaine's desire but he put the good of the service above personal considerations.

A WHITE HOUSE PICTURE

It was my good fortune to get several intimate pictures of life in the White House while the Harrisons occupied it, but none that I recall so truly reflects the atmosphere of a typical American home as the statement recently made to me by Major Halford. "In the afternoons when we would need the President's signature or have some information for him, we would often find him seated at the window of his sitting-room reading. Opposite him would be Mrs. Harrison engaged in decorating china. Often he would be reading aloud to her while she kept on with her painting. The White House did not change the family life of their Indiana home."

Harrison had one characteristic that saved him many worries. He never expressed regrets for things done or settled. He would say, "I did that with the best information and judgment I had at the time. I closed the case then and I don't want to hear anything more about it."

175

CHAPTER XXI

"THE BILLION DOLLAR CONGRESS"

Also A Billion Dollar Country—As Joyous In Washington As A Donnybrook Fair—Immigration And Anti-Trust Policies Started On Their Way—A Gun At The Head of Every President—Harrison Responsible For Flag Over Every School-House—Some Harrison Epigrams.

IT WAS a joy to be in Washington in the days of Harrison —that is if you had any liking to be where the fighting is good and there is news aplenty. I enjoyed my frequent visits on newspaper errands—some lasting several weeks. The two Congresses—one Republican and one Democratic—had the enthusiasm for turbulence of a Donnybrook Fair, particularly the Congress known as the "Reed Congress." Because of Reed's famous ruling to count a quorum if one was, in fact, physically present, also because of the narrow Republican majority of 12, there was scarcely a day without its sensational charge and counter-charge in the House—with Kilgore of Texas, for example, kicking at the closed door to get out before Tom Reed as Speaker could see and count him. Constantine Buckley Kilgore was that statesman's real name, but Congress knew him as "Constantly Bucking" Kilgore.

Other Democrats vied with one another to shout loudest, longest and most defiantly, but they never budged Reed, who was always the coolest member of the House. When they finally tired of wasting time in shouting he made them put in more hours at business to make up for the delay.

The result was that that Congress transacted all the business it had to do, as Reed promised that it would.

As I Knew Them

It had much to its credit. The Democrats called it a "Billion Dollar" Congress, and started out to make an issue of the fact that for the first time in our history the government's expenditures totalled a billion dollars. Secretary of the Treasury Charles Foster met the charge with the calm inquiry, "Well, isn't this a billion dollar country?"

That reply was too swift and too warm for the Democrats to handle; in baseball parlance of the day it was called a "daisy cutter," though no daisies now adorn baseball fields. The quick response came from the people that they were proud of a billion dollar country. That silenced the critics.

The McKinley tariff bill and the Federal Elections bill, the latter known popularly as the "Force" Bill, were the conspicuous measures of the session. But the two subjects then urged by the administration that were destined to grow into great national policies were the Sherman anti-trust law and restriction of immigration. In 1890 the first outcry was heard against the "melting-pot" theory. The pot was boiling over; we had passed the 500,000 mark of yearly immigration; the quality of immigrants was deteriorating and the quantity increasing. We had ceased to be able to assimilate. In a message to Congress, Harrison said: "We should not cease to be hospitable to immigration, but we should cease being careless as to the character of it." Congress, however, waited until 1917—nearly 20 years later—before taking action.

A GUN AT THE HEAD OF EVERY PRESIDENT

I have spoken of Harrison's refusal of the Hill campaign contribution and his attitude toward the steadily increasing power of corporations in Congress and elsewhere.

Those not familiar with official life in Washington do not realize the tremendous pressure to place men in positions that command every avenue of information, influence and action. There is no let-up to it. It is exerted so subtly, so shrewdly, that even an alert President or Cabinet officer does not always sense its presence before it has done its deadly work.

Truly a gun is held at the head of a President the moment he is elected. Every big corporate and banking interest in New York City and Chicago, every big railway system, intrigues to have a friend at court. The Treasury Department is a principal objective of this predatory campaign—the State Department a close second; but the White House is the real target.

Many Senators and Congressmen join in this siege of the White House. No threats are made, no open opposition shown, but the President suddenly discovers that the wheels are not turning—that things just don't move. Nominees are not confirmed, executive recommendations slumber in committees, departments don't function, strange rumors seep into official gossip. There is an inertia that he cannot overcome, and for which no definite reason can be given. It creeps over everything like an incoming tide. You cannot put your finger on the centre of trouble and say "Here it is!" An administration that holds out against these influences has a trying time with Congress. Only a resourceful character in the White House can measure swords with them.

HARRISON AND ROOSEVELT METHODS

Harrison did not possess those qualities, Roosevelt did. Coming into the Presidency, twelve years later, Roosevelt fought the same influences—but he fought in a different way. Those who recall both Harrison and Roosevelt will know how they would differ even when seeking the same result. Both had the same antagonism to an "invisible government." Both saw it rooted deep in Washington. Harrison, however, stood on the defensive in his legalistic way—denying it opportunity, so far as his power extended, and ignoring its existence so long as it did not come before him officially. Roosevelt went out to meet it. He used the Northern Securities suit as the basis for an aggressive campaign to destroy it.

Roosevelt's way led to his triumphant election in 1904; Harrison's way led with equal emphasis to his defeat for re-election in 1892. The thing Harrison had scotched but not destroyed rose to smite him at the polls.

"BIG BUSINESS" TURNED TO CLEVELAND

I was in position throughout the Harrison campaign to know the currents that were affecting the result. Subsequent information confirmed my opinion formed by what I saw before election day—that Harrison was betrayed and defeated by a group of Republican leaders resentful because of his antagonism to the influences I have described. Big corporations regarded Cleveland as "safer." They contributed so lavishly to his campaign that the fund was the largest ever collected up to that time.

They saw only the candidate, not the party behind him. They did not realize that a "safe" President in the White House, forced to rely upon an unsympathetic party in Congress, meant chaos—and chaos is the one thing business cannot stand. In the four years following 1892, business was to learn a lesson and pay a heavy price for its tuition.

The lamentable feature of it all was that Harrison's opponents blindly assumed that he was determined to have another term as President. Those in his confidence knew that that was not his desire. Certainly there were many reasons against another four years in the White House. Mrs. Harrison was fatally ill (she died in October, 1892) and his own experiences had many unpleasant features. A return to Indianapolis seemed more inviting than remaining where he was. Platt and Quay, unaware of Harrison's mood, began to seek delegates pledged against him. Definite evidences of their defiance reached the President. They were out to beat his nomination.

"I don't want this, I did not invite it," said Harrison when he learned that they had opened battle, "but a Harrison never runs from a fight."

BLAINE'S LAST BID FOR THE PRESIDENCY

Persuading Blaine into the contest was one of the tragedies of politics. Old friends like Elkins, Kerens, and Powell Clayton advised him against entering, and for the only time in their political careers did not support him. It would seem that it was late in life for Blaine to ignore such friendships, but he did. He seems to have been moved more by a desire to drive Harrison into withdrawal than by hope of his own nomination.

Only a month before his announcement I talked with Blaine in the Secretary of State's office. It was evident then that he was a sick man—so far from well that I put aside as absurd the rumors that he would oppose Harrison. However, he got into the struggle and his last battle for the Presidency proved to be as futile as were his previous contests. A career saddened by successive defeats had its saddest chapter in this final effort. Seven months later, death ended all.

PUTTING THE FLAG ON OUR SCHOOL-HOUSES

I have no official record on which to base the statement that the flags displayed on our school-houses are there because of a Harrison speech; but it is a fact that following his address at the centennial anniversary of Washington's inauguration, April 30, 1899, there was a speedy nation-wide movement, which resulted in the present-day display of the flag while school is in session.

That was a most inspiring occasion. The Benjamin Harri-

son who as President made the speech was grandson of a
President and the great-grandson and namesake of a signer
of the Declaration of Independence. He was called the "centennial" President. Such a coincidence, you may be sure, did
not lessen Harrison's patriotic interest in the occasion, or that
of the great number of people who joined in the ceremonies.

The celebration was held in New York City. Pageantry,
oratory and public enthusiasm made it picturesque and inspiring. Harrison landed in the city, as Washington had landed,
from a barge rowed to shore at the same landing place. He
stood on the spot now occupied by the Sub-Treasury where
Washington had stood when inaugurated; he attended services
in St. Paul's Chapel, using Washington's pew, and at night he
addressed a great assemblage at the Metropolitan Opera
House. There he made the stirring utterance that started the
flag-display movement. Here is an extract from it:

> "These banners with which you have covered your walls, these
> patriotic inscriptions must come down; and the ways of com-
> merce and of trade be resumed again here; but may I not ask you
> to carry these banners that now hang on the walls, into the homes,
> into the public schools of your city; and into all your great institu-
> tions where children are gathered and to drape them there, that
> the eyes of the young and of the old may look upon the flag as
> one of the familiar adornments of every American home."

SOME HARRISON EPIGRAMS

Harrison never made a poor speech. Always he had something to say worth saying and he knew how to say it. I would
like to quote at length from many of his speeches but this is
not the place. Here are some lines showing the keenness of
his mind:

> The evil that works from a bad centre works both ways.
> A community where law is the rule of conduct and where
> courts, not mobs, execute its penalties is the only attractive field for
> business investments and honest labor.

As I Knew Them

Those who would use the law as a defense must not deny that use of it to others.

If our great corporations would more scrupulously observe their legal limitations and duties, they would have less cause to complain of the unlawful limitations of their rights or of violent interference with their operation.

We should not cease to be hospitable to immigration but we should cease being careless as to the character of it.

No other people have a government more worthy of their respect and love or a land so magnificent in extent, so pleasant to look upon, and so full of generous suggestion to enterprise and labor.

Justice and mercy should hold the reins of power and the upward avenues of hope be free to all the people.

When the harvest from the fields, the cattle from the hills, and the ores of the earth shall have been weighed, counted and valued, we will turn from them all to crown with highest honor the State that has most promoted education, virtue, justice and patriotism among its people.

They (working-people) are American citizens and it cannot be a perversion of the Constitution so to legislate as to preserve in their homes the comfort, independence, loyalty and sense of interest in the government which are essential to good citizenship.

The Society of the Unemployed, now holding its frequent and threatening parades in the Streets of foreign cities, should not be allowed to acquire an American domicile.

It is time that mutual charges of unfairness and fraud between the great parties shall cease.

There are no frontiers to our possible development.

No lesson needs to be so urgently impressed upon our people as this—that no worthy end or cause can be promoted by lawlessness.

CHAPTER XXII

THE LAST STRUGGLE WITH THE SOUTH

*The "Force" Bill of 1890, Protecting The Negro's Right To Vote—
Lodge's First National Activity—Harrison Expresses Himself—My
Own Experiences In General Mahone's Campaign—A Stubborn Fact
That Some Day Must Be Faced—Why The Electoral College Should
Be Maintained.*

THE same Henry Cabot Lodge who in 1919-20 as Chairman of the Senate Foreign Relations Committee fought Woodrow Wilson's League of Nations so bitterly, and won, is the Henry Cabot Lodge who, as a Congressman in his second term in 1890, fought the last battle by Republicans in Congress to secure national protection for the negro voter at elections in the South—and lost. Cleveland had withdrawn U. S. Marshals from the polls there; the bill sponsored by Lodge sought to put them back. Its printed title was Federal Elections bill, but the country knew it as the "Force" bill.

Lodge had been slowly winning prominence as an author and legislator, but while this legislation was under debate the attention he received equalled in intensity that which came to him thirty years later while the Versailles treaty was before the Senate. He was a "first page" feature day after day. With courage and skill he piloted the bill through the House, but the Democrats in the Senate made a bargain with a group of their Republican colleagues seeking other legislation and the Force bill was buried. It has not come to life since.

I have no desire to revive a discussion of the subject, but in its own way the South should find a solution fair to the north on national candidates. Under existing conditions one white voter in the South has the potential voting influence of 10 voters in certain Congress districts in the North, and he

183

averages three; the South has representation in Congress based on population, white and black; but voting is limited to whites. I do not know how to point the way to adjust this inequality, yet all fair men must know that it constitutes a stubborn fact which some day is bound to become bothersome.

President Harrison's presentation of the situation in his message to Congress is without equal as clear and forceful analysis. It is as well worth reading today.

"The colored people did not intrude themselves upon us; they were brought here in chains and held in the communities where they were chiefly bound by a cruel slave code. Happily for both races, they are now free.

"Notwithstanding all this, in many parts of our country where the colored population is large the people of that race are, by various devices, deprived of any effective exercise of their political rights and of many of their civil rights. The wrong does not expend itself upon those whose votes are suppressed. Every constituency in the Union is wronged.

"Surely, no one supposes that the present can be accepted as a permanent condition. If it is said that these communities must work out this problem for themselves, we have a right to ask whether they are at work upon it. Do they suggest any solution? When and under what conditions is the black man to have a free ballot? When is he, in fact, to have those full civil rights which have so long been his in law? When is that equality of influence which our form of government was intended to secure to the electors to be restored? This generation should courageously face these grave questions, and not leave them as a heritage of woe to the next. The consultation should proceed with candor, calmness, and great patience; upon the lines of justice and humanity, not of prejudice and cruelty. No question in our country can be at rest except upon the firm basis of justice and of the law.

"The qualifications of any elector must be sought in the law, not in the opinions, fears, or judgments of any class, however powerful. The path of the elector to the ballot box must be free from the ambush of fear and the enticements of fraud, the count so true and open that none shall gain-say it. It should give the advantage to honesty and the decision to majorities."

184

As I Knew Them

I have some recollection of campaigns and elections in the South years ago; they have changed in some respects but in result not at all. I travelled with General "Billy" Mahone, the fighting little giant of Virginia politics, when he ran for Governor in 1889, and from my own experience I knew that all Southern elections, conducted under local auspices, were not elections at all.

I was a visitor in the Mahone home in Petersburg, when a mob gathered and began shooting in the air as we were about to have dinner. It was the night before election. The demonstration was made to show disregard for Mahone's candidacy. Mahone weighed not over 110 pounds, and was not over five feet three or four inches tall. With his wide-brimmed white felt hat and "Prince Albert" frock coat, and long white beard, he was a picturesque figure. Mahone walked to the long old fashioned window of the living room and looked out at the crowd. Without a word, he put on his hat, opened the front door and with hand stuck in trouser's pocket, coat thrown back, walked slowly down the fifty-foot gravel path to the gate.

Leaning over the gate he fairly glared straight into the faces of the yelling mob, cussed them as only a Mahone could cuss; then turning his back on them, he walked with defiant slowness to the house. Not a shot was fired until he had disappeared in the doorway—then there was another outburst of shooting. This time a few bullets crashed through some of the windows. Mahone insisted on eating dinner as calmly as though the silence of peace prevailed, but his guests, including myself, had no great appetite.

At midnight the crowd gathered again. This time they aimed more directly at the house. Butler Mahone, the General's son, fired back, slightly injuring one of the mob. Within an hour he was arrested, though he had only defended his home.

All that night lines of negro voters awaited the opening of the polls. The election districts were formed like the spokes of a wheel with the Town Hall as the hub. All the polling booths in the Town Hall were located in one large room. Perhaps one colored man in five was, after much persistence, allowed to vote. So many negroes voted, however, that late in the afternoon it was thought safest to make counting impossible. Someone started a fight, the ballot boxes were smashed, and the ballots scattered on the floor. "No returns" was the official report.

PRESIDENTIAL VOTES AND THE SOUTH

The South now has its own way with its negro vote; and it probably will continue to have its own way until such time as the people determine to elect their President by popular vote instead of through the machinery of the electoral college.

When, if and as that happens, it is not to be presumed that the South will insist that the nation should continue to accept the undependable election figures and methods of the present day. No Republican candidate for President could ever overcome with Northern votes the totals that would come up from the South. The one hope for a Republican candidate would be immediate insistence upon recognizing every citizen's constitutional right to vote, whether South or North, and to have his vote honestly counted.

The agitation for popular election of President, therefore, has many possibilities for reviving old sectional animosities, though that is not the strongest reason for standing by the electoral college.

The strongest reason is that it is the last bulwark sustaining the "checks-and-balances" theory so thoughtfully worked out by the founders of our government. The electoral college represents the popular will for President as sifted through the States; until 1914 the Senate also represented the popular will after a sifting process through each State Legislature.

The House of Representatives was the one direct-election body.

Now the President stands alone as a "balance" against both branches of Congress; when the clamor for direct election of President succeeds,—if it ever succeeds—the structure of our government as originally planned will be materially changed. There will be no checks, no balances except the Supreme Court; the political will of the people will prevail at Washington immediately after being registered in the ballot-box.

This is the "pure democracy" against which students of the philosophy of history continuously warn us. In the field of pure democracy there always flourish the tares and weeds of disintegration and destruction. The long path of world history is strewn with the wreck of such experiments. The founders of our government knew this peril. To protect us from its evil, and yet give popular will opportunity for immediate expression, it made the House of Representatives directly responsive to the voters, reserving the Senate and the presidency to their more deliberate judgment. We are swinging far from that anchorage.

I have been fairly well acquainted with the membership of the Senate for many years, and I cannot see that the change to direct election has improved the quality of its Senators, to state it conservatively. Certainly it is no longer a deliberative body; that tradition has been swept away; so have many others —so many that the result, as we look over the Senate today, gives no encouragement to thoughtful people to favor a similar change in the method of electing our Presidents.

CHAPTER XXIII

TOM REED—JOHN J. INGALLS

*One Of New England, One Of The West, Both Brilliant Debaters—
George Harvey's Dinner To Mark Twain Was Reed's Last Appear-
ance—Strong In Convictions, Dislikes And Friendships—The Reed
Quorum Counting Rule No Sudden Impulse—He Goes To New York
Disappointed With Public Life—Ingalls Insistent That The Decalogue
Has No Place In Politics—"Purification An Iridescent Dream"—Car-
ried Away In The Bryan Flood.*

TOM REED, of Maine!—Czar! Truly a character,
virile, brilliant, witty, sarcastic, profound. He had by
right of birth all the characteristics that have made New
Englanders leaders in the spiritual and material development
of our country.

The last time I saw Reed was at a birthday dinner to Mark
Twain, given by George Harvey in the Metropolitan Club,
New York City, November 28, 1902. Though apparently
well and in fine humor that night, Reed died one week later
in Washington. In eight years Clemens followed. The
feature of the Harvey dinner was the exchange of badinage
between Reed and Clemens. They spoke of their friendship
of many years, each deploring the fact that at their advanced
age they could not expect to be long together in this world.
And, each regretted that they would be separated in the world
to come. One would go above; the other below. Who was to
have the reward of Heaven the two speakers left their highly
entertained friends to judge, but amidst roars of laughter
at their clever way of doubting each other's future they regretted in turn that the Fates were against both reaching the
same high station in the hereafter.

188

As I Knew Them

They did not dream that they were never again to meet on earth!

My relations with Blaine and then with McKinley, based upon my newspaper connections, obviously prevented me from having the same intimacy with Reed. He was never in sympathy with either man. He stood loyally but not aggressively by Blaine whenever the latter's interests nationally were

TOM REED—CZAR! LOOKING DOWN ON THE HOUSE

at stake, but he never even pretended to recognize McKinley as a capable leader. Nor was his dislike for Harrison concealed. I was, therefore, on the "other side of the fence." To go from Blaine to Harrison and then to McKinley was a logical step for a newspaper and with my editor's policy my personal inclinations went also.

Judged by the cartoons and violent discussions at the time, you would assume that as Speaker of the House, Tom Reed used a gavel as constantly as a blacksmith pounds on an anvil. My observation was that he used it less often than most presiding officers. When he did use it, however, it came down with a bang that everyone within hearing instantly knew meant decision and action. Once was usually enough. Then, too, back of it as it swung through the air was the tall, massive figure of Tom Reed—enough of itself to impress.

Many a time as I watched him from the press gallery, he towered so high above all else that he seemed out of proportion, even in that spacious chamber of the House of Representatives. He easily dominated the picture as he stood placidly looking down upon defiant Democrats crowding the "well" and the aisles, too excited, too exasperated, to cope with their masterful presiding officer.

"DOES THE GENTLEMAN DENY HE IS PRESENT?"

Reed's famous ruling was simply a denial of the contentions of Democrats—that a member physically present in the House was merely a ghostly apparition, not to be counted as part of a quorum unless he so desires.

"I deny your right, Mr. Speaker, to count me as present," yelled a Democratic member rushing wildly down the aisle, his closed fist extended at arm's length toward the Speaker.

"The Chair is making a statement of fact that the gentleman is present," responded Reed in a voice so calm as to infuriate the member still further. "Does the gentleman deny it?"

Of course, it could not be denied, and equally, of course, when the Democrats came into control of the next Congress they adopted the Reed quorum counting rule.

The Democrats were not exasperated so much by the rule as by its purpose to enact Republican legislation. The Republican majority in the House was not more than 12. It was necessary, therefore, that the entire Republican membership should be present and voting if Republican measures were to be passed. That, of course, was impossible, for the sick and necessarily absent members are numerous. The Democratic strategy, therefore, was to demand the presence of a quorum, and then refuse to answer when the roll was called to determine whether a quorum was present. Without Democratic votes, a quorum could seldom be counted. These tactics were called "filibustering."

Reed's ruling was no hap-hazard affair. He foresaw the situation when he took the Speaker's chair, and was prepared for the first attempt at filibuster. It came when the contested elections committee brought in a report in favor of seating a Republican contestant. The point of "no quorum" was raised. More than half the Democratic members remained silent while the roll was called. Then Reed began to count those he could see and name; he ordered the clerk to enter them as present. Many Democrats bolted for the doors; those who remained to protest, however, were counted by Reed. They were sufficient to make up a quorum.

THE ABLEST DEBATER IN CONGRESS

Thomas Brackett Reed did not reach the Speaker's chair to make this historic ruling without first participating in many battles in Congress in the exciting period from the late seventies to the close of the last century. Those were the days of quick political fluctuations, when Presidencies hung by the slender plurality of a single State, and Congress and Senate swung from one party to another like a pendulum. Reed's service began in the House with the extra session called after Hayes' inauguration in 1877. He quickly won a place in the minds of his colleagues by his clever cross-examination of Democratic participants in the Tilden cipher dispatches.

Through the next ten years Reed, now in minority, now in majority, emerged steadily as the strongest debater in the House. There was no bitterness in his retorts, but there was a strong, broad understanding and a hard logic that his opponents found difficulty in evading.

Sarcasm is the most dangerous weapon in all the equipment of a debater. Like a too-heavily loaded musket, it has a dangerous recoil. Yet Tom Reed used it freely, and was not a greatly-hated man. Some of his closest personal friends were on the other side. Perhaps his very bigness was disarming. Six feet two or three, weighing well over 250 pounds, he always seemed bigger than all around him.

No Congressional leader was ever so perfectly adapted to the functions of leadership in majority or minority. My judgment is that he was the ablest debater the Republicans have ever had in Congress. He never permitted himself to make sharp rejoinders without substance to back them up, for, above all, Reed was not a superficial man. He knew the peril of too great brilliance and too little facts, and always thoroughly prepared for debate.

WHY REED URGED VOTES FOR WOMEN

I doubt whether many men who knew Reed, knew that he favored woman suffrage—yet he was among the earliest legislators to urge it. It is interesting to read this extract from a Committee report written by him:

> "It is not surprising to find that the reasons on which the continuance of the inferiority of women is urged are drawn almost entirely from a tender consideration of their own good. The anxiety felt lest they should thereby deteriorate would be an honor to human nature were it not an historical fact that the same sweet solicitude has been put up as a barrier against every progress women have made since civilization began."

And again:

> "No reason on earth can be given by those who claim suffrage as a right of manhood which does not make it also a right of womanhood."

When you watched Reed in parliamentary battles you had to realize that he was the most forceful figure on the Republican side, and the man whom the opposition most dreaded to arouse to verbal combat. A response to Congressman Springer, the Democratic leader from Illinois, has been so often quoted in some form as to be almost too familiar for repetition, but perhaps it will bear repeating for those not so long on the highways of life as some of us have been.

NEVER BE RIGHT OR PRESIDENT

Springer was known as "Bounding Bill" Springer. He was one of the few members whom Reed thoroughly disliked.

During a debate Springer declared that "like Henry Clay I would rather be right than be President."

"The gentleman need give himself no uneasiness," interrupted Reed with that New England drawl that gave a peculiar emphasis to his words. "He will never be either."

As widely known in political circles is Reed's saying "A statesman is a successful politician who is dead," but not so widely known is this story once told by Senator Lodge in a magazine article. A newspaper editor telegraphed Reed "Why don't you die and become a statesman?" To which he responded: "No. Fame is the last infirmity of a noble mind."

When the 1896 convention gave him only 85 votes for President, Reed made up his mind to abandon public life. He had given 20 years to it, he was poor, and he was now without hope of greater distinction. The Republicans re-elected him Speaker, but his heart was no longer in a political career. He served his term out and then accepting the advice of his friend, Augustus G. Paine, went to New York city to practice law; four years later he died.

INGALLS, THE BRILLIANT SENATOR FROM KANSAS

There were many interesting characters in that Congress besides Tom Reed. One I knew well was as picturesque as

Reed and as interesting in debate, though a contrast with him physically—John J. Ingalls, Senator from Kansas and for four years president pro tempore of the Senate. Reed weighed almost twice as much as Ingalls, whose slim body was topped with a head broad and high at the forehead, narrow at the back and chin; his large eyes hidden by thick round spectacles; his nervous energy exceeded his physical strength. He had none of Reed's complacency; nor was he so sound in his thinking. Ingalls was the slave of his eloquence; Reed was always the master of his. Ingalls used brilliant phrases because he liked the flow of language; Reed used them only when they expressed some purpose more pointedly than other words would. Ingalls went down in the 16 to 1 tornado—swept off his feet and into the Bryan camp, whence he never emerged politically.

THE DECALOGUE HAS NO PLACE IN POLITICS

When Ingalls spoke in the Senate the country always listened, but nothing he ever uttered there equalled in attention an article he contributed to the New York World in 1890 in which he declared that the "purification of politics is an iridescent dream." The article provoked a storm of denunciation. Thirty-five years later we are still facing astounding primary expenditures totalling over a million dollars. Though the Senate unseats a Newberry from Michigan and a Clark from Montana—and hesitates to admit a Vare from Pennsylvania and a Smith from Illinois—as a penalty for spending too much money, the dollar continues to figure conspicuously in the rivalries of politics.

Hopeless to stop it? I do not think so, but I must quote against my faith the Ingalls talk—the most remarkable interview ever printed on the subject of politics, particularly as it came from the then President of the Senate. Let us think back to 1890, and ask with how much truth Ingalls saw into the future:

As I Knew Them

"The purification of politics is an iridescent dream. Government is force. Politics is a battle for supremacy. Parties are the armies. The Decalogue and the Golden Rule have no place in a political campaign. The object is success. To defeat the antagonist and expel the party in power is the purpose.

"The Republicans and Democrats are as irreconcilably opposed to each other as were Grant and Lee in the Wilderness. They use ballots instead of guns, but the struggle is as unrelenting and desperate and the result sought for the same.

"In war it is lawful to deceive the adversary, to hire Hessians, to purchase mercenaries, to mutilate, to destroy. The commander who lost the battle through the activity of his moral nature would be the derision and jest of history.

"This modern cant about the corruption of politics is fatiguing in the extreme. It proceeds from tea-custard and syllabub dilettanteism and frivolous sentimentalism."

CHAPTER XXIV

"FOUR YEARS MORE FOR GROVER"

Cleveland Not A Party Leader—The White House The Loneliest Place In Washington—The Tariff And Money Battles—A "Campaign of Education" That Democrats Did Not Want—The Populist Deal By Which Cleveland Withdrew From Many Western States— Four Years Of Party Strife, Then The Chaos Of 1896—What Might Have Been—Gorman's Withering Arraignment Of Cleveland.

> "Grover, Grover, Four Years
> More For Grover!
> In We Go—Out They Go
> Soon We'll Be In Clover!"
> —Song of the 1892 Campaign

IN the story of Cleveland just advanced from the New York Governorship to the Presidency in 1884-85 I endeavored to give the reader a picture of the Cleveland whom I found in Albany waiting the day when he was to take the oath of office as President, also the first years of his Washington experience. He plainly showed his baffled spirit. Like all other Presidents, his greatest exasperations were the pleadings of place-hunters. With Cleveland they were at their worst. Democrats had grown old without a chance for national office.

Here was their long-waited opportunity. They had their eyes on March 4, 1885, as keenly as horse jockeys watch the starter's flag. They expected, they insisted upon, a clean sweep of all Republicans. In two years Cleveland gave them all save 8,000 of the 57,000 appointive places. When he first took up this monumental task, he frequently said he was sick at heart at the conflicts.

"The d——d everlasting clatter for office continues," he wrote, at one time, later on, "and makes me feel like resigning and hell is to pay generally." There was no way to satisfy all, but for a President idolized by civil service reformers and

196

professing to share their views his two years' record was a swift one.

Had Cleveland's career ended when he handed the Presidency over to Benjamin Harrison in 1889, he would have been remembered, of course, as the first Democratic President in the White House since Buchanan, but I doubt if there would have been much else for fame to make note of.

His antagonism to legislation passed by a Democratic House and a Republican Senate was the conspicuous feature of his Administration. Out of 1649 bills sent him by the Forty-ninth Congress, going out of office with him in 1889, he vetoed 145, allowed 167 to become law without his signature, and left 55 unsigned (and therefore dead) after adjournment,—364 out of 1649 failed of approval by him. No other President has such a record of opposition to Congress.

Four years is too brief to accomplish much at Washington —certainly too brief for a man with no national background and no national associations. Cleveland had less preparation for his new responsibilities than almost any other man ever elected to the Presidency. He had hardly "found himself" before his term was over.

I have always held that Cleveland's broader outlook on national questions came to him between his first and second terms, while his mind was free of official harassments. He could then look back upon his Administration as one does on a speech already made and think how he could soar beyond it, if given another chance. He sought and got that chance.

"WE LOVE HIM FOR THE ENEMIES HE HAS MADE"

I do not say that Cleveland did not grow during his first four years. He did—steadily—except in his ability to hold his party back of him and to tolerate differences of opinion. He was never able to do either. He failed completely in both respects while Governor of New York and while President—

most completely in his second term, when earlier experience should have modified instead of emphasized that weakness.

His champions made a virtue of this inability. We still hear echoes of the boast epitomized by General Bragg, of Wisconsin, in the Democratic National Convention in Chicago in 1888: "We love him for the enemies he has made." It is significant of the highly personal application of Bragg's remark that as he uttered it from the platform he looked directly into the faces of the Tammany delegation seated in the front rows of the convention.

In some capable minds it is still debatable whether Cleveland's place at present in history is not largely for the Bragg reason. For we must not forget that certain characteristics, while commendable, lead only to disaster and defeat—to objects not attained, though battled for heroically. We may applaud their courage while we question their wisdom.

The qualities of true leadership have their certifying clauses in achievement. Cleveland had fine purpose, a deep appreciation of his responsibilities as President, but, judged by actual achievement, his career is a career of courageous failure, except on two measures—the repeal of the silver purchase law and his famous controversy with England.

Let us survey the record, as results reveal it.

ALWAYS A DWINDLING PARTY COLUMN

In 1885, Cleveland, elected President, found his party in control of the House of Representatives. They were then hopeful of the Senate also. Two years later control of the House was almost lost; another two years and the Presidency as well as both Houses of Congress were lost. Democratic leaders warned him against taking the course that led to defeat, but he took it.

In 1893, again elected President, Cleveland found his party in control of our national government, lock, stock and barrel. In less than a year it was involved in such bitter factional strife over his recommendations that defeat was inevitable in the Congress elections of 1894; in another twelvemonth, a majority of Democrats in both houses of Congress were out of sympathy with their President, to state it mildly, and in the national Democratic convention of 1896 almost a two-thirds vote was recorded against platform indorsement of his Administration. Instead the platform made "16 to 1" its central plank, and took issue against practically every Cleveland policy. The one thing left the President was to labor for the defeat of the candidate his party had named as his successor—and that he did.

Now, you may say that Grover Cleveland was a resolute, almost heroic figure in the White House; that he made a great battle for sound money despite his party, and I agree most cordially; but you cannot get away from the logic of the facts recorded in the two paragraphs just preceding this one, when estimating Cleveland as a leader of men. He was not such a leader.

You cannot make a leader out of one who is constantly arraigning those who differ with him; constantly complaining of his burdens and lamenting the loss of support—particularly support that frequently he might have obtained through conference without serious compromise.

A leader's function is to attract followers, not to repulse them. In government by parties such as our government is, results are essential to successful leadership. Without successes to give your leadership authority you face chaos, the chaos that tore the Democratic party apart while Cleveland was President.

Though callers at the White House were few during Cleveland's first term there was little comment about their scarcity, but it became a common saying during his second term that the White House was the loneliest place in Washington, especially during the last two years.

This isolation was due to some extent to his separation from so many party leaders, yet not wholly so. There were many supporters of the President's policies among Democrats in both branches of Congress, but not many callers at the White House.

EDUCATION THAT DEMOCRATS DID NOT WANT

It was in this second term, however, this period of greatest isolation, that many Republican writers like myself were supporting his silver purchase repeal bill; his persistent but vain appeals for other sound money legislation; his stand to make Debs and the railway strikers realize that the Government is supreme; and lastly his arousing notice to England apropos of Venezuela's boundaries. He then revealed to many people the character that had come to the surface only infrequently from 1885 to 1889.

In 1893 we saw a more developed Cleveland than the Cleveland entering the White House in 1885. We saw a President who no longer planned and moved with the caution of inexperience, the dread of bog lands under him. I would never accuse Cleveland of having dreams; he was too phlegmatic for dreams; but in 1893, as he looked into the next four years, his intense partisanship must have stirred him to plans of great party achievement. The executive, legislative and judicial branches of the government were Democratic for the first time in half a century. Opportunity and responsibility were theirs. Cleveland, assuming party leadership, struck out boldly for the things he believed in—accompanied, as usual, with much lamentation to his friends as to his burdens.

"I look upon the four years next to come as a self-inflicted penance for the good of my country," he wrote. "I see no pleasure in it."

"A campaign of education," remarked Senator Calvin S. Brice, his national chairman, of the Cleveland programme.

Unfortunately for Cleveland's hopes the Democratic party did not want education—certainly not the education he sought to impose upon it nor his way of educating it. "Perhaps he'll be able to break that team of wild horses to harness," was the quiet comment of ex-President Harrison as he looked over the membership of the two Democratic Houses of Congress. He couldn't. They made ribbons of the harness and kicked the buggy into splinters.

It was certain they would do so.

THE CLEVELAND-POPULIST BARGAIN

How could there have been any other outcome of the 1892 campaign than a Democratic party controlled by Populists, soon to be rechristened "Bryanites"?

I have never been able to reconcile the talk of Cleveland's rigid adherence to principle with his acquiescence in the campaign "deal" by which in nine of the then fourteen States west of the Mississippi Democratic voters were authoritatively directed in 1892 to cast their ballots for General James B. Weaver, the Populist and Free Silver candidate for President.

The Cleveland ticket was officially withdrawn from five of those States; in four others it was informally abandoned. The purpose, of course, was to insure the defeat of Harrison electors even at the cost of giving impetus to the Populist movement; and it succeeded in both respects too well, though Harrison defeated the combination in seven States.

THE SOCKLESS "JERRY" SIMPSON

In all that vast territory, Cleveland secured only one elector in Oregon and eight of the nine in California. Weaver had twenty-two electors; also there were elected by the combination many Populist Congressmen of the type of "Sockless" Jerry Simpson, of Kansas, and of Peffer, whom Kansas had elected to the Senate. Peffer became famous because of his abundant whiskers, Simpson because in his campaign he gloried in the absence of socks.

Wherever he went in his stumping tour he made much of

the poverty stricken condition of the people and used his own plight as an example. "Why, we can't even afford to buy socks for ourselves!" he would cry and to bear witness to this sad plight he would kick off his shoes.

THE PURPOSE OF THE POPULIST DEAL

The theory of the Populist deal was that the first purpose of the Cleveland campaign should be to prevent Harrison from securing a majority of electoral votes even though Cleveland also failed to do so. In the event that no candidate had a majority the election would be thrown into the House of Representatives, then overwhelmingly Democratic. The Democrats knew that Cleveland could not carry the West,— that the only hope for depriving Harrison of electoral votes from that section was to withdraw Cleveland, and urge Democrats out there to support Weaver. If Weaver could win the West, there were not enough votes in the East for Harrison possibly to get a majority in the Electoral College. That is the kind of political manipulation that, though it often attains its purpose, as it did in this case, always carries reprisals, as it also did in this case.

Neither Cleveland nor his managers got the larger conception of the result of having Democrats vote the Populist ticket. They did not foresee the inevitable wreck of the Democratic party throughout that vast section of the country; nor of the influence on the party in Congress of so many Populist members whom Democratic voters had been told to help elect. I made a tour of some of the western States during the campaign. Nowhere could you hear any other comment on that deal than that the Democratic party "had gone Populist." That indeed was truth, and no man was more responsible for it than Cleveland, for he was the candidate withdrawn.

No great political party ever sold itself so boldly and completely to achieve campaign victory; nor has any Presidential candidate ever consented, as Cleveland consented, to his own elimination in so many States.

Never since that surrender of party standards, now thirty-five years past, have the Democrats regained their former standing in the West. In many sections their shattered party is still only a feeble Farm-Labor creature. That Cleveland-Weaver compact was a shroud which Democrats have yet to unwind from the body of their party.

Naturally, the Populists were made hopeful of greater victories by the 1892 results. They grew in the Democratic party like weeds in a neglected garden. Cleveland had no right to expect a Congress so elected to favor his policies. The Populists argued that since the Democratic candidate had given way to them in the campaign why should he hold against them in legislation?

REPEALING THE SILVER PURCHASE LAW

The storm that Cleveland aroused when he determined to repeal the Silver Purchase law was made doubly furious by this feeling. And it surely was a storm—none like it in all the passionate conflicts between President and Congress, not even Andrew Johnson's impeachment troubles in 1868.

Evidences of a demoralized industrial condition through the country were plain. Manufacturers realized that the McKinley tariff was to be displaced by a new law. In the transition period they curtailed production. Unemployment increased. The weakest point, of course, was the first to feel the strain, and the weakest point was the Treasury's diminishing supply of gold.

President Hayes, when he vainly vetoed the Bland bill in 1878, had forecast this very situation. Nevertheless, Congress after Congress stood by the measure. In 1890 John Sherman saw that he could modify, though not repeal it. He took the half loaf. Hence the Sherman silver purchase law. But modification was no cure. The evil still existed. A silver dollar worth less than 90 cents was not wanted when a gold dollar worth 100 cents could be demanded. As industrial distress became more acute everybody sought safety in the more precious metal. The Treasury could not stand the drain. There was just one way for our government to escape being forced to a silver basis—that was to stop the purchase of silver. The Sherman Law had to go!

WHY CLEVELAND WENT FISHING

Cleveland acted promptly. He called an extra session of Congress, told his party frankly the government's plight and urged immediate repeal of the law. Then, if not before, he must have realized the consequence of his Populist campaign deal. The Democratic party—or that portion of it ready to respond to his call—was not in a majority in Congress. Populists and Populist Democrats were!

"I have a Congress on my hands," wrote Cleveland despairingly when the extra session he had called began its turbulent career. A few days later, he exasperated Congress by going to Buzzard's Bay, professedly to fish while his party was in the throes of strife over his proposal.

It was characteristic of Cleveland to remain silent as to the real reason for his absence. Actually he had left Washington to recover strength following a serious operation, secretly performed on the roof of his mouth early in July. It was done on board E. C. Benedict's yacht in the Hudson River.

His doctors knew he could not stand Washington heat. They had ordered him to Buzzard's Bay. Not for a year afterward did the public hear the story of his intense suffering.

Cleveland's absence, however, really had no effect on the struggle in Congress. Open revolt had followed his message.

Democratic leaders, unwilling or unable to furnish the necessary votes, urged him to give up the fight. He defied them and turned to Republicans to pass the bill for him. They did, though their party ranks split over it, too.

As I Knew Them

All this occurred between March and November 1893—the first six months following his inauguration. Effective party unity in Congress was thereafter hopeless. If he was not then a President without a party, he surely became one a year later following his vain struggle with the Wilson-Gorman tariff bill.

By acquiescence, Cleveland had joined with Populists to secure election; by direct appeal he had joined with Republicans to secure legislation; politically he was in No Man's Land; his leadership was ignored; his party went its way regardless of his wishes. Yet he stood out on the nation's horizon a strong virile figure, with the kind of rugged determination that people admire.

That sound money struggle with his party in Congress, as relentless on Cleveland's part as it was futile, continued through his entire four years' term. It was won finally not in his own party but in the Republican convention of 1896! Its history, written in his messages, will remain as Cleveland's clearest title to statesmanship as well as to the gratitude of his country.

FIGHTING FOR THE NATION'S CREDIT

Despite repeated rebuffs he sent one appeal after another to Congress, always sounding the note of national integrity, arousing the people to the evils of a free silver policy. His party would not listen. Vote after vote in Congress went against him. Read one of his last appeals to the Democratic majority to reunite behind him. On December 20, 1895, (while Congress and country were applauding his Venezuelan message) he wrote:

> "We are in the midst of another session of perplexity caused by our dangerous and fatuous financial operations.
> "The Executive Branch of the government will not relax its

efforts nor abandon its determination to use every means within its reach to maintain before the world American credit.

"I have ventured to express herein the hope that the Congress will not take a recess before it has by legislative enactment done something . . . to assure the world that . . . the ability and determination of our nation to meet in any circumstances every obligation it incurs do not admit of question."

But Congress, not then a Democratic Congress, recessed as usual for its Christmas holiday and did nothing!

TOO LATE! TOO LATE! TOO LATE!

Cleveland realized his plight. He accepted it stoically. He saw his party more and more enmeshed in Populism. Knowing his whole Administration would be sacrificed should he fight it, he fought it anyway.

"If Populism is to control," he said to George F. Parker, "it is our duty to stand by our guns and let the party go."

Too late! Too late! Too late!

If only Cleveland had so declared in 1892 when his campaign managers made their bargain with the Populists by which Weaver, not Cleveland, became the candidate of Democratic voters in so many States; if only he had "stood by our guns" then; if he had taken such a stand as Alton B. Parker took in 1904 when Parker found himself nominated for President by the Kansas City convention on a platform which on the money issue satisfied the delegates because it said nothing. Only silence could have their unanimous consent! So their platform was silent. The one man from whom no protest was anticipated was Parker, the nominee. Bryan had been assailing him as a candidate urged upon the convention because he had no opinions.

PARKER'S COURAGEOUS TELEGRAM

Parker nominated, however, staggered convention leaders with a telegram showing an emphatic opinion on the issue

closest to Bryan. The convention had not yet adjourned.
The Bryanites demanded a new candidate, but a courageous
stand always wins in politics as in all else, and it won then.
They couldn't escape Parker. In political history his telegram
has no parallel for courage.

Here it is:

> "I regard the gold standard as firmly and irrevocably established,
> and shall act accordingly if the action of the convention today shall
> be ratified by the people. As the platform is silent on the subject,
> my view should be made known to the convention, and if it is
> proved to be unsatisfactory to the majority, I request you to decline
> the nomination for me at once, so that another may be nominated
> before adjournment."

That message sounded the death-knell of "16 to 1" as an
issue in any campaign in this country. Silver has never since
been heard from.

WHERE CLEVELAND LOST OPPORTUNITY

Just such an opportunity came to Cleveland in that 1892
campaign to stifle Populism within his party by a similarly
bold declaration, and thus keep the Democratic party free of
its strangle hold!

Ask those who know their Cleveland far more intimately
than I knew him—(though I have fairly good knowledge of
the man)—how he could remain silent when he found himself officially taken from the ballot as a presidential candidate
in five States and unofficially, in four other States;—his
candidacy abandoned in fact in the West so that Populists
might win there.

Contrast his complaining letters about his coming burdens,
his acceptance of the Presidency as a "self-inflicted penance,"
with acquiescence in his effacement in so many States, in order
that the Populist presidential candidate and Populist Senators

and Congressmen might triumph over Republicans, since his own party could not! Contrast his willingness to bring about such a result, with his declared antagonism to Populism; then try to reconcile the two!

WHAT MIGHT HAVE BEEN

Had Cleveland promptly denounced and repudiated that "deal"; had he risen above partisan desire to defeat Republicans, no matter how it was done; had he declared that he did not desire election by surrendering party standards in any State, the country would have risen to his candidacy overwhelmingly. By such a declaration he would have engaged in debate with his party before the people, where he was sure to win, instead of in Congress, where he finally had to battle, and, where, in the circumstances, he was sure to lose.

Had he done this there might have been no "cross of gold" speech four years later in the 1896 Democratic convention, and Grover Cleveland might have been throughout his second term the accepted leader of a united party! Instead, four years later he had to aid in the triumph of the Republican party, the party he hated intensely, because his own party organization had been shattered, for above all else he could not permit Populism to achieve the success his own course in 1892 had encouraged its spokesman to seek.

The like of that opportunity in 1892 seldom comes to any man and is even more rarely seized. It never came to Cleveland again—he was never again the master of such a situation. As President he could not dominate, and he did not know how to persuade. His messages to Congress had the status of recommendations to a body of coordinate power, well aware that it derived its authority from the people precisely as he himself did, and jealous of its equal right to interpret its instructions. This the combination of Democrats and Populists in Congress proceeded to do.

As I Knew Them

A DESPERATE, FUTILE STRUGGLE

Cleveland's messages on money and the tariff were always candid and vigorous; also they were provocative of bitter denunciation. On several occasions I sat in the press gallery of Congress and heard the jeers of Democrats, then half-turned Bryanites, as they listened to his words.

But his formal messages aroused less resentment than his personal letters to Congressmen Wilson, Catchings and others; letters written to be read on the floor of the House, arraigning those Democratic Senators who did not agree with his tariff bill.

The struggle to force Congress to yield to him grew steadily more desperate, and more hopeless. In that period Cleveland showed his lack in leadership. On not a single issue did he win his party to his views. He did not know how to mollify opposition. Antagonism was embittered if not increased by his methods. He knew how to "stick to his guns," however, and he did that resolutely. He would have voted for McKinley as his successor if the Palmer and Buckner ticket (the Gold Democratic ticket) had not offered him a way to defeat Bryan, and yet remain on record as a Democrat.

In those four baffling, humiliating, disheartening years Cleveland made his place in history. Though he faced vicious opposition from his party leaders, he did not flinch. He met defiance with defiance. He labored along day by day, hopefully waiting not for his party's candidate to succeed him but for his party's rival.

"We must let the party go!" he declared.

It reads well in print, as we read it today, but there was nothing to the utterance when it was made. The party had then deserted him. No wonder he wrote after he left the White House in 1897: "I am tired of abuse. I am going to know now how it feels to be really a sovereign, for that is what every American citizen is."

As I Knew Them

No President has yet succeeded in making himself bigger than his party; Van Buren, Tyler and Wilson tried it and failed; though Lincoln was sorely tempted on several occasions—even in his own Cabinet—he knew that unity was essential for the success of his great purpose, and he subordinated all, even himself, to that success. A President cannot stick to his own policy "if he is the only man in the country to do so," as Cleveland told Carlisle of his "free wool" message—that is, he cannot do so and expect his party to remain with him.

The party that elects him and to whose platform policies he pledges himself has the right of a community of interest. Cleveland never recognized that right.

Blaine in his "Twenty Years of Congress" speaking of Andrew Johnson's fate wrote: "At least twice before in the history of the Federal Government it has been demonstrated that a President who for any cause runs counter to the views and wishes of the party that elected him is doomed to disappointment and is fortunate if he escape disgrace."

It may be of interest here to quote a more recent analysis of the relations between President and Congress, by a leading member of Cleveland's party—Senator James A. Reed, of Missouri. The Missourian was one of the "willful eleven" Senators to whom President Wilson once referred, and later he openly endeavored to defeat Reed's renomination. Probably, therefore, the Missouri Senator spoke with some personal feeling when he said in an interview in the New York Sun, September 15, 1926:

> "The most dangerous trend today is the custom of creating an atmosphere of omnipotence about the Chief Executive, whatever his party. The idea has grown that the legislative branch of the government should bend its will and set its course to the mandates of the White House.

"There is no more similarity between this conception of Government and that established by our Constitution than there was between Government as conceived by George Washington and that conceived by King George III.

"In recent years we have switched the cart and horse all around. The President should not be the czar of his party but the product of his party, placed in the White House to carry out what the Congress, representing the people, directs."

Cleveland won honor, not disgrace, by his course, but he certainly doomed his party and his measures to defeat.

"STAUNCH OLD BOY!" SAID MCKINLEY

"Staunch old boy!" "Great old character!" McKinley would exclaim in the White House as he read Cleveland's thin copperplate handwriting on papers on file giving his reasons for action taken on different matters. McKinley liked to read them. There were no typewritten documents in Cleveland's files. He never dictated. He tried it once and then declared he was so poor at it that he would never try it again; he never did. His habit of handwriting added to his day's labors; he worked incessantly but so slowly and going so much into detail that he seldom caught up with his desk. In the White House of today he would be overwhelmed as indeed he was then.

"A BADGE OF PARTY PERFIDY AND DISHONOR"

Cleveland's keenest humiliation was the collapse of the tariff legislation on which he had set his heart. Such a bill was to be a vindication of his stand in 1888. Imagine his disgust when he found the tariff bill sent him for approval mangled by a Democratic Senate, despite his protest, beyond recognition as a Cleveland measure!

I was in Washington during that great fight. What a battle it was! Cleveland and William L. Wilson, Congressman from

West Virginia and a former college president—had framed their ideal free trade bill. They had a narrow time getting it through the House, but after Gorman and other old-time Democrats got through with it in the Senate the bill had no resemblance to its original.

"A wild orgy of the trusts," was Calvin Brice's description of the Senate proceedings.

"The deadly blight of treason has blasted the counsels of the brave in their hour of might," wrote Cleveland in his ponderous style.

"It is a badge of party perfidy and dishonor," he added.

Upbraiding letters, however, only embittered the strife.

It was not the rising tide of Populism within his party that Cleveland in his tariff fight had to stem.

Populism had opposed his repeal of the silver purchase act but on the tariff it was as rabidly free trade as he was. On the tariff he was opposed by Democrats who had stood by him on the other issue. They were the reactionaries—led by Senator Arthur Pue Gorman, of Maryland, then the most powerful figure in the Democratic Senate. Gorman used no timid language denouncing Cleveland's tariff letters arraigning his opponents as traitors to the party.

He declared that Treasury Secretary Carlisle had indorsed the Senate amendments, and called on Senator after Senator to tell of their conferences with the President. "If there has been deceit anywhere it has been with the President, not with Senators," he insisted.

GORMAN'S WITHERING SPEECH

How many recall that withering speech by the Maryland Senator? It was a national sensation. Its boldness was emphasized by the character of the speaker. His cold, suave, beardless, thin-lipped face that rarely showed emotion reddened with passion as he spoke, and those keen, steel-gray eyes that penetrated your secrets but never revealed his own, blazed scorn for a President who had so bitterly assailed his fellow-Democrats.

Gorman's speech is political history, and worth reproducing from the Congressional Record of July 23, 1894:

> "As I have said, sir, this is a most extraordinary proceeding, for a Democrat, elected to the highest place in the Government and fellow Democrats elected in another high place, where they have the right to speak and legislate generally, to join with the commune in traducing the Senate of the United States, to blacken the character of Senators who are as honorable as they are, who are as patriotic as they ever can be, who have done as much to serve their party as the men who are now the beneficiaries of your labor and mine, to taunt and jeer at us before the country as the advocates of trusts and as guilty of dishonor and perfidy.
>
> "Mr. President, it is time to speak. The limit of endurance has been reached. The Senate owes it to itself. Every Senator here who is a part of this Democratic majority owes it to himself.
>
> "There is no power, no matter how great, in this country—even the President with his patronage—that would keep me silent longer under such charges, under the imputations so freely made from such distinguished quarters.
>
> "I hurl back the accusation and say that this treatment of their fellows is discreditable. It is destruction to the Government that men in high position should attempt to lower this body, a conservative body, consisting of 88 worthy representatives of States."

Gorman forced surrender to his will. "The communism of pelf," as Cleveland termed it, had its way. "Professor" Wilson yielded in the House. Cleveland yielded, too. Though he would not sign the bill as amended by the Senate, he permitted it to become law.

It is the only revenue law without a President's signature!

And what a time the Republicans had in the House, led by Tom Reed, as they watched the free trade House Democrats (including Bryan) vote to agree with every protectionist amendment sent over by the Gorman Democratic Senate.

213

As I Knew Them

That whole struggle was simply the old, old story of theory against the practical. No tariff bill ever has been, or is likely to be, enacted over the protest of our industrial and farm interests. In "spots"—in big spots, the Democratic party is as highly protective as the Republican party—and no new party is on the horizon.

In the 1880 campaign, General Hancock's declaration that "the tariff is a local issue" cost him many votes. Hancock was assailed by Republicans for his military ignorance of statesmen's problems, yet no greater truth about the tariff was ever uttered.

It *is* a local issue—in Louisiana, where sugar-growers want protection; in California where fruit-growers want protection; in Montana, Texas, and Ohio where wool-growers want protection; in Nebraska and Michigan where beet sugar farmers want protection; in Pennsylvania where iron and steel manufacturers want protection.

Those who have closely followed tariff legislation, as I have for many years, know that every protective tariff enacted by Congress is merely a patchwork of local interests threaded together by a national policy intended to develop home industries and a home market. You cannot make anything else out of it and there is no reason for seeking to do so. It is justified by its purpose and its results. We have not a single industry subjected to foreign competition whose development is not solely due to the tariff protection accorded. As Tom Reed said, the only place you can pass a perfectly balanced tariff bill is in your mind; Congress certainly will never pass one. To talk of absolute free trade is to talk of moonshine; to talk of lower rates than actually afford protection is like advocating a 3-foot dam to hold back four feet of water.

I attended many hearings while the McKinley tariff bill was being framed, and talked almost daily with McKinley about it.

That measure was the ambition of his life; night after night, following a long day's session, he worked at it while watching at the bedside of a very sick wife. Every line in it was dictated by a deep desire to be of real help to the home market. He was so sure of his own purpose, so sure that the country understood and would indorse it, that he unwisely permitted the law to be enacted in October—less than a month before election.

It was impossible in those few weeks to secure results that would vindicate the new rates. McKinley went down in defeat (the Democrats had gerrymandered his district) and the Republican majority in the House of Representatives disappeared, being replaced by the largest Democratic majority in Congressional history.

CREATING A TIN PLATE INDUSTRY FOR AMERICA

Let me give one example illustrating the helpful influence of that bill on American industries.

The most vicious attack was centered on the tin plate schedule, and I am proud to be able to say that I devoted time and space to defending it. It appealed more strongly to McKinley than any other schedule, for it meant an absolute demonstration of the benefits of Protection. At that time, no tin plate was made in this country: every pound we used was imported free of duty. Several iron and steel manufacturers were anxious to engage in making it but could not do so without tariff protection. McKinley put on a provisional duty; it was to cease in two years unless a minimum tonnage of tin plate was being made in America.

More than the required tonnage was turned out in less than two years—and the industry thrived so well that when the Democrats repealed the McKinley bill they did not interfere with the tin plate duty. Yet on that schedule more than on any other they based their denunciation of McKinley's work— and won the election of 1890.

CHAPTER XXV

HAWAII—CLEVELAND'S GRAVEST ERROR

The Stars And Stripes Had Been Hoisted In Honolulu, And Harrison Had Approved, But Cleveland Hauled Them Down, Only To See The Flag Go Up Again Five Years Later—"Paramount" Blount Finds An Impossible Task—Queen Lil Addresses Her "Great And Good Friend"—The New Government Functions And Cleveland Reluctantly Acknowledges It.

HOW many readers of these lines have visited the Hawaiian Islands? How many of them, if any, have failed to be thrilled with pride that our people, our flag, our aid, has encouraged and protected the schools, the churches, the business houses, everywhere to be seen—has led the natives from conditions not far removed from savagery into living on the plane of our own home towns?

If while in Honolulu you have driven up the mountain to the thin peak called the Pali, and have stood there with admiration for the heroism that only a hundred years ago stirred hundreds of natives to throw themselves to death from its heights rather than accept subjugation by an invaders' army— and then recall that thirty-five years ago this same native stock earnestly sought our sovereignty only to be rebuffed, sought it again five years later—that time to be accepted;—if you have looked upon those scenes, as I have, and are familiar with this history, then you must regard Grover Cleveland's refusal to allow them to come under our flag as wholly and unpardonably wrong.

If Cleveland is to have justification for his relentless antagonism to the annexation of Hawaii it must be found in events of the future, for to date there is no basis for anything but condemnation.

As I Knew Them

The Hawaii of today—contented, busy, prosperous—well-schooled—is an example of government FOR the people by contrast with its past, unequalled anywhere else in this world. Every American whom I have heard express any opinion after visiting the Islands has been thankful that this nation had the opportunity thus to serve a people unable by themselves to secure the blessings of stable government.

THAT CRY OF "THE INTERESTS!"

Oh, I have not forgotten President Cleveland's arraignment of American sugar-planting interests nor the action of the ridiculous "Paramount" Blount, Envoy Most Extraordinary of the President, commissioned to do all in his power to restore a repugnant monarchy.

I still have it all well in mind—and when I contrast it with the results, I wonder that such a man as Cleveland failed to realize what annexation would mean for this nation as well as for the Islands.

I thought at the time that Secretary of State Gresham intensified Cleveland's attitude. In the early eighties Harrison had won from Gresham the nomination for Senator from Indiana and in 1888 had defeated him in the contest for delegates for the Presidential nomination. These experiences had embittered Gresham.

When he became Secretary of State and found Harrison's unratified Hawaiian treaty he made the most of his opportunity to hit back at his old opponent. Recalling Cleveland's long-continued but futile effort, I must say that if our nation at the urging of any "interest"—how folks like to talk of the "interests" when no other argument is left them—can ever again have an opportunity to achieve elsewhere all that has been achieved in Hawaii since annexation, then let more and more "interests" come on to Washington from any people struggling as the Hawaiians were struggling when they appealed to us, and let us as a powerful nation, unafraid, lend our strength to the helpless and welcome them in the name of a common humanity.

The fine achievements of our government in our insular possessions bring Cleveland's antagonism to Hawaiian annexation into interesting reminiscence now. We may well rejoice that when our army aviators ended their long flight across the Pacific they landed their plane on soil over which the flag of our country was flying.

HOW AND WHY LILIUOKALANI WAS DETHRONED

How well I remember those fun-provoking figures—"Paramount" Blount, Presidential Envoy to Hawaii—and Liliuokalani, the dethroned Queen whose "MY GREAT AND GOOD FRIEND" letter to Cleveland seeking "your friendly assistance" as well as her subsequent visit to Washington caught the cynical attention of the satirists and cartoonists. They were quick to picture the dusky Queen and the man in the White House fighting together against what McKinley later termed "Manifest Destiny."

The cartoons had at least one helpful influence—they lightened the serious side of the situation.

Cleveland, following Harrison, found our flag firmly planted in Samoan soil, far out in the Pacific, as a protective influence, thanks to the vigorous diplomacy of Harrison and Blaine. Due to the Senate's inability to act in three weeks' time, the annexation of Hawaii was an uncompleted job when Harrison left the White House, and Cleveland determined to prevent it.

Liliuokalani, then Queen of the islands, was a monarch cut to the pattern of Hawaiian tradition. She assumed all the rights of monarchy as well as a few of her own creation.

In January, 1893, conditions having become too tyrannous, a revolt broke out, the Queen was arrested, dethroned and pensioned, a new government was established, and commissioners were sent to Washington with a treaty of annexation.

The American Minister meanwhile had secured the landing of American marines to protect American interests. As those interests, and indeed all foreign interests, were identified with the revolt, the presence of the marines aided the cause of the anti-monarchists, though not a shot was fired. The commissioners reached Washington in February and brought their proposal before Harrison for action.

"This should have come earlier or else too late for me," Harrison remarked. "I don't like to undertake things I cannot finish."

He recognized the new government and sent the treaty to the Senate, urging ratification. Unfortunately, too short a period remained for him to secure action from that too deliberate body before his retirement.

CLEVELAND SAW A CONSPIRACY

Cleveland promptly withdrew the treaty "for consideration," moved by a cry of conspiracy to steal the islands. It was asserted that a worthy Queen had been made the victim of exploiting "interests"; that the real revolters were not natives but selfish American sugar-planters; and that the American resident minister had united with the conspirators. Talk of that kind always appealed to Cleveland. It did in this case. His mind, responding to distrust and suspicion, visioned conspiracies out in the Pacific. He saw the painted picture, not the real one. Indeed, he could not be persuaded to look upon the real one.

The President ignored the fact that for several years the natives had been bitterly resisting the Queen's efforts to rob them of their liberties; that every other government had joined with us in recognizing the new government of Hawaii; that not one government had uttered a word of protest against the course of our minister there, or against Hawaii's annexation proposal. In the whole world of rulers Cleveland was the *only* accuser of his own people!

As I Knew Them

Congressman Blount, of Georgia, was hurried to Hawaii as a Commissioner with "paramount authority." Blount did his duty and then some. He hauled down the American flag raised in Honolulu, and sent the marines back to their ships.

But Blount found it impossible to restore Liliuokalani to her throne. Nowhere in the islands could any demand for her be developed. As this truth grew plainer it became more exasperating to those who without knowledge had insisted that she was the victim of a sugar-planters' conspiracy.

Cleveland was frankly eager to re-establish Liliuokalani—to restore what he called the "status-quo"—but how?

With armed force? He had no authority as President to use force, and he knew that Congress would never grant it; nor would the country tolerate it.

Could he negotiate with the government that had supplanted the monarchy?

That government was functioning, he had no ground for withdrawing the recognition accorded it by Harrison; obviously he could not negotiate with it for its own extinction.

A QUEEN THEY COULD NOT INDORSE

To use an expression, Cleveland was "in a hole." Public opinion, inflamed by Blount's hauling down of the flag, was flouting the President's vain quest for a way to put Liliuokalani back; his own Congress was restless and divided; yet as usual he stuck to his knitting.

The one hope left him was to have an understanding with Liliuokalani as to her purpose if reinstated, and offer that agreement to the new government as a basis of compromise. He wrote to Congress that he was seeking such a basis.

The American minister in Hawaii was instructed to get the Queen's mind. This was not a difficult task. Liliuokalani had courage and frankness.

Newspaper dispatches stated that she inquired in surprise: "What? Are there to be no beheadings?" But that was subsequently denied. However, the query reflected the ex-Queen's point of view. If it was not literally exact, her other responses so clearly revealed her determination, if restored, to adhere to the tradition of her dynasty in disposing of revolters, that in his first report of his interview Cleveland's representative did not dare to speak with entire frankness.

He simply cabled that her views were "too extreme." In a later report, he made it clear that restoration of the monarchy would mean another revolution; he stated that American warships, constantly watching, would be needed to maintain it.

Thus, Cleveland, early wrought to indignation by his suspicion that a great wrong had been done a helpless people through a "selfish interest" conspiracy, came to realize,—but never to admit,—that a greater wrong would be done those same people by imposing upon them the monarch they did not desire. He could not put her back except as the type of ruler she was and that those who had dethroned her knew her to be. That responsibility was too perilous to assume.

JUST STUBBORN

Cleveland never budged from a position once taken, however. With him every decision was irrevocable. It was so in the case of Hawaii. He would not change his attitude but he abandoned the whole problem by passing it on to Congress. He wrote a lengthy message to that body, saying he had been "balked" by conditions he could not control. He might have summed it up more frankly in these few words: "I have made a mess of it. I have failed. Liliuokalani is impossible and I am through with her; the new government is getting on well. I have recognized it. Now do as you please."

No other meaning attaches to his message to Congress, where he well knew not a step would be taken. Events and conditions had proven too much for him. He could not denounce them as he could individuals. They carried their own vindication. He had to accept them. On August 7, 1894, he formally recognized the new Republic of Hawaii, controlled by the same men he had been characterizing as conspirators.

So the net result of eighteen months' agitation was that when Cleveland despairingly wrote Hawaii off his Administration books as a hopeless task he had not changed by one iota the situation existing when he took office. The government recognized by Harrison had worked out its own destiny and was ultimately recognized by Cleveland, the Queen ignored by Harrison was finally ignored by Cleveland, and, later, under McKinley actually the same flag that had been hauled down by Envoy Blount was raised on the same spot and same flag-pole in Honolulu!

EVERYONE HAS EARNED BY ANNEXATION

Thus ended the poorest chapter in Cleveland's career—at least that was then and is now my opinion of it.

Finally, let me take you back, reader, to the beginning of this Hawaiian story, and let me repeat that those who have visited the Islands and have seen the achievements of our sovereignty realize what it has meant to those people to be aided out of barbarism and oppression.

Taking the selfish point of view, and assuming that this world is not through with murdering people under the guise of war, the strategic value of Hawaii to this nation is, according to naval authorities, beyond estimate.

Thus we have gained, the Hawaiians have gained, civilization has gained—but not with Cleveland's consent.

CHAPTER XXVI

VENEZUELA BOUNDARY NOTE

Cleveland At His Best—The Country Gets A Fright—Standing By The Monroe Doctrine—All's Well That Ends Well—Cleveland's Words And Wilson's In Comparison.

IT IS pleasant to turn from such an episode in Cleveland's career to one that is intensely inspiring—from the hauling down of the flag in Hawaii to the bold, defiant assertion of that century-old American policy—the Monroe Doctrine—at the peril of incurring the hostility of Great Britain, then concededly the most powerful nation on earth.

This occurred in December, 1895. The world was at peace —no nations more so than this country and England. Quietly Cleveland and Olney had been forging their thunderbolt. Not a word, not even an intimation, leaked in advance.

Congress assembled in regular session. Of course, it anticipated the usual message from the President—but not the additional message it received a few days later. Congress knew little or nothing of Venezuela's dispute with Great Britain and cared less. The suddenness and tenor of Cleveland's demand created a sensation that startled the world, but no country more than our own.

At first, people here felt certain that the language of the message would instantly unleash the British lion for an angry leap across the Atlantic; in certain quarters, too, the American eagle, fluttering uneasily, indulged in some screeching about the crudity of a document really addressed to a neighbor nation, and the inevitable break-up of friendly relations. Once Congress had caught its breath, however, it stood by Cleveland overwhelmingly. So did the country. The people liked

223

his vigorous, outspoken declaration. A spirit of nationalism surged from coast to coast. The event was a high point in Cleveland's Administration, and it is interesting thirty-two years later to recall what it was all about. Let us do so before going further.

THE FACTS IN THE CASE

Seven or eight years in advance of President Monroe's historic declaration that the United States would not look with favor upon future European aggression in the Western Hemisphere, Dutch Guiana had ceded to Great Britain three of her South American provinces bordering on Venezuela. Later, Great Britain insisted that this cession included approximately 35,000 square miles of territory over which Venezuela claimed sovereignty.

Almost every American Secretary of State found it necessary to give consideration to the dispute, but the question never emerged from the chancelleries of the governments involved into public view. On several occasions, and particularly while Thomas F. Bayard was Secretary of State during Cleveland's first term, our government suggested arbitration. In 1895 Cleveland renewed the suggestion.

But Salisbury, with traditional English strategy of diplomacy, procrastinated. He did not propose to admit the United States as a party to the negotiations; Britain would have nothing to worry about so long as it dealt only with weak Venezuela.

Cleveland held a different view; the Monroe Doctrine made us a party to any claims of territory in South America, made by any nation. In July, 1895, Secretary of State Olney submitted to the President a letter of instructions to Bayard which Cleveland called "Olney's 20-inch gun." It must have been such, for even Bayard thought it dangerously strong. Bayard had hoped to keep the question "in an atmosphere of serene and elevated effort," to use his own words. But the Olney letter forced this significant revelation of Great Britain's contention—that the Monroe Doctrine did not apply to boundary disputes.

HE HAD A CAUSE TO DEFEND

This astonishing claim reached Cleveland a few days after his annual message to Congress. It was the first attempt to limit the sweeping character of our settled policy. The question was no longer a Venezuelan dispute; it was now a matter of interpreting America's policy in the Western Hemisphere. Thus, Cleveland felt that he had a cause to defend—the highest interest of his country. He decided to ask Congress for an appropriation covering the expense of a Commission to determine Venezuela's true boundary lines, independently of the British. The report of that Commission was to be used to notify Great Britain exactly where her sovereignty ended under the Dutch Guiana concession; our government proposed to maintain the lines so defined.

Congress made the appropriation, Republicans joining with Democrats in approval. Before the Commission got far in its investigation, the Salisbury Government proposed arbitration, and a satisfactory treaty with Venezuela was signed in Washington.

Nothing in Cleveland's career will endure longer or more admirably than his quick resentment of this first attempt to modify the Monroe Doctrine. Of course, if Great Britain could have maintained that boundary lines could be lengthened and widened without infringing on our policy against new acquisitions, the Monroe Doctrine would look like a sieve. Cleveland's strongest qualities came out in that crisis. His rugged Americanism, his unimaginative, stolid determination, his increasing pursuit of a subject to settlement, his readiness to accept consequences, however unpleasant—these characteristics show nowhere so splendidly as in this triumph in behalf of a great American tradition.

Of course, some thought, and still think, Cleveland's action a "tempest in a teapot." James Lord Rhodes and other historians condemn it as a piece of unworthy jingoism. It is true that Britain established her boundary rights substantially as claimed. If judgment against Cleveland is to be given on that ground he certainly did go far for small results. But that was not the heart of the issue once Lord Salisbury endeavored to draw some of the teeth of the Monroe Doctrine by questioning its application to boundary lines. When Great Britain challenged us on that point, the matter of more or less territory faded as an issue, and the integrity of the Monroe Doctrine loomed as the question to settle. Cleveland settled it in a way to insure its remaining settled.

CLEVELAND AND WILSON IN CONTRAST

In his greater offices as in the minor ones in Buffalo, Cleveland worked wholly and laboriously in an atmosphere of his own conceptions. I never heard any man claim he had persuaded Cleveland to any policy or had succeeded in changing his views. I doubt whether any other President save possibly Woodrow Wilson ever kept people—I mean people who could be of real help—at such a distance. And none needed help more than those two men!

In every other respect, however, Cleveland and Woodrow Wilson were opposites. Wilson visioned over a wide horizon; Cleveland saw only directly before him. It was hard labor for Cleveland, as he frequently said, to tackle all the problems that cross the threshold of the White House, and to broaden his view from Buffalo limitations to a nation-wide scale. He did it—slowly, but when he advanced into new ground he never abandoned a foot of it.

TWO SPEECHES THAT REFLECT THE MEN

No interpreter was ever required for Cleveland's language. His phrases while sometimes ponderous were always forceful and candid. Such expressions as "innocuous desuetude" only added interest to his utterances.

For illustration of the difference between Cleveland and Wilson—the two Democratic Presidents in nearly 70 years— let us contrast the utterances made by each of them on two critical occasions. Let us take the closing paragraphs in Cleveland's message to Congress, when aroused by Great Britain's final refusal to arbitrate the Venezuelan dispute, and contrast those paragraphs with President Wilson's utterances just after a German submarine had torpedoed the Lusitania and while our people were still reading the lengthening list of victims of that outrage.

Here are the two utterances side by side:

CLEVELAND IN ADDRESS TO CONGRESS, DEC. 1895:

. . . The dispute has reached such a stage as to make it now incumbent upon the United States to take measures to determine . . . what is the one divisional line between the Republic Venezuela and British Guiana.

When such a report is made and accepted it will, in my opinion, be the duty of the United States to resist by every means in its power, as a willful aggression upon its rights and interests, the appropriation by Great Britain of any lands or the exercise of government jurisdiction over any territory which after investigation we have determined of right belongs to Venezuela.

In making these recommendations, I am fully alive to the re-

WILSON IN PHILADELPHIA

May 10, 1915, at Convention Hall to Newly Naturalized Citizens:

Just because you brought dreams with you, America is more likely to realize the dreams such as you brought. You are enriching us if you came expecting us to be better than we are.

See, my friends, what that means. It means that America must have a consciousness different from the consciousness of every other nation in the world.

I am not saying this with even the slightest thought of criticism of other nations. You know how it is with a family. A family gets centered on itself if it is not careful and is less interested in its

sponsibility incurred and keenly realize all the consequences that may follow.

I am, nevertheless firm in my conviction that while it is a grievous thing to contemplate the two great English-speaking peoples of the world as being otherwise than friendly competitors in the onward march of civilization, and strenuous and worthy rivals in all the arts of peace, there is no calamity which a great nation can invite which equals that which follows a supine submission to wrong and injustice and the consequent loss of national self-respect and honor, beneath which are shielded and defended a people's safety and greatness."

neighbors than it is in its own members.

The example of America must be a special example, not merely of peace because it will not fight, but of peace because peace is the healing and elevating influence of the world and strife is not.

There is such a thing as a man being too proud to fight. There is such a thing as a nation being so right that it does not need to convince others by force that it is right.

CHAPTER XXVII

McKINLEY—MAN OF KINDLY WAYS

You Hit Hard-Pan When Integrity Or Principle Was At Stake—George B. Cortelyou Names Courage As McKinley's Dominant Trait —How He Delayed The War With Spain—Crowds Brought Him No Problems, But He Met Death In One—Silence, And The Presidency At Stake—Garfield Bows To The Chairman's Ruling And Nomination Follows—Blaine Smashes His Silk Hat While Urging Reciprocity—Harrison, Blaine and McKinley Rejoice Together And Later Are Rivals.

IT MAY be that William McKinley was no intellectual giant. It may be too that in the Presidency he was an example of Tom Reed's frequent remark that parties seldom nominate their great men but those who represent the average of party opinion. Perhaps the average man is a safer selection, for great men have greater ambitions not always consistent with the best interests of their countrymen.

McKinley made no claim to greatness; he was content to learn what the people wanted of him and then to endeavor to meet their desires. This led to the charge that he always had "his ear to the ground." He probably would not have denied that charge.

He was called by many "The Napoleon of Protection"; cartoonists delighted to caricature him as such. Except that there was a slight resemblance to Napoleon in McKinley's build and face, there was no basis for the term. McKinley had no soaring ambitions such as led Napoleon to disaster. He had the conservatism of his Scotch-Irish ancestry, overlaid with a deep veneer of kindliness which many mistook for weakness. You could go far with McKinley where essentials were not involved, but you hit hard-pan when integrity or principle was at stake.

229

As I Knew Them

No other man was so close to McKinley during his five years in the White House as was George B. Cortelyou. I once asked Cortelyou to state McKinley's chief characteristic.

"Courage," he answered promptly.

DELAYING THE WAR WITH SPAIN

McKinley's courage came time and again to the attention of those close to him. He knew how to resist pressure, and he resisted it on many occasions the public never heard about. Not until long after his death was the story told of his refusal in 1898 to send his war message to Congress, despite the heated demands of Senators and Congressmen. A committee large enough to crowd the Cabinet room called to insist upon an immediate declaration against Spain. The President told them that he had prepared a message, but he was awaiting a cable from Havana saying that all Americans were safely out of Cuba.

The committee was suspicious of delay; for there was a feeling in Congress that McKinley might find a way to avert war. They intimated that Congress might act without waiting for the President. While the conference was going on, a cable arrived stating the impossibility of getting all Americans away at once.

Quietly turning to Cortelyou, the President said: "Put that message in the safe until I call for it."

Then, turning to the excited, insistent war committee McKinley said: "That message shall not go to Congress as long as there is a single American life in danger in Cuba."

MCKINLEY SAID "CROWDS BRING ME NO PROBLEMS"

In the White House as during his fourteen years in Congress McKinley preferred to please rather than to displease; to help rather than to hinder; to smile rather than to frown. In one of our talks I deplored the burden of the handshaking receptions in the White House. He interrupted me to say that he enjoyed them, they inspired him.

"Everyone in that line has a smile and a cheery word," he said. "They bring no problems with them; only good will. I feel better after that contact. It is the visitor to the Cabinet room pressing some policy or seeking some office who tires. He comes determined to persuade or convince me; he is full of his subject, intense. I have to meet and resist all that force not once or twice each day but all day without interruption. Few visitors to the President's office come without a purpose. There's where the wear and tear is."

Yet McKinley met death not in his Cabinet room but in just such a crowd as he had told me he loved to greet! Characteristically, as McKinley fell, stricken by the assassin's bullet, he exclaimed, "Don't let them hurt him."

MCKINLEY'S STRENGTH AS AN ORATOR

McKinley easily held the mileage record as a circuit-riding stump-speaker, until Bryan outdistanced him. Bryan's speaking was always for himself, however, while McKinley spoke wherever he could be helpful. East and west, McKinley rode in more torchlight parades, now out of fashion, than any other campaigner. As a candidate for the Presidency, his speechmaking was practically confined to the porch of his little home in Canton.

Though I have heard most of our statesmen orators, I cannot name one more graceful in gesture, more pleasing in voice, than McKinley. He did not depend upon stentorian tones to carry conviction; there was a quiet earnestness about him, a modesty of manner, a directness and simplicity of expression that quickly won confidence.

McKinley could go into the corn-belt States and convince farmers of the increased value the tariff had given their crops; the same in the wheat States. In industrial centres he always had figures to prove the benefit in wages and profits. He had no equal in presenting statistics in an interesting way, and he never failed to use one or two local industries to illustrate. Nor do I recall anyone whose memory equalled McKinley's for names and faces. Once known ever so slightly to McKinley, you were rarely forgotten. Blaine, too, was proud of this ability; he also could couple names with faces,—but McKinley was a master in that art.

SILENCE—AND THE PRESIDENCY

One picture of McKinley rests in my mind revealing his firmness when loyalty was involved. No one needs to be told that only a man of decision can withstand the lure of the Presidency. It is sought with intense, desperate endeavor in every national convention; in the conflict of ambitions, the finer qualities which most men possess are at times forgotten. Often, two principal contenders wear each other out, and a third or "dark horse" candidate rushes to the front.

The first "dark horse" in our presidential politics, as is well known, was James K. Polk in 1844, but Hayes, Garfield, Harding, Cox and Davis are also more or less of that class.

It might easily have been true—many persons at the time thought it would have been true—that the Republican national convention of 1888 would have turned to McKinley as its "dark horse" candidate had he not stood firmly against it.

McKinley was the Sherman floor leader, just as Garfield was Sherman's spokesman in 1880. Several votes had been cast for McKinley on different ballots as had been done for Garfield; the galleries whispered prophecies of a stampede to McKinley. It might have come, had McKinley remained silent.

Silence and the Presidency!—an unsteadying prospect to most men; not to McKinley.

I can see him now as he stood on his chair in the centre aisle asking for recognition. The tumult of the convention ceased. Every eye focussed on McKinley's serious countenance. Then, indeed, it seemed to me, he looked Napoleonic. It was one of those tense moments in conventions when no one knows just what is going to happen, though everyone knows that it will be unusual. Then in that quiet, firm tone that all who knew McKinley well remember, he said:

> "Mr. Chairman: I am here as one of the chosen representatives of my State. I am here by resolution of the Republican State Convention commanding me to cast my vote for John Sherman. I accepted the trust because my heart and my judgment are in accord with that resolution.
>
> "It has pleased certain delegates to cast their votes for me for President. I am not insensible of the honor they would do me, but in the presence of the duty resting upon me I cannot remain silent with honor. I cannot with fidelity to John Sherman, who has trusted me in his cause and with his confidences; I cannot consistently with my own views of personal integrity, consent, or seem to consent, to permit my name to be used before this convention.
>
> "I do not request, I demand, that no delegate who would not cast reflection upon me shall cast a ballot for me."

Thus died the stampede that might have landed another Ohio "dark horse" in the Presidency.

WHEN GARFIELD BOWED TO THE CHAIRMAN'S RULING

Fairness to President Garfield requires that I should not close this incident without recording the fact that had not Senator George Frisbie Hoar as chairman of the 1880 convention rapped Garfield to order, compelling him to resume his seat, Garfield might have turned the delegates to some one other than himself exactly as McKinley did. That indeed was his purpose when he rose to protest against votes being cast for him. On the 34th ballot, with the "306" and their opponents worn out by the struggle, 16 Wisconsin delegates declared for Garfield. Here is the official record of what followed that announcement:

Mr. Garfield: I rise to a question of order.

The Chairman (Senator George F. Hoar): The gentleman from Ohio rises to a question of order.

Mr. Garfield: I challenge the correctness of the announcement. It contains votes for me. No man has a right, without consent of the person voted for, to announce that person's name and vote for him, in this convention. Such consent I have not given—

The Chairman: The gentleman from Ohio is not stating a question of order. He will resume his seat. No person having received a majority of the votes cast, another ballot will now be taken. The clerk will call the roll.

So ended the 34th ballot; so began the Garfield stampede. On the 36th ballot he was nominated.

A POINT OF ORDER MAKES A PRESIDENT

"I recollect the incident perfectly," wrote Senator Hoar in his Autobiography. "I interrupted Garfield in the middle of his sentence. I was terribly afraid he would say something that would make his nomination impossible, or his acceptance impossible if it were made. I do not believe that it ever happened before, that anybody who attempted to decline the Presidency was to be prevented by a point of order, or that such a thing will ever happen again."

"YOU, SIR, HAVE CLOSED THE DEBATE"

McKinley, strong in his personal loyalties, could keep in the middle of the road on public questions as skillfully as any man who ever sat in Congress.

Early in his career he made up his mind that one would travel further in the middle of the road than on the extreme of either side, particularly if he advanced only when the going was good. As Congressman, he stuck to this course, except on the tariff.

On that policy, frankly reflecting the interests of his home district and his State, he made himself the leading spokesman. Yet the McKinley tariff law of 1890—on which he based all his hopes of the Presidency—retired him from Congress and the Republican party from national legislative control.

NAP. McKINLEY: "OH, TAKE ME TO THE HOTEL—DES INVALIDES!"

"McKINLEY AFTER 1890"

The year 1890 marked a record of national prosperity. All seemed serene for the Republican party. Confident of the popularity of any tariff framed by McKinley, and with election day near, every legislator was eager to be identified with it. As chairman of the House Ways and Means Committee, McKinley made up the daily list of speakers. Tradition entitled the chairman to speak last, closing the debate on his side.

A Congressman from Kansas—I cannot recall his name—was anxious about his own reëlection. He thought his chances would be strengthened if he could show the home-folks that he had been accorded the honor of speaking last, and closing the debate. He made that unusual request. Good-natured

McKinley gave way to the Kansan, and spoke earlier in the Kansas man's time.

His speech concluded, McKinley stood for a moment receiving congratulations. The Kansas Congressman rushed excitedly down the aisle of the House exclaiming loudly:

"Major, by your kindness I shall speak last, but you, Sir, have closed the debate!"

BLAINE CRUSHES HIS HIGH SILK HAT

All Republicans did not share this enthusiasm for the McKinley bill; Blaine was at first a critic. He believed it should provide for reciprocity with Mexico and the Central and South American States. He went to the extreme of attending the Senate Finance Committee's hearing, where he denounced the measure so excitedly that instead of pounding the table he brought his fist down on his high silk hat, smashing his headgear so badly that a Democratic Senator had to lend him a hat to wear home.

"Pass this bill," then declared Blaine, "and in 1892 there will not be a man in the Republican party so beggared as to accept your nomination for the Presidency."

But when Blaine had his way and reciprocity was included, he changed his mind about the unpopularity of the measure. How each of us regards his own idea as the pivot of the whole structure!

Blaine's eyes as Secretary of State were turned toward South America. Despite his long experience with public opinion he felt that where he looked the people looked too. He was so sure that he had cured the defects in the measure that he accompanied McKinley to the White House to be present when President Harrison signed it.

Harrison wrote his signature and then took up a blotter to dry the ink.

"Don't blot that signature," cried Blaine. "Let it stand out bold and clear. Let the ink dry."

McKinley kept the pen.

Note what followed this last meeting of those three men:

In a month, the Republican party had lost control of Congress:

In less than two years Blaine resigned as Secretary of State, and was contesting Harrison's nomination for the Presidency! McKinley, presiding over the convention, allowed 182 votes to be cast in his own favor—only one-half a vote less than Blaine received. Harrison had a majority. The three men who had gathered to rejoice together over the signing of a tariff bill had become rivals for the Presidency!

Thus runs politics!

CHAPTER XXVIII

McKINLEY, SILENT, GETS 662; REED, FOR GOLD, 85

*Not Until The Last Moment Did McKinley O. K. The Gold Plank—
"I Don't Give A Damn What Wall Street Thinks" Said Hanna But
He Finally Yielded—How The Two Conventions Divided On The
Money Issue—"Joe, God Almighty Hates A Quitter!"—Tom Reed
The Only Gold Candidate—He Had Only Three Delegates West Of
New York.*

O N the gold and silver issue, McKinley, until nominated,
kept in the middle of the road surely enough, with both

IN THE MIDDLE OF THE ROAD

feet planted squarely and stubbornly in silence. Had his personal inclinations prevailed with the Republican platform-

238

makers at the St. Louis convention, the gold plank would not
have been of 22-karat quality. He was convinced that the
country was not ready to vote for an immediate single standard basis. He was certain that national defeat awaited the
candidate who went to the polls on that one issue. Developments in the campaign justified this belief.

For weeks before the nomination, the East hotly demanded
a "gold" declaration from McKinley; the West as hotly demanded "Silver or Silence." Silence left both sections claiming him.

At the last moment, with the convention assembling and a
majority of the delegates securely pledged, McKinley put his
O.K. to a gold plank brought to Canton by Senator Charles
W. Fairbanks, of Indiana, afterward Vice President.

Mark Hanna, seated in his Cleveland office less than a
month before, had pounded his desk with his big fist, saying,
almost shouting at me:

"I don't give a damn what Wall Street thinks of McKinley's
silence; they can go to hell down there. We are not going to
nominate McKinley on a Wall Street platform."

But at St. Louis Hanna did all he had declared so ve-
hemently in Cleveland he would not do. McKinley stood on
a Wall Street platform, and in the East became Wall Street's
candidate.

STRENGTH OF SILVER IN THE TWO CONVENTIONS

Thomas B. Reed—"Czar Reed," "Tom" Reed—was the
one honest-to-goodness gold standard candidate before that
convention. He polled 85 votes against 662 cast for McKinley on the one ballot taken. Two delegates from Chicago and
one from Oklahoma Territory cast the only votes for Reed
from the vast region west of New York. A few weeks later,
Senator David B. Hill, of New York, led a struggle for the
single gold standard in the Democratic National convention
with even poorer results. Those who now assume that the

political opinion of the country was then against silver as a money metal are confuted by the roll-call of the national conventions of the two parties. More than two-thirds of the Democratic convention and about 30 per cent of the Republican convention favored silver.

In the Republican convention the McKinley vote reflected the feeling among western delegates that, despite the gold plank in the platform, McKinley's long silence proved that he was not an extremist; they believed the folks back home could be persuaded that, if elected, he would "do something for silver." Of Tom Reed, however, the same could not be said. The people knew him as a "gold" man, out and out, and western delegates were convinced that in their territory the candidacy of a gold man was hopeless.

A DEMORALIZED JOE MANLEY

"Joe, God Almighty hates a quitter!" yelled Sam Fessenden, of Connecticut, at Joseph H. Manley, of Maine, when he met Manley in a hotel corridor after reading the latter's suggestion that it might be better to withdraw Reed.

I had travelled with Manley and W. Murray Crane from Albany to St. Louis. All the way west Manley kept saying it was wrong to expose Reed to what he regarded as humiliating defeat. As Blaine's manager for years, Manley was accustomed to great demonstrations of enthusiasm; he was depressed by the poor response to the Reed boom. Nearly all his friends were in the McKinley camp. The Reed men knew, of course, that they were beaten; Manley thought they should acknowledge it. Veteran in politics as he was, and though warned by Murray Crane, Manley's demoralization was complete even before he reached St. Louis. There he talked.

Fessenden's exclamation gave importance to the Manley statement. It was on everybody's lips; together the two utterances made the rollcall on the Reed candidacy perfunctory.

CHAPTER XXIX

BEATING BRYAN IN HIS OWN TERRITORY

The West Was Lost To McKinley On The Gold Issue, So He Switched To Protection—"Make Them Talk Tariff, Think Tariff, Dream Tariff" Declared Hanna—McKinley "The Advance Agent Of Prosperity!"—Sends His Greetings To Congress—His Mother Prays God To Keep Her Boy Humble.

NOT to disturb history too much but to record one of those facts that history has a way of ignoring—or of not discovering—I would like to say that the bald truth about 1896 is that had Reed been nominated he would have been defeated by Bryan; and had not McKinley, during the campaign, abandoned the gold issue west of the Mississippi, substituting the tariff, he, too, would have lost the election. Despite tremendous effort during July and August to convince western people, they remained suspicious that gold standard meant Wall Street domination; no argument could prevail against that prejudice.

At a conference in McKinley's home in Canton, Ohio, early in September, it was decided that the chances were strongly against carrying any State west of the Mississippi unless the people could be diverted from discussing "16 to 1." McKinley could not win without many electoral votes from that section. There were not enough electoral votes east of the Mississippi to overwhelm Bryan, backed by a solid west added to a solid south.

By direct orders from McKinley, there was a quick "recall" of the gold issue except in the east. Campaign speaking and literature were centered on an appeal to vote for "McKinley, Protection and Prosperity."

As I Knew Them

Hanna instructed all spell-binders in the west to "make people talk tariff, think tariff, dream tariff." "Tell 'em, McKinley means good times."

Not a word on the money issue was uttered in western meetings the last six weeks of the campaign unless the audience insisted. The one cry was "Elect McKinley, the Advance Agent of Prosperity."

That switch of issues brought California, Kansas, North Dakota, Oregon, Minnesota and Iowa into line for McKinley by a small plurality in each State. Before the switch only Minnesota and Iowa were on Hanna's list—and they were classed only as "probable."

In the east, of course, gold remained the vote-getting issue; there it was emphasized. The result was that the east voted for gold while the west voted for protection, and one candidate so managed his campaign as to satisfy both sections!

I have personal knowledge of these facts. Before and after the St. Louis convention I travelled the west thoroughly as correspondent, instructed by my newspaper to learn one definite thing—what the people there really thought. My investigations made me certain that Bryan would get most of the electoral votes of that section unless some change were made.

On my way east, in late August, I stopped over at Canton, Ohio, and gave McKinley my judgment. He said that it coincided with other reports he had received and acknowledged that he and Hanna were disturbed.

"I believe that if we could get the tariff issue to the west it could be won back," he added, "but how are we going to do it?"

A few days later Senator Thurston, of Nebraska, and several other western leaders were called to Canton and at the conference then held it was decided to abandon gold and talk tariff in the west. Wilbur F. Wakeman, then General Man-

242

ager of the American Protective Tariff League, was selected
to do the work of blotting out the money issue with tariff
pamphlets—and those who know Wakeman know how thoroughly he did the job. The printing presses groaned with
their burden, but their groans meant McKinley hurrahs on
election night.

A STRONGER MCKINLEY AS PRESIDENT

Election to the Presidency meant another McKinley,—a
McKinley made stronger in purpose by his sense of his new
responsibilities. Now that he was the national leader of his
party he grew steadily until the day of his assassination after
a speech, the last words of which reflected the broadening
influence of his high position. It was the high protectionist
McKinley of 1890 who, after four years in the White House,
speaking in behalf of reciprocity, left as his last message to
the people: "Let us ever remember that our interest is in
concord not in conflict, and that our real eminence as a nation
lies in the victories of peace, not those of war."

MCKINLEY SENDS GREETINGS TO CONGRESS

No other administration has been so like the period of
James Monroe from 1817 to 1825 as McKinley's—an era of
good feeling. The new President struck the keynote when
he began his first annual message with these words:
"It gives me pleasure to extend greetings to the Fifty-fifth
Congress, . . . with many of whose Senators and Representatives I have been associated in the legislative service."
That greeting to his former colleagues won them to him.
He held his party together and even broke over party lines—
getting the Dingley tariff, for instance, through a Senate that
had a Populist balance of power. Even Democratic Congressmen who had avoided the White House during Cleveland's
time visited it freely and felt that they were welcome. The

loneliness of Cleveland's day was dispelled by a kindly, inviting atmosphere.

MOTHER MCKINLEY'S PRAYER FOR HER BOY

On the train from Canton, Ohio, to Washington, for the inauguration, McKinley's mother said that the night before she had made what she called a special prayer.

"What did you pray for especially?" she was asked.

"I prayed God to keep my boy humble," she replied.

And McKinley kept humble in the sense his mother desired but those who had known McKinley in Congress found a stronger McKinley in the White House,—just as those who had known Chester A. Arthur as a Conkling lieutenant in New York city politics found a different Arthur as President.

CHAPTER XXX

McKINLEY'S HANNA OR HANNA'S McKINLEY?

*The Campaign Manager Wants A House In Washington But McKin-
ley Says "It Would Never Do, Mark"—He Insists That Hanna Must
First Have A Title—John Sherman Goes To State Department And
Hanna To The Senate—Hanna's Keenest Disappointment—The Phila-
delphia Convention of 1900 When Dawes Received The Message That
Forced Hanna To Say To Roosevelt, "Teddy, You're It!"*

TURN now to 1896—McKinley, President-elect; Mark
Hanna, President-maker, and long-time friend. Hanna
wanted no Cabinet portfolio; all his life he had been a business executive; he was determined to lessen not to increase
responsibilities. He wanted to be the trusted friend and counsellor of a President but not to hold office. Probably he
wanted a home in Washington.

His famous corned beef hash breakfasts in Cleveland
(made after a recipe he had worked out years before in the
iron ore camps of Duluth) had brought many a doubting delegate into line for his candidate. Why not try the same breakfasts in Washington on temperamental Senators and Congressmen? No office, no title, just a citizen friend of the President!

Politicians wondered; newspapers kept guessing the future
of this Citizen President-maker. It seemed clear to Hanna;
it perplexed McKinley. He knew it could not be as Hanna
planned. He had been too long in Washington not to realize
that there could be no overlord. Of course, Woodrow Wilson
was not then even dreaming of the Presidency, or of making
Col. Edward M. House his personal ambassador-extraordi-

245

nary and other self here and in Europe. McKinley, therefore, had no precedent by which to determine Hanna's status except his instinctive feeling that there could be only one President and one White House.

"IT WOULD NEVER DO, MARK"

The two men talked it over.

"It would never do, Mark," said McKinley. "You know everybody would be running to you either before or after seeing me. You owe it to me to come to Washington with a title to office or not at all."

Still, Hanna demurred. He saw no reason why he could not sacrifice time, thought and money for the success of the President he had done so much to elect. Fourteen years later, Wilson turned to Colonel House and made him an ambassador without credentials, to whom those "in the know" would go quietly with their ambitions, and their troubles. McKinley foresaw the inevitable consequences of such a relation.

Together he and Hanna sought a way out. Just one way was possible—persuade John Sherman to resign as Senator and become Secretary of State. Sherman was consulted. It was known that he would like to have held that portfolio under Harrison. Had he the same ambition now? Hanna's future rested on the Senator's reply. Several weeks of uncertainty elapsed—then an unheralded letter of acceptance reached Canton.

Promptly Hanna was appointed to the Senate vacancy by Ohio's Governor. Thus, he went to the national capital in his own right and title, and his famous corned beef hash breakfasts in the old Cameron mansion facing Lafayette Park were accepted as the hospitality of a Senator, not of a President's spokesman.

It was McKinley, not Hanna, who foresaw the unwisdom of the latter rôle.

As I Knew Them

MCKINLEY WOULD NOT; ROOSEVELT DID

A modest, genial figure in national Republican politics those days was Henry C. Payne, then in control of the Wisconsin State organization—the last of the "Old Guard" to control before La Follette took it over. Hanna's deepest interest in the McKinley Cabinet was to have Payne made Postmaster General. All of Payne's colleagues on the national committee urged the appointment, too. In earlier years Payne had been about the Capitol in the interest of the Northern Pacific Railroad; McKinley was then a Congressman and familiar with Payne's activities. He told Hanna he could not name Payne. Always a good fighter for a friend, Hanna persisted.

"Mark," said McKinley during their final talk in Canton, "you know I want to do anything so close to you as this seems to be but I cannot bring into my Cabinet a man who has been a lobbyist around Congress."

McKinley did not appoint Payne; five years later, Roosevelt did.

Thus, in two matters of consequence before his inauguration McKinley made decisions that showed Hanna a better way than the way he urged. And no one realized McKinley's ability to make such decisions better than did the man who newspapers were then declaring controlled McKinley's mind.

MCKINLEY'S WAY MEANT HANNA'S KEENEST DISAPPOINTMENT

There were to be other occasions when McKinley's way had to prevail over Hanna's counsel, but only once throughout their long friendship was there any keen feeling of disappointment on Hanna's part. That was when he was unable to persuade McKinley to indicate a choice for Vice President to be nominated by the 1900 national convention. He not only refused Hanna but he authorized Charles G. Dawes to say to the delegates that he had no choice. Hanna keenly felt that double blow at his prestige.

That convention, held in Philadelphia, was distinguished by the fact that more men refused to be nominated for Vice President than in any other convention of either party.

Even Roosevelt tried to dodge it.

No one dreamed that it meant the Presidency in fifteen months.

There was nothing but the Vice Presidency for the delegates to quarrel over. McKinley was to be their nominee for President and his record was their platform. They had nothing to do but decide on the man to take the place made vacant by the death of Vice President Garret A. Hobart.

Thomas C. Platt wanted Roosevelt named so as to get him out of the New York Governorship. Matt Quay was interested to force any nomination that would show that Hanna was no longer in control of the national organization. The western delegates were clamoring for a nominee who would be recognized as a "liberal." Platt and Quay used this western sentiment to work up a Roosevelt boom.

The old convention saying that "you cannot beat somebody with nobody" came in here for another demonstration. Hanna found himself without a candidate except John D. Long, of Massachusetts, who had no following. More fatal still was the knowledge among the delegates that he was without support from the President—the man many said he dominated!

Nobody who could be nominated wanted the Vice Presidency!

Fairbanks had dreams of the White House. He preferred to remain in the Senate until the real call came; Allison, of Iowa, was comfortable and contented where he was; Jonathan Dolliver was indifferently willing; Cornelius N. Bliss had refused. Five-foot Timothy L. Woodruff, Lieutenant Governor of New York, had most of the New York delegates, in a complimentary way, and Senator Platt had said "it might taper down to Tim."

DAWES AND PERKINS BEGIN TO FIGURE

I do not know when so much pressure was exerted upon a President to express an opinion as was used to persuade McKinley to indicate a choice. Hanna, realizing that he faced a hard fight without the President's aid, pressed hard for the right to tell convention leaders that he was speaking with authority. McKinley continued to refuse. Here again McKinley avoided a pitfall—one into which Roosevelt eight years later plunged with disastrous results—the mistake of a President naming a candidate for a convention.

Of course refusal meant humiliation for Hanna—better that, than White House domination of candidates.

Two men destined afterward to be prominent in politics were active figures behind the scenes at Philadelphia. Charles G. Dawes—then Comptroller of the Currency, and now Vice President—and George W. Perkins. Dawes indorsed McKinley's attitude; Perkins stood with Hanna. Perkins even went to the extreme of hiring a special train to take him from Philadelphia to Washington to urge McKinley. Fairbanks and Allison also urged.

Under such pressure it seemed probable that McKinley would yield. Hanna believed that he would and so kept steadily making his fight more and more an administration matter. Dawes warned Hanna against his course, protesting that he would be defeated and a nomination made that would be proclaimed as a defiance of White House wishes. Hanna, however, persisted. Dawes then, by telephone, repeated the same warning to the President. McKinley, through George Cortelyou, promptly authorized Dawes to state: "the President's close friends must not undertake to commit the Administration to any candidate; it has no candidate. The Administration wants the choice of the convention."

As I Knew Them

No desire to humiliate Hanna actuated Dawes; he simply wanted to protect McKinley. The message he received was seen by Hanna only. There was no need to show it to others. At once, Hanna knew he was beaten. He accepted defeat good-naturedly, for everything was part of the day's work with Hanna. If he could not get what he wanted he made the best of what he could get. He promptly sent for Roosevelt and said, "Teddy, you're it!"

Thus, a great chapter in American politics was begun, with not one of the figures having the dimmest vision of what it all was shortly to mean.

What different history would have been made had McKinley given Hanna the authority he wanted!

CHAPTER XXXI

HAWAII AND THE WAR WITH SPAIN

Both "Manifest Destiny"—McKinley Delayed War Until Our Army And Navy Could Prepare—He Believed That If The Parliaments Of Both Nations Would Adjourn, Cuba Would Be Free Without War— Foresaw The Problems That Would Follow War—Tells Shafter To Hold San Juan's "Thin Line"—Seeking A Right Basis For Peace— McKinley Ways And Wilson Ways—The Philippines And Cuba "Our Opportunity And Our Burden."

ANNEXING the Hawaiian Islands by treaty was one of the important steps taken by McKinley. His remark to Cortelyou that it was "manifest destiny" was made before there was any thought of the Philippines or Porto Rico. He found a responsible government in Hawaii, functioning as well as an independent government there could function. But it faced local uprisings and possible acquisition by England or Germany. Both considerations settled McKinley's mind. He urged the Senate to ratify the treaty offered by the Hawaiians. Not until after Dewey had taken Manila, nor until Hawaiians had violated neutrality by coaling and harboring our warships, did the Senate ratify the treaty. Thus McKinley closed the chapter Harrison could not, and Cleveland would not, finish.

Perhaps our war with Spain was "manifest destiny," too. Congress evidently thought so,—even to the extent of seeking to speed up destiny by declaring war before our Army or Navy was prepared even for a single battle. McKinley was firm against haste. He made no angry protests against Congress; he won delay by calmly talking over the situation day by day with those who were rampant for war as well as those opposed.

It was true, too true, that we were not ready, but it was

equally true that McKinley hoped that, given time, Spain would relieve the tension by freeing Cuba unconditionally. A week or so before the war declaration he told me in the White House that if the Parliaments of both countries would adjourn, he and Sagasta, then Spain's Prime Minister, could free Cuba and peaceably settle all differences. He said also:

"I am not anxious about the result of war. There can be but one result and it will not be long delayed. What I have in mind is what will come after war—the problems we do not see now but that are sure to come in some way. And they will not be easy problems. Other nations have had that experience, and we shall not escape it."

War came; so did the after-war problems. Some of those problems are still unsolved.

MCKINLEY DIRECTED ARMY AND NAVY

History will never credit McKinley with having directed every move on land and sea—but he did. Night and day he followed closely every battleship, every regiment and every plan. In Cuba not a move was made without approval from Washington.

Take one incident as typical, yet an incident that really led to the quick ending of the struggle.

On the night of July 1, 1898, after the day's battle driving the Spaniards over the slope of San Juan Hill, the American troops, exhausted by the tropic heat, were a thin, tired line on the hill-top. I was on the hill that night, and I know the "all in" condition of officers and men. Shafter feared a counter-attack, and did not believe we could withstand one. He cabled Washington that he might retire to a less exposed position. McKinley replied that he must, of course, use his own judgment inasmuch as he was on the ground, but he urged him to hold the hill. The people at home would not understand a retreat. That cable decided Shafter. The hill was held.

Holding that hill as well as El Caney made Santiago Bay impossible for the Spanish fleet bottled up there. It was at the mercy of attack by land guns. It had no alternative but to sail out hoping that some of the ships would escape the waiting American battleships.

Such is the caprice of fortune that Roosevelt's name is much more frequently associated with the war than is McKinley's. Just as when you speak of Waterloo the one remembered Britisher is Wellington so when you speak of San Juan the one remembered American is Roosevelt.

In both instances this is unfair to others who contributed as much if not more to the achievement, but it is the way of the world, otherwise known as fate. History is full of it. At times it seems like a conspiracy against the facts. The regular army won the battle of San Juan and the war in Cuba.

SEEKING A RIGHT BASIS FOR PEACE

In all the years I knew McKinley I cannot recall ever having seen him more concerned than when, with the armistice signed, he faced the problems of peace with Spain. He had none of the superior, confident air of a conqueror when, just returned from Santiago, I called at the White House. The war spirit still possessing me, I expected to find him in the same jubilant mood. My first glance, however, told me another story. The power to exact terms of his own liking seemed to rest uneasily on him. Here indeed was a man who had no flare to be absolute. Were we to keep the Philippines and Porto Rico? Were we to interpret the "Platt Amendment" literally as to Cuba, leaving it a free country, or interpret it in the newer light of conquest and take Cuba over, too?

These questions and others only less important were on our nation's doorsteps like unwanted children. If turned away where were they to go? If taken in, what would the consequence be? There was no answer that was not followed by responsibility as closely as one's shadow.

253

As I Knew Them

Never were the methods and personality of a man more clearly reflected than in the manner in which McKinley entered into peace negotiations; never were one President's ways in sharper contrast with those of another President than were McKinley's with those of Woodrow Wilson twenty years later, when the latter faced the same problems.

Wilson formulated his own conception of the peace he was to impose upon the world; he consulted few, if any. He did not even seek to learn the opinion of the country. When it came to him in the election of a Republican Congress, he rejected it. His course is stated more in detail in the chapter on Wilson.

McKinley sought counsel everywhere. He brought Elihu Root into his Cabinet as Secretary of War "because I want a lawyer to handle the problems of the new islands and you are the lawyer I want." He brought Admiral Dewey from Manila so that he might have by his side during the treaty negotiations the "man on the spot" who knew whereof he spoke. He persuaded Senators Cushman Davis, Frye and George Gray to become members of the peace commission, with Secretary of State Day and Whitelaw Reid.

Furthermore, McKinley took pride in the ability of his Commissioners. He sent them to their task with his confidence *and his respect.* "Be magnanimous" were his instructions—"the true glory and enduring interests of our country would best be served by an example of moderation, restraint and reason."

But McKinley did not stop there. He went west and made speeches, talked with representative men, wrote letters of inquiry. He made a systematic effort to get the reaction of the people to every feature of the peace negotiations, particularly the Philippines, and Cuba.

Step by step he moved to stronger ground—always keeping

254

ahead of public opinion but not too far ahead to be beyond its influence. He knew the peril any man, particularly a President, invites by attempting to do the thinking for a nation, and he avoided it. In this way McKinley secured a peace that Congress and the country would approve.

MCKINLEY ASKED FOR GUIDANCE

Charles S. Olcott, in his "Life of McKinley," tells how McKinley spoke in November 1898 to a committee of Methodist ministers who had called to pay their respects. As they were leaving the President called them back and said:

"Hold a minute longer. I would like to say a word about the Philippines.

"When I realized that the Philippines had dropped into our laps I confess I did not know what to do with them. I sought counsel from all sides—Democrats as well as Republicans—but got little help. I thought first we would take only Manila; then other islands, perhaps, also. I walked the floor of the White House night after night until midnight; and I am not ashamed to tell you, gentlemen, that I went down on my knees and prayed Almighty God for light and guidance more than one night. And one night late it came to me this way—I don't know how it was, but it came: (1) That we could not give them back to Spain—that would be cowardly and dishonorable; (2) that we could not turn them over to France or Germany—our commercial rivals in the Orient—that would be bad business and discreditable; (3) that we could not leave them to themselves—they were unfit for self-government—and they would soon have anarchy and misrule over there worse than Spain's was; and (4) that there was nothing left for us to do but to take them all, and to educate the Filipinos, and uplift and civilize and Christianize them, and by God's grace do the very best we could by them, as our fellow-men for whom Christ also died. And then I went to bed, and went to sleep, and slept soundly, and the next morning I sent for the chief engineer of the War Department (our map-maker), and I told him to put the Philippines

255

on the map of the United States (pointing to a large map on the wall of his office), and there they are, and there they will stay while I am President!"

"OUR OPPORTUNITY AND OUR BURDEN"

No one who was present at the Ohio Society banquet in the winter of 1900 will ever forget the scene when McKinley there met the challenge of imperialism. McKinley was never more impressive, more earnest, more persuasive and never held an audience more silent and attentive than while he was uttering these words:

> "There can be no imperialism. Those who fear it are against it. Those who have faith in the Republic are against it. So that there is universal abhorrence for it, and unanimous opposition to it. Our only difference is that those who do not agree with us have no confidence in the virtue or capacity or high purpose or good faith of this free people as a civilizing agency, while we believe that the century of free government which the American people have enjoyed, has not rendered them irresolute and faithless but has fitted them for the great task of lifting up and assisting to better conditions and larger liberty those distant peoples who through the issue of battle have become our wards. A self-governed people will never permit despotism in any government they foster and defend. The burden is our opportunity; the opportunity is greater than the burden."

COMPROMISED RATHER THAN "RIDE A WHITE HORSE"

There was still another incident in the McKinley policy toward our new island possessions that brought his methods into contrast with those of both Cleveland and Wilson. Cleveland, it will be remembered, speaking of his free wool message had said, "If every other man in the country abandons this issue, I shall stick to it!" Wilson took the same rigid attitude on measures that he included among his policies.

McKinley, strongly believing in a prompt effort to make the people of Porto Rico feel at home with us, declared immediately after annexation in favor of repealing all tariffs against that island's products. "It is our plain duty," he insisted to Congress. But the protectionist Republican majority did not agree with him; he found himself in conflict with them as much as was Taft in 1910 when he urged his Canadian reciprocity bill. Taft passed the bill over the protests of his party in Congress with the aid of Democratic votes. McKinley refused to do this.

"I could ride a white horse in this situation and pass the original bill," McKinley said to me in the White House the afternoon a compromise for Porto Rico was agreed upon. "All the Democratic members are ready to vote to repeal the duties. There is more at stake in this country just now, however, than immediate free trade with Porto Rico. The vital thing is to keep as many votes as possible in Congress back of the whole programme of the Administration. We have insured that. Also, Porto Rico gets free trade in two years, the revenues collected in the meantime go back to the island, and the legislation has a practically unanimous vote. I am content with that result."

"THE FOREIGNER THE BETTER," SAID PLATT

Another example of McKinley's way of handling Congress was his approach to Senator Platt, of New York, when he wanted to send Joseph H. Choate as Ambassador to Great Britain and Horace Porter as Ambassador to France. Both had been fighting Platt in New York politics for years. McKinley wanted no contest in the Senate over confirmation, so he followed his policy of testing a situation before getting into it. He asked Platt to the White House.

"Platt," he said, "two men in New York whom you do not like politically and who do not like you are candidates for important foreign posts. I would like to have your consent to their nomination."

"Who are they?" inquired Platt.

"Choate and Porter," McKinley responded.

"Mr. President," answered Platt instantly, "nominate them quick and the 'foreigner' you send them the better!"

CHAPTER XXXII

"WE'LL STAND PAT!" SAID HANNA

McKinley Had Made Good—Prosperity Reigned Throughout The Land—"Bet-You-A-Million" John W. Gates Typified The Spirit Of The Day—Big Effort, Big Capital And Big Results—So McKinley Got A Mandate From The People "In The Interest Of Business Expansion," As Hanna Explained It.

"WE'LL stand pat!" replied Hanna when asked by a reporter to state the issue of the 1900 campaign to reelect McKinley.

And "stand pat" the McKinley supporters did with much reason for their confidence.

Following Cleveland's four years of conflict with Congress, the first four years of McKinley were a period of calm that the country prized and during which it prospered greatly.

Prospered? Yes—beyond all expectation. McKinley had made good as "The Advance Agent of Prosperity." Through most of his term prosperity had reached farmer, merchant, mechanic and capitalist with some degree of fair division. "Dollar Wheat," high wages, industrial profits, had infused the people with a jubilant, confident, aggressive spirit. Crossing the line into a new century, our "captains of industry" seemed to feel that they had entered a new land of promise, and that "no pent-up Utica" would hereafter contract their powers or limit their possibilities.

"Bet-you-a-Million" John W. Gates was typical of scores of men to whom new wealth was only an incentive to greater wealth. "Big business" knew no caution. It became a gamble—a gamble with fate. Every capitalist, real or fancied,

259

looking into the future, visioned only big effort, big capital, big results. Today was merely a way station on the great highway to tomorrow. No one thought in terms of the present, splendid as they were; no one was content with what had been and what was. The future was capitalized as confidently as though it were a tale that is told. Men of experience, men of stability, men of hard-earned fortune looked upon every industry as a new Eldorado, whose treasures were to pour into the laps of those who planned on giant scale. The United States Steel Corporation is one of the dreams inspired by McKinley prosperity.

HANNA AND BRYAN SAW DIFFERENT ISSUES

It was while that spirit prevailed that McKinley defeated Bryan a second time; even Bryan's west returned generous majorities for McKinley. It was a campaign without a moment of doubt. Bryan thought the issue was "imperialism," and devoted his speech-making to that issue, but on election night Hanna gave a different interpretation to the verdict. "The Republicans," he said, "have received a clear mandate to govern the country in the interest of business expansion."

Back of that "mandate" too, was the earlier Supreme Court decision giving legality to the Sugar Trust's purchase of two Philadelphia refineries, making absolute its control of the industry. The decision seemingly stripped the government of power over corporate wealth, and such wealth promptly made the most of its opportunity. It assumed that it had received a license from the court; it assumed also that the election gave it in addition, as Hanna expressed it, "a mandate" from the people. What more could be asked?

Apparently nothing. So combination after combination was made. In every industry the "big fellows" united for control. Finally the railroads, too, saw possibilities in combination, and the Northern Securities Company resulted.

As I Knew Them

McKinley watched these developments with doubting mind. He wanted prosperity, but not too much of it; he wanted business to expand, but not too rapidly. He left nothing on the record to reflect his reaction to the get-rich-quick tide surging all about him, particularly after his reelection, but it is known that he often expressed regret that the Sherman anti-trust law had not been better sustained by the Courts. Seven months of his second term had barely passed when an assassin closed his career and the duty of carrying out the "mandate for business expansion" devolved upon the Vice President, Theodore Roosevelt.

CHAPTER XXXIII

MARK HANNA—BUSINESS IN POLITICS

It Was Clean Business, However, For He Was Not A Speculator—A Man of Many Kindly Qualities And A Loyal Friend—Sensitive To Cartoons—A "Big Boss" But A Popular One—Adrift After McKinley's Death—"Of Course Since You Want It, I Will Support It" He Telegraphed Roosevelt About His Nomination—Dead Before The Convention Of 1904 Met—Hanna And Bryan As Balances.

IN the picture gallery of the men of politics, the portraits have no soft tones. Both tint and lines are strong and emphatic, accentuating good or bad, as the artist sees the character of his subject. The politician, not the man, is on the canvas. Thus Mark Hanna is portrayed in the political history of his time. There he personifies the coarse, ruthless business man in politics—the kind of business man we see in theatrical characters or in novels—the kind that delights mercilessly to crush opponents or sacrifice family, honor and friends for gain.

It is grossly unjust to put Hanna in that class, for he was not of that type at all. True, he had the decisive ways of the man at the head of big affairs, but he also had qualities of friendship and kindness. He was candid, genial and straightforward. No pretences, no intrigues, to gain his ends. He was openly for you or against you. He was a business man in politics, and naturally had a business man's judgment of the policies best to pursue.

HANNA SENSITIVE TO CARTOONS

I first met Hanna at the Republican national convention of 1892 in Minneapolis. Later I knew him well. Month by month as he marshalled the McKinley forces of the country, he gathered men about him who gave him a loyalty that lasted until his death.

The one trait, suppose we call it weakness, that Hanna never overcame was his hurt feeling when cartooned or wrongly condemned in newspaper editorials. Homer Davenport drew the most offensive cartoon of Hanna—that with the dollar signs all over him,—and Davenport lived to seek Hanna and apologize. Most men in public life become hardened to criticism, but Hanna never did. Frequently he would say that he loved a fair fight but did not like below-the-belt blows.

To McKinley's proposal that he take John Sherman's place in the Senate, his instant response was that he "couldn't talk on his feet." When appointed two months later, he determined to make good in his new job and to secure election by the Ohio Legislature on his own account. He realized his handicaps—he was a "big boss" in politics, a "big boss" in business, a millionaire. It was not a record on which to expect popular support.

Nevertheless, Hanna went after that support. He was no platform speaker; he set apart an hour of each day to make himself one. He was not acquainted with the smaller county leaders of his State—soon he knew them all. Finally, he undertook a stumping tour of Ohio. In his speeches he tried no flights of oratory; he kept to the levels with which he was familiar. His audiences liked his blunt, homely phrases; he spoke their language and had their ways.

When the time came for the Legislature to elect a Senator, Hanna's name, like "Abou Ben Adhem's," led all the rest. He was then established in politics with his own ambitions and his own following. Later Roosevelt, among others, was to realize it.

HANNA ADRIFT WITHOUT McKINLEY

With McKinley gone, Hanna was adrift for the three remaining years of his life. He frankly told Roosevelt that he could not be with him in certain contemplated policies, but he kept his word to stand by him to the end of his term. Undoubtedly he would have been glad to see a candidate developed against Roosevelt in 1904, but Roosevelt held the stage too completely, and Hanna died while reluctantly watching the tide flow by. There was talk that Hanna would seek the nomination for himself. The newspapers constantly were publishing such stories. He certainly had made himself popular; but he understood public opinion too well to believe that he could run for the Presidency with any hope of success.

Yet many prophesied that he would become a candidate. Hanna enjoyed the talk, but he kept his own counsel. His silence so baffled Roosevelt that the latter authorized Gov. Durbin, of Indiana, to announce that the President thought it time for Hanna to "fish or cut bait."

THE "FOR-ME" OR "AGAINST-ME" TELEGRAMS

About the same time in the Spring of 1903, Senator Foraker decided to challenge Hanna's control of the approaching Republican State convention in Ohio. He used the Roosevelt candidacy as his issue, declaring for his nomination and insisting that the State convention should commit Ohio to him. Foraker cared little for Roosevelt, but he sought an opportunity to show that Hanna no longer spoke for Ohio Republicans. He got from Hanna just what he expected— opposition to the proposed indorsement. Hanna rightly insisted that a year in advance was too soon to pledge a State delegation. He then telegraphed Roosevelt, who was on a tour in the Northwest, that he would have to oppose the issue raised by Foraker, but he was not doing so in any spirit of antagonism to his nomination. He added that he felt sure Roosevelt when apprised of all the facts would approve his course. But the President took a contrary view. He wired that inasmuch as the issue had been raised those who favor his nomination would support it and those who do not would oppose.

That settled Hanna's attitude.

"In view of the sentiments in your telegram," he wired back, "I shall not oppose the resolutions."

The sentiments settled more than the Ohio indorsement. They settled the nomination a year in advance of the 1904 convention. Hanna had died before the convention met.

Next to Roosevelt Hanna did more than any other man to make the Panama Canal a reality. He led the battle in Congress for it.

HANNA AND BRYAN AS NECESSARY TYPES

Hanna, of course, did not have a broad conception of public policies, but his views were honestly held. He looked over the nation as a banker looks over a balance sheet, hunting for "tangibles." He was not without appreciation of those intangible things that go so far toward making the character of men and nations, but their value as collateral was no greater in his eyes than in the eyes of the average banker unless backed by a definite objective. The smoke from a factory chimney had more meaning to him than the dream of the man in the office below.

He wanted results, not dreams, and in politics if results were not forthcoming from one set of men he quickly switched to another group. Power not politics, held his mind, and, like all who seek power, he believed that his use of it would be wise and best.

Such men have a place in the life of every nation, particularly in our own. They are a balance, a check, to extremists on the other side. One type would be as unsafe in complete control of a nation as the other; but one is as essential as the other in fixing the level on which millions of people can stand together contentedly under one government. Hanna had his contrast in Bryan. The year 1896 produced both men as national figures. The two types fought it out stubbornly in two national elections—Bryan getting the hurrahs of the multitude; Hanna getting their votes for McKinley.

CHAPTER XXXIV

DEPEW—MAN OF YEARS AND OF FRIENDS

Everybody Knows Chauncey M. Depew—Why He Abandoned Saloon Campaigning—Seven Decades Before The Public—Chauncey "De Peach"—Supported For President And Twice Elected Senator—Always Sought As A Campaigner.

WHO does not know Chauncey Depew? Who has not heard him tell a story or make a speech? Who has not found his philosophy—laugh and the world laughs with you —the stirring elixir of life when life seemed drab and empty? My recollection of him goes back many years and runs through many events and situations that were dark and confusing until his cheery disposition and clear mind found the way to light and new effort. Depew is not of a type; he is a type by himself.

Depew was two years later than Mark Hanna in entering the Senate at Washington. It was the spirit of the McKinley days not to be fearful of men who had won their way in the business world, but from the presidency of one of the largest railroad corporations directly to the United States Senate was a step never possible before or since Depew's election in 1889 by the Legislature of New York. Not content with giving him one term the Republicans reelected him in 1905. Election for a third term came in 1910 when the break in the Republican party lost Depew his seat to a Democrat because of the anti-Taft tidal wave.

Back somewhere in the eighteen-nineties I heard Depew in a speech before the New York Legislature say that when he was campaigning for election in 1861 and 1862 as Member of Assembly from Peekskill, candidates rivalled each other as to who could visit the most saloons in the district, who could call the most loungers therein to the brass-rail and the mahogany bar, and hand out the largest greenback to the saloon-keeper, with a nonchalant "never mind the change."

Depew followed this practice in his two campaigns but became so disgusted with it and with himself that he resolved never again to seek public office if he had to pay that price. He put the resolution into effect next year (1863) when nominated for Secretary of State of New York. He canvassed different parts of the State, and spoke at many more meetings than he could have addressed had he continued touring saloons. His election by a substantial majority satisfied him that no votes were lost by his different campaign method. He never again entered a saloon for electioneering or any other purpose.

SEVENTY YEARS OF PUBLIC LIFE

In that change of campaign headquarters from saloon to platform, Depew laid the basis for his career as railroad president, as United States Senator, and as orator. Though he has had seventy years of public speaking in Europe and America, he is still sought and honored at every banquet he cares to attend.

I doubt that any other man has had contact with the extremes of life such as Depew has enjoyed.

In New York city they know Depew on the Bowery and east side as "the Peach"; among New Yorkers of average station he is "Our Chauncey"; and among the exclusives he is Senator, or "Mr. President" of the New York Central Railroad. It is an achievement for any man to be accepted in three stations so widely separated. I once asked Depew how he managed it. He said he didn't manage it, he just went along with the day's work, and let nature take its course. Then he added, "with this exception, that I never made a pessimistic speech in my life; I have always looked upon the brighter side; I've always had faith in my country and our people; that strikes home more often than public speakers realize."

The title of "Peach" came to Depew in an interesting way. During the Presidential campaign of 1892 he addressed a Republican meeting on the Bowery for Harrison and Reid. In order to show the opportunity for everyone in America, he said:

"I started in life with these two hands and this head."

Someone in the audience called out: "That head is a peach, Chaunce."

The newspapers took up the phrase and from that time on Depew has been known as "de Peach."

It is not my purpose to use Depew's saloon story as an argument against liquor, but I do want to use it to demonstrate the unwisdom of those who assume that they must descend to low levels in order to be "popular" in politics or in other callings.

Real popularity—the popularity that counts—is not attained that way; rather is it soon lost. I could name a score of able, brilliant men in Congress and in the New York Legislature in the last thirty years who wasted so much time seeking that kind of popularity that they sacrificed their real opportunities. Men of rare ability have gone down like ten-pins, one after another, as I have watched them through their careers, cut short by their inability to realize, as Depew fortunately realized, that respect and confidence are not to be won with your feet on a brass-rail or your hand slapping somebody's, anybody's, everybody's—back.

SLOAT FASSETT'S GREAT MISTAKE

For obvious reasons I cannot use names, but any reader acquainted with the habits of men in public life—in fact with the habits of men in any walk of life—will easily recall many who have frittered away their talent and their chance by their will-o'-the-wisp search for "popularity" based on an appeal to the poorer rather than the better instincts of people. My observation is that those who respect themselves are most respected. Depew did not become a "Peach" to the Bowery-ites by pretending to be one of them; he remained the same Depew on the Bowery as on Fifth Avenue and he achieved popularity in both sections because he was just Depew in both.

A contrasting incident of interest was the experience on the same Bowery of J. Sloat Fassett, when he was a candidate for Governor. He was addressing a house crowded with east side voters. The night was oppressively hot, and many of his audience began taking off their coats. Fassett evidently thought he would win favor by doing the same thing. He threw off his coat and then turned to resume his speech.

Hisses greeted Fassett instead of the applause he had anticipated for getting down to the level of his audience. Though his hearers were shirt-sleeved themselves they did not care to listen to a Governor in shirt-sleeves. Fassett continued his speech until he could find a place to stop; he then gave up and amidst boohs and hisses put on his coat and left the platform.

Next day's newspapers carried the story of Fassett's bad night on the Bowery—wholly due to the fact that, unlike Depew, he did not stick to his own ways on the East Side as he would have done on Fifth Avenue.

ALWAYS SOUGHT AS A CAMPAIGNER

In the years while Depew was the active head of the New York Central Railroad, he was in constant demand as a campaign speaker—particularly in the up-state rural counties. No man has made so many speeches in so many counties. The railroad extends into most of those counties, and has the traditional antagonisms of a railroad in all of them; yet each year when local political leaders would send their list of desired speakers, the name of Chauncey Depew, president of the New York Central, was always there.

As I Knew Them

In 1888 the destinies of the Republican party in New York State were entrusted to the "Big Four"—Platt, Depew, Miller and Hiscock;—the party leaders were not afraid to name Depew as one of the four, despite his railroad interests. Nor were the New York delegates to the national convention of that year fearful of criticism from the folks back home because they supported Depew for President. He received 99 votes, ranking next to John Sherman and Judge Gresham on the first ballot.

BRIGHTENS H. G. WELLS' GLOOM

Depew's philosophy of life was aptly illustrated at a dinner given by Ralph Pulitzer to H. G. Wells, when the celebrated Englishman came over here to report the Washington naval limitations conference for the New York World. Pulitzer called on Wells as the first speaker of the evening. I never listened to a gloomier, more hopeless picture of the future than Wells gave us in his speech.

The banqueters were certainly a depressed crowd when Depew was called upon. I shall not pretend to quote his exact words but in substance he said that with all that Wells had published in his book "The Outline of History" down to Julius Caesar he agreed because he knew little about it.

"But I am a contemporary of Caesar," he added, "and I know history from Caesar to the present, and I do not agree with a word our friend has written about those centuries. Nor do I agree with what he has said here tonight about the present plight of the world and the still darker future ahead of us. We have light, not darkness ahead of us; we have a better understanding among nations, not a poorer understanding ahead of us; we have a realization of the horror and burdens of war to guide us away from war in the future. No, friend Wells, this is not the time for sorrowing, nor the time for despair. This is the time for hope—the time for straightening out for one great big effort to make up for all the tragedies of the past eight years. This world has never turned from bad to worse; it gets its jolts, and I admit we have had a hard one, but it is always getting better and it is not going to stop now."

When Depew sat down, the clouds had lifted from the dinner table, and we showed our relief by applause that must have convinced Wells that he was in the wrong company for the doctrine he preached.

THE QUALITY OF LEADERSHIP

This is no place to detail Depew's career. Personally, I believe that had he, as a young man, continued in public life he might have been President of the nation instead of President of a railroad. He has the outstanding quality of leadership—the ability to sense the purpose of the average man and to move along with him. He has another great quality in his determination never to look hopelessly on the dark side of any situation.

Taft was elected President on his smile, but Depew's laugh in the midst of a gloomy conference whether of business or of politics has taken the furrows out of many a brow. And his reward is in the full life he is still enjoying as I write—full of friendships, full of honors, full of health and full of years.

CHAPTER XXXV

BRYAN—A CAREER OF PROTEST

Two Pictures of the "Peerless One," Thirty Years Apart—Making and Discarding Issues—Urging a Peace Treaty In Order To Have a Campaign Cry—What Was His Motive In 1912?—A Tragedy in the State Department—His Last Appeal To His Party, and the "Boos" That Greeted Him.

IN 1896 I sat in the press section not fifty feet from William Jennings Bryan when he made his "cross of gold" speech in the Democratic national convention at Chicago; there I watched the tumult that startled a nation and almost won him a Presidency; in 1924 I sat in the press section in Madison Square Garden in New York City, again not fifty feet away, when he made his plea not to denounce the Ku Klux Klan by name; there I heard the "boos" that greeted his last appeal to his party—"boos" so loud and persistent that Chairman Walsh threatened to recess the convention.

Those nearly thirty years!

At first, a man in the full energy of ambitious life—flashing, gleaming eye, broad-shouldered, straight as an arrow, the physique of a gladiator, the spirit of a crusader; voice clear and vibrant; 15,000 spectators emotionally following every word, every gesture. Then the other picture twenty-eight years later—a worn man, eyes dimmed, shoulders stooped, the old spirit glowing faintly like the thin flame from a burnt-out log, voice no longer resonant, many of the delegates and spectators hostile to his pleading, scarcely tolerant of the leader they had followed so many years.

What a career between the day of hurrahs and the day of "boos"! It had led him into all the highways and byways of politics except the one he most desired to travel—the highway to the White House. Its triumphs were of the platform; the only office he ever held by election was that of Congressman—two terms from 1891 to 1895. In those years an anti-Republican tide engulfed the country, making the election of a Democrat possible from Lincoln, Nebraska, normally Republican.

Bryan was a product of his restless day. Such types come in the life of every nation reflecting its passing temper but not its character. They have their "exits and their entrances," and while on the stage seem destined next moment to make a tremendous hit. That moment never comes. Looking back upon their activities, one wonders, as he sees great waves of discontent rising at times perilously high, why such men hold their leadership so long without being swept into the place of power they seek. With that wonder comes a firmer faith in the wisdom of the ballot-box.

THREE MEN WHO HELD THE PEOPLE

I am far from classing Bryan with either Roosevelt or Wilson, but we must not forget that from 1896 to 1919 those three men held the political attention of the country more completely, indeed more exclusively, than any other three men ever held it. Bryan became of national significance before Roosevelt or Wilson, though he was two years younger than Roosevelt and four years younger than Wilson. "The Commoner," as he delighted to hear himself called, was only 37 when first nominated for the Presidency—a fact that led to his being referred to, sarcastically, as "the Boy Orator of the Platte." Roosevelt was 42 when he succeeded McKinley and was the youngest President to enter the White House. Wilson was 56.

The death of Roosevelt in 1919 left Wilson and Bryan the most conspicuous figures in the public mind, though Senator Bob La Follette was steadily emerging. In 1924 as a presidential candidate of his own party, the Wisconsin Senator

polled 4,800,000 votes. Wilson's death in 1924 followed by
La Follette's, left Bryan alone on the national stage for a year
longer—just as he had held it alone for two years before
Roosevelt achieved national prominence, and ten years before
Wilson dreamt of a career outside his college environment.

THE TWO BRYANS MY MIND HAS SEEN

There have always been two Bryans in my mind—the Bryan
in private life with religious convictions to which he clung
with firm, sincere though spectacular faith; the Bryan in public life with so many convictions that he seemed to believe that
he was ordained to discover and redress all the wrongs of
the oppressed, because no other human could do the job so
well. He had a passion for "issues." This habit brought
him under suspicion of constantly shopping in the market
places for something to "sell" the people. Like an omnibus
he carried a great variety of issues so as to be sure he had
gathered up all there were, and could accommodate everybody.

Let me illustrate with the "16 to 1" issue—the foundation
stone of Bryan's career. Cleverly he dramatized that issue
in a single speech that almost as it was uttered changed him
from an unimportant advocate to an historic figure in the fight
for silver. Yet Richard P. Bland of Missouri—"Silver Dollar Dick"—had been the leader of the silver forces in Congress for more than twenty years. The only triumph scored
for the metal was the Bland law of 1878 compelling the free
coinage of silver dollars—the Bland "cart-wheel" dollars.

It was that law, modified by the Sherman law of 1890,
that Cleveland forced Congress to repeal. The issue thus
created seemed to point to the Missourian as the man to lead
in the 1896 battle for silver's restoration. Surely if the
servant were worthy of his hire—and Bland was—Bland
should have been chosen. But Bryan pounced upon the issue
as an eagle does his prey. He knew the moment to act in the
convention. He asked permission to speak last—just before

275

the balloting for nominee. He was staking all on one opportunity to impress the delegates; he wanted his voice to ring in their ears unchallenged by subsequent speakers.

LEAVING THE TRIED SERVANT FOR A NEW STAR

The political orator, as he reads the "cross of gold" speech can visualize the whole thing as an actor does when he reads a play. He can see every high spot, every chance for effectiveness, every place where the audience will break into applause. And Bryan utilized such opportunities. It was this example of dramatic force and careful political play-writing which led to the gossip in those days that in his youth Bryan had been an actor. His dynamic climaxes moved the delegates to turn hysterically from the man who had served to one who suddenly appeared like a new star in the firmament.

But the new star was not to be as constant as the star grown dim in many battles. The new star was determined always to be of the first magnitude and, if one issue seemed likely to tarnish its brightness, another must be brought forward.

Writing of the 1896 campaign, Bryan called it "The First Battle." When he wrote he knew it was the last battle for silver; he knew he would never use it again as an issue. Promptly he went "shopping" for something else that would arouse the people and keep him "the Peerless Leader." He found it in anti-imperialism. All the passion with which he had appealed to voters in 1896 against the God of Gold was now transferred to the newer issue as readily as you change one coat for another.

The God of Gold had not ruined the country as four years before he had predicted; there was no crown of thorns pressing down upon the brow of labor. Instead the people had prospered mightily and so had Bryan. But Bryan could insist that another God—the God of Imperialism—was being worshipped by the opposing party and was certain to transform our Republic into an autocracy. And all because we had taken over the Philippines! When the votes were counted, and he again found himself denied the Presidency, there was nothing for Bryan to do but go shopping once more for an issue. For the twenty-five remaining years of his life he kept shopping and shopping but never again found another issue that interested the people in a national sense.

ISSUES WERE BRYAN'S STOCK IN TRADE

Some call this just politics; some call it insincerity; some call it opportunism. Call it all or any of these, for the difference is not great, the truth is that Bryan had an unexcelled talent for keeping himself before the public, and in the exercise of that talent he used "issues" as a storekeeper uses his stock. He tried to keep on hand what the people wanted; and if he was out of stock he undertook to sell them something "just as good."

As a grocer Bryan would not have put sand in the sugar or his thumb on the scales, but he would make a sale, as he sold Florida real estate, based on things hoped for rather than on things done. No man with sincerity of purpose would jump grasshopper-like from issue to issue as Bryan did, or could so easily convince himself as Bryan could that he had finished his job before each jump.

Bryan always insisted, for example, that his "16 to 1" issue would have remained an issue until it had won but for the increasing production of gold! Thus he reconciled his yesterdays with his todays,—content with his own dismissal of it and his own reasoning. When he made this statement as to "16 to 1" he confirmed Tom Reed's prophecy in Congress in 1892:

"He (Bryan) finds now that even the Democratic party has got to obey the everlasting laws of common-sense; they have got to act according to the eternal verities, and that is going to be a great shock to him on every occasion."

As I Knew Them

It is amazing that a man of whom that could be said with truth could travel the country over so many times and for so many years and hold so many voters through it all—over 6,000,000 votes were polled for Bryan at each of three elections. What was it Bryan possessed that made it possible for him to do that which no other man in our politics was ever able to do? He had no record of achievement on which to ask public favor; his was a career of protest. Not once was he able to say "I did thus and so," contrasting his own official acts and policies with those of men who had responsibility. Excepting his "cross of gold" speech, Bryan never uttered a sentence that survived longer than its day, or that political historians can use to illustrate his philosophy. Words? Yes—words by the million, but not one thought that revealed a purposeful mind. Nevertheless, Bryan must be credited with something that appealed strongly. No two men ever agreed as to what that something was. Some said a Presence and a Voice. The Voice was magical; few could use it better. And the Presence filled the eye.

His power over the political opinion of the country was a tribute not so much to his convictions as to his adroitness. Perhaps that is the appropriate word for Bryan's statesmanship—adroitness, to the point of suspicion of his sincerity even in policies, such as prohibition, for which he would have made any sacrifice.

RATIFIED A TREATY TO CREATE AN ISSUE

As far back as 1898—only two years after his first campaign for the Presidency—Bryan demonstrated his skill in shifting issues.

In the Senate in February, 1899, the struggle over ratification of the peace treaty with Spain had much the same inten-

278

MICAWBER-LIKE, BRYAN WAS ALWAYS LOOKING
FOR SOMETHING TO TURN UP

sity as the struggle twenty years later over the Versailles treaty. The proposed purchase of the Philippines from Spain for $25,000,000 split party lines. Senators Hoar, of Massachusetts, and Eugene Hale, of Maine, denounced the treaty as an imperialistic document. They did not believe in the transfer of the sovereignty of any people by bargain and sale, without consent.

Many Democratic Senators, politically disposed to make trouble for McKinley, joined in this view, and began to unite in opposition to ratification. Bryan, who had been Colonel of a Nebraska regiment of volunteers, had resigned his commission, and was again footloose, a candidate for the 1900 nomination. He turned up in Washington with the surprising request to Democratic Senators to vote to ratify. He insisted that no political party could take responsibility for keeping the country even technically at war. His view was reluctantly accepted by enough Democrats to put the treaty through. Bryan's entrance into that situation was timed to be dramatic and pivotal. When the roll-call on ratification showed only one majority in favor, the country did not have to be told that Bryan had saved the treaty. Bryan had seen to that.

HE WANTED THE LIMELIGHT ALONE

Here again, as in 1896, he set the stage with himself in the centre, and the limelight on him alone. He had made himself the decisive factor in confirming the purchase of the Philippines. He would now make himself, or seek to make himself, the decisive factor in setting them free. He demanded our immediate release to the Filipinos of the sovereignty we had acquired from Spain.

Bryan had stood on broad ground while favoring the treaty and had won commendation for his course, but his new turn threw a new light on his motive. The response came quickly from the country that in urging ratification he had been shrewdly building a platform for himself in the presidential struggle just ahead. It was his one chance for a nation-wide issue—the one chance to escape from another "16 to 1" battle. If the treaty were to fail, he could not evoke "Imperialism," for we would be out of the Philippines, but if the treaty were ratified, and the Philippines should come under our flag, then he could demand that we set them free, and pocket our loss of $25,000,000 for temporary sovereignty.

Only a mind with a peculiar bent for creating a situation would have resorted to such strategy, but it made the best issue he could find. "McKinley prosperity" had buried all other issues; the distant Philippines offered the only one available. In that 1900 election he made the poorest showing, proportionately, of any of his three struggles; at its close, anti-imperialism, no longer serviceable, promptly went into the discard along with "16 to 1."

TOOK NO CHANCES WITH T. R., BUT FOUGHT TAFT

No persuasion could lure Bryan into a candidacy against Roosevelt in 1904; he was aware of its certain end. But four years later, he knew that he could not keep his hold on his party without becoming its candidate. Besides he had some hope that he could defeat Taft. All that he did in that campaign, however—indeed the most definite thing of his career —was to make a speech against "Big business" that brought Charles E. Hughes into national attention as a masterful orator and thinker.

At Youngstown, Ohio, Hughes replied. The Hughes speech caught the country; thereafter the election, though six weeks distant, was only a matter of totalling the vote against Bryan. Bryan replied to Taft's speeches, replied to President Roosevelt's 'statements'—but he attempted no reply to Hughes.

I saw Bryan frequently during the Republican national convention of 1912. He was there as a reporter for a newspaper syndicate; he seemed to enjoy talking with Roosevelt and other Republican leaders. I did not attend the Democratic convention at Baltimore a week or so later, but when I read of Bryan standing on the centre of that stage denouncing Belmont and Ryan as unfit delegates, and challenging the election of Alton B. Parker as chairman, my mind turned to the picture of him seated in the press section, a few days before, the calm interpreter of an intense Republican conflict. It was a spectacular transition—few men could have made it. But Bryan did it well. And it was just the thing he liked to do— to come upon a scene as though shot through a trap door, astonishing all by his presence and his purpose.

BRYAN'S GREAT BATTLE AT BALTIMORE

Was he, too, really seeking his own nomination in Baltimore?

Had the spectacle of a divided Republican convention, insuring Democratic victory, stirred his thrice-thwarted ambition anew?

He had been elected to the Baltimore convention under instructions to vote for Champ Clark; the Nebraska delegation was a unit for the Missouri candidate.

When the "break" came in Chicago, however, Bryan frankly lost interest in newspaper writing; the opportunity to elect a Democratic President had his entire mind. In my presence he declared that he was going to Baltimore to fight the Democratic reactionaries to the death. Others in Chicago quoted him as saying that if, after Taft's nomination, Baltimore should nominate a conservative, he would feel that both parties had become reactionary; the only course then left for him would be to support an independent ticket—even Roosevelt. When Bryan's plan was mentioned to Roosevelt, his reply was "I'm not the same kind of cattle." By a "conservative" it was assumed that Bryan meant Underwood, Harmon or the man he was under instructions to favor— Clark.

Though the instructions he had accepted meant the nomination of Clark there can be no doubt that Bryan had a different nomination in mind, and his purpose to desert Clark was revealed the instant he arrived in Baltimore. He gathered his forces to defeat Alton B. Parker for Chairman—and polled 508 votes for himself against 578 for Parker! That near-triumph led him to a still bolder effort. In effect the second effort succeeded too, for in a fiery speech, he secured a four to one vote for the following resolution, after agreeing to omit the second paragraph:

> Resolved, that in this crisis in our party's career and in our country's history this convention sends greeting to the people of the United States, and assures them that the party of Jefferson and Jackson is still the champion of popular government and equality before the law. As proof of our fidelity to the people we hereby declare ourselves opposed to the nomination of any candidate for President who is the representative of or under obligation to J. Pierpont Morgan, Thomas F. Ryan, August Belmont, or any other of the privilege-hunting and favor-seeking class.
>
> Be it further resolved, that we demand the withdrawal from this convention of any delegates constituting or representing the above-named interests.

WAS HE FOR WILSON OR FOR HIMSELF?

Thus two emotional incidents built a solid foundation under Bryan's manœuvring to name the candidate. He was now the pivot of the convention—the man of demonstrated strength. The Murphys, Taggarts and Brennans had the numerical force of their delegations, but Bryan had the spirit of the convention. There was no limit to its possibilities. How would he use his power? When would his real purpose be revealed? Would he kill off every candidate but himself? He was watched closely, suspiciously. The Clark managers asserted that Bryan would remain true to the instructions from Nebraska; Colonel House and other Wilson advocates rested on his assurance that he had forgotten Wilson's plea that he should be "knocked into a cocked hat" and they believed he was friendly to the Jersey Governor; Roger Sullivan and Tom Taggart asserted that he was out for himself and they acted accordingly.

BRYAN DEFEATS CLARK AND CLARK MAKES RESPONSE

Bryan voted for Clark for nine ballots. He knew that Clark could not be nominated until Tammany swung into line for him. On the tenth ballot Tammany did so. That move gave Clark a majority of the convention; nomination by a two-thirds vote would probably follow on the next roll-call. Bryan's great moment had arrived. Standing on the platform he declared that he could not vote for a candidate. whose nomination, if made, would be secured by the votes of Murphy, Belmont and Ryan. He switched to Woodrow Wilson. The Clark column was shattered.

Through thirty-five more ballots Clark struggled vainly; so far as his candidacy was concerned, the end had come. All the time, the one question was, when would Bryan desert Wilson for himself? The Sullivans and the Taggarts, unable to name Clark, were nevertheless powerful to stand in Bryan's way. Rather than take the chance of another candidacy by "The Peerless One," they preferred to defeat him with his own candidate Wilson.

Was Bryan a traitor to Clark? Was the use of Tammany, as a reason for switching, merely a subterfuge? Speaker Clark in his "Memories" said:

"I never said, 'Great is Tammany and Croker its Prophet.' Bryan did.

"I never welcomed Mr. Murphy at a railroad station and had my picture taken clasping hands with him. Bryan did.

"I never sent a trusted friend half-way across the continent to beg Mr. Murphy not to defeat my nomination under the two-thirds rule by refusing to give him the New York delegation after I received a majority. Bryan did."

283

As I Knew Them

Most men in political life fail to see any humor in jokes about themselves or in cartoons. Bryan enjoyed them. So did Wilson. So did Roosevelt. The latter was delighted with Finley Peter Dunne's book "Alone in Cuba" and was eager to meet Dunne and laugh over it. Wilson often told stories at his own expense. Bryan got the originals of many cartoons and hung them on the walls of his almost-bookless library. He liked to tell the story of the drunk, who, thrown down the stairs of a dance-hall for the third time, picked himself up and said: "Those fellows can't fool me. They don't want me in there, and they think I don't know it." He applied the story to his own three defeats for the Presidency.

BRYAN IN THE STATE DEPARTMENT

It is a mercy to Bryan to say little of his career as Secretary of State.

That Wilson tolerated him so long is the best tribute I know to Wilson's self-control and patience. Of course, Bryan in the Cabinet was politics; but even politics has its limits. There must have been many embarrassing moments in the Wilson Cabinet sessions. The public could not know of them, but it did know that the serene and dignified office in which the Secretary of State is to be found was a distressing place while Bryan occupied it. Shirt-sleeved (literally) with handkerchief tucked in his collar and a big palm-leaf fan in hand, he sat in the Secretary's high-backed chair like a Hottentot chief on his tropical throne. Bryan's callers were chiefly the cheap grade of politicians who grub a living out of public office or public favor. Men of consequence frequently had to wait while Bryan tried to hunt jobs for the daily procession of "deserving Democrats." He would telephone from one department to another seeking places for the "faithful," as he called them, explaining to his fellow cabinet officers that he had to take care of 6,000,000 voters who had supported his three candidacies for President.

284

As I Knew Them

"A PECULIAR PRODUCT OF OUR COUNTRY"

Next to hunting offices for his followers, he busied himself with lecturing on tour. Condemnation made no impression on him so long as the receipts held up. He talked of a speaking tour of Europe. President Wilson was told in advance of the Chautauqua tours and consented. But he must have headed off the foreign trip, though the report had reached London that Bryan had arranged to go there. On February 13, 1914, Ambassador Page wrote to Colonel House:

> "It was announced in one of the London papers that Bryan would deliver a lecture here and possibly in each of the principal European Capitals on Peace. Now, God restrain me from saying, much more from doing anything rash, but if I have got to go home at all, I'd rather go before he comes. It'll take years for American Ambassadors to recover what they'll lose if he carries out his plan. They now laugh at him over here. . . . Mr. Asquith . . . met Bryan once and he told me with a smile that he regarded him as a 'peculiar product of your country.' "

In Washington, diplomats were at first amazed, then disgusted; they kept their distance from the State Department except when it was necessary to call on official business.

BRYAN'S LAST CONVENTION

The picture of Bryan pleading for his cause amidst the "boos" of the Madison Square Garden convention in 1924 is something that no witness can recall with pleasure. There were many incidents throughout that unhappy convention that were sad to look upon or to recall in later days. Not in all the history of conventions has there ever been one so pitiful as Bryan on the platform frequently halting his speech until his voice could be heard above the yells of derision. Here was the thrice-named leader of his party, here was the man to

285

whose daring the party owed eight years of Wilson as President, with all that goes with partisan control of government. Yet he could not command even the respect of attention.

Bryan's battle in that convention was not so much over the nominee as over the platform. He seemed to centre on the party platform. He wanted prohibition upheld by a law enforcement plank, and he was against any denunciation of the Ku-Klux-Klan by name. Florida named him as its member of the platform committee.

THOUGH HISSED, BRYAN WINS FOR THE KLAN

A national platform is a delicate thing to write, an exhausting task for the members of the Committee. It was doubly exhausting in seething New York—a citadel of "wet" sentiment and religious antagonisms. The Ku-Klux question moved both sides profoundly; perhaps never before were they so evenly balanced. All day and all night the committee debated. When at last calm came, Bryan suggested closing with prayer, so at six o'clock in the morning Judge McCunn, of Pennsylvania, a Catholic, recited the Lord's Prayer, and Bryan himself prayed fervently in his own words.

Two reports go to the convention for its choice—a majority report that does not name the Klan, and a minority report naming and denouncing it. Bryan urges the majority report. He tries to be conciliatory. But every delegate of Catholic faith has been made to feel that a plank inferentially against the Klan without naming it is directed against his religion.

The heavy, tired speaker seeks to touch some note of common purpose. There is none of the "We will defy them" spirit with which in his early years he had constantly assailed the "money power." He seeks to touch a note of common purpose. But he cannot bring harmony out of such discord. He is greeted with howls from the galleries; despite the howls, he persists. When all is over, the tabulation shows only a single vote margin for the "no name" plank. It is the barest victory possible, but it is a victory. He has his way.

THE STRUGGLE FOR A CANDIDATE

The cost of that victory Bryan is soon to learn. The same elements that were at odds on the platform are at odds on the nomination. Thirty-eight ballots are taken. A deadlock has come. It must be broken. Who shall give counsel? The three-times candidate, the father in Israel of the present Democracy, tries to lead the way to a choice, as he led at Baltimore twelve years before.

But his victory for the Klan still rankles. He rises on a stereotyped excuse—to explain his vote. His reception is hostile. Not even the formal narrative of the official proceedings can conceal it. He is greeted with "cheers and applause mingled with hisses and boos." He tells his hearers that every state has at least one man to whom the convention could safely turn—he will name some. He begins at home. "We have a man in Florida. He is president of our State University (Laughter). His name is Dr. O. O. Murphree (Voices) "We want Smith! We want Smith! (Laughter, applause and cheers). He is a scholarly Democrat." (Voice: "Never heard of one.")

The speaker goes on. Soon he says that this is probably his last convention. His enemies join in a round of applause. Quickly he responds: "Don't applaud, I may change my mind." (Laughter, applause and cheers). He refers to his three nominations and the words "never again" greet him. He speaks of likely timber and at last reveals his real purpose with a good word for McAdoo.

The minutes record "applause, and boos, considerable disorder on the floor and in the gallery." A delegate from New Jersey interrupts to ask about "Doheny and McAdoo and Oil." There are "continuous cries of 'Oil,' 'Oil,' and the Chairman orders the galleries cleared. Bryan asks the man who has heckled him what state he comes from. 'New Jersey,' responds the delegate. 'I voted for you every time you ran. I am sorry.' "

And so it goes. The record is full of such interruptions as "Who's paying you for this?" "Come off, come off," "Great disorder, shouting, boos, cat-calls and cries of out of order." At last Bryan finishes his speech while the Chairman's gavel is pounding for order and Mr. O'Brien, a New Jersey delegate, exclaims "The same old 'Dollar Bill,' the same old 'Dollar Bill.' "

Bryan resumes his seat. His speech has been a failure. Not till sixty-five more—one hundred and three in all—ballots are taken can a nomination be reached, and the nominee is John W. Davis, whose candidacy he had denounced as too close to Wall Street.

In 1912 Bryan had fought and defeated a "Wall Street" candidate. This time he surrendered. The cynical said that he got his price—his brother in second place on the ticket. It was the last use of his influence in a national convention and, like other incidents, it brought his sincerity into question even among his own party associates.

ALWAYS IN A RACE FOR WEALTH

At odds with Bryan's professions, was his greed for wealth. The Bryan one finds denouncing Wall Street's worship of the God of gold is a Bryan in swift and persistent pursuit of the same God. Even while holding the dignified post of Secretary of State the desire for dollars led him to go lecturing through the country like a barn-storming actor. Later, when Florida needed an orator for its land speculation, he joined in the land craze and became its spokesman. It, too, meant gold.

Of course, Bryan was in a numerous company in his desire for wealth, but why should he have regarded himself as the only member of the company with honorable intent? His followers in politics often hoped that he would step out of the ranks of money-seekers, but he became more devoted to money-making as his Florida acres sold higher. He lived to find himself a millionaire and to speak of it with satisfaction. The great fortune he accumulated is the strongest indictment of his sincerity—not because it represented wealth, but because of his constant preaching that the man with a dollar is to be feared as a selfish creature, while the man without a dollar must be accepted as unselfish.

Of course, there is good, a great deal of good, in every man, and more of it in most of our public men than they get credit for. There was good in Bryan. I am reminded of the reply made by a friend when I asked him why he did not seek the gold known to be on some land he owned in New Mexico. "It costs too much to get it out," he said. The gold in Bryan cost too much to get out.

ALWAYS SEEKING, NEVER GAINING, OFFICE

Our people estimated Bryan properly when they kept him always seeking but never attaining power. Half a century is a long penance period but many people believe it would have required almost that time for the country to recover from a Bryan Administration. He had no mind for the practical; none for organization, none for sound reasoning. Not many men with his contacts and experiences would have remained as Bryan remained from beginning to end of his career at the same intellectual level. He was not a student, not even a reader of enlightening literature. Newspapers with their daily offering of something new had his attention. He cared little for books. His collection would not have overtaxed a five-foot shelf. One book, however, he knew thoroughly—the Bible.

In 1907 he toured the world, visiting many of the leading capitals and meeting many leading men. After such opportunity for broadening experiences he was as unchanged as if he had spent his time on a Mississippi river flat-boat. The influence of years, of observation and of travel counted for little. Adroitness in speech, adroitness in manipulating conventions, adroitness in advancing his own opportunity for political power and for wealth remained his dominant characteristic. Against that record must be placed his religious convictions whose fundamental bases he never changed.

He preached against millionaires and died one; he preached against militarists and asked to be buried among them.

CHAPTER XXXVI

T. R.

His Real Interests Were Family, Country And Friends—His Last Ten Years Were Regarded By Many As His Greatest—Always Something Doing In The White House, But In One Direction Only—"Don't Move, We've Got It!" Exclaimed John Singer Sargent—Where Roosevelt Should Be Honored With A Monument—How He Found Money For The Battle-Fleet Cruise—His Loyalty To Friendship—"Teddy" The Whole World Round—The Wide Circle Of His Acquaintances.

TO have known Theodore Roosevelt well and to have enjoyed his confidence is a proud privilege for an American to claim. That privilege is mine—and I rank it among the richest of my life.

I knew him in his days of early ambition; I knew him on the battle-line at Santiago; I knew him in his days of power; I knew him in his days of storm and trial; best of all, I knew him in those later days when he realized that the world was behind him, that his work was done and that all that remained for him was to counsel his fellow citizens as best he could out of his own vast experience.

It would be hard to say definitely in which period of his remarkable career Roosevelt's qualities stood out in most commanding way; but it will always seem to me that he was greatest after titles had become mere symbols of the past and the man, not the office or the power, spoke.

It is not my purpose to write as an historian. Certainly I shall not attempt that rôle with Roosevelt. Joseph Bucklin Bishop, Lawrence Abbott and Roosevelt's own "Autobiography" cover that field thoroughly. What I place on record about that splendid type of vigorous, patriotic and fine-purposed American manhood must swing back and forth

"HE'S GOOD ENOUGH FOR ME"

through the years, as events and conversations range themselves in my memory—at times far apart in date. I prefer to write in a more personal way based on the impressions I gathered on different occasions.

The first statement I desire to make is one that has long been on my mind, but one that I realized could not be made while Roosevelt lived without being regarded as a partisan effort to defend him. I want to put it on record here, as I have said in an earlier chapter, that of all the men in public life I have known and met during nearly half a century of active newspaper work, I can recall none more ready to listen to the views of others, more willing when convinced to put aside his own ideas, more ready to accept group judgment in preference to his own, than Theodore Roosevelt.

Following his return from Africa in 1910, I sat in numerous conferences called to determine the course he was to pursue—including his candidacy for the Republican nomination in 1912—and I was always amazed at the patience with which he discussed the various points of view urged and his own. Once you had his confidence you had an open sesame to his mind.

There were times, of course, when Roosevelt felt deeply on certain matters and stuck to his colors. Nor did he ever fail to state his views with vigor, and one had to be well equipped with facts and reasoning to gain the verdict over him in conference. When his own interests were solely at stake the Colonel felt that his own judgment should prevail.

HIS LAST TEN YEARS

I have said above that I consider the last ten years of Roosevelt's life—the out-of-power years—as his greatest. Perhaps I should qualify that statement by saying that to his friends they are the greatest. Those of us who were privileged to listen to him during those years felt like one thrilled by the warm radiance of a setting sun; how splendidly its strength and beauty shone out in the glow of its fading moments.

Roosevelt was no man to reminisce. He lived in today and tomorrow. His yesterdays served only the purpose of building up his tomorrows.

After his retirement from the Presidency in 1909, and particularly after 1912, he would often preface his talk by saying, "Now I am free to express my own opinions because I shall not be endangering anyone but myself." It was then that his friends heard Roosevelt at his best, and got the true measure of the man.

EVERYONE INTERESTED IN ROOSEVELT

Those seven years in the White House ending in 1909 had a fascination for the people that no other President was ever able to excite. I recall a popular cartoon of the period portraying the head of a household putting aside his breakfast table newspaper and calmly resuming his morning meal.

"My dear," says the astonished wife across the table, "the paper must be dull today."

"It is. Not a thing doing in the White House."

Everybody was keenly interested to know from day to day in what new direction their versatile President would turn his vigorous endeavors. Some had good reason anxiously to seek early information, but people generally indorsed and applauded each day's budget of news because they knew that the activities at the White House, whatever they might be, were directed toward one end.

There was one comment, however, frequently heard, that always angered Roosevelt—the talk that he was a militarist who would delight in forcing America into conflict with another nation. He resented that charge. His militarism was his belief that the way to avoid war is to be prepared and have others know you are prepared. In Chicago in 1903, he summed it up in the phrase "Speak softly, but carry a big stick, and you will go far." He repeatedly cited our peaceful relations with other countries during his Administration as proof that his policy was sound.

Probably no man assailed Roosevelt as a militarist more frequently than did Bryan. Now that both men have passed away, we find one lying, at his own request, in the modest burial ground of his home village, while the other, also at his own request, lies in a conspicuous sepulchre in Arlington Cemetery, Washington, among the brave men whose calling he had always condemned.

The Great Moment plumbs our deepest instincts. When you tapped those wells in Roosevelt you found home, family, his country and his friends. He rests beside them in death, and no martial glory intrudes.

"DON'T MOVE! WE'VE GOT IT"

Perhaps at this point is as good a place as any to tell the story of the John Singer Sargent painting of Roosevelt, now in the White House. The photograph of that painting is probably more familiar than any other of Roosevelt. It shows Roosevelt at the foot of a White House staircase with his elbow resting on the newel post, one hand toying with his watch chain, standing in contemplative mood as though about to state a conclusion that had for some moments baffled him. Such, in fact, is exactly what did happen; the masterful brush of Sargent caught the pose and put it on canvas from a true situation.

For two afternoons President and artist had vainly invaded every nook and corner of the White House for an appropriate place to serve as background. Pose after pose was tried in place after place, without satisfying either man. Roosevelt was not deeply concerned about it, but Sargent was. He wanted the real Roosevelt and he knew that the real Roosevelt could be revealed to him only in the right surroundings.

Roosevelt tired of the search, Sargent was eager to continue it; the painter's keen ambition, the President's thoughts of pressing duties, grated on the nerves of both men. Finally, as they descended the staircase shown in the painting Roosevelt stopped at the bottom, rested his elbow on the newel, and turning to his companion said hopelessly:

"Well, Sargent, we had better give it up. We're after the impossible."

"Don't move, Mr. President!" exclaimed Sargent quickly. "Don't move! We've got it!"

And they had.

DUG THE CANAL—THEN DEBATED ABOUT IT

Roosevelt believed in ideals, but he had no faith in ideals so vague as to be impossible ever to get beyond words and phrases,—impossible of practical application. He wanted results,—deeds not talk.

Take the Panama Canal, as an example. For years Congress had been debating how, when and where to dig a canal across the Isthmus. Even Mark Hanna with all his power and aggressiveness could not force action. The President wanted no more debate. He acted, and let Congress catch up with him.

So it was when he challenged the legality of the Northern Securities Company. There was much uplifting of hands that Roosevelt was leading the country into chaos, but the Supreme Court upheld him even against its own precedents. So, too, with the canal. The debaters in Congress first criticized, then wondered, then applauded and gladly paid the bills.

The Panama Canal is Roosevelt's big historic physical achievement. That is his own judgment of it. In view of his deep interest in it, I cannot understand why the Roosevelt Memorial committee has neglected to appropriate a portion of its funds for a memorial in the canal zone.

Somewhere on the highest mountain top, on each side of the Isthmus, there should be a tower of light to recall to voyagers in the Atlantic and the Pacific the man who made that great waterway a reality. The pending splendid plan for a monument to be located in Washington is not likely soon to become more substantial than a controversy with Congress. Of course, in time, Congress will act, but meanwhile there would be instant, cordial approval of a monument in the

THE NEWS REACHES BOGOTA—From the *Herald* (New York)

canal zone. Like the canal itself it would be built while the Washington enterprise is still being debated.

SENDING OUR BATTLESHIPS AROUND THE WORLD

The enterprise that won Roosevelt's heart was the triumphant voyage of our battleships around the world. He fairly thrilled over every incident as the cables brought the day to day news. It never ceased to interest him. Nothing delighted him more than to tell the story of his manœuvres to get funds for the trip. Nelson Aldrich, chairman of the Senate Finance committee, would not agree to an appropriation. For a time Aldrich was confident he had thwarted the President's plan.

"Loeb and I got to work on the job of digging up funds out of unexpended balances in different departments," Roosevelt once said to me. "We finally found enough money to take the fleet around South America to Japan and China— possibly a little further. It would then be half way around the world. I made up my mind to send the ships that far and then let Aldrich take responsibility for leaving them there at anchor or appropriate the funds to bring them back. I felt sure the country would not stand for ordering the ships back across the Pacific; Aldrich would have no option; he would have to bring them home by way of the Atlantic, which was exactly what I wanted.

"I had the same experience in other matters as in that affair. Once I acted instead of sitting around talking and pleading, I found all the support I needed. Aldrich and his committee of Senators, convinced that I was going ahead with the battleships, surrendered handsomely and the fleet sailed around the world, to be greeted everywhere in friendly spirit."

THE HOSTILE CORPORATION INFLUENCE

"More spying on the corporations" was the outcry when Roosevelt urged Congress to stop talking about establishing a Department of Commerce and Labor, and establish one. The need for such a Department had been obvious for a long time. Its creation was another Roosevelt achievement, gained over powerful opposition. Corporations could not understand why a President was not content with merely recommending; or why he wanted a Department with more than swivel-chair power. What sinister motive prompted him?

The usual "underground" opposition was exerted against the measure by corporation lobbyists at Washington, but they had to give way, finally, and on roll-call it had generous support from both political parties.

As I write of this incident, I am led to say that nine-tenths of the legislation to which banking interests and corporations object, and often spend large sums of money to defeat, prove of benefit to them. The Federal Reserve system is perhaps the most conspicuous example of a helpful measure that met the vigorous protests of New York bankers—yet the men who most strenuously opposed it are today its most ardent supporters.

The same story could be told of nearly every law affecting banks and corporations. The banker and the corporation head seem to distrust nothing so much as change; today they know, but tomorrow is a stranger to them; no matter how long the night may be, no matter how hopelessly they grope in darkness, they dread the dawn of a new day with new conditions.

CORTELYOU AND LOEB

The Department of Commerce and Labor, besides serving its purpose, brought two young men to the front who influenced the Executive Department of our national government far more than is generally known—George Bruce Cortelyou and William Loeb, Jr. The President made Cortelyou the first head of the new department. Loeb was made Secretary to the President, and, as in the case of Cortelyou, the title meant confidant and counsellor. Cortelyou had also been secretary to Cleveland and McKinley. Three Presidents, far apart in temperament and policies, depended upon him with equal confidence. Cabinet honors then came to him—first as head of the Department of Commerce and Labor, then as Secretary of the Treasury. Here was a reward for loyalty, industry and modest wisdom. It reflected no "pull,"—just a tribute to one who had served ably and well.

Loeb's experience in the White House did not cover as many years, but it was more intimate. He had been with Roosevelt while he was Governor of New York. No one ever knew every thought, purpose and mood of a President as Loeb knew Roosevelt's. He was in truth the President's other self;—he was the one man who could act for Roosevelt in full confidence that he was doing as the President would have him to do. There is not much in the Roosevelt administration that does not, in some way, bear the impress of Loeb's judgment. To his last years Roosevelt turned confidently to Loeb, though Loeb had gone out of public life and was well established in business. A career of helpful, energetic loyalty to his chief is now crowned with his own success.

ROOSEVELT'S GREATEST TRAIT

I have read many estimates of Roosevelt. I have read of his wonderful vitality, his tireless energy, his courage, his restless eagerness, the amazing extent of his knowledge of and interest in so many subjects—and, of course, it is all true. Indeed, the half has not been told.

The trait that most appealed to me was his loyalty to friendships. Commodore Stephen Decatur's famous toast to his country might well have been paraphrased by Roosevelt to read "My friends! May they always be in the right; but my friends right or wrong!"

More than once I was with Roosevelt in moments of keen personal disappointment, but never did he show the same deep regret over any happening to his fortunes as over evidence that one whom he called friend had turned on him.

And there were some who did.

Those wounds sank deep, though they left no vengeful scar. Where there was a separation it was the friend not Roosevelt who took the diverging path. It was not necessary to agree with him to hold his friendship. "My dear fellow," he would say, "it's bully of you—just bully—to come here and fight it out with me. You're a trump and a fine fellow but on this we don't see it the same way. We'll talk of something else."

Then would come a temptation to abandon your opinion

and accept his—a fatal mistake for one desiring to keep the Colonel's confidence. He never wanted anyone to surrender to him because he was President. He lost interest in those who sought his favor by not battling for an opinion of their own.

TEDDY THE WHOLE WORLD ROUND

I claim neither right nor ability to reveal more clearly than others have revealed the Roosevelt whose personality held the attention and admiration of the world through seven years in the White House. Wherever America was known in those years, Roosevelt was known; and what America meant in the minds of peoples, whether the people of Greenland's icy mountains or those of India's coral strand, there Roosevelt meant to them the same thing.

No other American was ever accepted so completely during his own time by the average man everywhere as a sympathetic, understanding leader as Roosevelt was accepted. He was Teddy the whole world round and the intimacy of that term in no degree lessened the universal faith in his endeavor to get a "square deal," so far as government could secure it, for the man who found it difficult to get one for himself.

THE WIDE CIRCLE OF HIS FRIENDSHIPS

I like to think of that wonderful friendship with Henry Cabot Lodge, lasting from young manhood, unchanging through all the vicissitudes of nearly forty years of political strife. It revealed the quality that seems to me the foundation of Roosevelt's greatness.

I like to read his favorite hymn, read at his funeral in that little village church from which he was buried. "How Firm a Foundation, Ye Saints of the Lord, is laid for your faith in His excellent word." In its inspiring lines I see the Roosevelt I knew and followed—firm in his faith in the Lord, firm in his faith in you, his friend.

As I Knew Them

Both Roosevelt and Lodge were big enough to tolerate differences of opinion that would have separated most men. Lodge kept out of the 1912 controversy, but he voted for Taft for President, and not for his friend Roosevelt. That was a vote of principle and Roosevelt respected it.

But Lodge was only one friendship. There were many, many others. There was Jacob Riis, a police news reporter for the New York Sun, who won Roosevelt's friendship in the early police department days, and kept it to the last; there was "Joe" Murray, a Republican district leader, who gave Roosevelt his start in politics and sent him to the New York Legislature; there was Father Curran, of Wilkesbarre, Penna.; there was Bill Sewall, the Maine guide; and "Bucky" O'Neill, from Arizona,—he of the Rough Riders who, near San Juan Hill, had boasted just a moment before he was killed that "no Spanish bullet was ever moulded to hit me."

Then there were the men who had ranched with him in the Dakotas; and Matthew Hale, of Boston, who had tutored his children before getting into politics; Dr. W. T. Hornaday of the Bronx Zoological Gardens, and John Burroughs, Charles F. McKim, Raymond Robbins, Booker T. Washington, Jane Addams and Sir Edward Grey, now Viscount Grey of Fallodon. Even the fierceness of the 1912 campaign did not lead Roosevelt into one word of dispraise of Senator Murray Crane, although the Senator was a relentless opponent.

High and low in politics, in the professions and in business were within that circle of friendships of infinite variety, and to each he gave something out of his incomparable personality that none could find elsewhere. •

AN ARCHBISHOP, AN EX-PRESIDENT AND AN EX-PRIZE FIGHTER

There is one incident of a score that could be told illustrating Roosevelt's contact with men in every walk of life.

One day in the summer of 1916 Roosevelt was lunching at

302

the Harvard Club. A friend had brought Archbishop Ireland there, confident that the Colonel would forget the clash he had had, while President, with the Archbishop.

Roosevelt saw the two men as they entered the club, and relieved Ireland's doubts as to his welcome; he rushed up to him, exclaiming "My dear Archbishop, I am delighted to see you again."

They sat down for a chat while awaiting lunch.

Soon a tall broadshouldered, bulletheaded figure approached.

Roosevelt had left word at the door to have him shown in when he called. The Archbishop was surprised to see him smile at the Colonel and offer to shake hands.

"Archbishop," said Roosevelt, "meet another good Irishman."

"John," turning to the visitor, "meet the Archbishop."

"Archbishop," continued the Colonel; "this is John L. Sullivan. He has fought many battles that I admire and an Archbishop cannot; but he has fought one battle that an Archbishop can admire—the battle with himself."

"If it had not been for you, Colonel, I never could have stopped drinking," interrupted Sullivan. "I used to think of you busy in the White House taking time to send word to me to keep up the fight, and seeing me there when I called. I couldn't drink with all that on my mind."

"I'm glad to shake hands with you on your last fight," said the Archbishop.

And an Ex-President, an Archbishop and a prize fighter sat there together!

THE ROOSEVELT I KNEW

There may be those who knew, or thought they knew, a different Roosevelt than the Roosevelt I knew; I have no quarrel with them. The Roosevelt I knew is the Roosevelt I am endeavoring to outline. I can speak only from my own experience. I ought to have a fair knowledge of the man, for I knew him as Police Commissioner; I stood with him when the battle of San Juan Hill opened that torrid July morning of 1898; I knew him as Governor and as President;—greatest of all, I knew him as citizen those last ten years of his life —the most potent, most purposeful voice in the country.

I never sought and he never offered me a favor except the favor of his friendship. My newspaper did not always approve his course; we held to our own opinions, but we never questioned the sincerity of his purpose. On some matters on which we differed I realized later that it is possible for editors to be wrong. The one request Roosevelt ever made of me was to support Taft for nomination in 1908. That I could not do. My paper was supporting Hughes. After Taft's nomination I gladly supported him.

CHAPTER XXXVII

TWO MEMORIES OF ROOSEVELT

Opening The San Juan Battle, And A Midnight Conference That Ended At Dawn With Decision For New Party—Munsey Pledges His Newspapers And His Fortune—Only One Inevitable End At Chicago—Never Made Decisions For Expediency's Sake—An Early Dream Of The White House—Harrison Introduces Him As "Impatient For Righteousness"—An Epoch In Himself—The One Title That In His Last Years He Desired.

MANY interesting memories live, of course, in the minds of all who had relations with Roosevelt. Two hold their place firmly with me. One was a midnight-to-dawn session in his bedroom, in the Auditorium Annex in Chicago, when George W. Perkins, Frank Munsey and I discussed with him the possibilities of the step that led to organizing the Progressive party.

What a night that had been! I never saw the Colonel so fagged; for hours his fighting blood had been at fever heat. It was not the crowd that tired him, for he could always handle a crowd, but a score of important party leaders one after another had discussed with him all phases of the serious situation.

The last one (I have forgotten his name) had dragged the Colonel into the bath-room and closed the door against intruders. He was another self-appointed emissary with a plan of compromise but with no authority except his own. Soon we heard a loud voice that all recognized; the door opened and the Colonel stepped out with a hurried, vigorous step that matched the wrath in his countenance.

The crowd had left the Colonel's apartment; their loud cheers and louder oratory still filled the corridors and lobby.

Four tired men sat on the bedside planning the strategy of the morrow. The Colonel leaned heavily and wearily against the headpiece, Perkins next to him and then Munsey. I sat at the foot.

While seated on that bedside, Perkins and Munsey urged the Colonel to go on with the third party fight. They pledged their fortunes—Munsey declaring with characteristic intensity: "My fortune, my magazines and my newspapers are with you." Even before that meeting Roosevelt had strayed far off the party reservation; yet the peril of going further, the doubt as to how the country would react to a bolt, loomed larger and larger. For more than an hour discussion went on; we saw the streaks of dawn as we separated with the Progressive party started on its earnest way.

ONLY ONE INEVITABLE END

Of course, there was no one moment, no one conference, when the one big decision was made. All that week every moment had been a moment of decision as to some phase of the exciting struggle, and all decisions pointed to one end.

Roosevelt members of the convention committees were abandoning the scheduled meetings; delegates and spectators in the convention were in constant riotous revolt, Hiram Johnson, the two Pinchots, Medill McCormick, Raymond Robbins, Bainbridge Colby, William Hamlin Childs, Chauncey Hamlin, William M. Chadbourne, "Bill" Flynn and all the Republicans of the corn-belt States were in hourly clashes with the Taft forces, and were straining at the leash with which the Colonel was holding them in line.

Against those influences, an influence more intimate and more potent than politics, was counselling the Colonel not to bolt. Until that midnight-to-dawn conference, it was still possible for him to turn back, and he would have welcomed a compromise eliminating both Taft and himself. No such terms were offered from the Taft side. The midnight discussion therefore settled the course to pursue. The one problem to which all minds were thereafter directed was how and when the new organization was to be brought into being.

After breakfast next morning William L. Ward, who had decided to remain "regular," made a last effort to persuade the Colonel to acquiesce in the Taft nomination. Not so much what he said as what his eyes and snapping jaws indicated made Ward quickly realize that something decisive had happened over night.

NEVER MADE DECISIONS FOR EXPEDIENCY'S SAKE

Many who condemned Roosevelt for his attitude in that campaign were astonished that an astute politician could have believed he could smash through his party organization and elect himself President. Such critics did not know Roosevelt. He never made decisions on the basis of expediency. He always searched for the right or wrong of a proposition, and decided accordingly. Nothing else influenced him in Chicago. The politics of the situation did not interest him; the unrighteousness of it did.

Roosevelt had no illusions about his candidacy. He never thought he would be elected. During one of my visits to Oyster Bay before the Progressive convention in August, he said: "Taft cannot win whether we go in or not; we cannot win. What we can possibly do is to poll more votes in States like New York than the Taft ticket and thus be recognized legally as the second party. With the Democrats we would then be entitled to a party column on the ballot. Thousands of Taft Republicans would flock to us. Let us keep this in mind as our objective, but don't let us ever again say to one another, or even think, that we are not going to win. You cannot fight hard unless you think you are fighting to win, and we must fight hard."

As I Knew Them

The other memory of Roosevelt still vivid takes me back to Cuba, in July 1898—on the knoll called Grimes' Hill, facing San Juan Hill and just in front of the cross-roads called El Pozo. It was called Grimes' Hill because the battery commanded by Captain Grimes had been placed there the night before, with Roosevelt's Rough Riders in support. Col. Samuel Sumner was in command.

I call them Rough Riders because that was the name the regiment had acquired before sailing for Cuba. History knows them only as Rough Riders. They were not Rough Riders at all in Cuba, for their horses were never brought over. Down there we called them Wood's Weary Walkers. Leonard Wood was the Colonel in command and Roosevelt was Lieutenant Colonel—hence the alliterative change. They were a wild lot, those Rough Riders. They did not know what discipline meant, though they knew how to fight.

It was not the intention to take San Juan Hill that day. The only orders from Shafter were to keep the Spaniards there busy by intermittent firing so that they would not send men to reinforce El Caney, a village several miles away, which Lawton and Chaffee had assured Shafter they could capture in an hour or two of fighting.

El Caney is a suburb to the north of Santiago while El Pozo is to the east.

But Lawton and Chaffee found they had a hard and bloody day's work ahead of them. Grimes' battery also found that the Spaniards on the hill could keep us busy, too.

Thus San Juan Hill and El Caney developed rapidly into a stiff battle for possession of both places.

That night our tropic-wearied troops had gained both objectives. They had had twelve hours of fighting, however, instead of one or two as Chaffee and Lawton had anticipated.

Roosevelt stood with Sumner and Grimes when the Battery

308

opened fire. I can see him now, looking thro' his field glasses and then pointing excitedly to different locations on San Juan. He was trying to detect how each shell landed in the Spanish trenches.

Not a shot came in reply from San Juan nor was there a visible sign of life, for 10 or 15 minutes after our first shells went whizzing over. Then a shell must have landed where it hurt, for bang! came a swift one in reply from a Spanish battery well concealed.

So long as our firing got no response, I was interested with Roosevelt and others in trying to locate just where each shell had landed, but when the Spaniards, having our range, began landing shrapnel "in our midst" I lost interest in the skill of our own gunners. With Colonel John Jacob Astor I accepted Sumner's hurried advice to "get out of this hell spot."

Astor and I found ourselves out of the shrapnel zone but in the rifle fire zone.

Finally we reached the narrow valley road already crowded like a sardine box with soldiers waiting delayed orders to move. They were under shell and rifle fire—and yet expected to stand still in an exposed road! It was at that point that Roosevelt made his memorable dash through the almost solid ranks, crossed the road and went up the opposite hill into the dense undergrowth behind which the Spaniards were entrenched. He had been ordered into action. That was my last view of him for the day. The heavy firing told me, however, that there was something doing where he had disappeared.

AN EPOCH IN HIMSELF

"T. R." was an epoch in himself—as much its dominant figure as were Washington and Lincoln in their day. He was all there was to his period, which began when he entered the White House as President and closed seven years later as he rode down Pennsylvania Avenue with Taft to install him as his successor!

I do not mean that the influence of Roosevelt ended then, for it still persists; it is to be found in many laws of recent years and conspicuously in the present desire of great wealth to seek the protecting power of government instead of defying it. The driving force of intense purpose behind his policies ceased, however, when he ceased to be President. As he said himself we may slip back a little now and then, but never to the old levels. The standards have been raised; those who thought their safety was in keeping them low now realize that a square deal for all is the best deal for all.

So it is that many of the things Roosevelt left undone are only now in the way of being done—much too slowly, it is true, yet inevitably. The mills of progress like the mills of the gods grind slowly—but they grind. Roosevelt lives in this slow, eventual development. And as public opinion drives government toward those ideals for which he stood,—his name will remain its symbol and its inspiration for great achievement.

Who is to interpret him? Not anyone of this day. His words and acts are his only interpreters and history must appraise them by the acid test of years.

LIKED THE CENTRE OF THE STAGE

No one could have associated with him without acquiring never-fading memories of a friendship that made you feel its helpful influence. There was a candor, earnestness and vigor about T. R., possessed to the same degree by no man I have ever met, and they were not withheld because of race or color or condition.

Yes—it is true that T. R. liked the centre of the stage— loved it in fact; but when he sought it he always had something to say or to do that made the centre of the stage the appropriate place for him. He preferred to talk to the galleries and against the narrower ideas usually held by those occupying orchestra seats.

There were strenuous, often boisterous times in the White House with T. R. But Roosevelt knew the powerful influences in and out of his party that had to be overcome, if his policies were to prevail, and he realized the futility of soft-stepping and whispered persuasion. He had no faith in "gum-shoe" methods. His faults were not those of secrecy and intrigue; Roosevelt worked in the open, with startlingly frank avowals of his purpose.

His first effort always was to reach the people. He believed that if he got the people he was certain to get the politicians. He worked on the theory that led Charles G. Dawes to punctuate his testimony before a Congress Committee, five years ago, with "Hell and Maria."

Dawes knew that what he said would be printed on the front pages of newspapers if peppered with "Hell and Maria," and on the back pages if merely a dry recital of facts, however important the facts might be. He had a message to get to the country; he deliberately chose the one way certain to get it before it. That was Roosevelt policy, too.

ALWAYS WORKED FAR AHEAD

Of course, I have heard a great deal about Roosevelt's "impulsiveness." On immaterial matters it is true that he was quick and sharp with his "yes" or "no," but he never made a decision of consequence without thoughtful consideration. He acted quickly when he acted; but he always had the matter well in hand before uttering a word or taking a step.

Take his speeches, for illustration. He made many speeches that aroused intense discussion; they were at times denounced as utterances of the moment, the outbursts of impatience. Yet no public man ever prepared his speeches so long in advance of delivery as Roosevelt; none ever gave them more careful revision. Those "impulsive" phrases which his opponents by their denunciation made popular, were the most deliberately thought out phrases of all, and usually got the reaction he anticipated.

Roosevelt's day was always well organized for work. He had no idle moments. At Oyster Bay "on vacation," he was either pulling an oar out on the Sound, laying an ax to a tree, or riding horseback. Then he had hours for reading, for writing and for visitors. He wrote laboriously, and revised so freely that it amounted almost to re-writing. This was especially true when he attempted to dictate. He disliked it and did it poorly.

His reading was almost wholly confined to books; he would go for days without looking at a newspaper. I doubt if all his newspaper reading for twenty years averaged over ten minutes a day. His home reflected his characteristics. You found there none of the ostentation of wealth. Books and trophies of his adventures were the outstanding features. The furnishings were of the kind you would expect in the average country home; there were no gilded sofas and chairs; no grand pianos with elaborate carvings, no rare tapestries and no liveried servants. When you crossed the threshold at Sagamore Hill you stepped into the warm, cordial atmosphere of a real home—the home of an American in spirit, in purpose and in ways. Hayes, Harrison, McKinley and Coolidge went from just such homes into the White House at Washington, and took with them the dignity of modest living and simple ways.

Roosevelt had no time for "leisure" as some persons call it. Idleness was the thing he most detested—unless it was the wealthy idler. He simply could not tolerate the man who could be of use to the world and yet refused to do his part. His persistent denunciation of the idle rich was often charged to "playing politics," but that was not true.

His motive was to drive them to work. To him life had a purpose; it ceased when purpose ceased. To live and to do nothing meant to be dead. The Colonel's leisure was not

found in wasting time but in changing his occupation. Every
hour counted—and yet I never heard him say he was tired.

AMAZED AT THE DEMANDS OF WEALTH

Roosevelt's long struggle against the power of the group
he characterized as "malefactors of great wealth," his determination to have government in the open instead of govern-

THEIR ONLY TEAM WORK

ment by invisible power, were prompted by evidences that
came to him in part while Governor of New York State but
in full in the White House. They revealed the methods,
the purposes and the arrogant attitude of corporate wealth.

The thing that amazed him most was the presumption by
influential men that as President he would accept their idea
that great wealth, corporate and individual, was to be cared
for and protected as something more sacred than government

itself. Roosevelt felt that the Presidency was a big enough office to deny that theory, and he determined to give it battle.

He fought to establish the supremacy of the government over every other influence, to put the interest of the people as a whole in advance of all other interests. To him con-servation meant not merely conservation of the nation's forests, waterways and other natural resources, but conservation of the government's power to command obedience to its statutes.

Wealth was blind to this theory of government; its big lawyers had taught it how to be "law honest" and yet do as it pleased; it regarded as heresy the Roosevelt theory that there must be teeth in the law so that "law honesty" would be "dishonesty."

We have not yet reached the millennium in "big business" ethics; we still have lawyers whose chief practice is in coun-selling restless wealth how to do what it wants to do and yet not find itself "out of bounds"; but we have made a good start in the right direction. Whatever advance has been scored had its beginning in the Roosevelt stand for a "square deal," and in the Roosevelt insistence that the best protection for wealth is its fair attitude toward others.

WHAT ROOSEVELT HAD IN MIND

No man who ever sat in the White House knew his America better than T. R. No man has ever responded with more vigor—to the inspiration of its traditions.

He visioned a nation born to strenuous endeavor and am-bitious purpose—a nation in which all would strive for the common good,—and when as the head of such a nation he had the power and saw the opportunity to mould its future to its birthright he eagerly, whole-heartedly set himself to the task. Always to do more, to learn more, to progress, were Roosevelt's aims in life, and as President he sought to make those aims his country's aims. His opponents did not dare attack his purpose, so they attacked his energy, his determined effort to accomplish. He wanted government to be purposeful; he wanted an equal share in its benefits for all—no favor, no fear, no power behind the throne. The good and the bad that he found at Washington were used as a skilled workman sorts his materials—he found some good even among the poorest material, and did not hesitate to use it; he found some bad even among the best material and did not hesitate to discard it. Often it was thought that Roosevelt discarded too much, but when the facts came to light it was found that he had made an accurate estimate of the men whom he had thrust aside.

"IMPATIENT FOR RIGHTEOUSNESS"

President Harrison once introduced Roosevelt to an audience by saying good-naturedly:

"He is a young man, impatient for righteousness. He wants everything done before nightfall; some of us can wait until tomorrow."

Elijah Halford, Harrison's Secretary, later corrected this characterization of Roosevelt to read:

"He is a young man impatient with unrighteousness" which to my mind is more fitting.

All this was said of Roosevelt while he was Governor of New York.

Harrison, it may be remembered, gave Roosevelt his first national job—President of the Civil Service Commission. He always had a high regard for Roosevelt. He applauded his earnestness, rejoiced in his integrity, but constantly counselled him against trying to put the whole government under civil service regulation at one fell swoop.

ROOSEVELT'S EARLY DREAM OF THE WHITE HOUSE

Seated on the porch at Sagamore Hill with Roosevelt one afternoon in 1911, our talk went back to the period before

1893 while he was serving in the Harrison Administration. I had spoken to him of the possibility of a popular call for him to succeed Taft. "This is the only spot on earth for me," he said. "I am never satisfied away from here. You don't live in the White House. You are only Exhibit A to the country. I've had seven years of it and I know. I admit that I once felt differently about it—very differently.

"I recall that in those Harrison years as I passed the White House every day to and from my office, the thought often came to me that possibly some day I would occupy it as President. Of course it was only a dream. I had no more reason for it than has every other American citizen. Still, it thrilled me even to think of it as a possibility. Well, I did occupy the White House and now I have no feeling but one of gladness that it is over. The thrill was justified in its day; the absence of it is justified now. It has no lure for me.

"It isn't how long you are President that counts, but what you accomplish as President. I've had my chance; I did fairly well with it. I made some kind of a place in history for myself. Someone else might have done better than I did, but I could not, for I did my best. I might not do as well if I were to go in again—unless, possibly, I went in to do some one definite thing, greatly needed by the country. Nothing of that kind is in sight.

"There is no demand for me except possibly the demand of the party for a candidate who can win. There are half a dozen men who come under that heading. No—I've had the title of President once—having it twice means nothing except peril to whatever reputation I achieved the first time."

THE TITLE HE DESIRED IN LATER YEARS

A moment's pause before Roosevelt spoke again.

"Do you know the only title that appeals to me now?" he asked.

"I suppose it is 'Colonel'?" I ventured.

As I Knew Them

"Yes,—there's a lot in that title for me," he said. "I like it. But if I were asked what title I would prefer it would not be President nor Colonel; it would be Major General in the U. S. Army in active service. Remember I say active service—no swivel chair for me. Active service, however, is not likely to come in my day, so I suppose 'Colonel' I'll remain to the end. That's good enough.

"After all, what's in a title? A lieutenant—Lieut. Wm. L. Worden—commanded the Monitor when it made that historic fight against the Merrimac. How many people know or care whether he was Lieutenant or Admiral? He had a job to do and he did it well. Ericsson, who designed and built the Monitor, will always be remembered. He had no title. It's the deed and not the title that counts.

THE PATRIOT'S RESPONSE!

"Just keep it in mind though, should a war come while you and I are still around, that the one thrill I shall have will be to be Major-General in active service!"

War did come. The thrill for service took complete pos-

317

session of him; denial of opportunity undoubtedly was the most depressing disappointment of his life. He could give his four sons to the battle line—but his own service was rejected. I have seen Roosevelt take several disappointments,—things that hurt him deeply,—but not all of them together affected him so deeply as that.

After the last of his sons had sailed for the other side he said to me "there's a chance if the war lasts long that none of them will see me here when they return. There's a greater chance that I shall never see all of them again. One or more is likely to stay over there. I rejoice that they've gone; I wouldn't keep one of them back. But what would I give to know that we are all to be together again some day at dear old Sagamore."

CHAPTER XXXVIII

"MY LAST MILE AS A CAMPAIGNER"

When Roosevelt Closed His Tour For Hughes, He Declared He Was Through With Presidential Stump-Speaking—"I've Done My Bit," He Said—Looking Ahead To 1920 He Declared, "I Shall Not Be The Candidate!"—His Conviction That He Would Have A Hard Time Fighting For Health During His Early Sixties—A Midnight Motor Ride To Oyster Bay.

"OLD trumps, let me tell you something that will interest you—I'm finishing with you tonight my last Presidential campaign. I've done my 'bit' for Hughes; I am not going to tour for any future Presidential candidate; I don't know how many thousands of miles I had travelled across country when I closed in Philadelphia tonight, but I know it marked my last mile as a campaigner. I've done my full share of it; I am now entitled to go on the exempt list. I am positively through campaigning forever."

Theodore Roosevelt was the speaker. It was late October 1916—late in every way. He had arrived at the Pennsylvania station in New York city, after midnight, and we were motoring to Sagamore Hill, reaching there about 3 A.M. Before his Academy of Music speech in Philadelphia that night, he had telephoned to George W. Perkins that he was anxious to get home, that he would insist upon an early speech so as to catch a 10 o'clock train, if anyone in New York city would be good enough to arrange for a motor car to take him to Sagamore. Perkins thought the Colonel should not go alone.

Turning to me he said he would go if I were game also for

a midnight ride. I replied "dee-lighted"—and both of us met the Colonel.

We motored through a Long Island night fog to Oyster Bay.

ROOSEVELT'S DREAD OF HIS EARLY SIXTIES

Almost two years later—in September or October, 1918—I asked Roosevelt if he recalled his talk about no more campaigning, the night we motored to Oyster Bay.

"Of course I remember it," he replied, surprised at my inquiry. "Every word of it. I'll refuse to campaign even should the candidate personally ask me!"

"Well, you will have to refuse yourself then in 1920," I replied, "for you are going to be the candidate!"

"By George, I'm not!"

"There's no one else," I insisted. "The party, in fact the country, is turning to you. It's a unanimous call, Colonel. I hear it now."

"I hear just as much of it as you do and probably more," replied Col. Roosevelt. "It's all right, let it go on. It is well enough to have the anti-Wilson sentiment rally around me. But I tell you again that I shall never make another campaign tour nor shall I be the candidate. Of course, I shall make no public announcement now, but I will do so long enough before 1920 to get out of the way of anyone who wants the nomination."

"Why, Colonel," I insisted. "You are now the leader of the Republican party—you cannot get away from it."

"Yes, I can. I'm a tired man. Let me tell you I shall have trouble 'bucking' my early sixties. If I can get by them I can keep going for a fair number of years. My danger, though, is right in the next few years. At 56 I never should have undertaken that South American trip. It just put the jungle fever into me when I was too old to fight it out of myself quickly. It is in my system yet. I've got to buck it for four or five years before I shall be rid of it. Then I'll be myself again. That is why I am not going to do any more campaigning. Put that down as settled. Let the talk go on, let the party rally around me, if it will, for the present. We must organize to fight Wilson. I'll help in that work. I am not saying anything about 1920. Let 1920 take care of itself when it comes—but I shall not be the candidate."

And he gave a characteristic emphasis to the "not" that led me to understand that back of his decision he had more reason than he was acknowledging.

That was the last talk I had with Roosevelt—the last time I was in his presence until I stood in the Oyster Bay church as his flag-draped coffin was carried up the aisle.

A MIDNIGHT MOTOR RIDE HOME

On that night motor ride in 1916 the Colonel, though tired, was in fine spirits. We plunged through a Long Island fog too fast for safety, while he kept telling stories of campaign experiences. Suddenly our car stopped on the country road so that the chauffeur could clean his windshield of fog. Up stood the Colonel in the car.

"Fellow citizens," he shouted, "fellow citizens of" ——

Then he turned to Perkins and said: "George, where under the sun—no, where in this devilish fog are we?"

"Glen Cove or thereabouts," said Perkins.

"Oh, yes—Fellow citizens of Glen Cove or thereabouts, I am here tonight to say to you" ——

By that time the chauffeur had removed some of the fog banked on his windshield and started the car—the Colonel sat down. In fact, he came down with a crash.

CHAPTER XXXIX

WHEN ROOSEVELT SAID "TAFT"

Loeb Shows Him The Need For Stopping The Drift And Insuring Control Of The Convention—Elihu Root Thanks Roosevelt But Declines To Be A Candidate—Taft, Surprised, Says, "I Must Go In And Thank Theodore For This"—Why Roosevelt Remained Silent—Determined To Be An Effective President To His Last Day—Foraker Demands Of The President Equal Respect For A Senator—"Joe" Cannon Eases A Tense Moment.

ONE morning in January, 1908, President Roosevelt looked up from his breakfast table in the White House to find William Loeb waiting quietly.

"By George, Loeb," he declared, "what brings you here and how long have you been here?"

¡"Only a few moments," Loeb replied. "I'm here because I want to talk with you before you go over to the office. I want to talk about the national convention."

"What's the matter with the convention—except that it's a long ways off?" asked Roosevelt.

"The matter is that if things drift along as now our friends may lose control of it; if that occurs there will be charges that you would like to have been the nominee but couldn't get the delegates, or that you backed this or that defeated candidate. I don't think that's a good prospect. It puts you in an equivocal position and it should not go on any longer."

"It hasn't impressed me that way," replied Roosevelt, "but you may be right. What do you suggest?"

"Have a candidate," said Loeb. "You are under pledge not to run again. I propose to make people understand that you intend to keep it. Some people believe that a deadlocked convention might force you to disregard it. Others believe you will demand a nomination anyhow, and that you are manipulating things so as to force a deadlock. The air is full of such talk. The way to settle is to have a candidate."

SEE ROOT, SAID ROOSEVELT

"Do you know the man I'd like to see here as my successor?" asked the President.

"I do not," replied Loeb.

"Elihu Root. He's made a great record over in the State Department, and would make an equally great one in the White House. I would be for him against all comers, but I'm told he couldn't be elected."

"What does Root think about it?" asked Loeb.

"I don't know," replied Roosevelt.

"Well, you have Taft and Hughes to consider, too," Loeb continued.

"Yes, and Cortelyou as well. He's in my Cabinet and is anxious to get the nomination. You see it's embarrassing when there are rivals in your own household. Now, whenever I've talked Taft to our friends I have had a battle. He is not strong with the men closest to this Administration. I don't understand it. I think he would run well; they say not. We must above all else get a man who can win."

"Any nominee can win," replied Loeb, "if you back him— Taft, Root, Hughes, or Cortelyou. That's my judgment."

"Well, then, you see Root; have a frank talk with him; tell him what I have said to you, tell him what you think, and let us get his idea. Of course, if we can't get Root we must agree on someone else—Taft is the next best, probably; but see Root."

That same morning, when Secretary of State Elihu Root walked into his office, he was surprised to find William Loeb there. Like Roosevelt he asked him why.

323

"I've been talking with the President about the convention, insisting that we ought to straighten things out," said Loeb. "We ought to have a candidate. He authorizes me to say to you that he would rather see you in the White House than any other man, and that he is ready to endorse you."

ROOT SAYS NO

If Elihu Root is ever surprised by anything he sees or hears his imperturbable countenance rarely shows it. But it did that morning. His face plainly reflected surprise and pleasure.

"That's very fine of him," he said. "Please tell the President I appreciate deeply every word of it, but I cannot be a candidate."

"Why not?" asked Loeb. "This Administration will control the convention and can name the candidate."

"Undoubtedly you can nominate me," replied Secretary Root. "You couldn't elect me—there's the rub."

"This Administration is strong enough with the people to elect the man it gets behind," persisted Loeb. "That's all bunk that you cannot be elected. Your record here will elect you."

"No, Loeb, I've thought it all out. I know the situation. I shall not be a candidate."

"Is that final?" asked Loeb.

"Absolutely final," replied Root. "Thank the President most cordially for me, but tell him I'm not in the running."

Back to the White House and to the President's offices went the diligent Loeb.

He cut short the President's callers, and got down to business.

"Root is out of it," he reported to his chief. "He won't take it—says he couldn't be elected."

As I Knew Them

"I've been thinking it over since you left," said the President. "You have the right idea—we must have a candidate. We had better turn to Taft. He has the experience. See Taft and tell him of our talk this morning, tell him all of it so he will know my mind all the way through."

An hour or so later, Secretary of War Taft was closeted in the White House offices with Roosevelt's energetic private secretary. He was frankly told of the breakfast table talk, and the President's conclusion.

"The President feels that he wants to settle this nomination matter right away, so far as he is concerned," said Loeb. "He is going to throw the whole strength of the Administration back of you. This talk about his getting into the race is all nonsense. The only way to stop it is for him to declare for a candidate and he has decided to declare for you."

"I must go in and thank Theodore for this," said Taft. "Also I want to send a message to my brother. He's anxious, of course, to know every development in my campaign."

"No messages to anyone," interrupted the cautious Loeb. "Let this thing take its own course. Let us first talk it over with the President. It will be time enough then to settle the next step."

By this time the President had left the executive offices for lunch. Taft and Loeb joined him afterward.

"Yes, Will," said Roosevelt. "It's the thing to do. Our friends should control the convention; we don't want any uncertain note sounded there. We've all talked about candidates long enough; it's time for a decision. I'm for you, and I shall let it be known right away. That's as far as I can personally go. I cannot get into the detail of it. My suggestion to you is to put yourself in Loeb's hands from now on. He knows the politics of this country as well as anyone I

325

can think of; I can lighten up on him, and give him the time so that you two can work together."

That, to state it briefly, is how William Howard Taft came to know definitely that Theodore Roosevelt had ceased to be merely favorably disposed toward his ambitions to be President and had decided to make him his candidate for the nomination.

WHY ROOSEVELT WAS SILENT

For months before the Loeb talk Roosevelt was puzzled as to the best course to pursue. He was not going to accept another term—that much had long been settled. It was settled by the statement issued by him the night of his election in 1904; it was settled as certainly by his own desire, shared most emphatically by his family, to return to Sagamore Hill, there to enjoy a career as private citizen. He knew of the Jonathan Bourne plan in Oregon to nominate him for a "second elective" term; he heard much similar talk from others.

Neither was he unaware of the insistence by his opponents, in and out of the Republican party, that he was killing off other candidacies to insure his own nomination. When I say that he knew of such talk I mean that he knew of it in the shadowy way that gossip reaches a President, unless an alert secretary like Loeb decides that the President should have full information. That is why Loeb had that historic breakfast conference.

Those in Roosevelt's confidence had no doubt of his purpose as to himself. They knew that he felt under no obligation to reiterate what he had said in 1904; in the absence of any public withdrawal or modification he expected his friends to accept his statement as it stood. His opponents would treat a reiteration as skeptically as they were treating the original announcement. So he allowed the record to stand as it was.

THE CROWN PRINCE

As I Knew Them

He insisted that the more intimate side concerning his own desire to get back home after seven years of the White House did not deeply interest the public. Moreover, it seemed ungracious and perhaps ungrateful to advance his personal desire as a controlling reason for leaving the Presidency.

None the less it was his plan to take himself entirely out of the storm area of life. His strong desire for a public career had always had as a rival his longing for literary renown; he had a passion for both. Having satisfied the first with the rounding out of his term as President, the old love for the pen asserted itself.

He would write, lecture, put into permanent form the experiences of his career, and interpret world-events.

That thought was, in fact, the basis of his arrangement with the "Outlook"—a magazine that was selected by him because it had no partisan ties and stood high in public confidence.

He had thought it all out most carefully during those final days in the White House. There was not a doubt in his mind of his future. For a year or more he was to hide himself away in the African wilderness. By the time he emerged into civilization the new administration would have definitely shaped its policies, most of the patronage would have been distributed and Roosevelt would have escaped the demands which he could not have wholly ignored had he remained within reach. His "Outlook" series and his story of his African hunt would of themselves keep him too busy to think of politics.

Thus he planned while in the White House; thus he dreamed as he trekked across the game trails of Africa; it was not until he reached Egypt that he heard—then only faintly—the first murmurings of the storm that was ultimately to beat so violently about his own head. But in 1908 all that he saw ahead of him was a period at Sagamore during which he was to be a care-free citizen and he rejoiced at the prospect.

DID NOT WANT TO FADE AWAY

Roosevelt had another reason for silence. He was determined not to fade away as President. He wanted his Administration to remain 100 per cent effective until the last moment of his term; he would then be able to hand over a "going" concern to his successor. He knew that as a President approaches the "ex" period, his influence with Congress and party leaders dwindles. Only the old Guard of loyalists for loyalty's sake remain to the end. The dawning day always reveals a majority eagerly scanning the horizon for its new figure.

Many were now waiting for that dawn, eager to seize control of the party organization the moment Roosevelt's hand was lifted from the helm and to thwart him in every way. There were measures pending in Congress that he desired to have enacted into law while he was yet in the White House. Moreover, there was the approaching national convention. He was determined it should give whole-hearted indorsement to his Administration, should declare for a continuance of his policies and nominate a candidate committed to them.

Thus buttressed by platform and candidate, Roosevelt was confident that the effectiveness of his Presidency would remain unimpaired to the end. He would go out of office with a record of seven full years of achievement, and his friends would be in control to "carry on."

In his opinion, that prospect would be imperilled if he silenced rumor as to himself,—in a word if he took himself out before some candidate friendly to the policies of his Administration seemed likely to go in.

As I Knew Them

That was the picture Roosevelt visioned in the early days and weeks of 1908. It was not the picture some of his supporters saw; they painted a different picture to him—some of them so often that he grew impatient over the challenge of his judgment. They didn't believe in silence or in Taft,—to whom he was not then committed—as insurance against the condition he dreaded. Nevertheless he persisted.

The Republican national committee in Washington in December, after fixing Chicago, June 16, 1908 as the place and time of the convention, called upon him in a body, formally. Not a word of encouragement did they get that the 1904 declination had ceased to have force. A modifying word, even a hesitant manner, would have sent them home yelling "Four Years More of Teddy." Some enthusiasts returned to their States uttering that popular cry, concededly without authority.

Southern Republicans were practically a unit in advocacy of another term. They insisted that Roosevelt could carry several Southern States. As Roosevelt admitted in a talk I had with him at the time and printed later in this book, there was a temptation in the prospect of breaking the Solid South. But it did not outweigh other considerations. So Roosevelt's mind dwelt upon Root and Taft.

Governor Hughes was in the field backed by New York Republicans; Vice President Fairbanks was actively picking up delegates in Indiana and neighboring States; George Cortelyou had important backing from national committeemen controlling many delegates; Uncle Joe Cannon, then Speaker of the House, was projecting himself into the situation as an anti-Roosevelt candidate; Philander C. Knox had Pennsylvania, La Follette had Wisconsin and Senator Foraker was disputing Ohio with Taft. But with Roosevelt silent, no decisive strength was possible for any candidate.

As I Knew Them

That was a stirring winter around the Capitol. Cannon in private talk was more and more openly denouncing Roosevelt's policies; insurgent Republican Congressmen were desperately struggling against Uncle Joe's Czar-like grip on Committees and on legislation; the Senate, with La Follette as the insurgent leader, had begun to show evidences of a determination to supplant the House as the place of endless debate. Everybody seemed to be in a restless, impatient mood.

The Gridiron Club dinner typified the spirit then prevailing. The President was the guest of honor; J. Pierpont Morgan, Henry H. Rogers, George F. Baker, and other men of the financial and business world were present. Roosevelt and Senator Foraker had had their falling out, and a good deal of feeling was known to exist between them.

Roosevelt's speech was a lecture to Senators for their lack of respect for the Executive branch of government. As we listened we realized that his words were becoming more and more centered on Foraker, then strongly opposing the Administration. At the beginning of each sentence we felt certain that Foraker would be named before the end. He stopped just short of doing so. Foraker was the next scheduled speaker. His seat was at the far end of one of four tables extending like a gridiron from the presiding officer's table where Roosevelt and other guests of the Club were seated.

Foraker's face glowed with anger while Roosevelt was speaking; he was less stirred when he himself took the floor. At first he spoke in quiet tones, plainly under restraint; step by step he advanced up the aisle toward the guests' table until he stood directly in front of Roosevelt. When within a dozen feet of him—in fact, it seems to me now that only the table separated them—he pointed his finger at the President and with the emphasis of passion said:

"I want to say in this presence that I have great respect for the

330

high office of President of the United States—no American has
greater respect for it—but I want to say also to the President of
the United States that I demand that he should have equal respect
for the chosen representatives in the Senate of the sovereign States
of the Union."

Foraker walked slowly back to his seat.

A tense silence followed. All eyes centered on the President, whose countenance by now showed the anger he, too, felt. We wondered what he would do or say. Someone must relieve the tension—but how?

"JOE" CANNON EASES A TENSE MOMENT

The Chairman looked about him as one looks for a life-saver. He saw Uncle Joe Cannon puffing a cigar. Cannon seemed more at ease than any other person. Perhaps he could pour oil on the troubled waters! The Chairman decided to try him. I happened to be seated at Cannon's right. Surprised that he should be called upon, Cannon turned to me and asked:

"What in hell can I say about this mess?"

It was well that he did not wait for my reply, for I could make none worth while. Uncle Joe slowly unwound his long, angular form, bit a little harder on his cigar, and by the time he was standing at full length was ready with his speech.

"Now, fellows," he said, "we all think we're mighty important and that this old globe would stop spinning around if we weren't here to keep it moving. The truth is, though, that if at this instant we should have an earthquake and the earth should open up and should swallow this whole roomful of us, big fellows as we think we are, the morning papers would publish a list of those missing—and the world would go on turning and we would be forgotten. So what's the use of getting excited!"

That ended Cannon's speech and the tension. Everybody laughed and the Chairman resumed the regular order.

CHAPTER XL

THE STRUGGLE TO NOMINATE TAFT

"I Can't Understand This," Said Roosevelt When He Found His Choice Of Taft Criticized—"It's Taft Or Me!" He Finally Declared —Cortelyou Warns Him To Prepare Himself For A Different Life After The Presidency—The Taft Brothers, Eager For Delegates, Raid New York—Roosevelt Told He Will Have Responsibility Without Power—Let The Party Pick Its Own Candidate—The Tafts Always Suspicious Of Roosevelt—A Scene While Taft Was Being Nominated.

IT WAS shortly after the decision for Taft that George Cortelyou, then Secretary of the Treasury, discussing future plans with Roosevelt asked him if he was prepared for the great change shortly to come in his life.

"Next March 4," said Cortelyou, "you will ride up Capitol Hill with all the power of office; a moment later you will ride down that same hill stripped of power. Such a change is a tremendous test for any man, but for you, Mr. President, with your temperament, it is going to be especially hard and I wonder if you are getting yourself in the frame of mind for it."

"I have never thought of it!" exclaimed Roosevelt.

"Better get yourself ready for it," warned Cortelyou. "Once you are out of office, you will miss the opportunities to push policies, you will miss the power of the White House, you will miss all the activities that have made your life here so full. That's a side of your future that you ought to prepare for. If you do it will be easier when you have to face it."

"I intend to live in an entirely different atmosphere when I leave here," replied Roosevelt. "I am not going in for politics. Should I ever do so, it would be only in the broadest sense, entirely divorced from any personal motive. I've made

332

up my mind to go in for the things I like and have neglected. I've had my day and I know it."

"IT'S TAFT OR ME"

He turned to the task of creating a day for Taft. The response to that candidacy, following Roosevelt's announcement, was not as anticipated. Protests by letter and in person flowed into the White House. Though Loeb was watching the election of delegates, the President found that, despite his February statement to Taft that he could not personally get into the situation, it was necessary for him to do so. Cecil Lyon, boss of Texas, (whom Taft in 1912 unseated in the national convention), John G. Capers, of South Carolina, as well as many western leaders declared against the President's choice.

"I don't understand this," said Roosevelt, puzzled, after talking with a protesting State leader. "They don't seem to know Taft as I know him. I've got to explain him to nearly all of our fellows."

In order to force every possible delegate to Taft, two courses were followed by the President in his talks. To the reactionaries he would declare "It's Taft or me," which sent them scurrying to Taft. To Progressives he would declare "It's Taft—I'm out!" whereupon most of them reluctantly accepted Taft.

There was not an act or thought in the White House not wholly dedicated to Taft's nomination. Unfortunately this attitude was too whole-souled and unselfish to be comprehended in Cincinnati and New York city. In the minds of Taft's relatives in those two cities, suspicion stalked around every new evidence of Roosevelt's helpfulness, though one test after another brought the same response of strength for Taft.

Finally, Taft's brothers decided to raid New York and take as many delegates as possible from Hughes. William Barnes and William L. Ward led the bolt from Hughes. Ten delegates for Taft resulted. Candidates seldom go into the home States of their rivals, and Roosevelt did not approve of the policy. In January he had persuaded Taft to address a letter to Herbert Parsons stating that he would not seek to "divide in my interest the delegates from any State which has a candidate of its own." As usual, however, Taft's "court of appeals" overruled him. The raid on New York was made, though Taft then had more than enough delegates to nominate. Roosevelt again cautioned that he should not embitter his rivals. "You will need Hughes in the campaign," he said. "Better let him alone in New York; fight him as hard as you can elsewhere."

This wise counsel for which there should have been thanks to Roosevelt was regarded as a sign of weakening support, and at once the Taft camp was flooded with new suspicion.

T. R. WARNED OF RESPONSIBILITY WITHOUT POWER

I had an encounter with Roosevelt on the matter of candidates about a month before the convention. My newspaper in New York was supporting Hughes, then Governor. I sincerely hoped he would be nominated. After luncheon at the White House one afternoon, the President asked me why I did not switch from Hughes. I had no reason to desert the Governor of my State and my own personal choice, though I knew Loeb had captured some of the New York delegates for Taft.

"Your newspaper ought to be for Taft," said Roosevelt.

"No, Mr. President," I replied. "We're for Hughes. He's our Governor. He would make a fine President. We're going to stand by him to the end."

"Of course you know what the end will be?" asked Roosevelt, with the vigor of impatience in his voice.

"Oh, I suppose you will nominate Taft. There is nothing against Taft. But New York has its candidate, and I think we should stick by him."

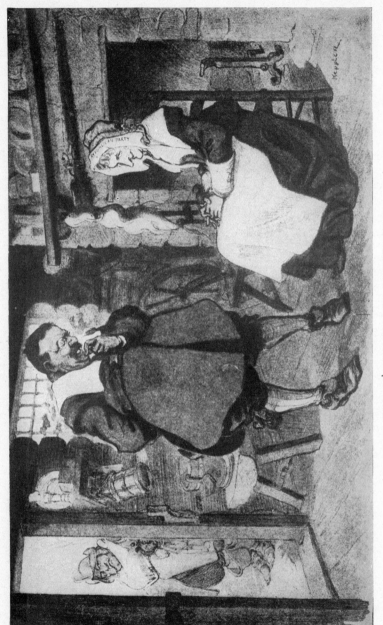

WHY DON'T YOU SPEAK FOR YOURSELF, JOHN

"There's more red blood in Taft's little finger than in Hughes' whole body," said Roosevelt. "If you knew Taft better you would realize it and switch to him."

"I shall not switch—that is impossible, Mr. President. I am going down with the ship. It's a good ship and if your hand were not on the convention Hughes would land the prize."

"You're wrong," he replied. "Do you know whom we have most trouble in beating! Not Hughes—but Fairbanks! Think of it—Charley Fairbanks! I was never more surprised in my life. I never dreamt of such a thing. He's got a hold in Kentucky, Indiana and some other States that is hard to break. How and why is beyond me. It is easier to win delegates away from Hughes right in New York than to win them away from Fairbanks in those States."

"LET THE PARTY PICK ITS OWN CANDIDATE"

"Mr. President," I said, "I recall that you once told me you liked to hear the truth, even an unpleasant truth, and so I am going to say to you that I do not believe you should pick the nominee of the convention. Let the party pick its own man. It may make a mistake. If it does it will be the party's mistake—not yours.

"If you are going to name anybody name yourself," I added—"You have a clear right to do that."

"I'm not in it," he interrupted.

"Then why not let the candidates fight it out?" I continued. "You are running a risk in naming a candidate. The party has done pretty well up to date in its selections—certainly well enough to be permitted to try it once more. You now take over the function of the convention, and you put yourself in a position of responsibility for the Administration the next four years without the power to see to it that it makes good.

"You will be criticized for every move Taft makes, and ex-

335

pected to correct it. The 'I-told-you-so's' will be the biggest crowd you ever listened to. Better let the convention find its own candidate and take responsibility for his course as President. It may pick Taft. I am not speaking against Taft. I am urging you not to take the responsibility when you are not to have the power. Better leave it to the convention."

ROOSEVELT HEARS THE "I-TOLD-YOU-SO'S"

All this was not listened to without interruptions, without signs of impatience, but I got my thought well into his mind.

"The trouble is that we have no one who fits the bill like Taft," he said. "The fellows don't like Hughes."

"Then the convention will select Taft," I replied. "That will be all right and much better than if you select him for the convention—better for Taft and better for you."

"You're an impossible man today," remarked the President as he ended the talk. "Come and see me after the convention."

[Let me here for a moment jump ahead to 1910. Soon after his return from Africa Colonel Roosevelt asked me if I remembered our talk at the White House about the Taft nomination.

I said I did.

"I do, too," he added. "It came to my mind one night over in Africa. You were right. It would have been better had I kept out of it. The 'I-told-you-so's' are as thick as leaves."]

WHY HE TURNED FROM HUGHES

"Let's talk a little politics," said Roosevelt to William R. Willcox after luncheon in the White House just before the 1908 convention. "I suppose you are for Hughes." Willcox was then chairman of the New York Public Service Commission. He had been Postmaster.

336

"I don't know that Hughes is seeking the nomination," replied Willcox. "Personally, I don't see why you should not be the candidate. I take no stock in that third term talk."

"I could be nominated all right," said the President, "but I do not know that I could be elected. If the third term tradition would not defeat me, my letter would. So that's settled. I have a high opinion of Hughes. He had a fine programme of legislation in his early days as Governor, and for some time I believed he would develop into a splendid candidate for President. So much did I think of him in that way that I said to Mrs. Taft less than a year ago that as much as I thought of Will, it might be that I would feel it my duty to be for Hughes. But Hughes got into the hands of the 'Evening Post' crowd in New York city and he also made public announcement that he did not want any assistance from here. That released me from considering him any longer. So now it's going to be Taft or me."

ALWAYS SUSPICIOUS OF ROOSEVELT

Willcox was not the only visitor at the White House whom Roosevelt found indifferent to or opposed to his choice of candidate. Loeb, however, kept pounding away at every delegate to declare for Taft. As one after another did so, the sigh of relief from Cincinnati was coupled with dread that the next delegate to speak would reveal a subtle Roosevelt plot.

Apparently, Taft himself was the one member of his family capable of believing that any man would relinquish the Presidency to another. The challenge of Roosevelt's sincerity never left the minds of those close to Taft until Senator Lodge as presiding officer of the convention formally declared Taft the nominee.

If Roosevelt learned of these suspicions, he kept his information to himself and went ahead with his plans to make

Taft certain. He made doubly sure to thwart a stampede in the convention. Few persons ever knew that he had the most expert White House telegrapher stand immediately back of Chairman Lodge prepared to flash a message from Lodge to the White House should a Roosevelt uprising seem imminent. Instantly the President would have imperatively demanded that his name be withdrawn.

I am sure, however, that had a stampede ever begun, it would have accomplished its purpose too quickly even for a telegram to interrupt it. The spirit of the convention was wholly Rooseveltian. Omit the demonstration whenever Roosevelt was named and the convention was distressingly dull. The delegates had no keen interest except in the man in the White House. Lodge, in the chair, knew that in the circumstances Roosevelt should not be named; also he knew the peril if someone put a lighted match to the powder.

One of the greatest demonstrations over Roosevelt came just before the roll call on nomination. Lodge watched closely and was tempted to telegraph Roosevelt for the message agreed upon. Finally, he decided to wait until Massachusetts was called, when the delegation cast a solid vote for Taft. That settled the stampeders. Roosevelt's closest friend and confidant was against them. Ten minutes later Taft was the convention's nominee.

WHILE TAFT WAS BEING NAMED

Joseph Bucklin Bishop, in his "Presidential Nominations and Elections" has an illuminating picture of a scene elsewhere while Roosevelt and Lodge were watching the convention as one watches a dam hard pressed by floods. Here is part of it:

> I remained with the President till about 4 P. M., when I went to the War Department, on personal invitation of Secretary Taft,

and was admitted at once to his private office, in which he was sitting with his wife, daughter, younger son Charlie and a half dozen or more personal friends.

Mrs. Taft sat in her husband's chair at his desk in the centre of the room, while he sat at one side in a group of friends. Bulletins were being received constantly from the convention by telegraph and telephone . . . When Taft was placed in nomination, successive bulletins were received describing the cheering, the length of time it was enduring, its volume and accompanying demonstrations. The Secretary sat calm and composed during this time, but Mrs. Taft was obviously in great agitation. "I only want it to last more than forty-nine minutes," she exclaimed. "I want to get even for the scare that Roosevelt cheer of forty-nine minutes gave me yesterday." The convention had cheered for that length of time for Roosevelt on the previous day. Mr. Taft merely smiled and said: "Oh, my dear, my dear!"

Word soon came that the nominating speeches had all been made, and the convention would proceed to ballot. There was a sigh of relief from the little company, and a brief period of breathless eagerness followed. Then Charlie came in with a bulletin which he handed to his mother. Her face went deathly white, and with visible effort she read (I quote from memory): "A large portrait of Roosevelt has been displayed on the platform and the convention has exploded."

A silence as of death fell upon the room. Mrs. Taft sat white as marble and motionless. Mr. Taft tapped with his fingers on the arm of his chair and whistled softly. No one said a word or looked at his neighbor. A minute or two later Charlie entered with another bulletin which he handed to his mother, and she read with impassive voice and face. (Again I quote from memory, but the substance is of unquestionable accuracy): "A huge American flag with a Roosevelt portrait upon it is being carried about the hall, and the uproar continues with increased fury."

That awful silence continued for several minutes, which seemed endless, when again Charlie entered with a bulletin and which his mother, almost leaping from her chair in excitement, read: "Massachusetts gives 25 votes for Taft." . . .

339

As I Knew Them

Quickly following the Massachusetts bulletin came others, and within a few minutes the nomination was announced. . . . It is needless to add that Mrs. Taft's face had more than regained its normal color. She was the personification of a proud and happy wife.

340

CHAPTER XLI

THE WRONG ROAD TO CINCINNATI

Taft Detours To Oyster Bay With His Acceptance Speech—There He Had His Last Intimate Talk With Roosevelt—He Faced An Issue And Stuck By Blood—A Silent Boycott Of T. R.—The Acceptance And The Inaugural Speeches Were The Last Heard Of "Roosevelt Policies"— Sherman Replies That The Vice President Is Not a Messenger Boy—A Winter Of Roosevelt Humiliation And Taft Silence—Charles P. Taft Makes An Effort To Get Burton Out Of The Senate And Himself In.

NOMINATED, Taft hurried from his office to express a whole-hearted obligation to Roosevelt. A day or two later he repeated it most profusely when he called at the White House to resign as Secretary of War. No two men could have been in happier mood than were the President and his named successor that afternoon. They gossiped of old times and of the new times ahead. Then it was that the references to his old Cabinet associates were made by Taft—then also it was settled that Luke Wright, of Tennessee, should succeed him as Secretary of War.

His mind cleared of departmental matters, his mood jubilant, Taft left for Hot Springs, Virginia, where he was to prepare his acceptance speech. The President went to Oyster Bay for the summer. No man could have been more confident that events had justified his course, that they had confounded those who had doubted, than was Roosevelt when I saw him a day or so later.

Meanwhile, Taft worked at the acceptance speech he was to deliver in Cincinnati July 29. Ten days before that date, with the speech completed, he left Hot Springs for Cincinnati, announcing, however, that he was going by way of Oyster Bay to discuss it there "and get the President's judgment and his criticism. I have the highest regard for his judgment." He spent the day with Roosevelt, accepted the few changes suggested, and continued on his way.

That visit to Oyster Bay marked the close of the Roosevelt-Taft intimacy. Taft did not talk with Roosevelt again, nor see him, until he called at the White House in December on his way to Augusta, Georgia, five months later.

TAFT STICKS BY BLOOD

What happened in Cincinnati?

I can only repeat the story as told by those who claimed to know, and to which Taft's course gives substance. It is that Taft had scarcely taken his hat off in his brother's house before he was asked rather abruptly why he had come to Cincinnati from Hot Springs by way of Oyster Bay when there was a shorter, more direct route—whether he did not realize that the country would interpret his roundabout trip to Roosevelt as a proof that Roosevelt, not Taft's relatives, had the direction of his fortunes as President. If Oyster Bay side-trips were to be continued his visits to Cincinnati would have the importance merely of rest periods.

Taft was not prepared for this criticism. Until that moment such an interpretation had not occurred to him. He had always gone to Roosevelt with his matters; by habit, he had gone to Oyster Bay. He now saw, however, that he would have to choose between two loyalties—it would not be possible to satisfy both. Those who know Taft best have always believed that he made a reluctant choice. However, he faced an issue and, as always, blood proved thicker than water. He stuck by blood.

A SILENT BOYCOTT OF T. R.

The cordial expressions of gratitude spoken in Oyster Bay died away into silence—silence for one week, then for two weeks, then for the campaign. Speeches were prepared, committee plans matured—but of these Oyster Bay heard only through gossip. National Chairman Frank Hitchcock was polite to his old chief, but after some experiences he decided that when he needed instructions he would travel to Cincinnati for them; also that he would not travel there by way of Oyster Bay.

It may be that in other walks of life men who have worked together intimately and with apparent unity of purpose for five years have separated as abruptly and as silently as Taft

DEE: LIGHTED: OR, THE RINGMASTER, *From The Eagle, Brooklyn, N. Y.*

separated from his former chief, but in politics, at least in American politics, there is no parallel.

No differences in policy or purposes were discussed, no reason whatsoever stated, but a "silent boycott" of Oyster Bay and of all men identified with Oyster Bay went into effect. At first it was confined to Roosevelt, but it widened steadily to others as Election Day approached. Then, with the returns showing Taft elected beyond dispute, the silence slowly developed into whispers,—whispers that led the alert to wonder what had happened, whispers that at once encouraged every Roosevelt opponent to feel confident that Taft as President would follow other policies and other men than those of the Roosevelt Administration.

THE LAST HEARD OF ROOSEVELT POLICIES

Not a word in Taft's public utterances justified such prophecies. Indeed, his speeches were in full harmony with the party platform. At Cincinnati, on July 29,—he had delivered his acceptance speech and had said:

> "The strength of the Republican cause in the campaign at hand is in the fact that we represent the policies essential to the reform of known abuses, to the continuance of liberty and true prosperity and that we are determined as our platform unequivocally declares, to maintain them and carry them on. . . .
>
> "The man who formulated the expression of popular confidence and who led the movement for practical reform was Theodore Roosevelt. He laid down the doctrine that the rich violator of the law should be as amenable to restraint and punishment as the offender without wealth and without influences. . . . In this work Mr. Roosevelt has had the support and sympathy of the Republican party, and its chief hope of success in the present controversy must rest on the confidence which the people of the country have in its platform that it intends to continue his policies.
>
> "The Chief function of the Republican administration will be to clinch what has already been accomplished at the White House; to undertake to devise ways and means by which the high development of business integrity and obedience to law which he (Roosevelt) established can be maintained."
>
> "Mr. Roosevelt led the way to practical reform. The chief functions of my administration shall be to complete and perfect the machinery by which the President's policies may be maintained."

As I Knew Them

These words, coupled later with his inaugural speech, are the last ever heard from Taft in a kindly way about Roosevelt policies; except that he vigorously pressed for and secured from the courts helpful interpretation of the Sherman anti-trust law.

Promptly after delivering his acceptance speech in Cincinnati, Taft had returned to Hot Springs—this time by the shorter, more direct route. There he played golf more persistently and with keener interest than he did anything else. To suggestions intended to enliven the campaign his usual reply, as he rested on a lounge after a golf game, was that they involved too much work. The remark was made at that time that apparently Taft was going to let someone else elect him President just as he had allowed someone else to nominate him.

Possibly that remark seems severe, but no one at Hot Springs at the time—and I was there—challenged its truth. Taft could not have been a more listless campaigner. A feature that was not detected until afterward was that no Cabinet member, no pronounced Roosevelt State leader, was bidden to Taft's presence. The men called to Hot Springs were from the other camp.

It was mid-August before Roosevelt realized that he was under boycott. He kept his own counsel, blinding himself to the separation that, deep down in his own mind, he knew had come. He could make no protest. He could cite no act against him, and Taft's only utterance was in strong support of him. Except by public profession, the candidate had simply forgotten that Roosevelt and his friends existed. Their part in the campaign, if any, had to be voluntary. Roosevelt made his part both voluntary and intense. Hughes stirred the country by his speech at Youngstown, Ohio; Roosevelt followed it with a series of vigorous statements hitting Bryan harder and harder. These were the only memorable incidents of an otherwise lifeless campaign.

As I Knew Them

"The King is dead! Long live the King!" broke out in loud and jubilant tones the moment returns made certain Taft's election. The cry came from those conspicuous in their opposition to all that Taft had supported and that he was to indorse anew in his inaugural. His former associates in the Cabinet waited impatiently to hear from him. They assumed that Taft would send for them and talk with them in the frankness of friendship. He never did. He told his varying purposes to others, who in turn told them to others. Thus, at last, the news reached those who should have been the first to know that they were to go. It was not until it was learned that a successor to Luke Wright was being sought that it was realized that Taft's course was a matter of policy and not merely applied to individual cases. No Roosevelt man was to "carry on" into the new Administration. Those who tried to keep on terms soon discovered that their identity with the old régime was a bar to intimacy with the new.

WHY LOEB WAS HELD

Before allowing this statement to stand in print I have tried to recall one ranking appointment or policy of the Taft Administration reflecting any suggestion from those with whom he had sat around Roosevelt's counsel table. I cannot.

Some reader will probably ask how about William Loeb, Jr., who was closer to Roosevelt than anyone else? The answer to that inquiry is that Loeb was made Collector of the Port of New York because his strategic energies had smoothed Taft's way through the nominating convention. If any man other than Roosevelt is responsible for Taft in the White House, that man is William Loeb. Taft remembered his obligation to Loeb. When appointed Loeb was wise enough to realize that New York city was distant from the White House

346

in more ways than mileage. He never wavered in his loyalty to Roosevelt, but also he never pressed his opinions on his new chief, with a mind made up to new men and new purposes.

VICE PRESIDENT NOT A MESSENGER BOY

How Taft himself veered in those days is illustrated by a statement made to me in December, 1908, at a dinner party given by me to Congressman James S. Sherman, of New York, elected Vice President—"Sunny Jim" as those who knew him well pleasantly called him. Sherman had just returned from Hot Springs, where he and William L. Ward, of New York, had been visiting Taft. Sherman told me that Taft had said to him he did not intend to have anything to do with Joe Cannon, then Speaker of the House, and a candidate for reelection.

"I am going to rely on you, Jim," Taft said, "to take care of Cannon for me. Whatever I have to do there will be done through you."

"Not through me," Sherman quickly replied. "You will have to act on your own account. I am to be Vice President and acting as a messenger boy is not part of the duties of a Vice President."

A month later, Cannon visited Taft by request. Four months later when Taft became President—he and Cannon were in conference at the White House and the Payne-Aldrich tariff was the logical outcome.

CHARLES TAFT'S EFFORT FOR THE SENATE

In that same month of December, 1908, occurred what was probably the crudest effort to grab a Senatorship ever made in politics. It will be recalled that back in 1897 Senator John Sherman was persuaded to become Secretary of State under McKinley in order to create a vacancy in the Senate to which Mark Hanna could be appointed. Immediately following

"UNCLE JOE"

Taft's election, Charles P. Taft announced from Cincinnati his candidacy for the Senate. Next came an offer from the President-elect to make Congressman Theodore Burton, of Cleveland, Secretary of the Treasury.

Burton was the leading candidate for the Senate and in the following January the Republicans in the Ohio Legislature elected him unanimously. The sudden ambition of Charles P. Taft for Senatorial honors; the plain implication that he planned to go to Washington as the Mark Hanna of the Administration; the lure to Burton to get out of the way; astounded the country and brought Ohio Republicans closer to disastrous faction strife than they habitually are.

Of course there could be only one outcome. Burton declined the President's offer and the Taft Senatorial candidacy was withdrawn.

Undoubtedly the President-elect realized the damage to his prestige caused by the incident; undoubtedly he bore the inevitable criticism uncomplainingly, for after all, he owed much to the brother who was to be the Warwick of his times.

Probably both men realized later that the humiliation of having failed to sidetrack Burton was easier to bear than the embarrassment of having in the Senate a brother of the President.

ROOSEVELT DEFIED, TAFT SILENT

Nothing more significant forecast the course Taft intended to pursue than his silence throughout the winter of 1908-09 while Roosevelt was struggling to carry out his purpose to remain a 100 per cent President until the last day of his term. It was largely to achieve that purpose that he had declared for Taft. He now found himself thwarted, defied.

Taft himself had once said that an important part of his duties in the Roosevelt Cabinet was to hold on to T. R.'s coattails so as to keep him from going ahead too fast. The time had come when as President-elect he could perform an equally helpful service. The Roosevelt measures in Congress were thrust aside, and it was made plain to him that only his title to office remained.

What such a condition meant to a spirited man like Roosevelt need not be told. One word from Taft would have changed it—would have saved Roosevelt much humiliation. That word was not uttered. In Hot Springs and in Augusta, Georgia, Taft explained his silence by stating that he did not care to begin his Administration with divided party support in Congress. The effect of this remark was to lead the reactionaries in Congress to greater defiance of the outgoing President. They knew then that they had nothing to fear from his successor; more confidently than ever they reiterated their prophecies that the new man would be with them at the proper time.

CHAPTER XLII

"I HAVE BEEN A CRUSADER HERE!"

A Remarkably Frank Talk By Roosevelt As To His Course As President—"There Was Crusading To Be Done And I Didn't Use A Feather Duster"—"We Have Raised The Standards"—"The Country Has Had Enough Of It And Of Me," And "Time For A Man Of Taft's Type"—Give Taft A Chance—We Will Have Four Years Of Up-Building.

TWO or three days before Roosevelt handed over the Presidency to the man he had chosen as his successor, I called at the White House to say goodby. There were so many waiting to see the President that I was determined to limit my call to a handshake and a quick farewell. The Colonel—it is difficult for anyone who knew him to call him by another title—had other ideas. He was in the mood to talk reflectively to somebody, and it was my luck to happen along. "Sit down," he said. "We'll hold up the procession for a while."

I began talking of Africa, but I did not meet his mind until I mentioned that he could have remained where he was, if he had so desired. That was the topic he preferred to discuss. As accurately as I can recall this is what he said:

"I suppose I could have had another term. There was just one lure in it, just one. I was told by Southern Democrats—I don't mean dyed-in-the-wool Democrats but Southern men who have been voting the Democratic ticket because there was no hope elsewhere—that my candidacy would break the "Solid South." They assured me I could carry surely Kentucky and Tennessee, probably Georgia and Texas and possibly Alabama. I felt that if I could do that I would be doing a great service for the country.

351

"Smash the South's solidarity once and it will be over forever," he continued. "Thousands of Southerners want to break it but they are timid about the first plunge. Once they realize they can vote for a Republican with safety to their local conditions, there will be a break away from the Democratic organization that will make several Southern States as doubtful as are the Northern States.

"They told me that I could cause such a break. I do not know that I could, but I felt that I would like to try. It was the one real temptation to run again.

"THERE WAS CRUSADING TO BE DONE"

"But I don't want four more years here, and there were larger considerations," continued Roosevelt. After a pause, and in a noticeably deeper tone he said: "I have been a crusader here, I have been a destructive force. The country needs a change. There was crusading to do when I took hold. There was something that had to be uprooted. I had to challenge and destroy certain influences or we would soon have had an intolerable condition imperilling everything.

"I have not been deeply interested in the tariff nor in what you call the business problems of government. They have no appeal to me. I know little about them. If the party leaders in Congress had ever come to me with a definite programme on those matters I might have backed it because they wanted it,—but no one ever came.

"If I had occupied myself revising the tariff, there would be another revenue law a little better or a little worse than the present one—and there it would end. The only result might be—a divided party, and possibly 1892 over again.

"Now, we are unified. We have revised government 'up' which is better than a futile effort to revise the tariff 'down.' I have concerned myself with the ethical side. I've wanted to make people in government and out of it realize that it is best to deal squarely by one another—to have a free field and a fair chance for all. I believe I have raised the standards. We may slip back now and then, but never to the old levels.

"I DIDN'T USE A FEATHER DUSTER"

"The conscience of business had to be aroused, the authority of the government over big as well as small had to be asserted. You can't half do that kind of a job; it must be done thoroughly. I think I've done it. I didn't use a feather duster. I knew I had to hit hard—and be hit hard in return.

"We have had four years of uprooting and four years of crusading. The country has had enough of it and of me. It is time for me to go and for a man of Taft's type to take my place. He's a constructive fellow, I am not. The country should not be asked to stand four years more of crusading. There is no reason why it should. The ground is cleared for constructive work; the man who clears is never the man to do the upbuilding.

GIVE TAFT A CHANCE, URGED ROOSEVELT

"I know that some of my friends are critical of Taft. They were critical before his nomination and are even more so now. But they're wrong to take that attitude. There's nothing to be gained by being doubtful. Give Taft a chance. He knows what has to be done here; he knows how it has to be done, and now he will know how to build on the foundations that have been laid. He has a legal mind—he can round out and shape up the policies of the last four years better than if I were to remain here. He has a big majority in Congress to back him, and the country is with him.

"Taft will give you four years of upbuilding and I'm going off to Africa for a real fine time.

"I have done my Sorbonne and Oxford lectures," he continued jubilantly. "I've paid all my political debts. I'm footloose and fancy free, and when I'm back in Sagamore in a year or so as a private citizen I'll be the happiest man you ever saw."

How dimly Roosevelt foresaw his own future!—how dimly Taft's!

CHAPTER XLIII

A PRESIDENT IN A PROPHETIC STORM

Still "Theodore" and "Will," But Not The Same Old Ring—"That Was A Fine Inaugural Address," Exclaimed Roosevelt—It Was A Good Programme Of Policies, But It Never Got Beyond Mere Say-So— Taft's First Conference Was With Joe Cannon And Aldrich—"Carrying Out Roosevelt's Policies" On A Stretcher—Taft Turns To The Old Guard—Every "Insurgent" Marked For Discipline—"I Am Leaving That To Aldrich," Would Be Taft's Answer—Canadian Reciprocity Made Party Unity In Congress Impossible.

WAS there ever a worse March 4 than that on which William Howard Taft was inaugurated President in 1909?

Cynical folk could have asserted that the day was made tempestuous so as definitely to mark the transition from Roosevelt to Taft. If so, it marked it well—but whether it was intended as a final clean-up of stormy Roosevelt times or a forecast of what was in store for Taft no one knew. For that matter, there was storm enough to serve both purposes, with still some to spare. Rain, snow, sleet filled the streets of Washington and halted railroads, telephones and telegraphs along the entire Atlantic seaboard. Taft was compelled to abandon the Capitol steps where most Presidents have been inaugurated and to hold the ceremonies in the Senate Chamber.

On the surface, all Republicans were jubilant. Party majorities had mounted high everywhere on election day; newly-elected Republican Governors were around Washington as thick as Southern Colonels; Republican Senators and Congressmen were so many that like a widening Spring freshet they flowed over into the half-empty Democratic side of each chamber.

355

As I Knew Them

The chief figures in the day's proceedings were still "Theodore" and "Will" to each other; but the old ring of close, unconcealing friendship was gone. Both men were still striving to make others believe that that shadowy something that often separates men when relations change had not been slowly acquiring too substantial form. There were whisperings of trouble but only whisperings. Years later, Roosevelt said to me: "Taft and I knew the true situation and its cause. It did not matter whether anyone else knew or not—best that they should not. There was too much at stake."

Heavily coated, Taft watched the inaugural parade from the White House reviewing stand. He greeted the Taft Club of Cincinnati by waving his silk hat in unison with the incongruous notes of "In the Good Old Summer Time." Meanwhile, a train making slow progress against the storm was carrying his predecessor to Oyster Bay.

Roosevelt had commenced the day by receiving his successor, posing with him for that famous picture of two portly men in the conventional "Prince Alberts" of the time. He had driven to the Capitol with Taft, listened in the Senate chamber to the storm-bound inaugural and before he left for his train said to Elihu Root, "My! That was a fine inaugural address."

Roosevelt had not seen it in advance. The Cincinnati warning had been effective. With his acceptance speech, Taft had gone to Oyster Bay "for the President's judgment and criticism" in July. His inaugural, however, was to be judged by Roosevelt as he heard it with others. He was curious to know what Taft would say and he was well content when he heard these words:

"I have had the honor to be one of the advisors of my distinguished predecessor, and, as such, to hold up his hands in the reforms he has instituted. I should be untrue to myself, to my

356

promises and to the declaration of the party platform upon which I was elected to office if I did not make the maintenance and enforcement of these reforms a most important feature of my administration. They were directed to the suppression of the lawlessness and abuse of power of great combinations of capital invested in railroads and in industrial enterprises carrying on interstate commerce.

"The steps which my predecessor took and the legislation passed on his recommendation have accomplished much, have caused a general halt in the vicious policies which created popular alarm, and have brought about in the business affected a much higher regard for existing law."

A FINE PROGRAMME OF POLICIES

Surely this was a keynote which must have pleased Taft's predecessor. Then Taft recommended relief for railroads from certain restrictions of the Sherman law which were "urged by my predecessor and will be urged by me." He pleaded for reorganization of the departments and bureaus having corporate matters in charge, so that there should be cooperation instead of conflict. Taft declared for tariff revision and announced that he would convene Congress in special session to secure it; he also spoke strongly for conservation of our natural resources "saving and restoring our forests and the great improvement of our waterways."

A good strong programme. Of course in picturesque idiom, "the proof of the pudding is in the eating," but at least here was a fine start.

THE BEGINNING WAS ALSO THE END

Unfortunately the start proved also to be the finish. The hopes aroused by Taft's words wilted like a full-blown rose when the news came that the first important conferees in the White House were Senator Aldrich and Speaker "Joe" Cannon. No two men in Washington had more bitterly opposed

STARTING ON A LONG JOURNEY

the Roosevelt policies to which Taft in his inaugural had paid such tribute, pledging also his own faith, and yet they were the men now selected by the new President to make the maintenance of those measures "a most important feature of my Administration"!

Newspaper dispatches spoke kindly of the conference as an effort to agree on making the Roosevelt policies effective; nearer the truth was a cartoon entitled "Carrying Out Roosevelt's Policies." It showed "My Policies" on a stretcher that bearers were carrying out of the White House.

TAFT TURNS TO THE OLD GUARD

No one in Congress, especially those who were opposing Cannon lost the significance of that conference. It was known for some time that Taft would not help defeat Cannon for reelection as Speaker. There are excellent reasons why a President should keep out of such contests and if Taft had kept out no one could have justly criticized him.

The revolt against Cannon's harsh exercise of his power had broken out in the previous session, and there was now an intense determination to have fair play for all. "Old Guard" Congressmen were the only ones who could get the favor of the Speaker—the only ones not "tainted with Teddyism," as Cannon termed it—and under existing rules unless you had his favor you might as well be in Timbuctoo as on the floor of the House.

Herbert Parsons, of New York, Augustus P. Gardner, of Massachusetts, Victor Murdock and Judge Edmond H. Madison of Kansas, George W. Norris, now Senator from Nebraska, Henry Allen Cooper and Irvine L. Lenroot, of Wisconsin, led in the struggle to revise the rules. In the beginning—that is, just after his election—Taft thought he was with them; then he wanted to think it over; the next heard from him was the news that he was seeking the counsel of Aldrich and Cannon.

PILING IT ON

TAFT TURNS TO THE OLD GUARD

As I Knew Them

Still the insurgents persisted in their battle for their rights. They could not win a complete victory, but they secured a revision of the rules giving every member the right to recognition. The outposts of Cannonism, of Czarism, were captured. But Taft, they discovered, was now in the citadel they were attacking. Here was a battle for justice—the opening skirmish of the fierce contest coming in 1912. Many historic battles have developed from such seemingly remote beginnings; but not until historians later searched for cause has it been revealed that a principle, or a great need, was from the first moment working its way to the fore, and that the final clash was an inevitable sequel of the early and smaller one.

So it proved to be in this situation. The Taft talk with Aldrich and Cannon was not a conference; it was a surrender. The reactionaries in Congress hailed it as such; the progressives accepted it as such. There was no middle ground of compromise. At least, Taft sought none. Steadily, he moved further and further away from the old moorings. "I am leaving that to Aldrich," he would say when asked to discuss some schedule in the tariff bill upon which Congress was then working.

Thus, little by little, progressives came to realize the hopelessness of seeking support at the White House, and the certainty of an unpleasant time there if, by chance, the name or policies of Taft's predecessor were mentioned. They were now not merely insurgents against Cannonism in the House; they were insurgents against the Administration.

Never was there such inept handling of legislation as in framing the tariff bill in 1909. Almost any effort at conciliation would have united all Republicans in Congress back of the new schedules; but conciliation was not what the men in control sought; their purpose was annihilation. Every

361

"insurgent" was marked for discipline, and every suggestion ignored.

Taft knew what was going on, shrugged his shoulders in a helpless sort of way, and gave the impression that he did not care to be burdened with the task of reconciling the warring factions. He must have foreseen what the split, ever growing wider and deeper, would mean to Republicans in the 1910 Congressional elections and later in 1912, but if he did his serenity was undisturbed.

THE CANADIAN RECIPROCITY BLUNDER

The worst was still to come, however. Taft insisted upon reciprocity with Canada. The measure had been refused indorsement in the Republican national convention, and a majority of Republicans, especially those from States bordering Canada were opposed to it. Still Taft persisted. When he forced it to a vote in the House on February 14, 1911, out of the 92 "noes" 87 came from Republicans.

Such extremes as Jonathan Bourne, progressive from Washington, and John Dalzell, a Pennsylvania stand-patter, voted "no"—demonstrating that the opposition embraced all kinds of Republicans. The Senate refused to act—and two weeks later Taft faced the newly-elected Democratic Congress.

PARTY CHAOS IN CONGRESS

Like Cleveland with his silver repeal measure, Taft now looked to the opposition party for votes to pass his bill. Apparently he gauged the popularity of his Canadian proposal by its acceptance by the Democrats—forgetting that any lowering of the tariff bars would have free trade support.

Again, like Cleveland, he called Congress in extra session. The House, now Democratic, passed the bill a second time with practically all the "noes" from Republicans; in the Senate, more Republicans opposed than favored it. With a majority of his own party against his principal legislation, party unity back of the President was thereafter hopeless. A minority of Republicans in both Houses had revolted against his tariff bill; a majority revolted against his Canadian reciprocity bill. Politically, Taft's plight was as bad as Cleve-

"SAY, BOSS, WHY DON'T YER HUNCH OVER A LITTLE TO DE ODDER SIDE? DEN DE MACHINE WILL RUN BETTER"

land's, and the result worse, for Cleveland stopped the coining of silver dollars. Taft's reciprocity was a dead letter. Canadian voters swept out of office the government of Sir Wilfrid Laurier with which Taft had negotiated. Thus the whole structure collapsed.

CHAPTER XLIV

TAFT'S ONE BIG TRIUMPH

He Won "Decisions That Decided" From The Supreme Court In The Anti-Trust Cases—Our National Policies Take Years To Develop— The Entire Supreme Court Membership Changed While The Sherman Law Was Before It—Only Harlan Stood By The Government From The First.

THE one Roosevelt policy which Taft did not abandon is the one triumph of his administration,—the effort to secure for the government through court decisions complete control of corporation activities. In this effort Taft shows at his best. His heart was in that work, and his mind was trained to the problem. There was need for "decisions that decided" despite the victory scored in the Northern Securities and "beef" trust cases under Roosevelt. They had greatly strengthened the law, but the "teeth" that Roosevelt had so vigorously sought had yet to be provided. It was Taft's task "to round out and shape up" (as Roosevelt had expressed it) efforts which had been made to secure helpful court interpretations. Through George W. Wickersham, his able and forceful Attorney General, this was accomplished.

As a nation and as individuals, Americans have a reputation for moving rapidly toward accomplishing the things they set out to do—much too rapidly, they tell us abroad. The history of our law making does not sustain this charge. Our government moves slowly; it has long periods of swaying back and forth before deciding. First Congress debates for years; then the courts take more years to declare and make effective what Congress really intended. "Half slave and half free," we stood on the brink of a precipice for thirty or forty years before we engaged in civil strife to end slavery. It took us ten years after the war to say that we would redeem our paper-money in coin, it took us a quarter of a century to establish the gold standard, longer to secure votes for women, the income tax and prohibition. Once policies are established we forget the long and doubtful period that preceded their enactment.

A STRUGGLE FOR TWENTY YEARS

So it was with the struggle to confirm the supremacy of the government over industrial enterprises and great wealth. For twenty years every President and every Attorney General had battled with it. The Sherman anti-trust law of 1890 was the corner-stone, but at first it could not be built upon substantially. The entire membership of the Supreme Court changed while, in case after case, the issue was argued before it, and futile decisions came down. In 1895, the Knight sugar case went heavily against the government. Associate Justice Harlan alone voted to sustain. In 1903 the Northern Securities case went in favor of the government by a five to four decision. Among the four dissenters was Associate Justice White who had voted against the government in the Sugar Trust case, and who now proclaimed that the two cases were exactly alike. He insisted that the law should be interpreted in "the light of reason," and not as the government contended.

Still, the Northern Securities case was won, which meant more than Justice White's phrase. Other suits were brought by Roosevelt and in these Taft, back from the Philippines, aided with suggestion. He was, therefore, well prepared to carry on the struggle in his own name. Approximately ninety suits were brought during Taft's Administration. Though not all of them were won, a body of opinion came from the courts that ended the effort of corporate wealth to deny the power of the government to regulate it.

As I Knew Them

Twenty years, however, were needed to establish this supremacy. The only man on the bench from the first test of the law to its final upholding was Associate Justice Harlan. He was also the only justice to vote consistently in support of the government and the law. Associate Justice White voted twice against the government. Not until 1910, in the Tobacco suit, did White change over to the interpretation of the Sherman law that now prevails. It would be tiring to list the number of Justices who sat in the different cases brought between 1895, when the Knight Sugar Trust case was decided, and 1911 when the Standard Oil case was decided with the full membership of the Court in favor of the government, but White and Harlan were the only Justices who sat through all. White as Chief Justice wrote the opinion in the Standard Oil case; and again as in the Northern Securities case he wrote of the "light of reason" in interpreting law. But the same light led him in one case against the government and in the later case in favor of the government—one of the peculiarities of judges that laymen like myself do not understand.

The point I had in mind, however, was not to discuss the attitude of individual Justices but to demonstrate that, despite all the talk that as a nation we hurry into decisions, the record shows that we deliberate long before acting.

CHAPTER XLV

WHY TAFT DID NOT SUCCEED

Two Reasons Why The Smile That Captured The Country Soon Lost Its Power To Persuade—The Comparison With Jackson's Naming of Van Buren—The White House Had Lost Its Real Meaning To Taft —Drift, Drift, Drift—Taft's Real Desire Was For The Bench—An Unusual Conference That Gave Him A Scotch Verdict—Trying To Help Jim Tawney—"God Knows," Said Taft Sympathetically, But Others Took It Differently.

WHY did not Taft get on well in the White House? Many reasons could be advanced but two fundamental reasons were: (1) his nomination did not reflect the party's will but the will of a retiring President; (2) he loved the title but not the work of President.

Whenever Roosevelt's nomination of Taft is discussed, reference is made to the nomination of Martin Van Buren by Andrew Jackson in 1836. Both Roosevelt and Jackson forced their will on their party. Both had the same motive— to insure continuance of their policies—but Roosevelt was by no means so well justified as Jackson. Van Buren was then Vice President; he had been Minister to Great Britain, a United States Senator, Governor of New York, and occupant of several less conspicuous offices. He had submitted himself many times to a vote of the people, and was identified with the issues of the day. In these various positions, he had gained a ripe experience for the Presidency—for the delicate task of knowing how to guide rather than to antagonize public opinion.

Taft lacked that equipment. For nearly thirty years he had held one appointive office after another. In Ohio, early in life, he had been elected to some minor judgeship, but in a broad sense his only experience with elections was as a candi-

367

date for the Presidency. In that candidacy he did not urge his election because of anything he had done, but solely on the ground that he was the standard bearer of the President he desired to succeed.

His nomination, like that of Van Buren, represented an unfortunate, unpardonable exercise of Presidential power over a party convention. Neither nominee represented party sentiment tested by a free roll call in convention. Inevitably in both cases the result had to be party schism and disaster.

DRIFT—DRIFT—DRIFT

The second reason for Taft's failure became apparent all too soon. The new Administration was on its way somewhere but whither it was going no one—not even the President himself—seemed to know. It was drift, drift, drift—little attempted, nothing done. No wonder Republicans grew restive. No wonder the country began to think it had made a mistake. There was a sag everywhere in Washington; the old vigor was gone; none of the familiar sharp calls to action were ever heard.

Those who went to the White House with suggestions were seldom welcome, and rarely came away satisfied. Those who wanted results turned to some department official for them. The department official usually replied that there was no use discussing matters until he could see the President "some time." Nobody seemed to be interested in getting things done. Officialdom found "the easiest way" was the White House way; quickly the whole Administration took its color from the top.

Possibly had this condition not followed seven years of Roosevelt it would not have excited so much criticism; but the change from decision to indecision, from action to delay, was so sudden, the contrast so sharp, that talk of a collapse of government efficiency soon filled Washington and spread through the country. The "Old Guard" in Congress promptly took the leadership of the party from the White House, and Senator Dolliver historically remarked: "Taft is an amiable man, entirely surrounded by men who know exactly what they want."

It was the judgment of men who had opportunity to know whereof they spoke that Taft did not even try to be a success. Of course, he wanted to make a good record and to be re-elected. No man could be in the White House without such desire. What I mean when I say "try" is to try with every ounce of effort in you—not once or twice, but until you get a result. Taft made no such "try." He relied on smiling through difficulties and finding the easiest way out of them—usually of course without settling them. They backed up on him like a mountain stream dammed.

Though no golfer myself, I do not share the criticism of his golfing or cite it as an example of indifference to his work. Those hours of relaxation were probably necessary to a man of Taft's build. He liked golfing and played the course well; he did not like the grind of the White House—for it is a grind unless you are temperamentally fitted for it—and he did not play that well.

THE WHITE HOUSE ONLY ANOTHER WAY STATION

I have always felt that as a member of the Cabinet five years, and earlier as Solicitor General in the Department of Justice, the White House had become too familiar to Taft before he occupied it. Its occupant had been "Theodore" to him and he was "Will." Crossing its doorsill as President gave him no deeper emotion than arriving at a familiar railroad station on one of the journeys he was always beginning or ending.

It had meant no effort on his part; like the engineer of the locomotive pulling his railway train on his travels, another person had the power to advance him to the desired place and did so. The nominating convention, which should have been the power, became merely the vehicle; delegates knew what was wanted of them and did it; so, later did the country. Thus the highest honor that can be gained by an American came to Taft so easily that I question whether it was prized by him at real value. The things you prize are those you struggle to attain.

For nearly thirty years before Taft reached the Presidency, he had been "kicked around," to use a frequent expression of his own. He was on the Ohio Superior Court bench when President Harrison made him Solicitor General; later Harrison appointed him to a Circuit Judgeship. He was on that bench when McKinley asked him to become President of the Philippine Commission.

TAFT'S REAL DESIRE FOR THE BENCH

Taft had three opportunities to go on the Supreme Court bench, and refused all three, before his nomination for President. President Harding's offer of the Chief-Justiceship was the fourth he had received. That one he accepted. No other man has ever had such a tribute.

They show the high opinion held of Taft's judicial mind by all who had opportunity to know it.

Twice while he was in the Philippines, and again in 1906 President Roosevelt vainly sought to place Taft on the bench. The first offer was cabled to him in Manila in 1902. He replied that he had promised McKinley to see the Philippine job through until a settled form of government had been worked out. He wanted to keep his promise.

"I long for a judicial career," Taft cabled, "but if it must turn on my present decision I am willing to lose it."

So far as I know this is the strongest utterance Taft ever made on any subject!

Roosevelt renewed the offer two months later; again Taft declined. In 1903 Roosevelt made him Secretary of War.

That department has supervision over the Philippines and Taft accepted.

HIS FAMILY WANTED HIM TO BE PRESIDENT!

The revealing declination came in 1906. Again Roosevelt offered him an Associate Justiceship. Again Taft declined— this time not for the excellent reason he had advanced from the Philippines. The new reason plainly stated was that his family preferred that he should seek the Presidency!

This was a commendably frank avowal of his intention to be a candidate in 1908. It could not have been made by a Cabinet officer to a President without an accompanying resignation unless the President was a staunch and genuine friend. If there is anything comparable to it in all the relations of our Presidents with their Cabinet members I have not read or heard of it.

It was an example of the finest kind of friendship possible between two men—how well Taft knew that his superior officer was also a friend to whom he could candidly tell his great desire; how splendidly Roosevelt responded to that confidence!

AN UNUSUAL CONFERENCE

On Taft's request, or at his own suggestion, Roosevelt went so far as to call Secretary of State Root, Attorney General Moody, and Secretary of Commerce Straus, into conference as to whether Taft should go on the bench or not. This most unusual proceeding to determine the future of a man uncertain of which honor he should seek resulted in what might be called a "Scotch verdict."

In the minds of all was a thought which none expressed. Taft had better go on the Supreme Court. One man present did suggest the familiar story of the bird in the hand. The conference broke up when Taft said he would write his brother. In a few days he gave Roosevelt the answer quoted above. Attorney General Moody was thereupon appointed to the vacancy.

Through the next two years Taft travelled and talked the country over. He seemed to be everywhere,—anywhere in fact, except in the War Department. His absences were encouraged by Roosevelt to give him his full chance with the people.

In that friendship Roosevelt saw only Taft. After the message he had received from Taft, he should have seen in the picture not Taft alone but Taft plus the family. For that message carried in it the seed from which all future trouble sprang. Taft was subordinating his own desires to the ambitions of others close to him who could share in the prestige of the White House, but not in the quiet dignity of the Supreme Court. The experience may have satisfied them, but it proved a nightmare to Taft.

A BIG TASK, BUT LITTLE EFFORT

I was one of many Republicans whose loyalty to Roosevelt did not lessen their desire to see Taft get on well. I realized that he followed an unusual man into the Presidency, that in method and temperament he was different. Moreover, I knew the peril of such a heavy vote as he had polled—the largest electoral and popular vote ever accorded. Great expectations were aroused; it was an almost impossible task to meet them. Even such an aggressive and resourceful man as Roosevelt would have found it difficult to keep such popularity at flood tide. Then there was the revolt against Cannon in the House. Try as he might to resist it, the new President was bound to be drawn into that maelstrom. Taft made no effort to resist —he just waded in waist high and was soon in deeper water.

These considerations were in my mind as I listened to criticisms. It was hard to reply. Taft gave no help by doing something, almost anything, that would show that he could master the big job he had undertaken. That something was never even attempted. Instead, there came from the White House either indifference or angry impatience according to Taft's mood for the day. Washington is a place of keen, cold judgment. It quickly judged Taft as a mistake in the White House just as it now has the settled belief that as Chief Justice of the United States he is in a position suited to his abilities and inclination.

Nor was the country long in making the same appraisement. Every evidence of the good will of the people had followed Taft into the White House. His smile had captured the country. But his Administration was less than two years old before it was condemned at the Congress elections of 1910, reversing a big majority into a pitiful minority; and in 1912, four years after he had received the largest electoral and popular vote then recorded for a President, he carried only Vermont and Utah, running behind both Wilson and Roosevelt also in popular vote.

THE WRONG WORD TOO OFTEN

A weighty influence in the wrecking of Taft's Administration and, temporarily, of the Republican party was his capacity for saying and doing the wrong thing politically. I do not wish to be misunderstood on this point, and I cannot emphasize too strongly that I mean no disrespect to Taft. His blundering was in the political field, and in dealing with men. It was largely inexperience. On the bench he is at home, and there, in lesser judgeships and now in the Supreme Court, he has been sure-footed.

In nothing did he differ from Roosevelt more than in his inability to gauge the effect of words. Roosevelt seldom spoke without seeing a picture of how the sentence would look in type, and how it would affect the mind of the reader or hearer. Taft was utterly unable to create such a picture. Before he became President this did not matter, and this Taft was never able to understand—a President cannot soliloquize in public like a private citizen. Every word a President utters is weighed and scrutinized. His words are often more potent than his deeds.

Wilson had some of this Taft trait; he too used words without always calculating their effect. He did not visualize the way "too proud to fight" would appear in print, or what effect it would produce. The angry roar that went up everywhere dumbfounded him. By noon a hurried explanation was issued from the White House to show that the President's meaning had been misinterpreted; too late. So with other phrases, such as "peace without victory," "with the causes and objects of this war we have no concern," and many another.

A TYPICAL CARTOON OF THE DAY

TRYING TO HELP "JIM" TAWNEY

But Wilson was not so frequently unfortunate as Taft. Take Taft's experience with the Payne-Aldrich tariff bill. That law was especially unpopular in the West. In all the West it was most unpopular in the Middle West, and in all the

Middle West it was most detested in Minnesota. And in all Minnesota there was no place where it was more detested than in Winona, where "Jim" Tawney was facing defeat for reelection to Congress.

Taft wanted to help Tawney. So, with unerring instinct for the wrong step, Taft picked Winona as a good place in which to advocate the new law, and journeyed out there to do it. The whole West was immediately vocal with rage. As letters, telegrams, newspaper editorials, began to pile up in the White House, Taft saw the necessity of saying something to meet the criticism. Unbelievable as it may seem, Taft explained the Winona speech by saying that he had "dashed it off hurriedly between stations!"

When people remembered that he had left the golf links at Bar Harbor, Maine, to go to Winona, the original mistake was immediately overshadowed by the explanation. The West was infuriated by the apparent confession that he had played golf rather than prepare carefully what he was to say to it. Everywhere there was dismay over the implication that the President of the United States gave little thought to grave public questions. Furthermore, instead of helping Tawney, the Presidential effort lost him hundreds of votes.

Undoubtedly Taft did himself injustice by his apology. He had certainly given more thought to the speech than he admitted. But he was on record as saying virtually that he was a careless man, postponing until train-time his review of matters vitally important to millions of people for whom he was the chief trustee. Nothing he could say or do afterward would efface the impression made.

ANOTHER UNFORTUNATE "BREAK"

Another of his mistakes came from his habit of thinking aloud and his inability to understand that while anybody else may think aloud, a President may not. Getting off a train in New York city, he was met by reporters who asked him what was to be the outcome of the labor situation. At that time there was a good deal of poverty and unemployment, and the subject was close to the hearts of a great many people not at all interested in politics. Taft mechanically replied with this historic sentence:

"God knows."

In these two words he had provoked a storm. The utterance was not so callous as it sounded. It was really uttered in sympathy—Taft meant it that way. But a President is supposed to be always thinking in definite terms and "God knows" was taken to show that he did not care.

"EVEN A RAT WILL FIGHT"

There is no need to call the roll of Taft's unfortunate utterances, so I will close the list of small but influential incidents with the celebrated one which completed the destruction of any hopes he might have had of carrying a single Republican State primary when he was seeking renomination in 1912. Taft's friends were urging him to take the stump against Roosevelt. At first he refused; no President had ever entered publicly into a contest for his own renomination, and he did not want to create a precedent. But Roosevelt was carrying everything before him with such a sweep that Taft finally yielded. Obviously, apology or explanation for his course was weakness, and so Taft made one. This was his explanation:

"Even a rat will fight when driven into a corner."

In every primary contest the Roosevelt supporters seized on this utterance and rang the changes on it. Taft was satirized as a frightened rat driven into a corner and fighting back hopelessly and unwillingly. The sentence even took the spirit out of his sincerest supporters. One may put some heart into fighting for a lion, but not for a desperate rat.

376

CHAPTER XLVI

CITIZEN ROOSEVELT

*Still Sees Himself Out Of The Turmoil Of Politics—Tells Me Of
The Greatest Battle Of His Life And How He Won It In Africa—
Frank Visitors Rare At The White House—Root Said In London That
Taft Had Broken Down—Roosevelt's Royal Welcome Home—Herbert
Parsons Uses A William Barnes Interview To Stir Roosevelt To
Action—The Colonel Tries To Stem The Anti-Republican Tide, And
Names Taft's Cabinet Officer For Governor.*

EVERY moment Roosevelt spent in Africa strengthened
the resolve announced before leaving the White House
to devote himself to things he desired more than he now
desired political honors. That vision of a figure remote from
faction and personal prejudices still filled his imagination;
he saw himself the accepted arbiter of differences, a court of
last resort. What an awakening was to follow such a dream!

"I have read what others have written about my battles
for health in early life, my battles in politics and my battles
with various influences and men," said Roosevelt to me after
his return, "but it was in Africa that I won a battle I had been
trying for years to win but had never succeeded in keeping
won for long. Yet no one ever knew I was fighting it—it was
a battle to control my temper.

"I tried to win it in the White House, but you cannot win
that kind of a battle while you have the immense power and
responsibilities of a President. Trying situations come up,
men come to you with unconscionable suggestions, others resort to petty intrigues. The man who speaks out frankly and
definitely is a rare visitor, though I can assure you from my
own experience he is cordially welcomed in the White House
and makes more headway. There were times when I just had

377

to tell such people what I thought of them and, of course, the newspapers would print a story about a scene in the White House. It would never occur to them to print the other side of the story—the side of the President, whoever he might be, forced to listen sometimes to untruths, sometimes to evasions, sometimes to office hunting and bargainings that the public never hears of.

From N. Y. Herald, April 2, 1909.

"THE CALL OF THE AFRICAN WILD"

"I suppose that is part of a President's job, but it tried my patience and my temper. I couldn't win the battle to control it when such matters were pressed upon me to the exclusion of more important things and I realized it. Over in Africa, I had some equally exasperating experiences but it was not difficult to master them. Back in my tent in the evenings I could laugh over them and talk with others about their ludicrous side. It was there that I came to know how to control my temper, and I have been able to do it ever since. It is a great battle won."

ROOT SAID TAFT HAD BROKEN DOWN

This frame of mind fitted the mood in which he had planned his life following his return to Oyster Bay. But other persons were shortly to exert a different influence. Scores of old followers were waiting all along the line home with protests against the Taft régime and insistence that Roosevelt alone could restore popularity to the party. He read their letters and listened to their stories, but his purpose remained unchanged.

In Egypt, Gifford Pinchot, since Governor of Pennsylvania, gave him his version of President Taft's activities and the consequences.

It was not until he reached London, several weeks later, in 1910 that the first definite impression was made upon Roosevelt—and Elihu Root was the man who made it. At least, that is what Roosevelt told me three or four years later. Roosevelt's statement to me was substantially this:

"Root told me that the Administration had completely broken down, particularly the State Department. He expected to see Congress go heavily Democratic, and he regarded New York as hopeless. Root spoke so unqualifiedly that I became convinced the party was in a bad way, but I could not see that I was called upon to throw myself into the situation. Moreover, what could I do? I could not ask the country to elect a Congress to support Taft in the way he seemed to be going, nor could I seek to elect a Congress against him. Root said something about the party needing me, but made no suggestion.

"In a way, his analysis of the situation was more hopeless than that of Gifford Pinchot, but I regarded Pinchot as naturally extreme; his experience with Taft had embittered him.

379

I believed that Taft was justified in dismissing Pinchot; Pinchot was right in his policies, but he should have resigned and fought his battle from the outside. His course was disorganizing the Department. There was nothing left for Taft to do but to drop Pinchot."

ROOSEVELT'S ROYAL WELCOME HOME

An emperor could not have had a greater welcome home than was accorded Roosevelt as his ship entered New York harbor. A reception committee met him, and a parade up Broadway followed his landing. It was a satisfying day in every respect save one—Roosevelt would not discuss politics. Many sought to get an expression of opinion, but not a word could be had. His first utterance of a political character was his telegram a month later from Harvard College to State Senator Frederick Davenport, of New York, urging the prompt enactment of the Hinman-Greene direct primary bill. That telegram followed his talk with Governor Hughes. After that flash from Roosevelt there came another period of silence.

Toward midsummer, Herbert Parsons, then Congressman, national committeeman and boss of New York City Republicans, called at the "Evening Mail's" office, and urged me to have our ship news reporter meet William Barnes, Jr., on an incoming steamer from Europe. He wanted Barnes asked whether he would favor Roosevelt as chairman of the approaching State convention. At that time Barnes was the acknowledged leader of the "Old Guard" Republicans in New York.

"Why should our ship news man waste time with that question?" I asked Parsons. "I can write Barnes' answer in advance. He's against it. He is for Sherman," (then Vice President).

"Of course he is against Roosevelt," came the quick response from Parsons. "I know that as well as you do. I want him to say so publicly. We have tried in every way to interest the Colonel in this convention, and have failed. He thinks he had better keep out of it. He's our only hope to gain control. A declaration by Barnes against him might stir the Colonel to action. Anyhow, we would be able to press him harder."

So down the bay on the revenue cutter went the "Evening Mail's" ship news reporter charged to induce Barnes to voice his hostility to the Colonel. The reporter did his work too well. That afternoon the "Evening Mail" published an interview with the returning Republican chieftain declaring against Roosevelt for chairman of the convention and in favor of Vice President Sherman. It was a characteristic Barnes talk —frank, positive, straight to the issue.

ROOSEVELT UNDERTAKES A LOSING BATTLE

Of course, I cannot say that the Barnes outburst led the Colonel finally to acquiesce in the movement to make him chairman of the convention and sponsor for the nomination of Henry L. Stimson, Taft's Secretary of War, for Governor. Parsons took the published interview to Oyster Bay, but I never asked how he used it there. All I know is that the Colonel's refusals grew milder. Finally he put aside his own settled purpose and yielded to the persuasion to get into battle. He tried to put hope into a hopeless gubernatorial fight in New York. He was named chairman over Sherman and he nominated Stimson, but the 1910 tide against the Republican party was too strong even for Roosevelt to stem.

It was a struggle that certainly had no promise for him. If he elected Stimson he would be handing the State over to a member of Taft's Cabinet as Governor. That surely was not furthering any political interest Roosevelt might have. If Stimson should be defeated, as seemed almost certain, the cry would go up that Roosevelt had been turned down by his own State in the first battle after his return.

As I Knew Them

The Colonel was advised to look upon that side of the question before identifying himself with such a hopeless prospect, but he refused. The result in New York was proportionately better for Republicans than in other States—(for the Democratic tidal wave ran high everywhere)—but that fact did not prevent the outcry that Roosevelt had been beaten in an effort to capture the Republican organization in the Empire State.

CHAPTER XLVII

THE TAFT BREAK, AS TOLD BY ROOSEVELT

"Preposterous To Believe I Would Want A President To Be Merely A Pale Shadow"—He And Taft Knew The Facts And In Their Own Hearts Could Decide—The Naming Of Luke Wright—"Tell The Boys I Want To Continue All Of Them," Said Taft, But All Were Dropped —All That Roosevelt Asked Was That Taft Should Satisfy The People.

NOW, permit me to recall to the reader my talk with Roosevelt in the White House a few days before the expiration of his term, for I want to reveal here what was deep down in his mind at the very moment he was urging others to give Taft a fair chance.

To tell the story properly I must state that in February, 1916, I was in Trinidad, West Indies, with Colonel Roosevelt and returned home with him on the steamer Matura. We had many talks on deck those twelve or thirteen days at sea. One afternoon I said to him:

"Colonel, all your enemies and a few of your friends think that you broke with Taft because you could not control him, and that you, therefore, are more to blame than Taft. I know that is not true, but I do not know, nor does anyone else know, the facts from your own lips."

"It's too preposterous," he interrupted.

"Maybe it is," I responded, "but you are not fair to yourself to remain silent."

"Taft knows it is not so; I know it is not so," he again interrupted rather hotly. "It does not concern others."

"Yes, it does," I insisted. "It concerns me as your friend; it concerns the four and a quarter million voters who supported you in 1912. They have to defend you against such charges; they do so because of their faith in you but you give them no help in the way of fact. I think you owe it to them to do so."

"It has never come to me in that light," Roosevelt replied. "I have regarded whether faith was kept or not as a matter that only Taft and I knew and in our own hearts could decide. So I have had nothing to say, but if you care now to take down a statement of the facts I will be glad to make one only to be released publicly after you and I agree that it should be."

Other matters engaged attention after our return home, and I never pressed for "leave to print." Here is that statement:

(STATEMENT MADE TO ME AND REVISED BY THEODORE ROOSEVELT ON S.S. MATURA, RETURNING FROM TRINIDAD, H. L. S.)

"There was no one incident on which I broke with Taft. It was a series of incidents, an accumulation of disappointments and of positive evidences of failure to carry out in action the intentions he expressed in words. None of these matters included in the remotest degree anything in which I had a personal interest—that is, an interest in which I as an individual was solely concerned.

"I never asked him to do a single thing; I was deeply concerned that the Republican party should continue to be the party of idealism and of advancing policies. I knew and recognized that it had a period of constructive work ahead of it, rather than destructive work, and I realized that in the evolution of things there would have to be adjustments and changes from the lines laid down in my own administration.

"It is perfectly preposterous for anyone to believe that I would want a President of the United States to be merely a pale shadow of his predecessor, no matter who that predecessor might be.

"In the case of Mr. Taft it must be manifest to everyone

that the only way he could justify the deep interest I had shown in his nomination and election was by making an Administration that would satisfy the people. His relations with me could not be made the test of his success or failure.

"Yes, it is true that before I left the White House I began to see another Taft than the Taft I knew as Secretary of War. When he came to me to go over his letter of acceptance, I gave him the best advice I could regarding it, and to a large extent he acted on it. At that time, he exhausted the English language for words with which to express his obligation to me.

"About that time, I had to name a successor to him as Secretary of War. I told him it was difficult to get a first-class man to take the place for a few months. He asked me if I had anyone in mind, and I replied yes. I wanted to name a Southern Democrat, and had Luke Wright of Tennessee in mind. I added that I did not believe I could get Wright for such a short time, but that if he felt that he would like to have him too, the fact might weigh with him. Taft replied that it would be a fine appointment, and he would be glad to have him in his Cabinet.

" 'Remember that I am not asking this as a favor to me,' I continued. 'I am trying to get a good man in the interests of the department. I would prefer to name a man whom you will continue, but if you do not care to commit yourself I will go ahead and do the best I can without involving you at all.'

"Taft reiterated that he would be more than pleased to continue Wright if I named him.

" 'Then I can tell Wright, when I offer him the place, that I am speaking for you as well as for myself?'

" 'You can.'

"I did so, but Mr. Wright's career as Secretary of War ended when Taft became President.

"About the same time, Taft brought up the subject of his Cabinet. 'I wish you would tell the boys I have been working with that I want to continue all of them,' he said. 'They are all fine fellows, and they have been mighty good to me. I want them all to stay just as they are.'

" 'Why don't you tell them so yourself?' I asked.

" 'No, I don't want to do that. I don't want to make any promises. I want to be in a position to say that I have no promises out. I wish, though, that you would tell them just how I feel and let them know that I want the Cabinet to stand just as it is.'

" 'That cannot be,' I replied, 'and should not be. Metcalf, for instance, wants to go back to California. Root wants to get out of public life unless he can be United States Senator, and I do not believe that you and Cortelyou would get on well together. Those changes must come, I believe. Straus, Meyer, Garfield and Wilson, however, would, I think, be glad to stay on, and if you really want me to talk with them about it, I will gladly tell them of your intentions.'

" 'Yes, I wish you would,' replied Taft.

"I acted on Taft's suggestion within the next day or two, and the matter seemed to be settled until shortly after election the men named heard from several quarters that Mr. Taft was considering their successors. Naturally, they came to me about it, and investigation proved that the rumors were true. All four men were slated to go.

"Senator Lodge, of Massachusetts, interested himself in behalf of George Meyer and persuaded Taft to reconsider his decision. In order to have this new decision hold until the appointment was made, I sent for Meyer one day while Taft was calling upon me, and told Taft that Meyer was on his way over to thank him for the assurance he had given Lodge the day before.

"Perhaps if the matter had been permitted to drift, Taft might have changed his mind again. As it was he and Wilson were the only men continued, although Hitchcock was restored to the place he resigned when he became Taft's campaign manager.

"Now, to go back to the period of the campaign, I found

as we got into September that Taft was drifting more and more away from the men with whom he had been identified. I do not refer to myself alone, for I tried hard to keep out of his affairs except to the extent that he and others with him believed I could be helpful. But a policy of exclusion of all the men who had any relation at all with me or what I stood for seemed to have been inaugurated, under the guidance of Charles and Henry Taft."

CHAPTER XLVIII

"MY HAT'S IN THE RING!"

The News Stirred The Deadened Party Waters Into Tempest-Tossed Waves Through 1912—Roosevelt's Early Refusals Cost Many Delegates—"Let Taft Take His Spanking," Said The Colonel—Taft Named Because "There's Nothing Else To Do"—"Gentlemen, They're Off!" Said Roosevelt—Walter Brown Urges A Columbus Speech And Promises A Crowd That Will Tie Up The Trolley Lines Of The City—It Does That, And More, Too.

"MY hat's in the ring!"—Roosevelt.

"Death alone can take me out now!"—Taft.

"I'm nobody's cloak. I'll fight to the finish!"—La Follette.

These three declarations in the early weeks of 1912 gave Republicans warning of a more destructive storm than the party had ever been called upon to weather. The Mugwump revolt in the Blaine campaign of 1884 was a summer breeze compared with the typhoon-like character of this new conflict, though in each year the Republican party was split and a Democrat elected President. It was not out of line with the emotional character of the 1912 campaign that, toward its close, the country was startled by the shooting of Roosevelt while in Milwaukee.

Clouds had been gathering over Republican councils ever since the 1910 Congress elections had demonstrated that the Taft Administration was not in favor. The Republican national committee, meeting at Washington in December, 1911, in the spirit of men arranging funeral services, had chosen Chicago, June 18, as the place and time for the national convention. The absurd idea that every President must be renominated, and the known power of a President to force his own renomination, led Republican leaders gloomily to accept

388

Taft as inescapable and to prepare to take their licking at the polls in November.

"There's nothing else to do," was the hopeless answer to inquiries.

The announcements from Taft and La Follette were accepted as perfunctory campaign literature. Not a ripple disturbed the mill-pond stillness of party waters. A fog-bank of inevitable defeat enveloped everyone. Nothing mattered much.

When later Roosevelt threw his hat in the ring, however, all knew stirring times were ahead; at once the waters lost their calmness.

NOBODY KNEW—NOT EVEN THE COLONEL

Before his announcement there had been rumors, plenty of them, that Roosevelt would be in the field. Many friends had been asserting it, many denying it, many hoping it, many deploring it. *Nobody knew—not even the Colonel himself.* Had he known it and decided it five or six weeks earlier than he did, his majority in the Chicago convention would have been too big to be tampered with; but that's another story.

Some people will always believe that Roosevelt eagerly sought the 1912 nomination, despite all that may be said to them by those close to him and who knew his mind. I realize the futility of endeavoring to change an unchangeable opinion. I have no illusions of that kind. The story I tell is my own experience, my own knowledge and my own interpretation. I must let it go at that.

Roosevelt had the privilege of every other citizen to seek the nomination, and if I believed that he did actually desire it I would offer no apology in his behalf. He was a citizen, a Republican, and out of office; no voters had to support him in the primaries unless they cared to do so. In the long list of delegates elected for him in the tremendous sweep of

state-wide primaries all had to win despite the antagonism
of a national administration's patronage and influence.

"NOT YET, BUT SOON"

"LET TAFT TAKE HIS SPANKING"

I suppose I talked AT Colonel Roosevelt a dozen times
during the last three months of 1911. My voice was only one
of many—most of the others being important Republican
leaders in different States. All had the same experience—he
did not want the nomination. The reader will recall the talk
I print on an earlier page in which he stated some of his
reasons.

When the National Committee in Washington adjourned
the gloom among the members led them to gather in groups
discussing the hopeless outlook. One group was composed of
Walter Brown, of Ohio, Frank Knox, then of Michigan and

now of New Hampshire, and Edward Lee, of Indiana. Each of these men was chairman of his State organization. They agreed that only a Roosevelt candidacy would have any hope of success, and determined to go to New York city to see the Colonel. They telephoned him they were going over to see him. He asked them not to do so. Their visit would be misconstrued.

"Some other members of the committee have said they wanted to see me," he continued, "and I have told them the same thing."

Still they persisted. It was finally agreed that the three State Chairmen would call at Oyster Bay next day.

When they arrived the Colonel did not wait for his visitors to state their views. He began the talk:

"I am not in this situation," he said, "and I am not going to be dragged into it. Taft created it and let Taft take his spanking for it. There is no reason why I should. If I wanted four years more in the White House I would say so and go after it; but I don't want it. I've had enough. I couldn't go back without risking all I gained in the seven years I was there."

NOT THE ONLY MAN WHO COULD WIN

"Colonel," interrupted Frank Knox, "I never knew you to show the white feather, and you should not do so now."

"What do you mean by that?" asked Roosevelt, astonished and angered.

"Why you are basing your refusal on the possibly bad effect another term might have on your reputation," replied Knox. "I contend that you ought to look at this thing from the party's interests and not your own. The party has honored you, and it now turns to you to do a service for it. It is in distress and it needs you."

"By George," said Roosevelt, "that would be a good argument if I were the only man available, but I am not. I agree that Taft cannot be elected. I do not know that any Republican can be elected, but if the party can win I am not the only Republican with whom it can win. I am not ungrateful for the honor I have had, but I think I have repaid in service. When I left the White House every State we had any right to expect was in the Republican column. It is not my job to put them back again."

The three chairmen left Oyster Bay convinced that Roosevelt could not be induced to run.

I knew nothing of this Brown-Lee-Knox interview. I, too, had been in Washington while the National Committeemen were in session; I, too, had returned to New York determined to try to change Roosevelt's point of view. I saw him at the "Outlook" office. It was the same old story,—no, no, no!

George W. Perkins, Frank Munsey, William L. Ward and others urged vigorously and had the same experience.

With the new year, however, came insistent demands from all over the country. Telegrams, letters, visitors crowded in on him. Little by little he began to modify his "no"; little by little he began to ask questions about conditions in one State and another.

"GENTLEMEN, THEY'RE OFF!"

I shall never forget the evening meeting in J. West Roosevelt's home in New York city early in February, 1912, when Roosevelt acquiesced. The house was a typical old New York home. A score of us had distributed ourselves in the nooks and corners of what New Yorkers once called their "back parlor." The hair-covered chairs and sofas with their curving mahogany frames were in keeping. Father Knickerbocker would have rejoiced at sight of them.

The Colonel sat in an arm chair, high-backed and wide, in the center of the room directly under the chandelier, the frosted glass globes of which only dimly-lighted the room. First, Governor Hadley, of Missouri, and other Governors present, talked, then the party leaders from different States; then the three or four editors.

Every man gave his frank opinion as to his own State as well as the nation. The Colonel made inquiries of each of us but expressed no opinion. Finally, we had had our say. There was an interval. Many of us began exchanging views in a low tone, while waiting for the Colonel to speak. He was evidently doing some hard thinking. Suddenly he raised his hands high, outstretching them as though in benediction. Quickly closing them he brought his fists down like a flash, each fist striking an arm of his chair with a bang and in a tone almost a shout, exclaimed:

"Gentlemen, they're off!"

We knew the presidential race had started!

BROWN GETS THE COLONEL FOR COLUMBUS

Walter Brown had come on from Ohio for the meeting and also to persuade Roosevelt to address the State Constitutional Convention then in session at Columbus, Ohio.

"Colonel," he said, "Wilson came out to Columbus and didn't cause a ripple, Taft came out and there was not enough of a crowd to halt a trolley car; if you will come there will be such a crowd that the whole traction system of Columbus will be tied up."

The Colonel was strongly against a speech-making campaign. He thought the contest should be conducted on higher lines. Brown, however, argued that a Constitutional Convention dealt with organic law; it was not an ordinary gathering. The Colonel could accept the invitation of such a body without being compelled to speak elsewhere.

Finally the Colonel said he would go provided certain men would approve. William L. Ward, of Westchester County, New York, George Perkins, Medill McCormick and two others whom I cannot recall were named. I was the sixth member of the group. We met next afternoon at the Perkins

393

house. The final vote stood five in favor of going to Columbus. Ward asked for time to think it over. So far as I know, he is still thinking it over. The Colonel accepted the verdict of the jury and agreed to go.

ROOSEVELT OBJECTS TO TWO-REVOLUTION MEN

Meanwhile La Follette's followers were crowding into New York city, to urge Roosevelt to accept their platform and become their candidate. Governor Hiram Johnson, just then emerging as a national figure, was in the group, which comprised all types of radicals.

La Follette's collapse physically in Philadelphia made it doubtful whether he would ever regain his health, still more doubtful that he would be able to carry on his battle for the nomination.

"I can stand one-revolution men," commented Roosevelt when he heard the names of some of those who were to call upon him, "but two-revolution fellows are too much for me; they want to be revolting all the time. I cannot be their candidate."

CHAPTER XLIX

THAT COLUMBUS SPEECH

La Follette's Lieutenants Sought To Edit The "Recall of Judicial Decisions" Address, But Roosevelt Stuck To The Lines Of His "Outlook" Editorial—Nevertheless, The Country Was Astounded And The Colonel Knew He Had Made A Mistake—It Surely Tied Up More Than The Trolleys Of Columbus—Roosevelt Surprised And Depressed—A Campaign Of Real Spirit—Where Roosevelt Won—Barnes And La Follette As Allies.

IT was unfortunate that the visit of the La Follette men to Roosevelt happened while he was preparing his Columbus speech. They insisted that he should say something to justify them in going over to him in a body. They made a number of suggestions; some he accepted, many he rejected. The big battle between them came over the recall of judges. That was a popular issue in the western States, as dear to the La Follette men as 16 to 1 was to Bryan. The Colonel flatly refused to endorse it. He had them read his signed editorial in "The Outlook" of January 6. Several days of discussion resulted in Roosevelt's concession that the recall of judges might be advocated "as a last resort" but he insisted that the "last resort" was far in the future and not justified by existing conditions. On this basis he resumed work on his speech.

Many others besides the La Follette men saw the first draft of the document and urged their widely differing views. Some did not like the subject, urging other topics; but so far as I ever heard no one foresaw the damaging effect of the speech. The final revision was read by Frank Munsey, E. C. Converse and William L. Ward in the Vanderbilt Hotel, New York

City. When the Colonel heard from that group he turned to me and said: "Don't let anyone know you have that speech. Give it to the Associated Press. I don't want to see it again. I want to be able to say that it is out of my hands."

TYING UP THE COLUMBUS TRAFFIC

Meanwhile, out in Ohio, Walter Brown was hustling to make good his assertion that the Colonel's appearance in

From the Cincinnati Enquirer.

IN THE RING AFTER IT

Columbus would tie up the city's traction system. The State seemed to be awaiting his arrival. On his way out, Roosevelt stopped over-night in Cleveland. Of course the local reporters sought an interview; of course they wanted to know whether he had decided to run.

Then came that historic declaration that flashed over the country like a streak of lightning.

"My hat's in the ring! The fight is on and I'm stripped to the buff!"

Next morning he went on to Columbus. It snowed hard. Nevertheless the crowd that Brown had prophesied was on hand to tie up the trolley system.

It was not the tie-up of the trolleys, however, that concerned Roosevelt and others next day when they read the newspaper headlines featuring the recall of judicial decisions, and adding interviews with lawyers strongly denouncing the Colonel's utterance.

"It looks to me as though we had tied up the whole campaign as well as the Columbus trolleys," I wired to George Perkins, who had gone to California.

Newspapers and politicians opposed to Roosevelt pounced upon the speech as though it were a new and surprising declaration by the Colonel "to catch the crowd." Yet they should have known that substantially every thought in it was printed in his signed editorial "Judges and Progress" in "The Outlook" six weeks earlier.

THE STORM AMAZED ROOSEVELT

Many theories might be advanced for the explosion that followed this reiteration of his views. Their first publication had created no such consternation. Of course, in January, he had not declared himself a candidate, while only the night before his Columbus speech he had thrown his hat in the ring. Probably that accounts for the different reaction. Whatever the explanation may be the fact is that it was the most sensational campaign utterance since Burchard's "Rum, Romanism and Rebellion" speech in 1884.

Roosevelt, like Blaine, was amazed. Just as Blaine refused for several days to make any effort to repair the damage Burchard had done, so not until a week later, when he visited the Massachusetts Legislature, did Roosevelt look upon the agitation as more than a flurry. In Boston he was staggered and depressed by the fierceness of the assaults upon him.

He had never been called upon to meet such a storm, and he could not understand it.

I do not share the opinion that the speech cost him the nomination. I do not believe that in the net result at Chicago it cost him a single delegate. In the East, the delegates he failed to secure were under "organization" control and would not have been for him anyhow. In New York City, for instance, with or without the Columbus speech, he had no chance against the local machine headed by Samuel S. Koenig. Koenig fought fair, but he fought to win. The West liked what Roosevelt had said.

The Columbus speech hurt because it intensified the opposition not because it cost votes in the convention. It always cut Roosevelt to the quick to be assailed as a reckless radical, and on this occasion the assaults depressed him because some came from men who he thought knew his purposes in life.

ROOSEVELT, FIRST DEPRESSED, THEN VIGOROUS

The letters and telegrams that deluged Roosevelt following his speech and the incidents of a visit to Boston, where he addressed the Legislature, put the Colonel in a frame of mind to abandon the whole campaign.

Such spells of despondency never lasted long with him, however.

He went to work on his reply to the Governors of seven States who had united in a joint request for him to enter the primaries. All his old-time vigor came out in that reply. He knew precisely what he wanted to say and how he wanted to say it, and no revisionists dotted an I or crossed a T. In that letter you will find the real Roosevelt.

Steadily the contest developed. Reluctantly Roosevelt agreed to speak—first in one place, then in another—until at last he was booked for a tour as in a Presidential campaign. He had resisted that kind of a contest, but the appeals for him to speak here, there and everywhere were beyond his control. Had he foreseen them I doubt whether he would have undertaken the fight.

"FIGURE OUT HOW MUCH YOU WANT," SAID MUNSEY

With the struggle in progress, however, he put himself in the hands of Senator Joseph Dixon of Montana, and Oscar King Davis, chairman and secretary of the campaign committee, and like a trained soldier he obeyed orders. When Dixon and Davis came over from Washington to New York in February to be told that they were to conduct the fight for delegates, they asked the obvious question how much they could spend for publicity and where the money would come from.

"Figure out how much you want," said Frank Munsey.

After some discussion Dixon finally said, "We ought to be sure of $50,000."

"I'll underwrite that much if you two will take the midnight train back to Washington and start work tomorrow morning," replied Munsey.

"Done!" was the joint response.

The campaign thus begun brought out every energy and enthusiasm of those engaged in it. If you were interested in it at all you were overwhelmingly interested. Sacrifice of time, of money, of comfort, meant nothing; to win delegates was the one thought. Sacrifices were never made so freely as in the fight for Roosevelt's nomination. Certainly in the subsequent Progressive party campaign for election, individual ambitions were thrust aside as never before. For many persons, their course meant exile from party honors for years to come. All knew it and all accepted.

If the experience was not the biggest thing in our lives it was the finest—the one we knew would be the best remembered by each of us in years to come; there were no doubters, no timid ones; we believed we were engaged in a battle for the right, and we battled with the fervor of the righteous.

As I Knew Them

THE "STEAM-ROLLER" CONVENTION

Of the struggle to elect delegates to the convention, of the fight in Chicago against the steam-roller that ousted enough Roosevelt delegates to give Taft control, the story is too familiar to be told again. William L. Ward, George Perkins and Frank Munsey were the directing heads. It was the first experience in politics for Perkins and Munsey, but Ward, of course, was even then a veteran.

You couldn't pull a trigger faster than Perkins could act. Time and again in the late afternoon he would have a dozen telephone conferences with as many different States, so as to have action everywhere at once. Down in Washington, Senator Dixon and Oscar King Davis were also fighting with tireless energy, for they had Congress as well as the country to look after.

Roosevelt did not lose a State in which a primary was held, except Wisconsin and North Dakota, where La Follette won. Those victories meant that the great Republican States of the nation were lined against the Republican President they had supported four years before. One of the strongest influences in the primaries was a series of articles in Munsey's Magazine by Judson C. Welliver, entitled "Catching up with Roosevelt" —revealing Taft's inability to do so. More than a million copies were distributed.

A vote-making campaigner and a real joy to all of us was Bainbridge Colby. He was never more ready in wit, brilliant in phrasing or vigorous in assault than when he was darting out to fill over-night speaking engagements. Enthusiastic, tireless and determined, he inspired everyone to greater effort. Colby also led the battle for the Roosevelt delegates before the national committee. Had the Southern delegates, chiefly colored, controlled by office-holders been taken out of the Taft column, Roosevelt would have had almost two to one of the convention. As it was, he had two-thirds of the delegates from

Republican States, and a clear majority of the whole convention, but the national committee saw to it that the temporary roll of the convention was made up with a majority for Taft.

Making up that roll was the last work of the committee before it officially ceased to exist. It had been chosen in 1908. As soon as the convention met, each State would name a committeeman and a new committee would thus be formed. Could the contests have come before the new committee, chosen by the just-elected delegates, the Taft forces would have had only a minority of its members, and no unseating would have succeeded.

The absurd custom still prevails that a national committee which goes out of office with the opening of a convention dictates the temporary officers and makes out the roll of delegates. It is a sort of dead man's hand over the initial proceedings. However, in 1912, the dead man's hand had a lively knowledge of its baleful influence, for Bainbridge Colby and other speakers did not spare them.

BARNES AND LA FOLLETTE AS ALLIES

I have always insisted that two men were chiefly responsible for the defeat of progressivism at Chicago—Robert M. La Follette and William Barnes, Jr., then boss of the Republican machine in the State of New York, and field marshal of Taft's working forces in the national convention. No two men in politics were further apart in purpose than La Follette and Barnes. They had not one thing in common except defeat of Roosevelt. It was an unusual coalition. It exemplified the old saying that politics make strange bedfellows, but never stranger than these two men with heads on one pillow dreaming the same dream—Barnes, a reactionary of the straitest sect, La Follette, progressive.

Barnes, resourceful and daring, directed the ousting of Roosevelt delegates by the national committee. He furnished the brains and the courage. The Committeemen furnished the votes. Barnes' task was to get enough Taft delegates on the temporary roll to elect Elihu Root as temporary chairman. Control of the convention would naturally follow.

La Follette, self-centered and vindictive, declared that the leadership of the Progressive cause belonged to him and to him only. He was determined that no one should displace him. He preferred to have the reactionaries remain in control—even nominate Taft—rather than have anyone but himself come out of the battle as leader. His own candidacy for

THE OLD ORDER—THE LASH OF THE BOSS

the nomination had degenerated from an ambitious hope that he would be named to a vengeful determination not to allow any other Progressive, especially Roosevelt, to be named. North Dakota was the only State supporting La Follette outside of Wisconsin. The delegates from those two States pleaded with him to release them from their instructions so that they could vote for Roosevelt, but he threatened lifelong antagonism to anyone who broke from his column.

Holding his delegates in a detached group, varying from seventeen to forty according to circumstances, was the La Follette way of cooperating with Barnes. He meant just that many less votes for Roosevelt.

LA FOLLETTE'S ONLY PURPOSE

When the test vote came, Root had 558 votes or a majority of 38 in a total vote of 1078.

Thus, "Fighting Bob's" rule or ruin attitude made him the ally of reactionary forces he had been denouncing for years. He and Barnes made Taft possible. Had Barnes been less daring or La Follette more true to the cause than to his own revenges, Taft would not have been nominated.

CHAPTER L

THE PROGRESSIVE CONVENTION

Personality, Plenty Of It, Reigned And Rejoiced—A "Call" Or A Plat-
form—Munsey Talks Dieting To Roosevelt—Beveridge Insists On His
Day—"I Want To Be A Bull Moose"—A Great Speech By Bever-
idge—"We Stand At Armageddon."

IF YOU did not attend the convention of the national Progressive party in 1912, you missed a thrilling and memorable occasion. Whether or not you agreed with its purpose, you
couldn't help applauding its spirit, its tensity, its honest belief
that it stood at Armageddon and was battling for the Lord.
Its equal has not been held in my day. Every delegate was his
own commander, and delighted in nothing so much as in challenging the right of anyone to stop him thinking and advocating anything he pleased.

Perhaps this independence was emphasized by the fact that
every delegate and alternate paid his own expenses, and
naturally felt entitled to something out of the usual. Those
not familiar with political conventions may not realize what
it means when I say that every delegate and alternate paid his
own expenses. Such a thing never happens in a regular party
convention. Rival candidates for nomination are anxious to
pay the bills of their supporters. The total often reaches high
figures. We had no rival candidates in the Progressive convention. There was only one man to nominate.

There was a deeper reason, though, for compelling all who
attended to pay their own way. No one knew what kind of
a convention could be assembled in Chicago in midsummer at
a month's notice. We knew that it would tell us, by the size
and earnestness of its membership, whether or not there was a

real response "from the bushes" to the revolt from Taft. We wanted that test made on the right basis.

There would be no test if railroad fares and hotel bills were paid in advance. Two convention halls easily could be filled if that were done. A real test could be made only by establishing a rule against providing a dollar for such expenditures, and trusting to luck for a quorum in the convention. At least we would know whether we had a convention or only a caucus. This rule was rigidly adhered to,—even when it was evident that men who had attended the Taft convention could not actually afford a second one. This pay-your-own-way plan proved a success.

PERSONALITY REIGNED AND REJOICED

Instead of lessening the number of delegates as some feared, there were double delegations from many States. A finer body of men and women never were gathered. Personality reigned everywhere,—there was plenty of it and to spare —from Gov. Hiram Johnson, of California, who was in the Seventh Heaven of delight, because he was in revolt; to Charles Sumner Bird, of Boston; "Bill" Flynn, of Pittsburgh; Cuney, the Texas Leaguer unseated in the Taft convention; Francis J. Heney, of California; the suave and eloquent William A. Prendergast, of Brooklyn (who made a brilliant speech nominating Roosevelt); Bainbridge Colby afire with indignation over the national committee's steam-roller; E. A. Van Valkenburg, of Philadelphia; William Allen White and Henry Allen, of Kansas; Oscar S. Straus, Chauncey Hamlin and Paul Block, of New York; and the famous western Governors who had round-robined Roosevelt into running.

You could get a spark, a flash, of hot discussion from a group of delegates as easily as a smithy hammers one out on an anvil. The joy of friction began long before the convention assembled.

It began early in July with the call for the convention.

Burdened and perplexed with many other demands, Roosevelt had undertaken to write the call. As usual, he showed the draft to one person; then to another. All had suggestions. The Colonel had his hardest struggle to keep the term Republican out of the new party title. He insisted that Republican

From the N. Y. Sun.

"THE OPEN ROAD"

was a hopeless name down South; with a party having some other title, he could gain thousands of votes there. He might even carry one or two States. Roosevelt thought splitting the "Solid South" would be a great political service.

A "CALL" OR A PLATFORM?

By the time he had accepted many suggestions the "call" was a document of 3,000 words. He sent it to Senator Joseph

Dixon, in New York city, with instructions to lock it in his desk until released next day (Sunday) for the Monday newspapers. Dixon put it in his desk but failed to lock the desk. I happened along while Dixon was out to lunch; seating myself at his desk I looked around for something to read until he returned. There lay the call! Without any thought of its contents I picked up the manuscript, and began to read it. Frank Munsey came in at that moment and asked me what I had found to interest me so deeply. I told him and began to read it aloud to him. I had not read far before he stopped me and said, "That's not a call, it's a platform. We don't want to send out anything like that."

"It's all interlined with T. R.'s handwriting," I replied, "and I guess it will have to go."

While we were talking, Dixon returned with Perkins. His eyes fell on the document in my hands, and if he were not a Quaker I am sure he would have used unprintable language. Munsey insisted on cutting more than half of the "call." I agreed with him. For an hour we discussed it. Then Perkins telephoned the Colonel that it wouldn't do. What was said I do not know. Perkins laughingly said he did not care to be shot; he would not go to Oyster Bay to discuss it. He left for home. Finally, another telephone talk, and Munsey and I were asked to go to Oyster Bay, to supper—and discussion.

When we got there, a hot July night, we found the Colonel in anything but a placid mood. "There are no two men I would ordinarily welcome here more cordially than you two," is the way he greeted us, "but tonight, in view of your mission, there are no two men I want less to see."

MUNSEY TALKS DIETING TO ROOSEVELT

At the evening meal, Munsey sat on the Colonel's right and I sat on his left. Every moment I felt there would be an explosion, for Munsey had been studying dieting and he kept telling the Colonel how wrong it was to eat cold roast beef and

baked Idaho potatoes. Roosevelt was taking a plentiful helping of both. Nor did Munsey believe in salt, which the
Colonel indulged in heavily. The peril of heavy eating and
the benefits of light eating were told us with the deadly
earnestness of a revival preacher. Still the Colonel kept on
eating. He would look—almost glare—at Munsey and then
take another mouthful; look again, listen a moment, and then
go at the roast beef with renewed gusto.

All the time our threatened revision of the "call" was also
on Roosevelt's mind—and nerves.

Several attempts were made by others at the table to divert
the conversation to other topics than dieting. But Munsey
was always deeply in earnest in anything that interested him,
and it was difficult to get him away from a subject until he
felt that he had enlightened and convinced his listeners. On
that occasion he was doing almost everything but convincing.
He did not lessen by an ounce the Colonel's meal. My own
appetite went unsatisfied because I kept trying to decide on
what I would do when the Colonel would blurt out his impatience. The Colonel, however, stuck to his food and his
patience.

Soon, we were in the library discussing the "call." It was
midnight before the document was cut to half its original
length.

"Now, gentlemen," said the Colonel as we left for New
York city, "we have had our battle tonight and you have
won. You were right. It would have been a mistake to have
allowed that call to go as it was."

That was a typical Roosevelt surrender,—frank and complete.

BEVERIDGE INSISTS ON HIS DAY

The Progressive convention was called for August 5 at
Chicago. Senator Albert J. Beveridge, of Indiana, who was
slated for temporary chairman, was also to make the opening

address. Roosevelt was anxious that every delegate should know at the outset precisely what the new party meant. It was arranged, therefore, that he was to speak immediately after Beveridge. When the Indiana Senator learned that he and Roosevelt were bunched in the same afternoon, there was an outburst that threatened for a time the whole convention schedule. Beveridge declared, quite properly, that the papers would publish the Roosevelt speech and minimize his. Two stars could not shine in the same firmament. Beveridge telephoned from York Harbor, Maine, insisting upon a day to himself or no speech.

Gov. John N. Parker, of Louisiana, who was scheduled for permanent chairman, was entitled to his opportunity on the second day, and there were a score of orators for the third and last day. Thus the task of arranging speakers was as delicate as arranging the precedence of diplomats at a dinner. There were not enough days to go around. The Colonel had prepared what he called a "Confession of Faith." It contained 20,000 words, even after Oscar King Davis had edited it down to a point at which the Colonel stoutly demurred. But Roosevelt still insisted upon speaking the first day, and so did Beveridge.

Finally, in the Colonel's library, Davis evolved the theory that a big 16 inch gun should follow and not precede a little gun. Roosevelt should have the second day, provided Parker would yield as permanent Chairman. Parker generously yielded—and Beveridge and the Colonel each had his day.

Such were two of many incidents in that gathering destined to make political history. They tried one's patience and one's nerves, but they were the outcroppings of intense earnestness, and finally melded into a great enthusiasm that swept us along through three months of hard, up-hill campaigning until the last ballot was cast on election day.

We did not win the election, but we had been in battle, and the zest of conflict, the thrill of a stubborn fight for what we believed was right had stirred us more deeply than any other political contest ever had before or is likely to do again.

The convention was in the mood for a jubilant, heroic time. Every State delegation entered the hall in marching order cheering and being cheered. Governor Hiram Johnson marched at the head of the Californians, whose banner read:

> "I want to be a Bull Moose,
> And with the Bull Moose stand
> With Antlers on my forehead
> And a Big Stick in my hand."

The Michigan men got the whole convention parading to the tune of their song:

> "Follow, follow,
> We will follow Roosevelt,
> Anywhere, everywhere,
> We will follow on!"

And the New York delegation, headed by Oscar S. Straus, marched through the aisles singing "Onward Christian Soldiers!" Surely, we were all set for a fine, care-free time;—in just the mood to greet Senator Beveridge's opening sentences as Chairman: "Knowing the price we must pay, knowing the sacrifice we must make, the burdens we must carry and the assaults we must endure,—knowing full well the cost, yet we enlist for the war!"

The Beveridge speech was one of the strongest ever delivered in a political convention; had it been made in a regular party convention, it would have been accorded a place in political oratory with the Conkling, Ingersoll, Garfield and Bryan speeches.

No wonder Roosevelt greeted him afterward with the exclamation "A great speech, Albert! I'm glad you insisted on your own day. It's worth two days!"

As I Knew Them

The speech was a splendid summary of Progressive purposes. These extracts give an indication of its trend:

"We stand for a nobler America. We stand for an undivided nation. We stand for a broader liberty, a fuller justice. We stand for social brotherhood as against savage individualism. We stand for an intelligent co-operation instead of a reckless competition. We stand for mutual helpfulness instead of mutual hatred. We stand for equal rights as a fact of life instead of a catchword of politics. We stand for the rule of the people as a practical truth instead of a meaningless pretence. We stand for a representative government that represents the people. We battle for the actual rights of man.

"For the party comes from the grass roots. It has grown from the soil of the people's hard necessities. It has the vitality of the people's strong convictions. The people have work to be done and our party is here to do that work. Abuse will only strengthen it, ridicule only hasten its growth, falsehood only speed its victory.

"The root of the wrongs which hurt the people is the fact that the people's government has been taken away from them. The government must be given back. And so the first purpose of the Progressive Party is to make sure the rule of the people. The rule of the people means that the people themselves shall nominate as well as elect all candidates for office, including Senators and presidents of the United States. What profiteth it the people if they do only the electing while the invisible government does the nominating?

"The first work before us is the revival of honest business. For business is nothing but the industrial and trade activities of all the people. Men grow the products of the field, cut ripe timber from the forest, dig metal from the mine, fashion all for human use, carry them to the market place and exchange them according to their mutual needs, and this is business.

"Present day business is as unlike old time business as the old time ox-cart is unlike the present day locomotive. Invention has made the world over again. The railroad, telegraph and telephone have bound the people of modern nations into families. To do the business of these closely knit millions in every modern country great business concerns came into being. What we call big business is the child of the economic progress of mankind. Warfare to destroy big business is foolish because it cannot succeed and wicked because it ought not to succeed. Warfare to destroy big business does not hurt big business, which always comes out on top, so much as it hurts all other business which, in such a warfare, never comes out on top."

Beveridge concluded:

"The Progressive Party believes that the Constitution is a living thing, growing with the people's growth, strengthening with the people's strength, aiding the people in their struggle for life, liberty and the pursuit of happiness, permitting the people to meet all their needs as conditions change.

"The opposition believes that the Constitution is a dead form, holding back the people's growth, shackling the people's strength but giving a free hand to malign powers that prey upon the people.

"The first words of the Constitution are 'We the people' and they declare that the Constitution's purpose is 'to form a perfect union and to promote the general welfare.'

"To do just that is the very heart of the Progressive cause."

"WE STAND AT ARMAGEDDON!"

The same turbulence lasted throughout the three days' session. Roosevelt's appearance on the platform the second day led to an hour's demonstration, which was repeated when he closed with these words:

"To you men who have come together to spend and be spent in the endless crusade against wrong, to you who face the future resolute and confident, to you who strive in a spirit of brotherhood for the betterment of our nation, I say now as I said here six weeks ago, we stand at Armageddon and we battle for the Lord."

It was in the color of such a convention that no one should ask a formal roll call on any question or demand a ballot for candidates. We were voting enthusiasms, and they could neither be counted nor divided. It probably is the only national convention of which it can be said that it never had a roll call or cast a ballot.

The great climax came when the two nominees, Roosevelt and Johnson, appeared on the stage, walking side by side

THE SPIRIT OF 1912!

to the front, while a banner was unfolded from the rafters above them reading:

"Roosevelt and Johnson!
New York and California
Hands across the Continent!
For there is neither east nor west
Border nor breed nor birth,
When two strong men stand face to face
Though they come from the ends of the earth."

Naturally, that convention has a tender place in my memory. I shared its spirit fully, and I prize the recollection of every moment of those three days as a lifelong treasure. If the earnestness and high purpose of those delegates could be put into the conventions of the regular party organizations, there would be no need for protests such as that of 1912.

413

CHAPTER LI

WAS 1912 A MISTAKE?

An Earnest Purpose, Even In Politics, Is Never A Mistake—An Endeavor To Save The Republican Party From Defeat With Taft—No Other Thought Back Of The Roosevelt Movement Until The Theft of Delegates—La Follette Would Not Do—Taft's Weakness, Not Roosevelt's Strength—A Result That Might Have Been Secured—Norman Mack's True Forecast.

WAS 1912 a mistake?

To many persons a lost battle is always a mistake. Historians then call it a revolt while if the battle had been won they would call it a revolution.

It is not what you say when you buckle on your sword that counts; it is what you are able to say when you take it off.

An earnest purpose, however, is never a mistake, even in politics. Those who strive honorably to achieve it and fail may well regret defeat, but they have no reason to regret their effort.

There is one place above all others in which to justify yourself—that place is in your conscience—

> Yet still there whispers the small voice within,
> Heard through Gain's silence and o'er Glory's din,
> Whatever creed be taught or land be trod
> Man's conscience is the oracle of God!

It may be that of the 4,150,000 voters who followed Roosevelt in 1912 there are some who in their own conscience—call it their political conscience if you care to do so—now believe they were unwise in doing so. I have not happened to meet many who take that view and personally I am not of the

414

number, whether large or small. My impression is that it is small.

If a refusal to see the Republican party go down to defeat, without endeavoring to save it, is a mistake, then the struggle to prevent Taft's renomination was a mistake.

If a refusal to condone the unseating of elected delegates to force the nomination of Taft after he had been clearly defeated in the primaries—particularly the primaries in all Republican States—is a mistake, then the Progressive party was a mistake.

It is conceded, I presume, that no one who opposed Taft's renomination had any thought at the outset that the movement would result in the organization of the Progressive party.

It may not be conceded, though it is none the less a fact, Roosevelt was made the candidate in the primaries not because he desired the nomination but because no other candidacy was likely to insure Republican success after the collapse of 1910.

It may not be conceded, though it is none the less a fact, that until the wrong decisions of the Chicago convention made it impossible for the anti-Taft delegates to do anything else, a bolt was not contemplated.

A FIGHT TO INSURE PARTY VICTORY

These points should be kept in mind by those who, either from prejudice or from lack of knowledge, insist that the protest against Taft's renomination was primarily an effort to put Roosevelt back in the White House. It was not. It was an effort to insure a Republican successor to a Republican President who could not be reelected.

The unpleasantness of opposing a President of your own party, the difficult task of overcoming in a nominating convention the power of presidential patronage, led many Republicans of the "organization" type to reconcile themselves to

Taft and defeat. Many justified their stand by the fact that they held office, or as patronage dispensers had secured office for others. Loyalty to the Administration controlled them, though it meant disloyalty to the party. Others insisted that a political organization must stand by its men in office and their record whether they have carried out its pledges or not. They

1912—THE RETURN FROM MOSCOW

declared that it meant defeat if they failed to renominate, and defeat if they renominated. Hence they favored renomination.

LA FOLLETTE WOULD NOT DO

Other Republicans beyond the influence of those two theories believed a candidate should be found. Throughout 1911 efforts were made to find one. The only candidacy that met with response was Senator La Follette—"Fighting Bob," of Wisconsin. Between defeat with Taft and possible success with La Follette, however, the bulk of Republicans, at least in the East, would have taken defeat. Ten or twelve years later, as the 1924 vote suggests, they might have accepted La Follette rather than defeat—but not in 1912.

Until Roosevelt threw his hat in the ring there was hope that someone else could be developed who would be strong enough, despite Taft patronage, to win the nomination. I know Roosevelt had this hope.

When he finally abandoned it, and became a candidate, it looked as though the Republican party would be able to crawl from under the Democratic avalanche of 1910. Its only chance to do so was by nominating Roosevelt. I do not believe there was one Republican leader, whether in the Taft column or out of it, who in January, 1912, honestly thought that Taft could be reelected.

TAFT'S WEAKNESS—NOT ROOSEVELT'S STRENGTH

The State-wide and district primaries for delegates to the convention reflected this Taft weakness. Substantially Roosevelt carried all of them. His delegates came from Republican territory while the Taft delegates came largely from doubtful or Democratic States, and from Congress districts controlled by Presidential patronage. Taft's weakness, not Roosevelt's strength, showed in the long list of Roosevelt delegates.

Had that condition been other than a guess before the primary tests, had it been realized that Taft's hold on his party was as feeble as his seven electoral votes from Vermont and Utah in November indicated, there is every probability that such a man as Herbert S. Hadley, then Governor of Missouri, would have been the anti-Taft candidate. Hadley might have secured almost as many delegates as Roosevelt. But contesting a nomination with a President in office is no holiday undertaking, and even some who were not over friendly to Roosevelt supported him finally because they believed he could be nominated over Taft and they were certain he could be elected over any Democrat.

As I Knew Them

Take a glance at the situation.

I repeat the statement I made as to the opinion of Republican leaders early in 1912—that Taft could not be elected—and assert that every delegate who voted for Taft's renomination in the Chicago convention knew he was nominating a candidate certain to be defeated, even were Roosevelt to support him. Most delegates candidly admitted it.

Some reader may ask here how I know the mind of every delegate in that convention inasmuch as I did not poll each delegate. Since they were all more or less in politics, they had the 1910 defeat in mind; they had in addition the indisputable evidence of the primary contests that that weakness continued to exist in 1912; in fact those contests showed Taft weaker. Assuming, therefore, as I do, that the delegates were competent to judge the situation, they must have known that a Taft candidacy was hopeless.

One might justify the Taft nomination by insisting that his defeat would be preferable to Roosevelt's election. Delegates had a right to that belief and to vote that way; but the exercise of that right carried responsibility for the consequences to the party on election day.

I do not contend that they should have turned to Roosevelt. I do not contend that they should have disobeyed telegraphic orders from the White House, and from Attorney General Wickersham and other Cabinet officers, to vote for Taft and defeat. I do insist, however, that any considerable number of them could have united on a compromise candidate and forced his nomination. This they talked about doing, but never did.

Just before the convention Taft was quoted as having said, "Whether I win or not is not the important thing; I am in this fight to perform a public duty—to keep Theodore Roosevelt out of the White House." Unfortunately, he kept out Roosevelt, the Republican party and himself. It was in his power to keep the party in, by keeping both Roosevelt and himself out, but he made no effort to do so.

NORMAN MACK'S TRUE FORECAST

I remember that Norman E. Mack, then chairman of the Democratic National Committee, said to me in New York City a week or so before the convention:

"We can beat Taft hands down if you nominate him; I am not so sure about beating Roosevelt but I think we can. You fellows will be split up if either man is named. If it is Taft we will nominate a liberal Democrat and get the liberal Republican vote; if Roosevelt is your candidate we will nominate a conservative and get the conservative Republican vote. That is why our folks believe we have you beaten."

"Suppose we don't nominate either man?" I asked.

"Then the Democrats will have a harder battle," replied Mack, "but you won't get away from Roosevelt and Taft. Neither of those fellows will give up."

This experienced Democratic authority gave a true picture of the possibilities of the Republican convention. His opinion that a new man would give the Democrats a hard battle was a correct analysis. Obviously, the suggestion of a compromise candidate could not come with controlling strength from the Roosevelt camp. After the adoption of the temporary roll, Roosevelt delegates were in a minority in the convention. Responsibility rested with those in control. They shrugged their shoulders at defeat and took Taft.

That determination was responsible for the change in political history that occurred in November; the Progressive party emphasized but it did not cause Taft's defeat. Had Roosevelt acquiesced in the Taft nomination, he could not have persuaded voters to follow his example. The tide was too strong. Taft seemed to have lost the power to interest the people—to interest even the partisans who vote at party primaries, for they had declared against him.

NOT A SUNDAY-SCHOOL

No one expects a political convention to be conducted like a Sunday-School. It is a battle ground and those engaged in combat know that the hardest blows are the only blows that count. Hard blows were anticipated at the 1912 convention, but not the kind of blows that would have ruled out any contender who delivered them in a fair fight. The unseating of delegates has been practiced in nearly all conventions. The contests usually reflect merely local factional dissensions. Occasionally they mean a handful of delegates for one or two out of half a dozen candidates for nomination; they seldom have broad significance. In 1912, however, the unseating was done to control the convention, its candidate and its platform. It was a duel. The 4,125,000 votes polled by Roosevelt are the best answer to those who ask which side in the convention voiced the spirit of the Republican party, which side was striving to do what Republicans wanted to have done. Those 4,125,000 votes also answer the question whether 1912 was a mistake.

CHAPTER LII

GEORGE PERKINS AND FRANK MUNSEY

Two Men, New to Politics, Whose Pledge Made Possible the Progressive Contest of 1912—as Strange as Any Friendship That Ever Existed—Perkins Liked Politics and Kept On, but Munsey Sought to "Amalgamate"—Perkins Tireless in Welfare Work.

GEORGE PERKINS and Frank Munsey influenced the politics of this country in 1912 more than any other men with whose activities at that time I am familiar. And, of course, the events of 1912 had their marked influence on national politics until 1920.

There certainly would have been no national Progressive party but for those two men; there probably would not have been a Roosevelt candidacy for nomination in the convention against Taft but for them. Perkins had executive ability, great energy and money; Munsey, in addition, had his newspapers and magazines. Governors, State chairmen and local leaders aplenty were urging Roosevelt into a contest with Taft; but I doubt whether he would have acquiesced had he not known that Perkins and Munsey would organize and finance his battle. He realized that, without organization, his forces would not be effective.

Six months later, in Chicago, when the decision was made to bolt the regular party convention, they were the men on whose word Roosevelt depended to insure a proper campaign management.

Deliberately, I have used "probably" as to the battle for nomination and "certainly" as to organizing the Progressive party. I speak with full knowledge of the facts as to both. Had either Perkins or Munsey faltered in Chicago, the call

421

for a national Progressive party convention would never have been issued. Therefore, I repeat that Perkins and Munsey influenced the politics of this country in 1912 more than any other two men.

The amazing feature of their activities that year was that neither of them had ever figured in politics before, and that Munsey had an intense dislike for politics and politicians. He avoided both whenever possible. Perkins, on the other hand, liked the activities and the excitement, and got deeper and deeper into the game. They had no other motive in urging Roosevelt to become a candidate for nomination than to save the Republican party from defeat with Taft.

In Chicago, they resented the theft of Roosevelt delegates and in that frame of mind refused to abide by the decisions of a convention that in their firm opinion had been stolen.

THE FRIENDSHIP BETWEEN THE TWO MEN

As strange as any friendship that ever existed between two men was the friendship lasting thirty years between Perkins and Munsey. They differed in temperament and in many characteristics. Both were positive individualistic men, each had to dominate in whatever he undertook; both were quick in temper and quicker still in action. Seldom a day passed that they did not meet. They knew each other's traits, and guided themselves accordingly. I knew both men intimately, sat with them often in discussion of public men and measures, and I never heard either of them advocate a course for a wrong motive or for his personal gain.

Frank Munsey, sitting alone in his apartment before a blaze of Maine maple logs, had a rare talent for seeing into the future, for analysis of a situation. It was there that he habitually sought the solution of all his problems and there that he made his plans. The day's work was merely carrying out those fireside decisions.

As I Knew Them

Once his course was thus determined, only actual experience would change him. He would insist upon a demonstration; no change was possible until it was proven that he was wrong. Then he would quickly change and admit his error. But he was not wrong often, though he frequently had to wait long to be justified. Let me cite one example.

I spent an evening with Munsey while Woodrow Wilson was returning from Paris acclaimed at home and abroad as a world leader. Wilson had his League of Nations covenant with him; opposition to it seemed small in number and less in hope. "The Senate will never ratify it," said Munsey, "and if it ever gets before the American people they will vote it down two to one. Every year that goes by will make us more and more thankful that we never entered the League."

I did not accept Munsey's prophecy—but it has come true.

PERKINS DEEP IN WELFARE WORK

Perkins was not so sure of himself as Munsey. He liked to confer with others and to search for facts. Once his mind was made up, however, he was never timid. I have known many men generous with their wealth but I know of no one who equalled Perkins in giving time, thought and money to the welfare of others. When he resigned from J. P. Morgan & Co., he told me he had all the money any man should possess; henceforth he would devote himself to public affairs— not public office. I know that he did so with a devotion that meant many sacrifices—in fact that really cost him his life.

Roosevelt as Governor had put him at the head of the Palisades Park Commission, some years earlier. He took hold of the enterprise as though it were his own, and made it the wonderful playground it now is for thousands of people unable to meet the cost of outings elsewhere. When the right man was needed to go to France, in 1919, to straighten out the

423

Y. M. C. A. tangle there, Perkins was chosen—and in that work he so exhausted himself that he was never well again.

Perkins and Munsey, so strongly united in friendship, never had a business transaction together; each sought and gained fortune in his own way. And they knew that their friendship would endure longer if business transactions were not involved. The one exception was the National Progressive Party of 1912. Perkins managed that battle, but Munsey agreed to share the deficit. Just the word of one friend to another, without a line in writing, was good enough for those two men to undertake a national campaign.

MUNSEY WANTED AN "AMALGAMATION"

True to his habit of abandoning experiments that did not work out Munsey abandoned the Progressive party promptly after the 1912 election. The figures, great as they were, proved that the party could not displace the Republican organization; division meant that the Democrats would continue to win. He made an elaborate analysis of the vote cast by the Republicans, Progressives and Democrats in each State, and showed that, by uniting, the Republicans and Progressives would control two-thirds of the States, as well as the Presidency and Congress.

Munsey promptly urged them to unite—an "amalgamation," as he called it in the terms of the day. In his signed appeal to "get together" Munsey cited the success of industrial amalgamations as an example, and insisted that political parties could be merged with similarly good results. In politics, however, two and two do not always make four, and the Munsey amalgamation did not gain the confidence of politicians.

However, other forces were slowly uniting the two wings of the old party, though it was not until 1920 that Time had accomplished what Munsey had so keenly visioned in 1912 as the real thing to do.

PERKINS STUCK IT OUT

Perkins did not accept the Munsey viewpoint. He did not believe in amalgamation. He had gone wholeheartedly into the Progressive party; he had seen it poll more electoral votes and more popular votes than the Republicans; his confidence and enthusiasm were not lessened because the party had come out second instead of first. He was for fighting on—and he did. Perkins, unlike Munsey, was an idealist. He gave much of his time to the Progressive organization, and abandoned it in 1916 with great regret for the same reasons as those that controlled Roosevelt. Criticism that Perkins was dominating Roosevelt through the years following 1912 did not affect the intimate, confident relations between the two men.

Perkins was not dominating—he was doing. While others talked, Perkins acted. The thing was done before others had started. Roosevelt saw that quality in Perkins and admired it. When the possibility of Roosevelt's return to the Presidency was discussed, a question often came up regarding his disposition of Perkins. Many thought Perkins would insist upon being Secretary of the Treasury, but Roosevelt told me that Perkins had notified him that he would never accept office. He did not care to be tied to a desk. The one office with any attraction for him was Secretary of Commerce and Labor— there he might help work out some welfare measures for labor. Nevertheless, he believed he could do better work out of public office than in it. So he freed Roosevelt of all obligation.

CHAPTER LIII

ROOSEVELT'S ONE PURPOSE: BEAT WILSON

Never Had Any Other Desire In 1916, But His Name Stalked Through Republican Committee Meeting Like Banquo's Ghost—Sails For West Indies To Avoid Situations—My Voyage To Trinidad And The Resulting Message To The Country To Get Into An "Heroic Mood"— A Letter From Elihu Root That Never Got To The Public—T. R. Hits Hard From Trinidad—Wilson Wanted Roosevelt As Opponent.

ROOSEVELT'S name and purpose attended like Banquo's ghost the meeting of the Republican National Committee in Washington, December, 1915, when the 1916 convention was fixed for Chicago, June 16. The same rumors of a Roosevelt candidacy heard at the meeting four years earlier disturbed the councils of the party chiefs.

In 1912 the rumors had been listened to with hope that they were true; now with dread. The committeemen knew that in the minds of the people Roosevelt was the only sharp contrast to Wilson, but 1912 was too close. Many Republicans were unwilling to accept a Roosevelt leadership even though it might lead to victory. Nevertheless, they were fearful of another contest in Republican primaries, and of another campaign of divided opposition to Wilson. Who could command unity? The committeemen looked inquiringly to the U. S. Supreme Court, where the sombre robes of an associate justice were an uninviting prospect for politicians; when they turned from that picture and looked upon other possible nominees the figures seemed so pale and thin that the Roosevelt apparition assumed substantial form; the committee meeting

426

adjourned with many members confessing their inability to find a candidate so strong as the man they would not have.

ROOSEVELT'S ONLY CONCERN: BEAT WILSON

How little they knew that man!

More intent even than they to have Wilson defeated, moved by patriotic impulses to make every sacrifice that would insure unity and success, Roosevelt had no thought of a primary contest, and no desire except to find a candidate, who, if possible, would unite all Wilson opponents.

He, too, had vivid recollections of 1912. While he believed that there was common ground on which Republicans and Progressives could stand to fight Wilson there was still much ground that, in his opinion, they could not then occupy together. Therefore, while he was not concerned over their attitude toward him, he was concerned as to whether they would name a candidate that Progressives could accept. Whatever differences of opinion may exist as to Roosevelt's desires in 1912, there can be no honest belief that he had any purpose in 1916 other than to find the man most certain to beat Wilson. And his supreme reason for desiring Wilson's defeat was his conviction that the President's timid policies were forcing the nation on the rocks.

Far back as October, 1915, Roosevelt said to me: "At best this war will be a stalemate for the Allies unless America gets into it. I don't say that Germany will win, but I do say that the Allies cannot. They may check Germany, but not more. For us the question to determine is whether we will get into this war with the Allies cooperating with us, or go into a later war against Germany without help from the Allies. Wilson ought to see that we must make a choice. I wish he would realize stern facts and not keep up in the clouds. I don't want to be constantly criticizing him; I would like to stand shoulder to shoulder with him—if he ever takes a stand I shall be with him."

As I Knew Them

It was not difficult that year for Roosevelt to prevent independent Republicans from using his name as a candidate in the party primaries; he promptly stopped the first efforts. It was difficult, though, to determine an attitude toward the Progressive National Convention. Should it precede or follow the Republican Convention? Should it be held at all? Many Progressives were against a convention. They argued that it would end all hope of unifying the anti-Wilson forces. It would put new life into an organization that if left alone would disappear before campaign time. Other Progressives argued that a convention was necessary as a club to force the Republicans to an acceptable nomination; they believed that agreement on such a nominee could be brought about.

In that belief the convention was called for the same time and place as the Republican Convention. It was a mistake that led to the most humiliating episode in Roosevelt's career. He would have been wiser had he promptly faced the inevitable and allowed the Progressive organization to drift out of existence, as it was doing, for delay only made his position more difficult. But Roosevelt was controlled by loyalty to old friendships; he did not want to be charged with abandoning a cause. He was confident that when the convention met he could persuade it to his view.

With that course settled, he began holding conferences, beginning with one in the apartments of William Hamlin Childs, with Horace Wilkinson, George W. Perkins, E. A. Van Valkenberg and others. All agreed that the nomination of a "reactionary" by the Republican National Convention would compel a Progressive ticket, but there was more than one interpretation of "reactionary." The divided opinion then expressed should have warned the Colonel of the spirit that would surely prevail in the Progressive Convention, but it did not. He never lost faith that it would see the situation as he saw it. He

428

had to notice, however, that others did not share that faith.

AN UNPUBLISHED LETTER FROM ELIHU ROOT

Finally, in January, to take himself out of embarrassing political situations, he sailed for a tour of the West Indies. It was agreed that he was to remain silent while away. Before his steamer had reached its first port of call, it was stated in New York City by someone who claimed to have seen it that Elihu Root had written a letter to be read a month hence, at a meeting of Republican leaders in Chicago, in which, while he declared he was not a candidate for President, he outlined a sort of platform for Republicans that was substantially a summary of Roosevelt policies.

It was alleged that despite his refusal, Root was providing a platform for himself. Some Republicans opposed to a Root candidacy urged that the Colonel should anticipate the Root essay by a new statement of his own views. The Root letter was addressed to Frederick C. Tanner, then Republican State chairman. Its fate is a political mystery. It was not read at the Chicago meeting, nor, so far as I know, has it ever been made public. The discussion in New York city regarding its contents led to a series of cables to Roosevelt, which in turn led to a suggestion from him that I should catch up with him in Trinidad, and explain what was desired of him in such a hurry and in view of the understanding that he was to say nothing.

Germany's sub-marines were then making ocean travel anything but a pleasure trip, but it seemed to me that if Colonel Roosevelt could risk a tour of the Atlantic with Mrs. Roosevelt there was no reason why I should hold back. The steamer leaving next day carried Mrs. Stoddard and myself to Trinidad. There I met the Colonel and from there I cabled his one thousand word statement—a statement that stirred Republican politics. It took nearly two days to give the proper tone and phrasing to the document. I was impatient to get it on the cable, and the delay in preparation left me in no mood to meet with equanimity the slow processes of the English censor in satisfying himself that no secret conspiracy in behalf of Germany lay concealed in Roosevelt's words!

It seems incredible that a statement from an ex-President of the United States, especially from one who at the moment was being fêted in Trinidad, should be held up "for consideration." Nevertheless I had to abandon a trip to the asphalt lake with government officials and the Colonel, to waste time persuading the censor that there was no hidden help to Germany in the document. I sat by the cable operator's side until the last word had gone, so as to be ready for any new objection from the censor.

"UNLESS THE COUNTRY IS IN HEROIC MOOD"

A few days later we were amazed to learn from home dispatches that the statement was regarded by some Republicans as a bid for the nomination. This feeling was reflected at a banquet in Trinidad, where the Colonel was greeted as the next President of the United States. He tried to explain the situation, but they would not see it. Nevertheless, he told the banqueters that his sole purpose was to arouse the country to the peril of a pacifist mood, and that he regarded his own nomination as too unlikely to be discussed seriously.

In that statement the Colonel said:

> "I am not the least interested in the personal fortunes either of myself or any other man. I am interested in awakening my fellow countrymen to the need of facing unpleasant facts. I am interested in the triumph of the great principles for which with all my heart and soul I have striven and shall continue to strive.
>
> "I will not enter into any fight for the nomination, and I will not permit any factional fight to be made in my behalf. Indeed, I will go further and say that it would be a mistake to nominate me unless the country has in its mood something of the heroic;

unless it feels not only like devoting itself to ideals, but to the purpose measurably to realize those ideals in action.

"This is one of those rare times which come only at long intervals in a nation's history when the action taken determines the life of the generations that are to follow. Such times were those from 1776 to 1789 in the days of Washington, and from 1858 to 1865 in the days of Lincoln. . . .

"Nothing is to be hoped from the present Administration. The struggles today between the President and his party leaders in

A PAGE WRITTEN BY ROOSEVELT FOR ME AT TRINIDAD

Congress are merely struggles as to whether the nation shall see its government representatives adopt an attitude of a little more or a little less hypocrisy and follow a policy of slightly greater or slightly less baseness."

"THAT WOULD BE A CRIME," SAID T. R.

As the date for the Republican and Progressive conventions drew closer, it seemed more difficult to avoid another division of Republican voters. Another division meant handing the Presidency over to Wilson a second time.

431

"That would be a crime!" exclaimed Roosevelt. "It is unthinkable that I could be a party to such a result."

It was in that spirit of intense disgust for Wilson's policies that Roosevelt worked to have one nominee come out of the two Chicago conventions, and it was in that effort that he met his most humiliating defeat. Neither convention responded.

"HE KEPT US OUT OF WAR"

At that time, too, incredible as it now seems, there was developing throughout our West a feeling that America's interests were not involved in the war, and that a President who had kept us out of it, and whose purpose was to keep us out, should be continued in office.

Gov. Glynn's "he-kept-us-out-of-war" speech nominating Wilson was not indorsed by the President until he had satisfied himself that, if a sharp issue could be raised the people of the West would reelect him to do that very thing. A close canvass made of the West had convinced him that the country was not in the "heroic mood" that Roosevelt desired, and he was ready for the test.

WILSON WANTED ROOSEVELT AS OPPONENT

Just before starting for the Chicago convention from Washington I met Samuel Untermyer, as he left the White House.

"What are you fellows going to do in Chicago—Roosevelt or Hughes?" he asked.

"Roosevelt," I replied, to get his reaction.

"Well, that will suit the man in there exactly," said Untermyer, indicating the White House. "He can lick Roosevelt on the war issue, and he wants to do it. If Wilson could name your candidate he would name Teddy."

The Democratic national convention knew exactly what it wanted in candidate and issue; the Republican convention did not. The Republicans made their first blunder when they called their convention to meet a week in advance of the Democratic convention. The Democrats were in power; they had held the government for four years and wanted four years more; under all the rules of politics they should have been the first to state their case and ask the judgment of the people; then issue could be joined by the opposition.

The Republican managers unwisely determined to lead off. They fixed an early date—June 7—deliberately, to show their disregard for anything the Wilson convention might do or say. When they got to Chicago, their platform committee discovered that, aside from the ordinary partisan condemnation, they had no target at which to direct their fire; "He-kept-us-out-of-war" had not yet emerged from Democratic councils. The result was the weakest platform ever written in a Republican convention.

CHAPTER LIV

1916—A CONTRAST IN CONVENTIONS

The Republican Gathering Colorless, The Progressives Loaded With Pyrotechnics—A Conference Committee That Knew It Could Not Agree—Lodge, Aroused From Sleep, Visions The Presidency—Roosevelt Refuses The Progressive Nomination And Centres His Efforts On Defeat Of Wilson—The Severest Trial Of His Career.

THE convention itself was as colorless as the platform. It had no real rivalries for nomination since Hughes was at all times the obvious nominee. Its proceedings, never exciting the slightest enthusiasm, forecast the campaign and the result.

With one exception that was the dullest convention held within my recollection by either party. The one exception was the 1888 Democratic convention in St. Louis at which Cleveland was re-nominated, only to be defeated. The St. Louis convention was so listless that the correspondents were forced to write of the muddy waters of the Mississippi, and of the old-timer river steamboats that Mark Twain immortalized.

In Chicago in 1916, they would have been compelled to do likewise but for the Progressive convention. The Progressives furnished the pyrotechnics of the week; let me say that they had quite an assortment of explosives, and used them furiously, especially at the close. As in 1912, it was a crusaders' gathering—and Roosevelt was still their leader, though now convinced that union not division was a duty.

In the big Coliseum five or six blocks away from the Progressive gathering, the Republicans went through their convention proceedings as though it was a mail order catalogue. Warren Harding, then Senator, made a long speech as Chair-

434

man; not a note sounded by him or by any other speaker had the vibrant quality of definite purpose. Many delegates would have preferred to go elsewhere for their candidate than to Hughes but there was no elsewhere.

AGREEING TO DISAGREE

A conference committee of the two conventions had sought for two nights to agree upon a candidate whom the Republicans and the Progressives could support. The Republican conferees were former Attorney General Charles J. Bonaparte, Senator Murray Crane, Senator William E. Borah, Nicholas Murray Butler, and Senator Reed Smoot. The Progressive conferees were Gov. John N. Parker, of Louisiana, Hiram Johnson, George W. Perkins, A. R. Johnson, of Ohio, and Horace Wilkinson, of New York. There, two immovable forces met.

"We'll take any one you offer but Roosevelt," were the first words spoken by the Republican conferees. Reed Smoot uttered them.

"We don't believe in barring any man," was the response from Wilkinson. "Let us put all the cards on the table and discuss which one is the best to play."

The one name the Republicans crossed off their list so arbitrarily was the one name that made up the whole Progressive list. It was soon found that unity on any candidate was impossible—1916 was too close to 1912. In factional politics memories are prejudices and they disappear slowly. Hiram Johnson gave up the conference. Then Gov. Parker gave it up.

Somewhere in the midnight hours, with a decisive ballot certain to be cast the next day in each convention, Roosevelt was telephoned, to suggest a possible nominee. When his telephone rang, the Colonel was engrossed in writing an article on birds, promised to his publishers that week. He had stayed up late to finish it. He asked Chicago for time to think it over. Soon the reply came, "Lodge." It astounded the conferees on both sides. They knew Lodge could not be nominated in either convention. Yet they felt it a duty to inform the Massachusetts Senator.

LODGE, SEATED ON BEDSIDE, VISIONS HONORS

A committee went to Lodge's hotel room and awakened him. Seated on the bedside, clad in his pajamas, his eyes blinking with sleep, he listened in astonishment, and took it seriously. He thought Roosevelt's indorsement would bring his nomination in the morning.

"Oh! that this honor should come to me at my time of life!" was his first utterance.

He exaggerated Roosevelt's strength at that time with a regular convention, and utterly misunderstood his motive. Roosevelt knew that Hughes would be nominated, but he did not care to indorse Hughes to the convention and have it charged that he had nominated another presidential candidate. This time he was evading, not seeking, responsibility for the nominee. What a change eight years had brought! He believed his message would bring Lodge some prestige and some votes—as it did—and that the Massachusetts Senator would understand the strategy. But Lodge did not see it that way. His mind was thrown completely out of balance.

I have seen other men while their names were before conventions lose their good judgment, but Roosevelt's telephone message surely should have been too slender a hope for a man who had presided over three conventions. How the strong light of the Presidency dazzles the most experienced! The committee talked with Lodge about the possibilities, and then retired. They made a report to the convention, as they were bound to do, presenting Lodge's name. It met with no response. By noon that day Hughes was the nominee.

As I Knew Them

While Roosevelt could thus easily dispose of the Republican convention, so far as he was concerned, he faced the severest trial of his career in the Progressive convention. He sincerely believed it was his patriotic duty to refuse another Progressive party nomination and to indorse the Republican nominee. It was a hard decision to make—his country or his party?

That broader view was not shared by the Progressive convention. Most of the delegates were emphatically in favor of another campaign. All the wonderful spirit of the first convention four years before was reflected in this second gathering. Despite the unwisdom of its insistence upon a third ticket, it merited a better fate than that which came to it when it named Roosevelt only to have him decline.

I shall never forget the scene of dismay, anger and defiance, with their old leader, in those closing hours. They little knew how deeply he felt back there in Oyster Bay, or how poignantly he regretted that the party of his creation had to be sacrificed for his country. The Colonel bowed his head, and unprotestingly accepted the condemnation of those who did not see the real issue as plainly as he saw it.

That was Saturday night; the following Tuesday Roosevelt dined with Hughes, the Republican nominee, in New York City, and pledged his full support.

CHAPTER LV

HUGHES: THE OFFICE SEEKS THE MAN

No Career In American Politics Compares With That Of Charles E. Hughes—Never Sought Honors, Never Asked Support, Never Expended A Dollar For A Nomination—The Archie Sanders Incident That Separated A Governor And A President—Hughes Would Never Use Patronage To Pass Legislation—Root's Arraignment of Hearst, "By Authority Of The President"—A Candidate Who Gave No Help —Roosevelt Urged Hughes For Governor In 1908—Some New Facts About Hughes And Roosevelt In The Struggle For Direct Primaries.

MY earliest recollection of Charles Evans Hughes goes back more than twenty years to the time when he was a citizen of New York City, not known outside of his profession. He lived on the upper west side of Manhattan Island; my home was in the same neighborhood. Hughes liked to walk—with quick, vigorous step, his thick heavy cane tightly held. On cool breezy afternoons his rapid pace against the wind would carry the tails of his unbuttoned light overcoat fluttering far out behind him. You could see in his stride that he was a purposeful man, who at all times knew where he was travelling. Not many of his neighbors were personally acquainted with him, but the brisk walker morning and afternoon was a familiar figure.

It is common-place to say of any man that there are none like him, but it is so true of Hughes that I cannot help saying it. You may search the careers of all the men in our public life for a century and a half and you will not find a career like his. He has never sought public office; he has never asked any individual to speak for him, or to work for his advancement. He publicly repudiated the announcement in 1908 that Hughes headquarters had been opened in Chicago, to secure

his nomination for President; his silence while on the Supreme
Court in 1916 was broken before his nomination only to disavow responsibility for Republican leaders who sought to
create the impression that they had his consent to seek delegates for him.

In a word, Hughes has been Governor, Associate Justice
of the Supreme Court, Presidential nominee and Secretary of
State without ever having expended so much as a postage
stamp and without ever having uttered, or authorized others
to utter, a single word in his behalf. Here is a remarkable
record. It is not one of indifference—for I am sure Hughes
is not indifferent to the honors he has had. It reveals a determined purpose to let the office seek the man, uninfluenced
by personal appeals or manipulation of delegates.

We have had men in our public life who believed in that
policy, but the temptation of new honors proved too strong
for them. Hughes, however, has adhered to it so consistently,
so firmly, that the man who would announce that he spoke for
Hughes on any subject would have to show credentials
stronger than his own say-so, whoever he might be.

AN INCIDENT WITH LASTING CONSEQUENCES

Once Theodore Roosevelt while President acted, as he declared, to aid Hughes, then Governor of New York, in his
struggle to enact anti-racetrack gambling laws. Archie D.
Sanders, Internal Revenue Collector at Rochester, New York,
and since Congressman, was believed to be the influence holding "on the fence" the votes of two Rochester Assemblymen.
Sanders' term was expiring. At the suggestion of Congressman Stevens, an enthusiastic Hughes man, the President refused to reappoint Sanders unless he first brought the
two Assemblymen into line. The White House frankly explained the purpose; the sincerity of Roosevelt's desire to help
was never questioned. When the news was brought to Hughes
at Albany, he stated that he was not interested in Sanders'

fate, had not requested the President's action and knew nothing of it.

The significance of this incident was large and lasting. Hughes as Governor always refused to use patronage to pass legislation. When legislation came before him for official action, he never inquired whether friend or foe sponsored it. He looked only to the proposal. Several times while Governor he astounded his factional opponents by naming one of them for office, because he believed him to be the best man for the place. He as freely refused to appoint from his own supporters unless they could furnish a man as capable as he could find elsewhere.

With his policy in this respect unbroken by any act of his own, Hughes felt even more strongly that he could not accept support secured for him by another, through patronage. He could not acquiesce in having the President do for him what he would not do for himself. Hence his prompt denial of any interest in the matter. He wanted the votes of the Rochester Assemblymen, but he did not want them that way. Hughes always has been a stickler for maintaining what he calls "the integrity of his position," and to the dismay of his friends he has sacrificed much in the way of immediate gain rather than break through the line. The real gain has come later.

ROOSEVELT FELT REBUKED

You can imagine the effect on Roosevelt. He felt that his friendly offices had been rejected in a most unfriendly way; he expected thanks rather than what he considered a rebuke. From then until 1916, he and Hughes travelled different paths.

I am not prepared to say that except for the Sanders incident Roosevelt would have supported Hughes in 1908, but I am certain that it led Roosevelt to feel that Hughes was almost the last candidate he cared to see nominated as his successor.

I use the Sanders case because of its undoubted influence in separating Hughes and Roosevelt politically; even though the Presidency may not have been directly involved, their inability to work together was unfortunate for the party and the country.

"BY AUTHORITY OF THE PRESIDENT"

The world of politics knew nothing of Hughes until his nomination for Governor in 1906. He was a stranger to it and was not thought of for public office. He owed that nomination to his success as counsel for the legislative committee investigating the big insurance companies in New York. I understand that his name as counsel was suggested by Bradford Merrill, then associated with the New York World, which newspaper was largely responsible for the investigation.

Hughes made good as an investigator and the Republicans turned to him to save New York for them. Their grip on the State was slipping and Tammany had nominated William Randolph Hearst for Governor in the belief that he would add to the Democratic strength enough politically unattached votes to win. It did not turn out that way, but there was a hard, uncertain fight until the last returns were in.

The feature of the campaign was a speech in Utica, New York, by Secretary of State Root, made "by authority of the President," in which he arraigned Hearst unmercifully. This most unusual proceeding was full of boomerang possibilities. I never understood why the Democratic leaders did not seek to arouse the people on the issue of presidential interference in State affairs. There have been many demonstrations of the sensitiveness of voters on that point. However, the Democrats thought it best to drop the matter as quickly as possible. When elected, Hughes announced himself as "counsel for the people" in all that he was to do as Governor, and acted accordingly.

A CANDIDATE WHO GAVE NO HELP

Party machines are never enamored of Governors inclined to do much thinking on their own account, and the New York Republican machine did not like that characteristic in Hughes. The people did, however. By 1908, Hughes had grown to Presidential size; the State machine reluctantly responded to the strong Hughes sentiment by accepting him as the State's choice for national honors. They gave him no real support, however. Nor did Hughes help himself. He gave no encouragement to those who really wanted to see him nominated. What might have developed into a formidable candidacy had New York's Governor followed the ambitious course of other men, was stunted in its growth because it could make no headway with a candidate who discouraged rather than encouraged. That is why, as Roosevelt told me in a White House interview, it was easier for Taft to win delegates away from Hughes than from other candidates. He had 67 votes in the Chicago convention.

ROOSEVELT INSISTS UPON HUGHES' RENOMINATION

Another two years of Hughes as Governor was not what the "organization" in New York wanted after the delegates returned from nominating Taft. New York was certain to return a heavy Republican plurality on President, and the swing could be depended upon to carry almost any Republican candidate for Governor with it. Conferences were held to agree upon a nominee, and for a time it seemed likely that Hughes would be dropped. Roosevelt, however, took a broader view, though he was still smarting over the Sanders matter. His attitude is revealed in the following reply I

received to a letter I had written him urging Hughes'
nomination:

Oyster Bay, N. Y.
August 29, 1908.

My dear Stoddard:—

 I share entirely your view. I think it will do damage to nominate Mr. Hughes, but that it will do far more damage not to nominate him. I think he has given just cause and offense to decent
men engaged in active political work, and that he has shown grave
ingratitude to men like Parsons; but nevertheless I am convinced
that the popular feeling about him is exactly what you describe, and
that, therefore, he ought to be renominated, inasmuch as there
is nothing to be said against his personal integrity.

    Faithfully yours,
      Theodore Roosevelt.

As usual, Roosevelt followed word with action. He made
the New York leaders see the folly of turning down Hughes,
and a second term for the Governor followed.

THE HUGHES STRUGGLE FOR DIRECT PRIMARIES

At once, Hughes went into a struggle for direct State-wide
primaries. The party "organization" opposed the legislation,
and the winter's development was the familiar story of conflict between executive and legislative branches. In the midst
of it came Taft's offer to Hughes to become Associate Justice
of the Supreme Court. The "organization" rejoiced that
Hughes would now be put out of the way, but the Governor
out-generalled them. He accepted the appointment with the
proviso that he would not be called upon to take his place on
the bench until the Legislature had adjourned. That meant
a finish fight.

 Roosevelt was homeward bound from Africa while the
battle was in the final stage. Albany was full of rumor that
he was not in sympathy with the Hughes programme. There
was no truth to such talk, for he knew nothing of the conflict,

but the rumor served its purpose of stopping the bills until Roosevelt could be heard from.

NEW FACTS OF AN HISTORIC STRUGGLE

Then came a letter from the Colonel, dated London, inviting Hughes to Oyster Bay when convenient after Roosevelt's return. Hughes would have gone there but both men discovered that they were shortly to attend the Harvard commencement exercises and their meeting was postponed until then.

I have always regretted that the conference was not held in Oyster Bay. Roosevelt, in London, must have had something in mind beyond a social engagement with Hughes, something big enough for him to write about it weeks in advance. Its political significance would have been beyond the power of the two men to explain away.

Moreover, there would have been no stories that they had met unexpectedly at a college commencement and that Hughes had there persuaded Roosevelt to undertake to win a battle which, without Roosevelt, was lost. Not knowing the facts, those stories were accepted as true. Neither Roosevelt nor Hughes ever attempted to silence them by making known that their Harvard meeting was a substitute for an Oyster Bay visit, and that both men went to Cambridge knowing that the New York situation was to be discussed. If the facts here related have ever before appeared in print I have failed to see them. The direct primary bill was, of course, the most important measure pending. Hughes had hardly mentioned it before Roosevelt interrupted with a short:

"I have determined to remain silent."

"I am not urging you to get into the struggle," said Hughes, "but your silence is used by the opposition as evidence that you are against the bill."

"They say my silence means opposition to the bill?" queried Roosevelt. "Of course it means nothing of the kind. I am for the bill. I'll wire Fred Davenport now telling him I think it should be passed."

And within a few moments the oft-quoted telegram was on the wires to the State Senator from Utica, now Congressman. The fight was ended, the bill became law, and in October Hughes took his place on the Supreme Court.

He was through, or thought he was through, with politics. In truth, however, the work on which his fame is to rest had not begun.

CHAPTER LVI

A SURPRISED AND SILENT JURIST

Though Lost To The World Of Politics For Six Years, Hughes Was Found And Made A Candidate For President—He Knew Politicians Did Not Like His Ways—His Real Desire Was To Return To His Law Practice—Finally, Allowed Fate To Take Its Course—His Campaign For Election Was Emphatically His Own—Crocker, Not Johnson, Responsible For Loss Of California.

THE remarkable feature of the demand for Hughes' nomination for President in 1916 was that there was not a word or an act on his part for six years to arouse new interest in him. As a justice of the Supreme Court, absorbed in its duties, he was lost to the world of politics. No one was more surprised than he that his name was mentioned. It was a long time before he believed that those Republican leaders who were declaring for him really meant it, or that they had any considerable public opinion back of them.

Crowded with court work, unable to make inquiries without encouraging the belief that he was seeking the nomination, Hughes blinded himself to newspaper talk, political talk and even the talk of friends lest he be misinterpreted. It seemed to him that any move he might make would be inconsistent with his rule about "maintaining the integrity of his position" —his position at that time being that of a judge too deeply immersed in his work to concern himself with what was going on outside his court room.

There was just one move he could have made that would not be misinterpreted—to take himself out by a flat declaration that he would not accept. This he did not do. His position was much the same as that of the young lady willing perhaps to marry but not willing to disclose her mind until formally asked. He was not a candidate and was not seeking to influence the convention's choice; he was under no obligation to assume in advance that there was anything for him to accept or reject. Statements by party leaders seemingly involving him were met with a brief public announcement disavowing them, but he steadfastly refused to anticipate the possible action of a convention not yet in session.

I know that the thought dominant in Hughes' mind that winter was that he should resign from the court and return to New York City, resuming his place there as a citizen and practice law. Two terms as Governor and six years on the bench had materially reduced his income, and he felt that longer public service meant continued denial to his family of the comforts to which they were entitled.

WOULD NOT ENJOY WHITE HOUSE TURMOIL

Another consideration that tempted Hughes to stop the talk of a possible nomination was the strong feeling that he then had that politicians did not like his ways, and that in the White House he would have to deal almost entirely with politicians; the prospect of unity of purpose was not bright. He had not forgotten his troubles at Albany and four years of similar contention at Washington were not alluring. He liked to deal with public questions on their merits, not on their political aspects. His experience on the bench had strengthened this tendency.

"Your friend Roosevelt can handle the work of the White House and enjoy it," Hughes said to me at one time when the Presidency was under discussion. "It would take me a whole day to dispose of matters that he could get rid of in an hour. The Presidency is the greatest honor that could come to any man; it is also the greatest burden."

More than once during that winter of 1916 when his silence made him the mystery of politics the considerations I have mentioned weighed heavily on Hughes' mind. They led him

447

close to an emphatic declaration, as he had declared in 1912, that his name must not be used politically while on the bench.

But the Presidency is too big for an American to turn his back upon. Confronted with what seemed like a certainty that he would be nominated and elected, he must have decided to let Fate take its own course. It did—and the silent jurist became the nominee of his party.

ONE FACTOR THAT DEFEATED HUGHES

No one will ever write the history of the campaign that followed without challenge of his analysis of its changing phases and its surprising result. I realize that my opinion cannot escape that fate, but I may say on behalf of it that it is based on familiarity with the day-to-day developments while the struggle was on,—a knowledge that led me early in September to doubt the election of Hughes despite my confidence in June that he would surely win.

Looking backward, it is my judgment that the seeds of Republican defeat were sown in the Republican and Progressive conventions held in Chicago in June. The Republicans adjourned in a deadened calm of over-confidence; the Progressives adjourned in a riot of defiance of Roosevelt. They had nominated him for President with all the enthusiasm of 1912. Then came his telegram that he would think it over and let them know later whether he would accept or not. Bainbridge Colby's quick response "we, too, will think it over" voiced the resentful spirit that swept over the convention, changing it in the last hour from an intensely Roosevelt gathering to an intensely anti-Roosevelt gathering. Had the delegates been polled then on their choice for President as between Hughes and Wilson, I am certain that a majority would have declared for Wilson. Antagonism to Roosevelt, not to Hughes, would have influenced that choice.

The delegates carried that feeling back to their homes, where, finally, it found its way into the November ballot box.

THE SPHINX AND THE CANDIDATES

It made no impression on the heavy Hughes majorities in the East, but in the West, where the Progressives had their greatest strength, it was probably responsible for the loss of the two Dakotas, Oregon and Washington. No man could control it. Roosevelt in particular could not. It was the feature of the campaign that Chairman Willcox always feared. There was also, of course, through the West the kept-us-out-of-war issue that brought States like Kansas into the Wilson column. That, of course, was the talked-of issue west of the Mississippi, but the Progressive bolt to Wilson was also a real factor.

HUGHES PLANNED HIS OWN CAMPAIGN

Hughes' campaign was emphatically his own affair. That is to say, that while he did not interfere with what other campaign speakers might say in public speeches, Hughes had his own conception of what he should say and do. He was also resolved to have no entangling alliances made by the national committee. To insure this policy, he made his friend William R. Willcox chairman of the national committee.

His across-the-continent tour was undertaken because of his desire that as many voters as possible should see him and hear him. He had been on the Supreme Court for six years; he had not concerned himself with public questions nor appeared in public places in that long time. He was only a newspaper name to thousands who were now asked to vote for him; they had a right to look him over, and to hear what he had to say. He did not want their vote merely as a name.

That was a fine position to take, but even an experienced campaigner would have regarded it as perilous. It was certainly extremely perilous for a candidate unfamiliar with the varying moods and temper of the people in different parts of the country, especially for one not given to setting his sails to catch every breeze. Hughes did not realize how completely the West had been deceived by the Democratic platform plank about the "splendid diplomatic triumphs" that had "kept us out of war." He knew the opinion of the East, but western Republican leaders did not enlighten him as to a different opinion across the Mississippi. His speeches show that he did not join issue with the "kept us out of war" propaganda until his return to the east. Then he denounced it vigorously, but too late to change the trend of the West.

The failure of the western Republican leaders to sense the opinion of that section is without parallel in political history. It cost a Presidency. I have known national committees to feel too certain of one State or another; I have known State chairmen to judge poorly the drift of voters in different counties; but I have never known so many State leaders so wholly unaware that their opponents had stolen a march on them and had captured the mind of the people.

The Republican effort was confined to a futile attempt to win back the rebellious Progressives, and election day was at hand before it was realized that, deeper than the Progressive bolt to Wilson, was the feeling of the West that Hughes meant war and Wilson meant peace.

I was permitted to read many of the reports received daily at national headquarters. I also had frequent talks with Murray Crane and John W. Weeks, both experienced campaigners, who, with Willcox, were directing the battle. Those daily reports and those talks prove that eastern headquarters had no advices indicating the real situation in the West.

THE DEMOCRATS RELIED ON THE WEST

The strategy of the Democrats was masterful. President Wilson and Col. House planned it and to the end remained its directing mind. The East was abandoned as "the enemy's country," as Bryan had termed it in 1896, but, more shrewd than Bryan, the 1916 campaigners did not advertise the fact. Wilson staked his hope of election on his ability to persuade the West that war sentiment was an Atlantic seaboard affair and that Hughes was its candidate. He linked Hughes with

Roosevelt as certain, if elected, to plunge us into war, a charge bound to make an impression, for the two men could not disavow each other.

I must not give the impression that better than others I knew the weakness of the Republican cause. But the remark made to me in Washington by Samuel Untermyer that Wilson would prefer to have Roosevelt as his opponent rather than any other man stuck in my mind. It gave me clearer light on some campaign developments. I repeated it to the Colonel.

"I refuse to believe that the people out there are pacifists," he declared, "or that they will indorse Wilson's flabby policy."

"But, Colonel," I persisted, "Wilson's people have studied the situation carefully and really believe it. They believe it so much that they would rather have had you nominated. They feel certain they could defeat you."

"That would be the keenest humiliation I could suffer," replied Roosevelt, "but Wilson would have a fight on his hands before he licked me."

CROCKER, NOT JOHNSON, CAUSED HUGHES' DEFEAT

California, of course, furnished the sensation of the campaign. Hughes' across-the-continent tour extended to the Golden Gate State where he failed to meet Governor Hiram Johnson. That failure is supposed to have cost him California's electoral vote. The newspapers made much of that unfortunate incident, but back of it was a situation of which that incident was only a part.

Anyone experienced in Pacific Coast politics could have warned Hughes of the peril of touring California. Johnson not only controlled the Progressive party but the Republican primaries as well. The old Southern Pacific Railroad crowd, led by William H. Crocker, ousted six years before, were in continuous battle with him to regain power. It was a duel, and no one can safely step between duellists. It was well known in the east that Johnson regarded the State as his bailiwick. He assumed responsibility for it, and the election figures year by year show that he always made good.

Hughes knew something of the situation, but he did not know its intensity. He did not know, either, that, when at the San Francisco meeting he greeted Crocker as California's leading citizen, and emphasized his error by failing to ask why California's Governor was not present, he overlooked the real political power of the State—a power unusually jealous of its due. In such cases, explanations seldom catch up with the offense.

When the election returns showed Johnson elected Senator by nearly 300,000 plurality and Hughes defeated by 3,773, Johnson was arraigned everywhere as the man responsible for continuing Wilson in the White House another four years. Such a wide discrepancy in the figures gives apparent support to that charge, but the figures are not the true guide to the cause of the disaster. I am of the opinion, and my view is shared by others close to the situation, that National Committeeman Crocker is the man who made Hughes' success in California impossible. The records of the Republican National Committee confirm this statement.

THE SITUATION IN CALIFORNIA

We can all recall the anxiety with which the country waited the day after election for the final returns from California. Hughes and Wilson alternated in the lead by a margin too close for comfort until finally it was settled that Wilson had it. The story leading up to the result has not been told, so far as I know, in the new light of the national committee records. I think it worth telling. Let us start at the beginning of the campaign.

Johnson, then Governor, was a candidate for the Senate, and undoubtedly the spokesman for two-thirds of the voters of his State. He attended the Progressive National Convention in Chicago, in June, where he urged Roosevelt's separate nomination, and the continuance of the Progressive party. When that body adjourned, with Roosevelt refusing to run, Johnson went to New York City, to determine his course. In New York City he conferred with Hughes. "He's my man for President," he declared with enthusiasm to National Chairman Willcox as he left for home.

Now, what was the situation at home—in California? It was different from that existing in any other State. Hiram Johnson as a Republican had been elected Governor several times over the opposition of the Crocker faction and controlled the state organization. He carried most of the California delegates for Roosevelt in 1912. In the election that year 283,000 votes were cast for Roosevelt and only 3,914 for Taft. Taft's total vote in 1912 was approximately the Wilson plurality over Hughes in 1916. After the 1912 campaign, Johnson entered all Progressive candidates in the regular Republican primaries, and won indorsement for them over the Crocker candidates. In 1916 he undertook to repeat that success—and in fact did repeat it—in the primaries by winning the nomination for Senator for himself. Both sides were hotly engaged in that Senatorial fight when Hughes toured the State.

WILLCOX APPEALS IN VAIN TO CROCKER

Such facts make it impossible to dispute Johnson's complete control of the Republican as well as of the Progressive voters of the State. Certainly he was a force not to be ignored. In other States, and particularly in Illinois in 1916, warring factions dropped their antagonisms while the Presidential candidate was within their borders. Honors were divided as equally as possible. All factions had representation in meetings and receptions.

Crocker, however, would not have it that way. He was

the regular Republican national committeeman for his State and he insisted upon all the prerogatives of his office.

But Chairman Willcox, in New York, was anxious to bring Progressives into helpful cooperation, and had added representative Progressives from several States as campaign associates to the National committee. The California Progressive chosen was Chester H. Rowell. Naturally Crocker should have shared authority with Rowell in arranging all national meetings, particularly those for the presidential candidate.

One cannot read the telegrams passed between National Chairman Willcox and these two ostensible collaborators, and believe that Crocker regarded the success of Hughes in California as equal to him in value to the success of the Crocker candidate against Johnson in the Republican primaries. The telegrams from which I use extracts have never been published.

WILLCOX VAINLY ASKS CROCKER TO DESIST

The first of the series of dispatches (July 8) was sent by Crocker's chairman, Keesling to Willcox, and pledged Hughes a "cordial reception" under the auspices of "a re-united party." It soon developed, however, that the Crocker idea of a "re-united party" was of a party to which the Progressives were to be like the young lady of Niger and at the end of the campaign the two factions were:

> ". . . return from the ride,
> With the lady inside,
> And a smile on the face of the tiger."

Evidently Chairman Willcox had heard of Crocker's real attitude for he sent him this telegram:

"Disquieting rumors are current here of lack of co-operation looking to the general support in your State of all forces opposed to the Wilson nomination. We feel that every effort should be made to harmonize all differences. . . . Will you kindly give this matter your personal attention?"

Progressive committeeman Rowell suggested that Johnson preside at the San Francisco meeting, and the Crocker candidate for Senator at the Los Angeles meeting, "although," he added, "my suggestion of Johnson considers him as Governor and not as a candidate."

This proposal seemed a fair division of honors between the two factions, but Crocker would have none of it. Apparently he appealed to Murray Crane to head Willcox off from urging peace. In a telegram dated July 16, Willcox refers to Crane and adds: "I sent the telegram as I did for I feel very strongly that in those States where there is a fight on for United States Senator, if continued until election, will work harm to the national ticket."

CROCKER'S REAL PURPOSE

Under date of July 19, Crocker reveals his purpose to control the Hughes visit in the interest of his candidate for Senator and against Johnson. He telegraphed among other statements "California must have Republican (meaning Crocker candidate) Senator. My efforts will be judiciously and unreservedly so directed."

On July 28, Rowell telegraphed: "In any other State the Governor and Hughes supporter would be obvious chairman and to refuse Johnson recognition will be taken by voters as indication of ostracism of Progressive participation. I shall therefore insist upon my suggestion of Johnson. I have no objections to postponing Hughes meeting until after primaries, but maintain Governor should preside if meeting is held on original date."

On July 30, Chairman Willcox telegraphed: "I might say personally and not officially that I think there is force in the Governor of a State who is supporting a presidential candidate having the privilege to preside at one of the meetings.

This is a courtesy that usually should be extended. . . . It does seem to me that during the two days that Hughes is in California all hands should pull together in an effort to make the meetings successful both for the interests of the national candidate and for themselves, thus removing local complications."

Finally, August 2, Crocker wired: "We believe we can handle the situation," which meant, as Rowell telegraphed on August 6, that Progressive participation in the two meetings was excluded and that only those Progressives whom Crocker invited as guests were included. Rowell asked that something be done "to prevent calamity to Hughes which Crocker's proposed exclusion of Progressives will produce. These plans if unchanged will arouse such widespread resentment as to render California a doubtful State for Hughes."

CROCKER REIGNS AND TAKES SOLE RESPONSIBILITY

On August 10, Willcox telegraphed Crocker: "I desire to record my earnest protest against any reprisals being placed on those who are supporting Hughes and who may not have supported our ticket in past years. . . . I state as emphatically as I can that if there are any grounds for Rowell's complaints they should be speedily removed."

Crocker's reply to this telegram was brief. He wanted no more argument. He curtly wired: "Replying to your telegram all arrangements for California meetings have been completed."

The series of telegrams ended as they had begun with Crocker insisting upon his own way regardless of consequences to Hughes. He presided at the San Francisco meeting, as he had always intended to do, and he named one of his lieutenants to preside at the Los Angeles meeting, leaving the Johnson forces out in the cold.

The Governor of the State was thus deliberately denied formal notice of the presence in the State of the presidential candidate he was supporting. An organization capable of delivering only 3,914 votes to its presidential candidate in 1912 took sole responsibility for Hughes; receptions, dinners and meetings were held with Crocker as the one directing authority.

Naturally Johnson resented this affront; naturally, his followers resented it even more deeply. They saw a presidential candidate for whom they were asked to vote completely surrounded by their factional opponents; they lost interest in him. In every speech Johnson continued to urge support of Hughes; had he not done so Hughes would not have come within 3,773 votes of winning the State.

It may be true, that aside from speaking for Hughes, Johnson concentrated his campaign efforts on his own election as Senator. What else could he do? Crocker had taken over responsibility for Hughes' political fortunes in the State. Despite the protests of Chairman Willcox, he used his place as national committeeman to treat the Johnson forces as outsiders. The latter had no responsibility in the campaign after Crocker's decree. Planning a return to control of the State under a Hughes Administration,—Crocker was determined that Hughes should understand that he, and he alone, had fought the battle. His mistake was that he could not wait until after election to make his purpose known. He had to dominate at once, he had to put his own ambitions ahead of Hughes' interests as a candidate—and California voted with Crocker more in mind than Hughes. The surprise is, that under such conditions the Hughes vote was so large.

HUGHES AS SECRETARY OF STATE

Of course, the honor of the Presidency is too great to lose without regret, and Hughes must have felt the blow keenly. No shock-absorber will blunt the sharpness of it for any man —not even Time, for most men. But Hughes has now resumed the place he really had in mind before the call of the

Chicago convention—his place as a citizen and in his profession—and as I see him on public occasions I get the impression that the four years he missed as President have been more than made up by his satisfaction with his six years as Secretary of State. Undoubtedly those years are the hap-

From the Glasgow News.

A FINE HAUL FOR HUGHES

piest of his career. In that office he did the work on which his fame will rest. Both Harding and Coolidge gave him a free hand. He was Secretary of State in fact. It was an atmosphere to his liking, and he quickly impressed the country and the world. He was as far removed from the political currents that swirl around an Administration as it is possible for a Cabinet officer to be. Aside from the World Court and the recognition of Russia he had no political phases to consider seriously. It is not my province to contrast the records made by the Premiers of various Administrations, but it would be difficult for me to name one who achieved greater renown than Hughes, who has to his credit so many treaties ratified, or who can point to a Department reorganized on a basis that offers a career to those who enter it. Every policy was thoughtfully studied, frankly declared, and vigorously pressed. There were no hasty judgments, no subtleties of language or of purpose, no timidities.

An earnest desire to be on good terms with other nations, to exert the good offices of this government in the after-war chaos of Europe, was translated into performance. It will never be known how frequently our State Department was called upon immediately after the war to adjust minor but irritating differences between other nations solely because there was confidence that the man at the head would see to it that right prevailed. It was in giving that character of exact justice to his administration that Hughes performed his greatest service to other countries as well as to his own, and made a record of substantial achievement.

Today he is our ranking citizen without title—what I call our first citizen for emergencies. Every big occasion needs him. Coolidge as President is spokesman for the nation, but when a voice from our untitled citizenry is desired, the people turn to Hughes.

CHAPTER LVII

HOW WILL HAYS BECAME NATIONAL CHAIRMAN

WHEN William R. Willcox in 1918 decided to resign as chairman of the Republican national committee, Senator Boies Penrose, ex-Senator Murray Crane and others agreed upon John T. Adams, of Iowa, as his successor.

The committee was called to meet in St. Louis, February 12, 1918. The election of Adams seemed settled. Ten or twelve national committeemen of the progressive type, however, did not like the choice. George Perkins finally became active in this minority movement, and the newspapers gave it attention. A week or so before the meeting Murray Crane telephoned me to take breakfast with him at his apartment in the Biltmore Hotel, New York city. After breakfast, he suddenly asked me, "What is the use of stirring up all this muss about the chairmanship? Perkins cannot defeat Adams. I wish you would tell him so."

I replied that I had no interest in the matter—that a newspaper editor had no business in purely "organization rivalries."

"We have from 36 to 40 sure votes in the committee for Adams," continued Senator Crane. "There isn't a ghost of a chance to defeat him. Try to see Perkins today and make him see that he is up against a stone wall."

I talked with Perkins, as requested, and a check-up of the national committee showed the "Old Guard" strength about as Crane had stated.

"They have the votes," replied Perkins, "but possibly we can produce something else. Walter Brown has just been here from Ohio. He says we are going out to St. Louis with only a pair of deuces to draw to, but if we can draw the other two deuces we will have a strong hand. I'm after the other two. Better come out to St. Louis with us, and help in the good work."

"No," I replied, "I've attended enough funerals the past six years and I don't care to go to any more. You and Brown can be the whole show."

I learned later that the other two deuces Perkins was seeking were a series of letters written from Germany by Adams in the summer of 1914 (just after the outbreak of war) and printed in Adams' home-town paper in Iowa. They were distinctly pro-German. Perkins believed the committee would not dare to go to the country with a chairman who had expressed such opinions. He had sent a man to Iowa to dig up the letters. Three days before the St. Louis meeting they had not been found. Nevertheless, he and Walter Brown started for St. Louis.

SOME LETTERS ARRIVE AND ADAMS RETIRES

There was just one hour to spare when the documents arrived in St. Louis. The committee was about to meet. Apparently the Adams candidacy had no serious opposition. Perkins showed Senator Calder, of New York, the Adams publication.

"I'm for Adams," said Calder, "but these letters, if true, make him impossible."

They proved to be true enough. Adams frankly acknowledged their authorship when Calder read them to his astonished colleagues. You never saw a body of men so startled. In less than ten minutes the Adams candidacy was withdrawn, and the Committee recessed in a chaotic search for a new chairman. Murray Crane always insisted that had he been present the committee would have ignored the letters and elected Adams. The Massachusetts Senator, usually so thorough, had assumed that Adams was certain of election, and had remained at home. He thus lost control of the situation;

he vainly tried to rally the members by telephone, but he found that the water was over the dam. The next problem was to find a man whom both Murray Crane and Boies Penrose would agree was not "the other fellow's" candidate. He was hard to find.

SULLIVAN, INDIANA, PRODUCES ITS LEADING CITIZEN

Back in the little town of Sullivan, Indiana,—said to be somewhere near the geographic centre of population in this country—there lived a young man whose unusual ability in politics had been recognized for several years by Vice President Fairbanks and other Hoosier Republicans. He was unknown to fame beyond the banks of the Wabash but for a year or more he had been the working head of the Indiana Republican organization. He had represented Fairbanks in the 1916 convention and had persuaded him to accept a second nomination for Vice President, despite reiterated refusals. In Chicago that year he met Republican leaders from other States—and, in particular, he met George W. Perkins, who at once shared the Indiana faith in the young man from Sullivan.

The young man was Will H. Hays. That was the name suddenly thrust into the situation in St. Louis. His strength was that he had no political ties outside of Indiana; he was young, tireless and able. He seemed the man of the hour, and the committee turned to him as to a life-saver. Not a vote was cast against him. Hays was speaking before a Presbyterian Church meeting in Indianapolis that afternoon, when the presiding officer asked him to stop for a moment and announced that he had just been unanimously chosen chairman of the Republican National Committee. A national career clean, honorable, forceful and achieving was thus begun—and has not yet ended.

CHAPTER LVIII

WHEN ACQUAINTANCE, NOT ISSUES, WON

The 1920 Convention Had Many "Ifs" To It But Harding's Acquaintances Carried The Day—Hiram Johnson Refuses To Go On Ticket—Oregon Interrupts The Lenroot Boom With Calls For Coolidge, and Delegates Insist Upon Naming Him For Vice President.

SO MANY "ifs" could be used in the story of the 1920 Republican national convention that it is still possible for any candidate before that body to believe that he would have been the nominee "if" any one of several particular things had happened as he had planned.

Of course the big "if" in everybody's mind was—if Roosevelt were alive, could he, or would he, have stopped his own nomination? Undoubtedly, he would have liked to see his return to the leadership of the Republican party authenticated by the vote of a national convention indorsing his views if not his candidacy. But I cannot forget his emphatic "no" not many months before his death when I told him he would be the unanimous nominee. In 1912 I never abandoned hope that he would finally acquiesce, but I had a different feeling about him after my talk in 1919. He was then beyond his sixtieth birthday, the strain of a persistent illness was telling on him, and I knew that he was in no condition for the return of other days and their burdens. His passing away was so sudden that he left no word to indicate the man of his choice, if he had one.

So we had another "if"—would Roosevelt have urged Leonard Wood? The General's supporters insisted yes. They declared that the mantle of Roosevelt had fallen upon his shoulders—others said no.

463

As I Knew Them

If Saturday had not arrived with the delegates anxious to avoid further hotel bills, would they have continued balloting instead of making a hasty choice so as to get away? If they had continued, would the steady increase of votes for Leonard Wood have gone on?

There was still another "if." Had Senator Warren Harding insisted, as at one time he was inclined to do, upon "filing" for reelection as Senator from Ohio on Thursday night (the last lawful date) he would have fallen out of the Presidential race next day. If that had happened, who would have been the nominee?

HIRAM JOHNSON REFUSES SECOND PLACE

Without dwelling upon other "ifs," however, or summarizing the rivalries for nomination, let me divert and speak of an "if" that as matters turned out really would have made a President.

If Senator Hiram Johnson, of California, had agreed to Warren Harding's personal request that he go on the ticket as Vice President, he and not Calvin Coolidge would have succeeded President Harding in the White House. Not many persons know that Johnson refused such a request, but he did. It came to him just as the delegates were "breaking" and Harding's nomination was assured. The Harding group of managers went hurriedly into conference to consider the man for second place. Harding himself suggested Johnson. Not all of those present could wholly forget 1912, however. Some argument was required to overcome their factional objection. The convention was moving fast toward its decisions. Any settlement on Vice President had to be made quickly. Johnson therefore was selected.

The California Senator was informed of Harding's wish. He promptly replied that if he could not be named for President he preferred to remain in the Senate. On several ballots Johnson had polled close to 150 votes; like other candidates

he resented the hurry-up programme of the Harding supporters; he was against forcing a nomination on the plea that
the convention should adjourn before Sunday. Other tactics
by the Harding managers had also displeased the California
Senator. His visitors, therefore, heard some rather strong
words from the man they wanted to make Vice President—
and Johnson knows how to be emphatic. In fact the Harding men felt uncertain as they left him whether he would support the convention's nominee and the ghost of California in
1916 came to their minds. But Johnson delivered a hand-
some majority to the ticket of which he might have been a
part and thus two years later achieve the eager ambition of
his life.

ACQUAINTANCE, NOT ISSUES, CONTROLLED

I have heard the 1920 convention referred to as a convention in which acquaintance rather than issues influenced the
choice of the delegates. And that is as good an appraisement
of it as any other, for the Harding nomination had no deeper
significance.

He stood for no particular issue. He was a party man,
ready to do whatever everybody thought best. All that week
in Chicago he was smiling and buoyant throughout the usual
ups and downs of convention manipulation, apparently the
least concerned person in town. He had more acquaintances
in the convention than any of his rivals, and in a real sense
he put himself in the hands of his friends. They did the work
and the worrying.

I believe that Harding was the most astonished man who
ever sought the Presidency when Harry Daugherty and others
convinced him Thursday night that he could safely ignore
his last opportunity to file for reelection as Senator. He had
signed his nominating papers for the Senatorship, and they
were ready for filing in Ohio. Reluctantly, he allowed the

last moment to go. Then, and not until then, did he take an active interest in the convention result. He had to get the nomination or go back to Marion as Editor of the Marion "Star" after March 4, 1921.

The Lowden candidacy at the outset had the most votes on roll-call, though it never had a strong hold on its delegates. Hiram Johnson was a definite figure among the candidates. But among seventeen men formally nominated for President, Leonard Wood had the longest identity with public affairs. As against the Wilson Administration, he meant something in the public mind. So did Calvin Coolidge, whose candidacy was based on the issue raised by the police strike in Boston. While the strike was a local affair the issue was national.

NATHAN MILLER THE ONLY MAN WHO EVER BEAT "AL" SMITH

Another candidacy that had greater possibilities than the roll-call indicated, was that of Herbert Hoover, now Secretary of Commerce. His name was presented by Nathan L. Miller, soon to be Governor of New York. Miller has the honor of being the one man who ever defeated "Al" Smith for Governor. Smith turned the tables on him in 1922, but not before Miller had made a record as one of the ablest Governors of the Empire State. It was a record that appealed to Harding in the White House, for he offered to make Miller an Associate Justice of the Supreme Court—an honor that Miller, for financial reasons, reluctantly declined.

Had the move to Harding failed Saturday forenoon, the convention surely would have adjourned until the following week. There would then have been only three candidates in the "likely" list: Calvin Coolidge, Herbert Hoover and Leonard Wood. The Lowden column had broken, but the Wood column did not weaken until Harding was too far ahead to be overtaken. There were rumors that the Lowden delegates were to turn to Wood. They might have done so had there been time for negotiation but the convention leaders refused a recess and forced a nomination.

THE NAMING OF COOLIDGE

The one surprise of the convention came in a most dramatic way when Chairman Lodge asked for nominations for Vice President. Failing to persuade Hiram Johnson, the Harding people had no candidate for second place. Senator Medill McCormick of Illinois, got recognition, and walked to the platform to make a nominating speech. To reach it he had to pass my desk in the press section.

"What are you going to do, Medill?" I asked.

"We're going to put over Lenroot," he replied.

"The hell you are!" broke in a correspondent seated at an adjoining desk.

McCormick glared at him in surprise, and as he climbed up the ladder steps to the platform, called back, "Watch me and see."

A Senators' ticket—top to bottom—Harding and Lenroot! It seemed a narrow structure for a national appeal. However, that was the slate, so I awaited developments.

McCormick had not uttered fifty words before a voice from the rear delegates' seats interrupted with "Coolidge! Coolidge!" It was not a heavy voice, but it penetrated the convention hall. All kinds of voices and all kinds of interruptions are heard in a convention. They are accepted as part of the proceedings and merely swell the volume of noise. This voice, however, had a different sound—it seemed to say something worth heeding.

Senator McCormick went on with his speech to the next period. Again came that voice from the rear benches—"Coolidge! Coolidge!" Once more it filled the hall. This time it was echoed by other delegates. From individuals in a dozen State delegations came an echo to the cry "Coolidge!"

McCormick closed by naming his candidate, Lenroot, but from the delegates and galleries came insistent calls for Coolidge.

Probably two-thirds of the Republican Senators were delegates. Most of them rose to shout for Lenroot. Edge, of New Jersey, Calder, of New York, Brandegee, of Connecticut, just in front of me, jumped upon their seats and hurrahed as though they were cheering a home run by their local base ball team. But the Senators could not out-cheer the ordinary delegates, who by this time had grown into a substantial group demanding Coolidge.

OREGON NAMES THE BAY STATE GOVERNOR

The voice that had started the Coolidge demonstration was a voice from Oregon—truly across the whole continent from Massachusetts; the Pacific calling to the Atlantic. At once all eyes turned toward the Oregon standard to see the man who had broken in on the Senatorial slate. Delegates asked his name, and wondered how it happened that far-off Oregon—the pathless wilderness that Daniel Webster preferred in 1848 to let England own rather than have America burdened with it—had become so deeply interested in the Governor of Webster's State. Conventions are often moved by their great orators but rarely by men unknown beyond their own State lines.

In one of Bernard Shaw's comedies, the critics, when asked to give their opinion of a play they had just witnessed, responded by asking the name of the author. "How can we tell whether it is good or bad unless we know who wrote it?" So it is in large assemblages—the crowd mind seeks a big name to guide it. In this instance, however, the convention only knew that a man from Oregon was insistently calling for Coolidge, and that on every call he was getting a louder response. Perhaps in those final hours the delegates were glad to be free after three dreary days of balloting for President, under the restraint of "organization" decrees.

As I Knew Them

THE DELEGATES WANTED COOLIDGE

On the Vice-Presidency, the bars were down, and the delegates streamed out of the old, beaten, follow-the-leader path into new pasture like colts turned out on June grass. There were calls for "Oregon," calls for "platform," but the man whom nobody knew modestly stood on his chair and nominated for Vice President a man whom shortly the whole world was to know. Wallace McCamant made no long speech. He merely said that the Oregon delegates had come to the convention to nominate Calvin Coolidge for President. Since they could not get him in first place, they now wanted him in second place.

By this time the Coolidge boom was everywhere. The delegates themselves were in control of the convention; leaders—especially Senators—did not count. Not since Garfield was nominated in 1880 had there been an uprising so entirely "from the floor." Senator Joseph S. Frelinghuysen, of New Jersey, moved to make the nomination of Coolidge unanimous before Lodge, surprised and chagrined, could put the motion.

CHAPTER LIX

"DON'T LET'S CHEAT 'EM!"

Harding Always Anxious To Tell The Whole Story In His Speeches—My Visit To Harding's Home Town And A Breakfast Prepared By A Statesman—A Last Talk with Harding Before He Left for the West—"You've A Better Job Than I Have"—He Was "Warren" To The Whole Town—Fighting Illness To Do His Duty—"It Must Not Be Again! God Grant It Will Not Be!"—His Last Act Was To Gain An 8-Hour Day For Iron And Steel Workers—A Fine Record Through The Chaos Of War.

I SHALL never forget my first visit to Harding a week or so after his return to Marion. With Senator Coleman Du Pont, Harry Daugherty, and two others, I went down on the night train from Chicago, reaching Marion before six o'clock in the morning. There was no one "at home" so early in the Marion Club, but nearby we found a bakery and a butcher shop open. Du Pont fried the ham and eggs, heated the rolls and boiled the coffee. Others set the table, I acted as waiter. Never was a breakfast better cooked or more thoroughly enjoyed.

About nine o'clock we walked over to call on Harding. There in one of those modest village homes that are the greatest asset of American life we found the candidate—physically a splendid type of manhood. He asked my opinion as a newspaper editor as to how long an acceptance speech should be. Spread out before him were proofsheets that would fill a newspaper page.

"About half that much," I said.

He looked surprised.

"Candidates try to say too much at one time," I continued,

470

"and the people will not read it all. Give it to them little by little; then they will read it all."

"You're right from one point of view," he said, "but an acceptance speech is a sort of confession of faith; it's a record. The folks ought to know it all in one story. They expect it that way and we mustn't cheat 'em. Let them know it all, and then let them decide. Don't let's cheat 'em; let's make the record full and fair."

The speech when published filled almost two newspaper pages, or sixteen columns.

"DON'T LET'S CHEAT 'EM!"

After the campaign I learned that "Don't let's cheat 'em!" was a usual phrase with Harding when discussing the completeness of his speeches. Richard Washburn Child was one of those in charge of Harding's speaking engagements. Every morning they would have a conference about the speech for that particular day. Harding would ask for the data that had been gathered and listen to arguments about emphasizing or omitting different features. Invariably he would end discussion by saying: "Well, boys, let's tell them the whole story. Don't let's cheat 'em! They'll like us better."

Whenever there was doubt around the Harding headquarters in Marion as to what to do in public utterances, the candidate's "Don't let's cheat 'em!" became the guide. Finally, it spread to national headquarters, where Will Hays began using it in talks with campaign spell-binders.

Frankness was a strong Harding trait. And he always meant what he said. When the adjusted compensation bill —the "bonus bill"—was before him for approval or rejection in September 1922, he had decided not to sign it. He knew, however, that he had made a number of campaign speeches on the subject. Obviously, he could not recall every word he had said, but he wondered whether he had ever made any statement that could be regarded as a pledge to

471

favor such a measure.   He sent for Will Hays, then Postmaster General, who had managed the campaign.

"Will," he said, "you know my campaign speeches.   Did I ever say anything that would lead anyone to charge me with breaking faith if I should refuse to sign this bill?"

"I think not," replied Hays, "but I would have to look it up to be sure."

"Then I'll give you two days to have it looked up," replied the President.   "Put enough men on the job to read every word I ever uttered.   I am sure my record is clear, but make doubly sure, for if I'm pledged to sign it I'll sign."

The speeches were gone over, no pledge was found, and the bill went back to Congress with a Harding veto.

A LAST TALK WITH HARDING

"This is the most distressful decision of my life," said President Harding to me in the White House as he held up before me the contract, just signed, for the sale of the Marion "Star."   "It tears at my heart.   But what else is there for me to do?   I do not expect ever to live in Marion again, and there is no joy in running a newspaper from a distance.   Besides, every community is entitled to a resident editor for its newspapers.   It is hard for me to think that my days as editor are over.   An editor has the finest job in the world— I envy all you fellows.   You've a better job than I have."

For nearly two hours, we talked "shop."   It was a day or two before the President left on the trip from which he never returned.   He was in a strange mood.   I have since frequently recalled his tone, his words and his attitude that afternoon and as I have done so it seemed to me as though something hovering over him led him into a sort of spiritual mood.

I did not suspect that he was a sick man, for only his closest intimates knew that he was ill, but it was plain that something was sapping his strength and taking the color out of his face.

I realized as I left him that I was saying good-bye to a man who needed rest. I made up my mind also that Harding was not happy as President.

The austerity of the White House, the separation from companionships that meant much to him, created a void in his daily life that the honor of his title did not fill. This was reflected in his face the afternoon in July 1921 when he went to the Capitol to plead with the Senate not to pass the first bonus bill. Before making his address he sat with his old group at lunch around the familiar corner table in the Senate restaurant. Senator Frelinghuysen accompanied him from the White House.

"Don't make any early dates for me this afternoon," Harding called to his secretary. "I want to feel free."

And, as I watched him step into his motor car, I remarked that I had never seen him look so happy. That day, he told the Senate frankly what that particular bonus bill would mean to the finances of the nation. To the surprise of all observers, it was sent back to committee, and another year elapsed before the adjusted compensation bill succeeded it.

HARDING—HIS HOME TOWN'S "WARREN"

Fate was unkind to Warren Harding. It made him President almost against his will and certainly without his urging; it gave him the greatest popular and electoral majority ever recorded in a national election, and then, as he was growing into the bigness of his office, it robbed him of the opportunity to make good on the larger conception of his responsibilities that had slowly come to him out of the burdens and anxieties.

To get an accurate line on Harding you must go back to his days as Editor of the Marion "Star." He was the best known man in town. His office was the gathering place for all seekers after favor—the favor of publicity and the greater favor of no publicity. At the club, in the shops, everybody called him Warren, and he called every fellow townsman by

473

his first name. For him, the intimacies of a small town made life worth living; their boundaries marked the world of his desires.

He drifted into county conventions, state conventions, national conventions—always a popular figure. Then his road led to the Legislature at Columbus, to the Lieutenant Governorship, and to the Senate at Washington.

Even with these honors ambition did not stir him greatly. He remained "Warren," with all that that implied. With every advance he carried wholeheartedly the load of old associations. Each period back in Ohio had had its group of them. Slowly, without full appreciation of the changes he had outgrown them; but they clung to him and he clung to them. He was the last man in the world to realize their embarrassment to him when he entered the White House, also the last man to turn from them because they were embarrassing.

It seemed the task of gratitude, and the test of loyalty, to stand by them, and he did stand by them. He could see no wrong in their ways or their purposes, could see no reason why the ways of Marion and of Columbus as he knew them could not be the ways of the White House.

HARDING LOVED LIFE AND HIS FRIENDS

There was gratitude, there was friendship, there was a comradic warmth about Warren Harding that in every presence made him less a Senator, less a President, and more a genial understanding companion; life had finally turned its pleasant side to him and he tried to make it do the same for everyone he knew. He greeted every dawn with the sunny, cheery smile of the man who loved life and his friends, and whose record is made up only of kindly acts. It was so back in Marion days, so in the Ohio Legislature, so in the Senate, so in the White House, and so to his last breath in San Francisco. Truly a consistent record, for it was flesh of his flesh, bone of his bone.

As I Knew Them

Harding did not make a burden of his work, but he was an earnest President. He had Hughes in the State Department, Mellon in the Treasury, Hoover in the Interior, Hays in the Post Office, Weeks in the War Department, and Dawes at the Budget. What stronger group could be assembled, to relieve a President of perplexities, and to aid him in a wise solution of his problems? He knew he was in safe hands when he trusted them; he believed as confidently that he was in safe hands when with equal faith he trusted others who did not prove so dependable.

Then too, Harding was an undisciplined man in his day's work. The old times of care-free printer and editor were still coloring his cordial nature. Method rather than purpose stood in the way of rigid organized effort. But those who criticise must face the fact that Harding labored for a year with a blood pressure exceeding 180, defying the orders of his doctors and silencing those who had to know of his peril and might speak of it to others.

While the newspapers were publishing reports of Mrs. Harding's illness, they could with equal truth have published reports of the President's defiance of death, day after day, in order to attend to the affairs of the nation. The calm courage with which he endured that strain is shown by the way in which he kept it his own secret, shared only by his Cabinet, until finally, it was revealed to the world by his collapse in San Francisco.

FACING AFTER-WAR PROBLEMS AND CHAOS

A colossal task faced the man who became President in March 1921. Returning the country to a peace basis—(to "normalcy," as Harding described it)—was quite as difficult as directing it on a war basis. The spirit of united effort left the people when war ceased. Every nation was in chaos. We had our railroads emerging, almost bankrupt, from government control; we had ships by the score that had never sailed the seas, and scores of others destined never to sail again; we had millions of men demobilized from the army, but not yet gathered back into industry; we had industrial and farm over-capacity and over-production that finally forced a deflation period through which the country staggered but did not fall. In our great agricultural States more banks closed than remained open. In truth all the chaos of war in our own country as well as its terrific ravages abroad came to Harding for adjustment.

THE RIGHT MAN FOR EACH TASK

He was a newspaper editor and a politician. He had no experience equipping him for the situation he had to deal with. He could not be a Mellon, but he got Mellon; he could not be a Hughes, but he got Hughes; he could not be a Hoover, but he got Hoover; he could not be a Hays, but he got Hays. The experience he lacked was to be found in those men. Yet in their selection, except with Hays, he ran against the narrow views of his party leaders. They could see no politics in the choice of such men, but Harding had a larger conception of the country's need.

There was the unemployment conference with Hoover and Davis at the head, with leading employers of labor gathered together in Washington to find a way to put men to work. That, too, was not politics, but it was service for the country. A railroad strike was settled, a coal strike was settled, farmers were financed as well as possible through the War Finance Board, Dawes was brought on from Chicago to budget government expenditures, and the one big constructive after-war measure upon which all nations agreed—the limitation of naval armament—was carried to success. I have no exact figures, but my guess is that that agreement has already saved taxpayers close to a billion dollars which would have been spent for war ships.

SOUGHT THE RIGHT WAY AND RIGHT MAN

Sum it all up from the record of Harding's two years in the White House and it will be found that he proved greater than his conceded limitations; and that in every large policy and task the intuitions of a deep patriotism led him in vital matters to search for the way and the men that would accomplish most. His judgment was not infallible; some mistakes were inevitable. But when suspicion reached him, he corrected two mistakes in men. The scandals attaching to those men are discussed by scandal-mongers as though Harding had not moved in the matter, though the date of his action, in each case, is easily available.

HIS VICTORY FOR THE 8-HOUR DAY

Harding found approximately 200,000 men in our iron and steel mills working twelve hours a day. He made no public announcement, but a few months before he started west he took up the subject with Judge Elbert H. Gary and Charles M. Schwab. As he was leaving for Alaska, he made public the written pledge of the iron and steel companies to change from a twelve-hour to an eight-hour day. Harding did not live to see the change made. But he died knowing what he had accomplished for labor. The eight-hour day in that industry is a Harding day. He told Judge Gary that he would regard it as the greatest triumph of his Administration.

"IT MUST NOT BE AGAIN"

I witnessed that scene on the long Hoboken pier when the first bodies of our soldier dead were brought home for burial. I followed behind Harding as he walked the length of the pier, viewing the long row of coffins, visibly agitated by the sight. In the speech he then made he brought tears to many eyes as well as to his own as he said:

> "They have served, which is the supreme inspiration of living. They have earned everlasting gratitude, which is the supreme solace in dying. . . .
>
> "There is ringing in my ears like an admonition eternal, an insistent call—'It must not be again! It must not be again!' God grant that it will not be, and let a practical people join in cooperation with God to the end that it shall not be."

And the same sentiment ran through his speech later, at the naval limitation conference in Washington when he declared to the assembled statesmen of the great nations:

> "The United States welcomes you with unselfish hands. We have no fears; we have no sordid ends to serve; we suspect no enemy; we contemplate or apprehend no conquest. Content with what we have we seek nothing that is another's. We only wish to do with you that finer nobler thing which no nation can do alone."

Of war, he said in the same address, "How can humanity justify, or God forgive?"

OUR PROTECTION IS OUR FRATERNITY

No better picture of Warren Harding, man of sentiment, of friends and of patriotism can be painted than his own words. And he spoke no finer sentiment than is to be found in his address at Vancouver, British Columbia, on July 26— only a week before his death. Here is an extract well worth reading:

> "Thousands of your brave lads perished in gallant and generous action for the preservation of our Union. Many of our young men followed Canadian colors to the battlefields of France before we entered the war and left their proportion of killed to share the graves of your intrepid sons.

478

As I Knew Them

"When my mind reverts and my heart beats low the recollection of those faithful and noble companionships, I may not address you as fellow citizens, as I am accustomed to designate assemblages at home, but I may and do, with respect and pride, salute you as 'fellow men' in mutual striving for common good.

"What an object lesson of peace is shown today by our two countries to all the world! No grim-faced fortifications mark our frontier, no huge battleships patrol our dividing waters, no stealthy spies lurk in our tranquil border hamlets.

"Only a scrap of paper, recording hardly more than a simple understanding, safeguards lives and properties on the Great Lakes, and only humble mile posts mark the inviolable boundary line for thousands of miles through farm and forest.

"Our protection is our fraternity; our armour is our faith; the tie that binds more firmly, year by year, is ever increasing acquaintance and comradeship through interchange of citizens; and the compact is not of perishable parchment, but of fair and honorable dealing, which, God grant, shall continue for all times."

CHAPTER LX

WHO *KNEW* WOODROW WILSON?

No One Convinces Others That He Knew Him—A Many-Sided Man—Would Never Get Anywhere If He Listened To Suggestion—No Use For Cabinet Or Senators—Write And Wait For Your Type-written Answer—A Solitary Figure, Battling Alone—The School Master Sure Enough.

I WISH that I could say I *knew* Woodrow Wilson.

I have never met anyone who makes that claim and who at the same time validates it in any mind but his own.

Of course, you can always hear two contrasting opinions about our Presidents, usually more than two, but never were so many diverse opinions heard as could be heard of Wilson in his day. Such a thing as being in his confidence deep enough to know beyond challenge the real man, to understand his moods and impulses, seems to have been impossible.

"A cold intellectual," some folks said; "an inspiring, stimulating companion," others said; "the most curt, opinionated man of all I know," another said; "a man of superb ability and the most workmanlike man I was ever associated with," is another direct quotation to me from the leader of a group.

These utterances, though from different sources, echo the estimate made to me, seven or eight years ago, by one who knew Wilson intimately at Princeton and for some time thereafter, "a many-sided man, so many sides that there is room for a variety of honest opinions." There were those who found in him much to admire, and with good reason; there were those who found in him much to deplore, and with good reason. There were those who were baffled by his swift, pitiless, unexplained changes from friendly relations to cold dismissal, and with good reason.

As I Knew Them

Those who saw the good in Wilson acclaimed him with Islamic faith and adulation; those who saw the other side were equally intense in their condemnation. The in-betweens were not so numerous during his first term as either of the extremes; during his second term, the idolaters were not so many as in the earlier years of his Presidency, but they grew more emotionally devout as their ranks grew thinner.

The groups I have quoted were in the Cabinet, in Congress, among the leaders of his party, and among those who though not in politics had contact with him on public matters.

Sifting these varied opinions plus my own observation of the man, my guess is that Wilson held himself from you unless he felt you had something to bring him that he lacked, and that there was not much that in his own opinion he lacked for long. He had few around him whom he regarded as on a level with himself, and to whom he felt it worth while to listen.

NEVER GET ANYWHERE IF HE LISTENED TO OTHERS

During his first year as President one of his intimates urged him to establish better relations with his party leaders in the Senate and House, to ask for suggestions, and discuss contemplated policies with them.

"Utterly futile," he quickly replied in decisive voice. "A waste of time. I would never get anywhere if I should do that. Every fellow has his own views; I would be swamped."

"Even if they have no ideas worth adopting, Mr. President," persisted this visitor, "you would get their cooperation in things you want to accomplish. They would feel that you at least had given their views consideration."

"Futile! I tell you, futile!" again replied Wilson, "I can make better headway by giving consideration to my own ideas, whipping them into shape, testing them out in my own way, and insuring their adoption by their own fairness and merit. I waste no time while I am engaged in such work."

It was not Congress alone that was thus held at arm's length.

One night I found Franklin K. Lane, his Secretary of the Interior, sitting on a hotel corridor lounge deeply absorbed in reading an address just delivered by the President. "Great stuff," he said to me, "great stuff that is. I like to have him talk that way."

"Didn't you know he was going to say it?" I asked.

"Not a word of it," he replied. "I haven't seen the President for a month, and don't know when I shall."

NO USE FOR CABINET OR SENATORS

From that talk and from others I learned that Wilson's Cabinet officers rarely saw his public addresses until they read them in the newspapers; they were not privileged, either, to have an advance reading of his messages to Congress except such portions as concerned their individual departments. Wilson was not distrustful or suspicious of people; he ignored his Cabinet and Senators because he did not regard them as his equal, and wanted to hear their views only when he asked for them. Cleveland maintained the most cordial relations with his Cabinet and he gave his confidence to those Senators and Congressmen he trusted. The latter were few, it is true, but they were a crowd compared with Wilson's intimates.

Yet it was this same Wilson who in his inaugural address in 1913 had said:

"I summon all honest men, all patriotic, all forward-looking men to my side. God helping me, I will not fail them, if they will but counsel and sustain me."

AN INCIDENT IN TRENTON

Wilson's curtness and unwillingness to listen to discussion were attributed sometimes to the inability of men to "get" him, to understand how to approach him and the arguments that would appeal to him. I have had cited as an illustration an incident at the State House in Trenton while he was Governor of New Jersey.

Wilson was then jamming his famous "Seven Sisters" bills through the Legislature. The measure attracted nation-wide attention and was heralded as a cure-all for corporation evils. Its only result in fact was to give Wilson a place in the public mind, and to lose New Jersey several million dollars in taxes on foreign companies.

Wilson was not pleasing Jersey Democrats with his distribution of patronage. A group of legislators determined to hold up the "Seven Sisters" bills until they could have an understanding. They called upon the Governor, but their line of argument quickly showed no meeting place for their minds and Wilson's.

Presently they began to hint that his legislation might suffer. The light blue of his eyes when in friendly conversation deepened at once into the dark blue of the ocean when tempest tossed. He got up, took a quick turn about his desk (a habit of his when excited to anger), and cut them off in a series of short, savagely contemptuous answers. They went out silent and bewildered.

WRITE—AND WAIT FOR YOUR ANSWER

In a larger way, the same incidents frequently occurred at Washington. They strengthened his distaste for "conference" and for meeting people. Some in anger, some in admiration, all in silence, left him at his bidding to his own thoughts. More than once, when reminded of his abruptness he seemed surprised. He would curtly say, "Well, I can't make myself over."

This practice of "self-determination" grew with Wilson as he found himself with the dazzling power of a President. He listened reluctantly, if at all, to oral suggestions; he gave as his reason that he did not want his mind swayed by the personality of the proponent. You were asked to present your views in writing. He insisted that in that way only could he consider them dispassionately, and without regard to the source. Even Cabinet officers were forced to do this, and to wait, sometimes for weeks, the famous typewritten memo from Wilson's study in reply. This much must be said for that memo—it always bore evidence that he had thoroughly considered your paper.

But a President cannot carry on a government on a typewriter. Most essential to him is the open conflict of many minds, searching for the best conclusion—the enlightening contact of a round-table discussion. A product of the cloister cannot escape its rigid environment, and our ocean-to-ocean continent is too big for one man, unaided, to grasp its needs.

A SOLITARY FIGURE BATTLING ALONE

In that sense, Wilson became almost a recluse after his second election. Constantly he would reiterate that he had no time for discussion. More and more angrily he resented efforts to change his mind, more and more he stripped himself of old friendships—eventually even of Colonel House—and stood a lone, slim, pallid figure on an eminence as unapproachable as Mount Everest—

> ——such a man, too fond to rule alone,
> Bears, like the Turk, no brother near the throne.

If you will look over the Wilson friendships, you will find that they were ever-changing. He took none of his associates out of Princeton into public life; he took only Tumulty out of Jersey political life and left only antagonisms behind him; and after his eight years in the Presidency the men remaining close to him in private life were Bernard M. Baruch, Norman Davis and Bainbridge Colby, who were of the last not the early vintage of his friendships. The separations were his choice; not the choice of his early supporters. Even Tumulty was dropped, his wonderful loyalty spurned. Wilson is the only President of the last half century who failed to honor in a conspicuous way some friend or friends of other years. In his view, friendship meant service to him and not by him; friendships were bridges burned behind as he himself moved on, a solitary traveller.

While writing this chapter I asked one of Wilson's most loyal supporters in his last days how he accounted for this marked absence of long-time associates in his Administration. "In pursuit of what he believed to be right Wilson was as relentless as time," he replied. "Public office was to his mind most emphatically a public trust and he acted as a trustee. It might and would grieve him deeply to refuse to appoint a man whom he liked immensely but he would surely refuse unless he believed the man was capable. He had the stern sense of duty that would lead him to send his best friend to the scaffold, though it would break his heart to do it."

ANOTHER WILSON IN PRIVATE LIFE

The Wilson in private life, in social intercourse, was an entirely different man. He was genial and witty; he could tell a story magnificently, and he had a highly developed sense of humor. He was not the cold unresponsive overlord but a lively companion. His sense of his own dignity was less than Roosevelt's; he did not seem to value it, while Roosevelt sometimes over-valued his. Wilson did not get himself across the footlights, though. He was pleased beyond words when, while stumping in 1912, some one in a crowd called him "Woody." His face was one big smile whenever he talked of that greeting and he took it as an indication that he was putting over with the people the Wilson of his own mind. But he was not, and never did.

As I Knew Them

THE SCHOOLMASTER SURE ENOUGH

During the early days of Wilson in the White House it was said in Washington, chiefly by those politically opposed, that he was a schoolmaster in public office, and that no event or experience would be powerful enough ever to take him out of the rôle. At the national Capitol one is accustomed to cynicism and criticism and I tried not to allow that particular estimate to take hold of me. It was to be expected that some of the atmosphere of the school-room would cling to him, but I believed that the wider outlook and contacts of the Presidency would quickly dissipate it. That belief was to be slowly shattered. As the months rolled by I heard the early opinion echoed by members of his own party. But not until the memorable night of April 2, 1917, when he appeared before Congress to deliver his war message, did Wilson seem to me to justify his critics.

As he entered the crowded House of Representatives through a narrow stage-door back of the Speaker's rostrum, he was the schoolmaster beyond all question—the perfect product of the conventional mould. His pale, immobile face, his protruding chin, his long thin nose firmly supporting eyeglasses, his carefully brushed hair, his slender figure seemingly elongated by a close-fitting frock coat, his dark gray trousers painstakingly creased, his ease, the manner of one conscious of his commanding place and of the importance of what others were now to hear from his lips;—yes, he was the schoolmaster from head to foot.

When he looked out upon the faces in front of him, he saw the revered justices of the Supreme Court seated in semicircle around the "well"; back of them were ranged the somewhat less revered members of the Senate; in their seats were the Congressmen, whom no one seems to revere. Diplomats and their wives crowded their assigned gallery, important folks from all parts of the country filled the public spaces to over-

WOODROW WILSON IN CHARACTERISTIC POSE WHILE SPEAKING

flowing. We knew war must come and its brutalities and
tragedies even then cast a shadow of solemnity over the brilliant scene.

THE COOL AND COLLECTED WILSON

I studied Wilson from the press gallery. As he advanced
to the space in front of the Speaker's desk I searched his face
and manner for some emotion responsive to the vital importance of that moment. Not a sign! No man ever was more
at ease. To the correspondent who sat next to me I remarked
that Wilson took his manuscript from the pocket of his frock-
coat and began his address with the calmness of a clergyman
announcing the evening meetings of the coming week before
service; he read it with as little emphasis. If his manner was
deliberate restraint it was a masterpiece; if it was just Wilson,
he certainly was the coldest man I ever looked upon.

He got from that great audience what he gave it—the cool-
ness of an academic address.

Oh, for a Roosevelt! the thought came to me as I listened
to paragraph after paragraph without a handclap, without a
change in the placid faces of the audience, without any notice-
able depth of feeling in the speaker's tone.

Perhaps Chief Justice White had much the same thought,
for after vainly waiting for someone else to punctuate the
President's speech with applause, he dropped on the floor the
felt hat he had been holding on his lap, and started a vigorous
first round. Wilson was then half way through. Of course,
at the close, there was a wave of enthusiasm, for the peroration was thrilling, but nothing in his manner or tone gave
encouragement to go much beyond respectful hearing and
courteous response.

And no one did.

CHAPTER LXI

SAW HIMSELF THE WORLD'S ARBITER

Wilson Sure At First That He Was To Be Arbiter Of The World War—Other Methods Would Have Brought Us Into The League Of Nations—An Amazing Secret Agreement "Probably" To Go To War —"You Know My Mind And How To Interpret It" He Told House— Kitchener's Words "Worth Serious Consideration"—"We're Just Backing Into War" Said Senator Stone—Wilson's Liking For "13"— "How Far From Paris To Versailles?" Asked Senator Martin.

FROM the first beat of the drums abroad, the World War drew Wilson into a wider field than any President was ever called upon to work in—as wide as the world itself. It was not given to any man alone to foresee its tremendous scope, to know and appraise its developing phases, or wisely to guide a nation desiring peace, but being steadily drawn into war. Wilson undertook to do it—alone. It seemed to him an opportunity almost as great as came to Washington and Lincoln to make himself immortal, and it was in his nature to want no rivals for that fame.

The dimensions of the picture gave him no concern; he never doubted he could measure up to them. He had always worked alone; he was now President of the most powerful nation. Alone he stood at the peak of fame; with the poet his one thought was:

"What shall I do to be forever known,
To make the age to come my own?"

The prospect fascinated, controlled him. His great power coldly, dispassionately, held aloof from the intense conflict seemed to him certain to make him the chosen arbiter of the fate of nations. Many strange and baffling situations were to arise, but Wilson never lessened faith in his ability to master them, nor in his purpose to be the central figure; rather he emphasized both. He lost his opportunity to leave deeds instead of words as his record because it was not possible for one mind to force every other mind to its single point of view; and he lost his life because, physically and mentally, it was not possible for one man alone to carry the burdens and solve the problems of a 100,000,000 nation at war.

There were three distinct periods in Wilson's career as it relates to the World War.

The first period was dominated by his early determination to keep America "ready to play the part of impartial mediator, not as a partisan but as a friend"; "neutral in thought and deed."

The second period covered our participation in the war.

The third period was dominated by his re-awakened purpose, after having gone through war, to make himself the peacemaker of history. Alone so far as America was concerned he outlined the terms of a world settlement; alone he sat at the peace table in Paris; alone he passed on the wisdom or unwisdom of every line of the treaty; alone he carried the treaty back with him to Washington, personally submitting it to the Senate and demanding that that body ratify it precisely as it stood because, in his judgment, it was the embodiment of the sum of human hopes.

WHY WE ARE NOT IN THE LEAGUE

The result of this unyielding attitude is that the United States is not a member of the League of Nations, and that Wilson, his personality and his policies still remain in controversy.

When the historian analyzes Wilson's course, he will find that the Versailles Treaty in all probability would have been ratified by the Senate without a serious fight over the League of Nations, had Wilson sent to Paris a peace commission representative of America, with power, purpose and ability to negotiate with other nations, even with Wilson present.

Again, when the historian reads the series of Wilson notes to Germany and England covering more than two years and sees how the two nations at war persisted in their own way— one with sub-marines and the other by seizing our ships and taking them to port—he will be astounded at the claim of the 1916 Democratic national platform of "splendid diplomatic triumphs" that had "kept us out of war."

He will search in vain for diplomatic triumphs; the record shows an unbroken line of diplomatic turn-downs and evasions. The response from Mexico in 1914 to our demand to salute our flag was a pattern later for the responses of both England and Germany to our notes of protest. Mexico never saluted, England continued to search our ships and Germany sub-marined more ruthlessly than ever. Toward all three countries we adopted a policy of "watchful waiting" for something that never came—and that everybody but Wilson knew would never come.

Three days after the torpedoing of the "Lusitania" Wilson proclaimed an "America too proud to fight." With that sentiment crossing the Atlantic to Germany simultaneously with our note of protest, the Kaiser knew, as indeed the whole world knew, that the head of the American government had other aims than war in mind. No matter how loud we might thunder, "too proud to fight" was accepted by Germany as a roving commission for her sub-marines; the subsequent warning that we would hold her to "strict accountability" did not stop a single attack; nor delay or change a single German purpose.

WHEN THE GERMANS ERRED

Von Bernstorff and other Germans had studied their Wilson and they thought they knew him; then came the 1916 triumph of his kept-us-out-of-war platform. That result confirmed them in their wrong assumption that the President could not be dragged into war, whatever Germany might do. The defiant "unrestricted" sub-marine policy shortly announced by the Kaiser was a consequence of that judgment. It held good so long as war events failed to arouse Wilson's patriotism to the peril of his pride of opinion. For no one can truly say of Wilson that he lacked intense love of country; he was deeply patriotic. But his supreme confidence in himself created a certainty that his own purposes were best for the nation and he did not hesitate to let others know it. Nothing was so precious to him as his own opinion, his own future; nothing so valueless as what others might say or think to the contrary.

A SECRET AGREEMENT "PROBABLY" TO WAR

Has anyone ever explained the staggering fact that at the moment Wilson was giving his O.K. to Governor Glynn's keynote utterance in the 1916 Democratic National Convention, "He-kept-us-out-of-war," there was lying on the desk of England's War Minister, Sir Edward Grey, awaiting England's approval, "at an opportune moment," a secret document (signed of all days on the calendar for a foreign alliance by America, February 22nd) and approved by Wilson, reading as follows:

> "Confidential. Col. House told me that President Wilson was ready, on hearing from France and England, that the moment was opportune, to propose that a conference should be summoned to put an end to the war. Should the Allies accept this proposal and should Germany refuse it, the United States would probably enter the war against Germany.
>
> "Col. House expressed the opinion that if such a conference met, it would secure peace on terms not unfavorable to the Allies, and if it failed to secure peace the United States would leave the conference as a belligerent on the side of the Allies if Germany was unreasonable. . . ."

Only within the last year, through "The Intimate Papers of Colonel House" and Sir Edward Grey's "Memoirs" has this document become public; had it been known to exist at the time the Democrats were hurrahing in convention over the Glynn speech, or had it become known during the campaign while western voters were convinced Wilson would continue to keep us out of war, a tornado of protest against secret war agreements would have swept the country.

The only change Wilson made in the original House memorandum was to insert the word "probably" before "enter the war against Germany." "Probably," of course, was a saving clause that ordinary precaution suggested.

HOUSE AS THE PRESIDENT'S SPOKESMAN

House had sailed for Europe on December 15, 1915, with the definite understanding reached between Wilson, Lansing and himself that he was to supersede all Ambassadors and represent the President directly. Wilson thanked him for consenting to make the trip, and provided him with a "To-Whom-It-May Concern" letter as his trusted and confidential spokesman. In effect, those in Europe to whom the letter was intended to be shown realized at once that House reflected the President's mind. It is now in Yale University Library but it properly belongs on the files of the State Department at Washington, for no man ever went abroad to pledge this country in any circumstances to war, authorized only by a private letter. Only an Emperor of the most autocratic type would make the fortunes of a great nation his sole personal concern.

Thus in considering Wilson before the war we have a Wilson "neutral in thought and deed," "ready to play the part of an impartial mediator," a Wilson nominated for reelection because his avowed purpose was to keep us out of war, and in contrast at the same moment a Wilson with an outstanding pledge to go to war if "Germany proved unreasonable." I leave it to the reader to judge had England accepted Wilson's condition what chance there was for America to escape war under the terms of that memo—the only document in existence in which this government was ever committed even remotely to a foreign government to engage as its ally in war. House insists in his diary that this was an effort for peace, but he concedes that if England had accepted the result would have brought us into war.

Of course, the Grey memo was in fact a Wilson document; but how Wilson could go through a Presidential campaign as a kept-us-out-of-war candidate with that we-will-go-in document lying around like a ton of dynamite is beyond me. Every morning he must have given a sigh of relief when he found that the newspapers were still without information of the most daring negotiation ever carried on in the name of our government. Fortunately for Wilson's political fortunes the newspapers never learned of it. Downing Street proved rumor-tight.

KITCHENER'S WORDS WORTHY OF CONSIDERATION

Here, indeed, we see the many-sided Wilson his friends described—so many sides, as one friend had said, that there is room for a variety of honest opinion. It was at this time, too, while the Grey memo still awaited England's "opportune moment," that Wilson frankly stated that he was impressed by a voice from England—that of Lord Kitchener. Only a short time before Kitchener sailed on his fatal voyage, he had said to House, "God forbid that any nation should become involved in this war, but if the United States should feel compelled to come in, it would shorten the war, save an untold number of lives, and lighten for the world the burden that will otherwise crush it for years."

Of all the soldiers and statesmen of the world Kitchener alone in 1914 sensed the duration of the struggle just begun. By 1916 events had confirmed his conception of it and when Wilson that summer heard Kitchener's words as to our own

From London Punch 1916.

BRINGING IT HOME.

"TUT! TUT! GERMAN SUBMARINE BLOCKADING NEW YORK? IMPOSSIBLE!"

participation he promptly accepted them as "worth serious consideration."

Reelection, however, turned Wilson's thoughts back to his rôle of "an impartial mediator"—more suited to him than any other. Again he visioned the monument he was building for himself with the grateful inscription by his countrymen "He kept us out of war" and he went to work at it with new determination. The Roosevelt onslaughts, vigorous, scathing and persistent, only hardened him to his course. He continued to speak of war as an Atlantic seaboard affair with which people west and south had no sympathy. He insisted that they believed with him that it was "no concern of ours" and that the election had proved that they wanted him to continue "neutral in thought and deed."

Wilson's message to Congress in January, 1917—three months later we were at war—that "this country does not intend to become involved," and later his plan for "peace without victory," were a logical sequence to his December letter to the belligerents that they should declare their purpose in war and seek an adjustment. Never was Wilson so strongly against our getting into war, never so resentful of reminders that events were making our entrance into it inevitable, as during the months immediately preceding our war declaration. His own judgment was against it—hence it could not be. Orders became more rigid against any preparation of our army and navy, and Cabinet officers whose unexpressed views were known not to agree with the President's found themselves ignored.

"WE'RE JUST BACKING INTO WAR!"

A President has facilities for learning the true situation available to no individual, but the only facts Wilson sought were those that seemed to sustain his position. His course recalls a statement made after the 1912 election by one closely associated with him at Princeton: "He will make a fine President so long as he is right, but God help the United States should Wilson be wrong!"

While the perplexities and uncertainties were reaching their climax in the winter of 1916-17, Senator Stone, of Missouri, —"Gum Shoe Bill," as he was commonly called,—then Chairman of the Senate Foreign Relations Committee said to me in a tone that reflected the existing chaos, "We're just backing into war."

"I'LL DO MY DAMNEDEST!" SAID WILSON

War had to be; Wilson had to abandon his dream. When he faced the reality he went whole-heartedly to his new task. At their first conference, the Allies told him of their exhausted condition, of the imperative need for haste. Wilson's instant reply was "Gentlemen, I'll do my damnedest!" And he did. He shunted his Cabinet to the side lines and picked men in whose organizing ability he had more confidence. They formed his "War Cabinet" and with them he sat in conference every Wednesday. In that circle were Newton D. Baker, Bernard M. Baruch, Charles G. Dawes, William G. McAdoo, Herbert Hoover, Vance McCormick, Edward N. Hurley and Dr. Harry Garfield, president of Williams College. There Wilson listened to criticism as he listened nowhere else, but he insisted upon having suggestion with it. An illustrative incident occurred when one of the War Cabinet said that a certain member of a leading commission was incompetent.

"All right," said Wilson, "get me a successor who will do better and I'll appoint him. Put up or shut up."

Two weeks were spent in vain search for the better man. Everybody who was sought professed to be too busy. Finally the Cabinet officer abandoned the effort and reported to Wilson.

"Now you have had your chance to put up," said the President, "and you couldn't. So it's your duty to shut up."

As I Knew Them

But with all its man-power, its spirit and its factories, America could not hide its unpreparedness for war. Wilson did his best to make up for this humiliating consequence of his peace dreams; the whole country went to work with a will; yet the sad record is that not an American cannon of real power was ever placed on the battle lines of France, not an American aeroplane ever flew over enemy country, not a wooden ship ever felt the splash of an ocean wave against its prow.

Wilson's damnedest, however, did give the Allies something most effective—his speeches and addresses. Lord Northcliffe had them printed in German and from aeroplanes covered Germany with pamphlets as with a blanket of snow. Such propaganda outdid the Allies' cannon in breaking down the morale of the German army; it led the German people to doubt, for the first time, whether their Kaiser was right, but particularly whether they could win the war. That kind of fighting appealed to Wilson; he was at home with words and phrases; he could produce them without the aid of factory or furnace, or farm. He did it well.

THE PEACE TABLE ALWAYS WILSON'S GOAL

Never for an instant during the nineteen months we were engaged in war did Wilson regard the conflict as his place of opportunity; the peace council not the battlefield was always his goal. And when the peace-making came we had again the two Wilsons—the Wilson sincerely intent upon making the world "safe for democracy" and the Wilson determined, alone, to dictate and control the manner of doing it. He could see no difference in the aims of the two Wilsons, so sure was he that, better than any or all others, he knew what was best.

In his letters and speeches from the moment of the armistice you will find many appeals for support for what he was undertaking to do, but never a suggestion that he desired cooperation.

When he announced to Congress that he was going to France he gave as his reason that the Allies "very reasonably desire my personal counsel," though there is no record of such a request; he asked for "undivided support," and then assured the listening legislators that the cables would make him "immediately available" for any aid or counsel *they* might desire of him. Not a word in that address could even by inference be accepted as indicating that he felt in need of counsel from the coordinate branch of government. He wanted support—not advice.

SEEKS, THEN IGNORES, ELECTION VERDICT

Yet at the time he was on notice definitely from the country that world peace was neither a one-man affair nor a one-party affair. Two months earlier, just before the Congressional elections of 1918, he had amazed the people by his letter addressed "To My Fellow Countrymen" asking them to express themselves unmistakably by returning a Democratic majority to Senate and House, "if you have approved of my leadership and wish me to continue to be your unembarrassed spokesman in affairs at home and abroad."

Here are some other paragraphs in that most remarkable of all campaign appeals:

> "I am your servant and will accept your judgment without cavil. But my power to administer the great trust assigned me by the Constitution would be seriously impaired should your judgment be adverse. . . .
>
> "I have no thought of suggesting that any political party is paramount in matters of patriotism. I feel too deeply the sacrifices which have been made in this war by all our citizens, irrespective of party affiliation, to harbor such an idea. I mean only that the

THE PARADE TO PARIS—WILSON, HOUSE, LANSING, WHITE, BLISS, BARUCH, HOOVER AND CREEL

differences and delicacies of our present task are of a sort that makes it imperatively necessary that the nation should give its undivided support to the government under a unified leadership and that a Republican Congress would divide that leadership.

"The return of a Republican majority to either House of Congress would, moreover, be interpretative on the other side of the water as a repudiation of my leadership. . . . I submit my difficulties and my hopes to you."

The response from the people was the election of a Congress Republican in both branches—and Wilson promptly refused to accept their judgment "without cavil" or to assume that "his leadership had been repudiated."

It was still his duty to think, speak and act for America and he remained convinced that he could do all three with certain benefit to the world—that other minds would only confuse, perhaps thwart, the consummation of a purpose almost inspired.

WANTED NO ONE BY HIS SIDE

If he had only realized it, Wilson's long sought opportunity for achievement was now open wide to him—here was the time for him, by frank exchange of views with others, to make himself the accepted spokesman for all. But it was not in his nature to do so. When he expressed that desire in his campaign letter it would seem that he really meant spokesman *to* not spokesman *for* the whole nation. Never had he held himself apart more than in those days when his decisions were to be of such consequence to the world; even an autocrat would then have sought counsel.

The armistice had scarcely been signed before he was urged to bring men of all parties into conference, and seek to learn what the people had in mind regarding the peace to be made. As President he could draft into such service the experience, the wisdom and the patriotism of the nation. Everywhere it was hoped that he would. With such cooperation, his peace plans would have been invincible. He gave no heed to such suggestion. One man who urged it too strongly was met with angry flash from the eye, and those tightly gripped lips that indicated that the speaker was restraining unpleasant words.

We must remember that Wilson, despite his idealism, was an intense partisan. His reply that he did not propose to bring Republicans to the front in the peace negotiations was a true reflection of his partisanship, but it was only a small part of the truth—the part he could admit. The whole truth was that he did not propose to bring anyone to the front.

NOT WHAT YOU THINK, ONLY WHAT YOU KNOW

For peace commissioners he did not seek counsellors. He selected men who, with the single exception of House, would do no thinking on their own account, who would understand that Wilson was to do it all. One of the commissioners, anxious to be of real help in Paris, asked after six days of uncertainty on the George Washington, how he should go about it. "Never offer the President advice, never plead a cause with him," came the reply. "He is interested only in what you know, not in what you think. He will listen to your information but not to your opinion."

WILSON'S LIKING FOR "13"

With that deadened spirit among those who accompanied him, and in the mood himself that I have described, Wilson sailed for France on the George Washington. I think it was George Harvey who said that the ship speeded across the Atlantic at 18 "May-I-Nots?" an hour. The George Washington could have made Brest a day or so earlier than Dec. 13, but Wilson had it slowed down so as to arrive on that date. He had a liking for that unpopular number. Frequently in the White House he spoke of the 13 letters in Woodrow Wilson and of the fact that 13 States were the "originals"

AT 13 "MAY-I-NOTS?" AN HOUR

From Harper's Weekly.

in the Union. He grew to believe that there was something more than coincidence in the two thirteens. He thought it would be a good omen if, Columbus-like, he should set foot on French soil on the 13th and the George Washington's May-I-Nots were regulated accordingly.

"HOW FAR IS IT FROM PARIS TO VERSAILLES?" ASKED MARTIN

That voyage across the Atlantic was watched with deep anxiety by Democratic leaders back in Washington. They did not like the idea. Senator Martin, of Virginia, Democratic leader of the Senate, was especially disturbed. One day, during a dull session, he strolled over to Senator Lodge, and leaning far over Lodge's desk, asked in a low voice:

"Lodge, how far is it from Paris to Versailles?"

"Oh, about nine or ten miles," replied the Massachusetts Senator. "Why do you ask, Martin?"

"It seems to be too damned far for President Poincaré to go out there to meddle with Premier Clemenceau's conduct of the peace negotiations, but 3,000 miles does not seem to deter our President."

Whenever Democrats talked that winter as frankly as Martin talked with Lodge the same doubt of the wisdom of Wilson's course was heard. If there were any members of his party who believed the President was right, they did not make their opinion known.

CHAPTER LXII

THE "WILSON OF PARIS"

Amidst The Premiers Of The World He Was Acquiescent And Treated Them As Equals—"If We Could Only Bring This Wilson Back Home With Us!"—But Wilson Of Paris Could Not Cross The Atlantic—His Silent Break With House—Was House A Sage? A Myth? A Svengali?—One Or All?—Men Too Keen To Be Wrong Sought House As The Real Power.

WILSON pleaded constantly for a world of brotherhood and of heart; he lived in a world of loneliness and of what he himself called a single-track mind.

It is unfortunate that the track had neither sidings nor terminals, for if the *good* that was in Wilson could have been fused with the average purposes of men, a record of great achievement would have been made.

"Oh if we could only bring this Wilson back home with us!" a loyal Southern Democrat exclaimed in Paris. As a visitor at Versailles he had watched Wilson through many sessions presiding over the commission formulating the covenant. "What a hit he would make! He would have the Senate eating out of his hands!"

The Wilson of Paris, seated at the head of that table, saw as his associates those whom he felt he could accept as his equals. They were the premiers of the nations of the world, the flower of the world's statesmanship. He treated them accordingly.

The man whom I have quoted could contrast the Wilson of Paris with the Wilson of Washington, for in Washington he had seen and deplored Wilson's attitude of icy separation, even from his associates in the government; his not wholly concealed contempt for the Senate. In Paris the considerate, acquiescent Wilson whom he saw day after day so enthused him that he had dreams of a changed Wilson returning to America; a Wilson who had come to realize the wisdom of conference and of considerate treatment.

But the Wilson of Paris could not cross the Atlantic. The nearer his ship approached his native land the taller in his own eyes he grew; and in those same eyes the smaller grew those at home who by election, or by appointment, were entitled to share with him the responsibilities of government. Instead of the changed Wilson he had with partisan pride hoped to see, this Southern Democrat on his return found in Washington a Wilson made more austere by his contacts abroad—more convinced than ever that, as he had said several years before to another supporter, it would be utterly futile and a waste of time for him to listen to others.

WILSON'S EARLY DOUBTS

In Paris Wilson at first doubted the wisdom of making a supreme issue of the League of Nations, as an integral part of the Versailles Treaty. Twenty-nine nations were seated at the peace table. He knew how far apart their views were. Each nation, regardless of size, believed it had been essential to victory, each felt its voice should be heeded. Indeed, the smaller nations were more certain than the larger ones that they had won the war.

To Wilson the prospect of unity seemed dim; he questioned whether he should thrust another brand into the fire. Some of his peace commissioners favored making the effort—Colonel House in particular. They believed that a treaty without the League in it would simply be one of the numberless and forgotten treaties of past centuries. A treaty with the League in it would be the most forward step ever taken for permanent peace; it would stand out by itself in all history. Wilson liked that prospect, and the League of Nations as a separate settlement was abandoned.

First, though, he had to settle the wisdom of sitting personally, as a member of the peace conference. It is the traditional policy of rulers of nations to have ambassadors represent them in such negotiations. No monarch had ever participated in an international tribunal, and, of course, that seemed to establish a precedent for the President of the United States.

Besides, no head of any other nation was then in Paris; Wilson outranked all who were officially there. Should he ignore that fact in an atmosphere where rank counts for so much—and hold himself in reserve, as a Court of Appeals? Lloyd George, Clemenceau and others thought so.

Wilson took a few days to consider the point; then decided to go in. Clemenceau, who presided, seated him at his right —the place of highest rank. He promptly made him responsible for the covenant. As chairman of the commission to formulate the covenant he became the "Wilson of Paris," a presiding officer more tolerant in his attitude toward all who desire to speak to their own time; so, also he became a member of the "Big Four"—Lloyd George, Clemenceau, Orlando and Wilson.

NO TRADING NEEDED TO SAVE THE LEAGUE

He bowed to their will as he had never bowed in Washington to any will. The "Big Four" got all they really desired—even the obligations of the secret treaties about which not a word had been said to Wilson during the war or until they were brought forward to be incorporated in the peace treaty. It is asserted in explanation of Wilson's surrender to the Allies' most important demands that he was fighting to save the League of Nations and that he sacrificed in order to do so, but not one scintilla of evidence has been produced that the League was ever in danger—that Wilson was any more eager for it than were his colleagues excepting Clemenceau. In America Wilson was accepted as the champion and spokesman for the League; in Paris he was only one of many.

It is not fair to the others around the peace table to picture Wilson as constantly engaged with them in a desperate battle over the League. A world in grief, in distress and in chaos crowded about them; peace was the prayer and purpose in every mind. Clemenceau alone regarded the old balance-of-power theory as the best assurance of peace; the other principals in treaty-making were as firm as Wilson for the League. They, or their successors, now constitute the League. Wilson's battle in Paris was over other features of the treaty, and into the struggle he threw himself with high purpose and a passionate energy that made its deep impress apparent on mind and body before the treaty was signed.

THE SILENT BREAK WITH HOUSE

It was at this time that the historic "break" with Colonel House occurred. Who knows the facts of that sundering of the most intimate ties that ever existed between the Executive of a great nation and a man in civil life? The relation began in silence, it continued in silence, it ended in silence. Was it a myth—that unity of purpose and of mind? Or was it real? Mystery of mysteries! Politics never saw its like!

Strange in its beginning, stranger still in its development through seven years of momentous problems, strangest of all in the mystery that still surrounds it, impenetrable, with the darkness of the grave on one side, and on the other side the only written evidence held back in deference to request.

Was House a sage? A sphinx? A Svengali?—one or all? In his day of power such queries were whispered among gossipers as softly as a spider spins his web. Since the "break" loud assertion has taken their place. Thus the glory of this changing world passes; surely we have here new evidence that its triumphs are of the moment—a frown, and they are gone!

I have studied with great interest the varied pictures of the Wilson-House intimacy as drawn by those who assume that they can fathom its depth and measure its extent, and I have reached the conclusion that until the entire correspondence— the letters *from* Wilson as well as those *to* Wilson—have been published, no man can judge the relations that existed, for no man knows.

What was Wilson's motive? What was House's? Here was a President who habitually shut the world out of his confidence—except this one man. Here was a President, new to public office and public policies, who yielded his judgment to no person except this one man. Here was a President unfamiliar with the problems growing out of a foreign war, who looked for guidance not to his Ambassadors in the Capitals of Europe, not to the leaders of his party, or of the nation, but to this one man.

Not once but several times this one man visited nation after nation at the suggestion of the President with the *written* authority of a supreme representative, and heard the potent voices of the world's leading men.

"As usual I listened" would come back to Wilson as, one by one, House conferred with the responsible men of Europe's great empires. Even in the Kaiser's presence he listened, as Germany's war lord laughed at the thought of committing Germany to a year of deliberation before engaging in war. The Kaiser's government was the only large nation that refused to sign the treaty prepared by Bryan. It failed in its main purpose because of the Kaiser's refusal. "With the German army and navy trained to the moment!" said the Kaiser, "why should I give another nation a year to prepare?"

ALL TURNED TO HOUSE

Perhaps you do not like this picture of the House relation; perhaps you are inclined to reject it; there are no official documents on file to attest it, no title gives it authority except the title of friendship, which, of course, has no place in government archives. Incredible it truly seems to be; incredible that another White House should be functioning in New York city, in addition to the official one in Washington. Yet European statesmen addressed their most confidential cables to New York because they believed it; our own leading men sought the House apartment in New York because they knew its power.

Were they right? And if they were right was such a condition right? I shall not attempt here to answer. My purpose is to show that men too keen to make a mistake in such matters acted upon that belief until after President Wilson's return to Paris in March 1919. There can be only one opinion about the relations of the two men up to that time; there is room for more than one opinion from that time, until Col. House in Madison Square Garden, New York city, listened to the radio report of his dead friend's funeral services instead of sitting, as he sought permission to sit, in the church in Washington, where the last words were being said.

THE STAGE IN PARIS AND ITS FIGURES

Now, let us look at another picture of House. We need not go into those seven years during which the President was his "grateful friend." Let us start with the assembling of the peace commissioners in Paris. There was the stage of tremendous events; the men to play a part upon it were destined to be historic figures. All eager, properly enough, to be in the limelight; all seeking to be identified conspicuously with any phase, every phase, of that difficult struggle to assess the penalties for a great tragedy and adjust the world to a better day.

Into that scene came Wilson, at once the central figure. Foreign statesmen did not know him; they had heard stories of his austere ways. Is it strange that at first they thought it best to continue using the channel he had indicated as an open and direct one to him? Even habit would have led them to do so. Evidently they did not realize that the House proxy from Wilson ceased when the giver of the proxy was present. The House apartments in the Crillon Hotel were the centre of many conferences that should have gone on where a President resided who wanted to do all and see all—even though the task must shatter him, as it did.

It is said that after an unsatisfactory talk one afternoon with Wilson, Lloyd George had hurried to the Crillon to talk it out with House. While the two men were thus engaged, Wilson entered. He excused himself for interrupting and said he would call again when House was at leisure. That later call was never made. At another time Lord Balfour, discussing with friends the differences still unadjusted, said:

"If we could only deal with House we would have nothing to worry about."

EAGER TO CARRY THE NEWS

On seven league boots that statement was rushed to Wilson; there were many persons eager to carry it and its like—so many that when Wilson left Paris on his first trip home in February, his mind had begun to close against House, though he was still on friendly terms with him. Back in Paris three weeks later the biggest budget of gossip awaiting Wilson was about House. He was told that during his absence House had cut the ground from under him, by agreeing to so many Allied demands that there was nothing left for trading purposes on other features of the treaty. Wilson's mind was so firmly fixed on doing everything himself that it yielded readily to suspicion that someone was intruding. He began an increasing avoidance of House.

"In Paris Wilson did not want tea party talks," said one of Wilson's Paris intimates to me, "he needed practical suggestions. House was good at tea parties where he agreed to everything and undertook to carry it through with Wilson.

As I Knew Them

The President needed a man who would take orders from him and not make compromises with others. House simply couldn't fill that bill. They had captured him as they had captured Page, and Wilson turned from both."

One can get the indictment drawn against House in Paris only bit by bit, from different individuals, he must then put the pieces together. President Wilson never uttered a word to House to indicate his separation from him. He just forgot, more and more each day, that such a man existed. No charges, no dissensions, no explanations. House saw him off for home, exchanged cables with him after he reached the White House, but there was another tone to their relation and shortly it died away entirely. I have never heard of a person to whom Wilson afterward ever mentioned the name of House.

The differences in April, with the "Big Four," that led Wilson, in temper, to order the George Washington made ready to carry him home, were laid by many persons at House's door. The President flatly refused to acquiesce in any of the understandings entered into by House during his absence. He let it be rumored to the other treaty conferees that House no longer knew his mind, or could interpret it. In the resulting tangle, he lost his balance in Paris, and came close to sailing home in pique. Finally with slight modifications he agreed to all that had been tentatively mapped out. The incident brought Wilson to the front as his own adviser; it also ended House.

After Paris, they never met again on the old terms. Finally sickness came to Wilson and meetings and letters ceased.

What did this man without title contribute to Wilson, that led him to make him his confidant, his spokesman, and, apparently, his guide? Colonel House's "Intimate Papers" give the clear impression that he was all three; the only authentic challenge to that picture of their relations lies in the unpublished letters from Wilson to House.

CHAPTER LXIII

THE EFFORT FOR "A SOLEMN REFERENDUM"

Wilson Was Determined To Make The Senate Yield Or Force An Issue In The 1920 Elections With Himself As The Candidate—Kellogg's Offer To Ratify Goes Unheeded—The Twelvemonth That Marked The Highest And Lowest Levels Of Wilson's Fortunes—Colby, Burleson and Daniels Worked for Wilson's Nomination—Colby's "Mingled Feelings" Returning to Washington—Wilson Said: "We Would Have Gotten That League Through Had My Health Been Spared—It Is God's Way and He Knows Best."

THE Wilson who on July 10, 1919, presented the Versailles Treaty to the Senate in person rather than by the usual messenger was neither the Wilson of Washington nor the Wilson of Paris, but a Wilson who had burst all narrower confines and now rated himself as a world figure without rival. You can get his own appraisement in his statement to Editor James Kerney four years later, as revealed in his enlightening book, "The Political Education of Woodrow Wilson"—"I realize that I am everywhere regarded as the foremost leader of the liberal thought of the world."

Happening to be in Washington at the time of his address on the treaty, I went up to the Capitol to hear it. I wanted to study the reaction of the Senators to what he had to say as he handed the document over for ratification. I was anxious, also, to contrast the Wilson I had heard deliver his war message with the Wilson now delivering his peace message.

Had I not known of his emotional breakdowns under the strain of Paris, I would have been shocked by the pallor of his face, the worn look that told a story no effort could wholly conceal. Zeal had plainly taken heavy toll. No thought of the tragedy then shaping itself crossed my mind. I realized, however, that I was looking upon a man who had returned to his native land with the hurrahs of Europe still ringing in his ears as a world call to leadership, who now regarded himself as the crusader for an inspired conception of the world's needs, the Messiah of his day, guarding his distinction with the avarice of a miser counting and recounting his gold to make certain that no one had robbed him of any of it.

There was a sureness about Wilson as he stood before the Senate that was almost defiance, the manner of one confident of the reality of his dream of a world Utopia with himself as its immortal figure.

WILSON'S FAITH IN A DEMAND TO RUN AGAIN

And on that July 10 began the period in Wilson's career yet to be fully revealed by those who know the facts, with all its intolerance of opposing views, its firm determination, if the Senate did not yield, to take the issue to the country; the tragic collapse on his western tour, the pathetic clinging to power while stricken and, finally, the abiding faith that his party and the people would re-elect him President and instruct the Senate to ratify his treaty.

Wilson's belief in such an outcome was so supreme that even those who knew his physical inability and the political unwisdom of his candidacy had not the heart to undeceive him. From his sick-room in the White House he waited expectantly day by day, hour by hour, for word from San Francisco that the national Democratic convention had put aside all lesser candidates and lesser issues and had chosen him to lead in what he had called "a solemn referendum." That word never came, but instead there came to him with crushing force the realization that the sceptre of power had passed to other hands, and with it the issue on which he had staked all.

Exactly one year from the day at Versailles when with glowing countenance he attached his signature to the peace treaty the Democratic convention met in San Francisco. Those two days, twelve months apart, marked the highest and the lowest levels of Wilson's quest for fame. On June 28, 1919, in Versailles, the signed document seemed a crowning triumph; on June 28, 1920, in San Francisco, his own party registered its preference for another as its candidate, and forced Wilson to a place with figures of the past.

KELLOGG'S OFFER TO RATIFY GOES UNHEEDED

It is not my province to rehearse the incidents of that year. I would like to say, however, that Wilson could have insured the ratification of the treaty within two weeks after his return to America had he chosen to do so on the basis of reservations suggested by Senators friendly to the League of Nations. I understand that the fact has not been published—certainly not widely published—that Senator Frank B. Kellogg, of Minnesota, now Secretary of State under Coolidge, called on Wilson at the White House about July 15 as the spokesman for a group numbering from 32 to 34 Republicans. The group did not include Senator Lodge. He explained to the President the reservations desired. Wilson listened attentively, but told Kellogg that their proposals were already covered in the covenant or by our Constitution. They were, therefore, not material to the treaty. "If that is so," urged Kellogg, "why not accept them? They can do no harm. We can furnish from 32 to 34 votes on this basis and with the Democratic votes you control you will have a safe margin for ratification."

"Thank you for the offer," replied Wilson courteously. "I appreciate your purpose. I'll think it over and if I can agree with your view I will let you know."

One week, then two weeks, passed without a word from the White House. Kellogg, Norris, and others in the group concluded that they would never hear from Wilson—and they never did. Nor did any other Senator ever get the slightest indication that any reservation, however mild, could break down the barrier in Wilson's mind.

As I Knew Them

In that battle with the Senate you have a Wilson striving solely for personal mastery—not a Wilson striving to achieve a great purpose in cooperation with those who by position had equal right with him to a voice in the decisions. His, and his alone, must be the treaty ratified. In November, 1919, in a letter to Senator Hitchcock he warned all Democrats against voting for it with the Lodge amendments; in January 1920, he revealed his mind more frankly when he wrote the Jackson Day banqueters in Washington:

> Personally I do not accept the action of the Senate of the United States as the decision of the nation. . . .
>
> If there is any doubt as to what the people of the country think on this vital matter the clear and simple way is to submit it for determination at the next election to the voters of the nation, to give the next election the form of *a great and solemn referendum*— a referendum as to the part the United States is to play in completing the settlements of the war and the prevention in the future of such outrages as Germany attempted to perpetrate.

No one who was not himself a candidate would have penned such a letter, for no national convention could have adopted such a platform without calling upon the man who embodied it to lead in the campaign. "We would have gotten that League through had I been spared my health," said Wilson a year or so later.

HE ALONE WAS THE ISSUE

In the weeks from the date of that letter until the Democrats met in San Francisco, the effort for recovery was buoyed and strengthened by his determination to be physically ready for the campaign battle he anticipated. That is why he had no regrets when in March 1920 the treaty failed of ratification a second time. Perhaps it furnishes a reason for his continued refusal to save it. Seven or eight Democratic votes would have given it the necessary two-thirds and men whose loyalty he could not challenge urged him to permit that to be done. The White House atmosphere, however, had then become surcharged with thought of the coming campaign with Wilson as the candidate. The President looked upon counsel to save the treaty as the counsel of surrender; he was in the mood of martyrdom and he had no other thought than that the people would rise en masse behind his banner once it was raised. He was looking out upon the world through the windows of a sick-room, and with a mind long burdened with a single purpose. There was no other leader to carry on the battle—not even to Crown Prince McAdoo could the succession safely pass. In that mood, with body wracked by disease, this pitiful figure in the world's greatest tragedy met with stoic calmness a disappointment that shattered a dream such as few rulers ever dared to dream.

COLBY PRIMED TO NOMINATE HIS CHIEF

The men upon whose strategy at San Francisco hope chiefly rested were Postmaster General Burleson and Secretary of the Navy Daniels. Burleson went so far in his prophecies of success that he never recovered his place in the President's confidence. Not for months afterward did he have conversation with him. But I am told that the man who hurried 3,000 miles across continent with polished epigram and brilliant peroration to rouse the convention to a noble duty was Bainbridge Colby.

Colby says no, and Colby ought to know.

But Colby was Wilson's Secretary of State; he had many world problems in his great office demanding his serious consideration; diplomats from thither and yon were paying their calls of courtesy and urging and pressing for audience,—and Colby breaks all precedents of his dignified office as to political activities, grabs a suitcase, takes the fastest train to San Francisco. It would be a fair guess that Colby under similar circumstances today would take an aeroplane.

He paused only for a call at the White House.

Why the sudden resolve? Why the parting call? Indeed, why should a Secretary of State—the high-hatted member of every Administration—attend a nominating convention at all unless the interests of his chief were involved in a most important way? And what was at stake?

Certainly not the party platform. So far as the Wilson Administration was concerned the delegates were of one opinion. The President had no candidate to urge—even McAdoo had been disavowed; scores of loyal Wilson leaders were on the ground ready to defend their chief if need be. It was not defense that was needed but offense.

Colby like Sheridan was miles away—three thousand instead of twenty. Someone was needed to rally and enthuse a confused convention; someone was needed to reform the line of battle, to point the way to victory, and Colby was the man ordained by fate to be the Sheridan of his day:—San Francisco needed him.

And why?

Not to nominate "Jimmy" Cox; Colby didn't buy a ticket to Trail's End.

Nor was he seeking to bring to a close the Administration of which he was then the guiding and conspicuous member.

No, Colby had other motives in the Golden Gate city, and Wilson back in the White House awaited their consummation. The radio was on, preparations were made for newspaper photographers to gather and click their cameras at the thrice-named candidate when the news was flashed that Colby had begun to speak, that the delegates were in rapturous approval and that the new battle of the ballots was to be led by the man who had made the one real issue.

It was not to be. Somehow the cards didn't fall the right way; and a Democratic convention missed an opportunity to hear Bryan's cross of gold speech made to look like tinsel, for Colby would have done it.

What could the dependable Secretary of State telephone the eagerly-waiting White House of the developing conditions? Certainly not a blunt statement of the true situation. That shock was for the convention, not for him, to administer. He could telephone, however, that while prospects were not over-bright, he still had hopes, and that he was prepared to take the platform at the right moment. So Colby's "right moment" drifted from roll call to roll call but never came.

What a scene there would have been in that convention had it come! Far back in 1912 when Colby and I were engaged in that puritanic effort to return Roosevelt to the White House, he was a daring leader for the right, a spokesman who could face a thousand foe. And he would have been equal to that great occasion in San Francisco had there been a "right moment." There was not.

Think of Colby's poignant feelings as he saw the Cox vote climb to the needed two-thirds; think of his planning how to tell his chief the whys and wherefores of the failure—the "mingled feelings" with which he contemplated the disappointing result of the convention. There was so much to tell that it was nearly a month before Colby wrote the President he would like an opportunity to do so,—and neither Burleson nor Daniels ever found the courage even to go that far.

"THE WORLD NOT READY FOR IT"

And thus it was that Wilson resigned himself to defeat. He refused to be saddened. No one ever heard him complain. He let others do the talking. He lived to see two men follow him into the Presidency both sharing the opposition of their party to the League of Nations. "It is all right," he would say. "Perhaps we shall be all the better for the delay; the world was led to it by its sufferings; it might not have worked just yet; to be a sure success a League of Nations must not come from suffering but from the hearts and spirit of men. We are still in darkness but I am sure it is the darkness that eventually lightens. I realize now that I am only an empty tenement, a tool that has served its purpose in God's hand. I was stricken because it was His way of doing things. It was His will to set me aside; He knows what is best. I am content with the record as it stands."

CHAPTER LXIV

DAWES—POLITICIAN AND BANKER

TO MANY persons Charles Gates Dawes is an after-the-war development in national affairs. This presumption merely means that following his activities in the 1900 Republican national convention, as detailed in the McKinley chapter, Dawes undertook to build one of the big banks of Chicago, and, true to his character, put himself wholly into that effort until he had accomplished it.

The political public heard little from him for twenty years or more but Dawes was all the time looking over the fence into the old political pasture. When fortune came to him and gave him freedom of time and action, he found the World War a way back into the fold of public activities. "Over There" he acquired a pipe and a few mild swear words, but such things are only the outward evidence of a vigorous, hurry-up-and-get-there spirit,—intense, kindly and vigorous.

Dawes likes public service; he is really an old-timer at it—if the McKinley days are far enough past to be so classed. He was the first convention strategist—certainly the first to my knowledge—to card-index the delegates to a presidential nominating convention. Frank Hitchcock gained that reputation in the 1908 campaign to nominate Taft, but Dawes really began the practice in national politics back in the winter of 1896.

"A YOUNG MAN NAMED DAWES"

He had then moved from Lincoln, Nebraska, to Chicago, where he was establishing himself. As an ardent McKinley supporter, he was Mark Hanna's personal representative in

520

the Illinois struggle to secure McKinley delegates. Illinois Republicans were then as ever since in a faction war; fighting was fierce and plenty. I was then to learn the situation, and found it baffling.

Someone in Chicago told me that if I really wanted the facts I would have to get hold of a young man named Dawes. So I hunted for Dawes. He had a little office up two or three flights of rickety wooden stairs in an old building on La Salle Street. I climbed the stairs, and found a room equipped with a roll-top desk, a wooden centre table, and two or three chairs. No pipe was in evidence.

I recall that whenever I asked Dawes about this or that county, he would rise from his chair, pull a little drawer from a case on top of his desk and look over half a dozen cards. Those cards had written on them the record of the day-to-day changes in each county. He would never answer a question until he had consulted his cards. He was so careful that I promptly made up my mind to accept his figures as the most dependable estimate to be had. When the State convention met, two months later, at Springfield, the Dawes prophecies of the number of McKinley delegates proved to be approximately correct.

A year later, Dawes became Comptroller of the Currency in the new Administration. He was known in Washington as McKinley's "white-headed boy." Next to Mark Hanna he was deepest in the President's confidence. McKinley's regard for him became deep enough to be called affection.

But banking on his own account was more attractive to the ambitious Dawes than office-holding, so he resigned as Comptroller and returned to Chicago to create the bank of which he was the head and principal owner when named in 1924 for Vice President.

ALMOST IN HARDING CABINET

How near Dawes came to be Secretary of the Treasury

under Harding is not well known; but for a week or so it was about settled that he was to be the man. Harding had called him to Marion, and had asked him if he could arrange his affairs so as to accept the Treasury portfolio if offered later on. Dawes replied that he could. Harding then said he had made up his mind not to make promises—he wanted to feel free as to appointments until the last moment for action; also he wanted others to feel equally free to decline.

"I expect and hope to offer you the place," said Harding, "but I shall not do so until I have my Cabinet complete and ask all members at the same time. I have no commitments. With this understanding let us both feel absolutely free to change our minds."

"That suits me perfectly," replied Dawes.

DAWES BUDGETS FOR AMERICA AND FOR THE WORLD

A week or so later, Senator Knox, of Pennsylvania, urged Andrew Mellon. Harding jumped at the opportunity; Mellon was willing. Dawes, when informed that Mellon would serve, heartily indorsed the Pittsburgh banker. Later, Harding sought a budget-maker, he asked Dawes to undertake that thankless task. Dawes agreed to do so for one year and with the definite understanding that he would be the direct representative of the President backed by his authority. He insisted that no budget could be made without supreme power over every Cabinet officer or bureau chief. Harding stood by him on that basis and the budget system of today, which has meant so much to the country, is the result.

Again, when a man was needed to budgetize German reparations, Dawes was brought into service—with the same fine results.

Back of Dawes' success, I have often thought, is that little case I saw on his roll-top desk in Chicago, thirty years ago, in which his card-index typified the thoroughness with which even in his young days he undertook everything.

Now he sits in the Vice President's chair—uneasily. He likes action, results, making each day count for something done and ended. The Senators like to talk, and while they indulge themselves in debate they expect the Vice President silently to listen. That is Dawes' job and he sticks to it, but with the Senate in recess the Senators hear from their vigorous presiding officer often enough to realize that he has some views of his own regarding the procedure of that "most deliberative body in the world." Moreover, having started on the road to political fame, there are many who believe Dawes has not yet finished his journey.

CHAPTER LXV

BORAH—INDIVIDUALIST

IF YOU are looking for an individualist among our national leaders, allow me to present the purest type in public service—William Edgar Borah, of Idaho, now serving his fourth term in the Senate, and, as chairman of the Foreign Relations Committee, the most potent voice on the subject next to the President and the Secretary of State. Europe, I suppose, wonders why we go almost to the Pacific for the man to conduct our foreign affairs insofar as the legislative branch of government is concerned. There must be a feeling of surprise over there, as there is here, that a Senator from Idaho should be so deeply interested in our attitude toward distant lands as to seek assignment on the Foreign Relations Committee when he could select committees whose work is closer to his constituents and seemingly more vital to them.

Borah picked the judiciary and foreign relations committees back in 1907 when he entered the Senate. Advancing by seniority in both committees he finally had to make a choice of chairmanships when Senator Lodge died, in 1924, and he chose foreign relations. So Idaho, the State of mountains, minerals, forests and distances, furnishes the parliamentary eyes, ears and mind for our country in matters across seas.

It is only a new demonstration that the east must face the fact more and more as time goes on that the Star of Empire westward takes its way. Next to Borah on that committee is Hiram Johnson, of California. Seven other members of the committee—making nine in all, or a majority—come from States west of the Mississippi River. When we keep in mind that Secretary of State Kellogg is a citizen of Minnesota, it is clear that our attitude toward other countries, for the present at least, except as the President voices it, has a distinct western point of view. It is not my province to say here whether that is a correct point of view or not, but it is certainly a more detached point of view, more of the isolationist pattern, than would be held if the majority of the committee were from the Atlantic States.

WANTS U. S. OUT OF EUROPE'S AFFAIRS

Borah in particular is an isolationist. He was more extreme as an "irreconcilable" during the League of Nations debate than was Senator Lodge; he was more responsible than any other Senator for hobbling our World court participation with so many reservations that Europe refused to agree to them; and he would be delighted if a way could now be found to recall our unaccepted acceptance rather than run even the slim risk that Europe may yet take us on our own terms.

You cannot get it out of Borah's head that Europe, still militaristic, only awaits opportunity to build larger armies and navies. He believes it is bred in the bone of her rulers and statesmen, and that the Versailles Treaty instead of serving the cause of peace is just so much dynamite to be exploded in a war more fearful than the war just ended. That is, largely, the ground on which he opposes cancelling the debt due us. Freed of that obligation, he believes that Europe would use the released credit to increase its military forces, and we would thus be uniting with her in a blow at peace.

If Europe would agree to cut down her present military expenditures, and relieve her people from that heavy tax burden, I am certain that Borah would be the first in America to urge that we do our share toward a world wide reduction of armies and navies by writing off the whole debt. Lacking such assurance he wants every dollar due us. He wants America to stand alone among the nations of the world,—in kindly but absolutely independent attitude—an individualist like himself. He believes that territorially we are big enough between the Atlantic and the Pacific and that our future is more secure if we remain in every sense between the two oceans.

Perhaps, I state it too strongly, but it seems to me that Borah favors letting the world take care of itself, believing that it will get along better without our intervention, and that we will have the same experience. That is why he urges recognition of the Soviet Government of Russia and independence for the Filipinos.

BORAH TRAVELS HIS OWN PATH

As a Senator for twenty years, Borah has gone his own way. He doesn't know how to follow. He so seldom travels a path another has trod that, if he were hunting bears in his Idaho mountains I doubt whether he would follow the tracks of Brother Bruin, as most hunters strive to do, lest he should feel that he was travelling a beaten path. He would get the bear, but in his own way!

If you were to study the Senate roll-call you would find that Borah votes more independently of party, of friends and of opponents than any other Senator. Nevertheless, he has more friends among his colleagues than have most Senators, and his attitude on legislation sways more votes. Why? Because of confidence in his integrity and ability, and because he makes no personal issues. He accords others the privilege he exercises of having his own opinion. There is nothing vitriolic about Borah; he never assails those who disagree with him; he fights their views but not them.

You will not find Borah in his Senate seat unless something important is before that body. Most of his time is spent digging for facts in the quiet of his office. There he determines whether he will support or oppose pending measures. He enters into no deals; he gives no votes as a bargain and seeks none. In all the gossip to be heard on Capitol Hill in Washington, I have never heard anyone claim that he had persuaded Borah not to speak his mind.

THE SENATE'S CONSTITUTIONALIST

Years ago William M. Evarts, of New York, and George F. Edmunds of Vermont were in turn known as the leading expounders of the constitution in the Senate; then John C. Spooner, of Wisconsin, then Elihu Root, of New York, Joseph W. Bailey of Texas and Philander Knox, of Pennsylvania. Today Borah is the accepted successor to that distinction. Borah studies the constitution, however, not to narrow it but to broaden it, and thereby keep it strengthened in the confidence of the people. He insists that its principles were intended to give effect to the fine purposes of the founders of our nation, and not to thwart them by technical interpretation.

Could a regular party convention be persuaded to nominate such a man for President? Who knows?

In 1924, he got out of bed in Washington after midnight to hear by telephone that the Republican national convention in Cleveland wanted him for Vice President; he promptly replied that he would not accept it and went back to bed. Borah would be the unhappiest man in Washington if he were fated to sit, silently, while the Senate was in debate. He delights in a conflict on the floor. Though he is "Bill" to most of his colleagues and they are "Jim" or "Frank" or "George" to him, those personal relations do not influence his attitude on legislation.

Borah's term as Senator expires in 1931—he will then have served twenty-four years. He has given the best years of his life to public service, and except for occasional newspaper writing he has limited his income rigidly to his salary. That means the sacrifice of many comforts. His reputation is his only asset as he moves into his later years; it assays of the finest quality but it is not convertible into those comforts that every man has a right to look forward to, and that every gov-

527

ernment should insure if it demands the kind of service that Borah gives it. He has now achieved the distinction of leadership of the Senate; that body holds no greater reward for him. The Presidency is the only promotion, but if Coolidge is to be reelected in 1928 the earliest date for Borah would be 1932— a long time to wait with many intervening uncertainties. Borah would then be sixty-seven years old. William Henry Harrison is the only man to enter the White House at a greater age. He was 68 when inaugurated.

The Presidency has yet to go west of the Mississippi—other places of power are going in that direction, and, of course, it is only a question of time when the presidency will go too. If Coolidge should refuse to run again, perhaps there will be a call for the able, earnest individualist Senator from Idaho,— the kindliest figure in the Senate personally, the most "uncertain, coy and hard to please" in legislation.

CHAPTER LXVI

CALVIN COOLIDGE

"THERE is no right to strike against the public safety by anybody, anywhere, any time," rang through the country in September, 1919, from the Governor of Massachusetts, like the clear, sharp peal of a Liberty bell.

It was a new voice. With thousands of others I listened, aroused.

"This is the people's cause," came a few days later in a proclamation from the same Governor of Massachusetts, declaring that he proposed "to support all who are supporting their own government," and that "the authority of the Commonwealth cannot be intimidated, coerced or compromised."

Again, with more thousands, I listened, aroused.

Here was a voice calm but firm, decisive but not defiant, capable of stating the substance of a great issue in a few understanding words.

Though Calvin Coolidge was the Bay State's Chief Executive, the Boston police did not know their man. They were now to know him better, so was the nation. Everywhere people applauded; everywhere newspapers gave columns to the struggle to maintain the supremacy of government. They were not slow to rally back of a Governor with the courage to challenge Samuel Gompers' contention that public servants had a right to strike even though such action imperilled public safety.

THE PEOPLE WANTED TO KNOW MORE OF COOLIDGE

The battle was quickly won, and the "news" was out of the incident. Like other nine-day wonders it soon faded away through the back pages of the newspapers. But Coolidge remained in the minds of the people as the defender and exponent of orderly government. Never did any man in public life win the interest and confidence of a nation so completely. Speeches delivered long ago—even his valedictory at Amherst —were dug out of a neglected past and widely discussed. A series of addresses were finally gathered into a book entitled "Have Faith in Massachusetts"; even that was seized by the newspapers for serial publication.

The Calvin Coolidge who had never sought to push his way to the front now found himself in the front line of national figures, well liked for his modesty, well liked for his philosophy of life, well liked for the courage with which he held to his beliefs.

Nor was this liking a political liking. The talk of Coolidge was not at first heard among politicians; it soon got to them, however, for a presidential contest was not distant and a candidate was needed. Since the days of Blaine and of Reed, the country had not looked seriously to New England for a President. In 1916, John W. Weeks, then Senator from Massachusetts, had sought nomination, but the support he received was largely a compliment to a man highly esteemed. The trend of political availability had long been steadily away from New England; Coolidge turned it back.

HE STUCK TO HIS DAY'S WORK

But not by seeking newspaper notoriety or indulging in stump speaking. He spread no propaganda about himself. Newspapers discovered that the people were interested in him, and gave him space on their own account to satisfy that reader interest. I was among those editors attracted by the Coolidge speeches and even more strongly impressed by his "approach," to use a golfing term, to the presidential nomination. He stuck to his day's work. All the progress he had made in life had been made by doing each day's work within the day and not crowding it with plans for ambitious tomorrows.

The possibility of the Presidency did not lure him away from that wise habit. He refused campaigning tours, refused alluring offers to write for magazines and newspaper syndicates, refused interviewers and photographers. If the people were to judge him he preferred to be judged on his record and not on any representations he might make to them as a candidate.

Take the Coolidge of today and recall the Coolidge who first came to your attention and you will find him following the same quiet habit of doing thoroughly his day's work and letting results tell his story.

LODGE COULD NOT SEE COOLIDGE

In the 1920 convention, my thoughts ran to Coolidge as more likely than others to interest the country. He had no antagonisms, he had made a good impression, and he had proven his courage in public service.

I said so frequently in my newspaper. Though new to the people in a national sense, I believed that he had secured a substantial following among them. I was prepared to see the Wood-Lowden forces end their deadlock by turning to the Vermont-born Governor of Massachusetts.

I have already referred to that convention as a convention of "ifs" so I may be permitted to add one more. *If* Senator Henry Cabot Lodge, head of the Massachusetts delegation and chairman of the convention, had not insisted that only a candidate acceptable to Boston's Back Bay aristocracy could possibly be the real choice of Massachusetts for national honors, a compromise on Coolidge might have been secured. But Lodge could not see a President in the occupant of a modest home in Northampton and he held a majority of the Massachusetts delegates in opposition.

"Nominate a man who lives in a two-family house?" he

exclaimed to me while at dinner in the Chicago Club. "Never! Massachusetts is not for him!"

That was not the comment heard among the delegates, however. They liked Coolidge. They believed that brains and purpose were more desirable assets in a President than wealth. Their liking was not reflected in actual votes on the nominating roll-calls for President because nearly all State delegations were committed to candidates with more "organization" backing; but a clear demonstration of Coolidge strength came in the quick responses to that unexpected call from far-off Oregon for Coolidge for Vice President.

The men sitting as chairmen of their delegations manipulating the convention did not have Coolidge in mind for a place on the ticket; in those closing hours, however, the bulk of the delegates got out of hand, and Oregon's demand had to go through. It voiced the uncontrolled desire of the convention, —too emphatically to be denied. In the chapter on the 1920 nominations I have described that scene.

THE PEOPLE'S FAITH IN COOLIDGE

The people see in Coolidge the fine simplicities, the sturdy patriotism, the firm unpretentious character, the spirit of New England; they have faith in him beyond any they have shown in any other President of my time. I say this without lessening in the slightest my admiration for Roosevelt. Roosevelt commanded an intense, emotional enthusiasm never equalled by any other man.

There is a different meaning to the faith the people have in Coolidge. His period is a period of world-healing, of restoration—of an effort toward what Harding called normalcy. Vision clear, judgment cool, course always marked straight ahead toward a fixed purpose, he inspires a deep, nation-wide confidence that all will go well with the country while he is in the White House.

We will live within our means and meet all our obligations;

By permission of Ladies Home Journal

CALVIN COOLIDGE BEING SWORN INTO OFFICE AS PRESIDENT IN THE HOMESTEAD AT PLYMOUTH, VT., 2 A.M., AUGUST 3, 1923. HIS FATHER, JOHN COOLIDGE, AS JUSTICE OF THE PEACE, ADMINISTERED THE OATH. THE ABOVE IS A REPRODUCTION OF THE PAINTING BY ARTHUR I. KELLER, WHICH APPEARED IN THE LADIES HOME JOURNAL AND IS NOW IN POSSESSION OF MRS. COOLIDGE

we will travel a sure road, taking no quick turns to prosperity nor quicker turns to adversity; we will respect the rights of others and see to it that others respect ours; every hope for permanent world peace will be strengthened by our example; every department of government will be well financed for its real necessities but not for extravagance; our house will always be found ready for any emergency, equal to any test.

A BIG TASK WELL DONE

It has been the good fortune of our people that in times of crises they have had at the head of their government the man suited to the task beyond any other man then known to them. Calvin Coolidge is in that class of Presidents. Harding's term was too brief for him to do more than realize the appalling extent of the chaos following war, and to undertake tentative plans; he did well all that was possible for him to do in two short years; the real task of making good on his plans and of making new ones came after Harding had passed on. Coolidge took over that task. I do not minimize its importance or the splendid results obtained when I rank another need as of equal importance. One hundred million people dazed by immense wealth, newly aroused to ambitious endeavor, thrilled by the consciousness of world-wide opportunities, needed the restraining example of a President whose own experience had shown him the wisdom of prudent living and of calm reasoning before acting.

AN EXAMPLE THAT THE NATION FOLLOWED

No example from the White House would be impressive if made for the occasion only; it had to have the backing of lifelong habit. Coolidge gave it that backing. He did not suddenly acquire those traits; they are his by intuition. Neither great power nor the pressure to seek quick solutions of pending problems has ever led him from them.

533

The people knew this of Coolidge—big people, little people, all people. It has influenced them to follow the same course. We have not had the "frenzied finance" of the McKinley days or the sensational industrial expansion which Hanna declared had been voted in 1900. Our prosperity is sound. Business men have kept their heads and wage-earners have put their savings into banks, into home-ownership or securities to an amazing amount. To no one person so much as to Calvin Coolidge is this due; by example not by preaching he has persuaded a whole nation to this habit. And the influence of his course is not lessening.

With him as President there will always be progress, steady and sure; greater progress, when the final accounting comes, than if it were too eagerly sought. Coolidge believes that back of every advance there must be effort and purpose if the advance is to count, and he knows that effort and purpose require time. He is willing to wait results, but waiting does not mean idly hoping; he is working to accomplish all the time.

COMPARISONS WITH LINCOLN

I am tempted to say that in this respect Coolidge suggests Lincoln, who was our most patient President, and who often waited long and anxiously for the thing he had in mind; but thought of a Lincoln comparison recalls to me a remark made by Roosevelt at a time when many extravagant comparisons of him with Lincoln were being made.

It was not long after my newspaper had published Homer Davenport's popular cartoon, "He's Good Enough for Me," showing Uncle Sam standing back of Roosevelt with his hand on Roosevelt's shoulder. We had followed that cartoon with another drawn by Davenport showing Lincoln in similar attitude. The second cartoon led Roosevelt to mention the subject to me. He said:

"I've got to let this talk about Lincoln and myself run its

course, but you must know that I am not fooled even a little bit by it. I am not in Lincoln's class. He had his work to do and I have mine; the two are far apart. He did his work mighty well, and I am doing mine the best I know how. I think I have a fair estimate of my possibilities. I understand myself, and I'm making no comparisons with Lincoln."

So, too, Coolidge is not to be compared with any of his predecessors, for, like the period during which he has been at the head of our government, he stands apart. His record when completed will be that of a President who knew at all times the exact direction and purpose of his undertakings, and who gauged with accuracy how far the people were prepared to go with him. Of all the men in the White House the past half century Coolidge senses most surely the desire of the average person; he has the keenest mind for knowing just how that person would react to each separate situation. He has referred to it as just plain common sense, and perhaps he is correct; if so then common sense is the one quality that hereafter should determine our choice of President.

A book of reminiscences is not the place in which to deal with an administration not much more than half-way through, or to estimate the work of a President with much still to accomplish. I shall not attempt it with Coolidge further than to repeat that, in my opinion, judged by the record as it stands to date, he has made good as the man best fitted to our nation's needs, the man who more than any other is regarded by the people as an accurate interpreter of their desires.

He has made no prophetic boasts, has fixed no ambitious outposts of achievement, and has sought no glory but the satisfaction of performance of the tasks at hand. The record as stated in figures of debt reduction and of tax reduction and in legislature is available from many other sources than here.

When Coolidge said in an Associated Press interview in the autumn of 1926 that he liked to do things for himself, that on his father's Vermont farm that was the habit and pleasure of his day's work, he gave the country a picture of its President that took him out of the austerity of distinguished office and into closer relationship with his fellows. The man who "likes to do things for himself"—he is the man in whom the people have an abiding faith.

COOLIDGE FURNISHES A SENSATION

Wednesday, August 2, 1927.—This book written and finally given over to the tender mercies of the Publishers. A perfect summer afternoon, the country calm, serene and prosperous.

"I do not choose to run for President in 1928!"

This time, it was not a new voice, but, as in 1919, I listened, amazed.

"I do not choose to run for President in 1928!"

Out of Dakota's Black Hills the voice came like a rifle shot—sharp, clear, direct at the target.

Amazed, not a nation but a whole world now listened. Those twelve words meant the turning aside from power and place greater than any man ever held, and the free choice of the life of a plain citizen of the republic. No fanfare of trumpets heralded this unexpected renunciation of the finest title in the world,—just the calling of the correspondents into the class-room of a modest Dakota schoolhouse and handing to them, one by one, a folded slip of paper, with the historic words typewritten.

Where is there such dramatic force as in the simplicities of life? And of all the men in the Presidency who more than Coolidge has illustrated in his manner of life, and in the things he has sought and prized, that splendid, outstanding quality of American birthright that values contentment more than titles and one's own fireside more than the seats of the mighty?

As I pictured that scene with the newspaper men filing one by one past the President, I could not repress a feeling of keen regret that Time had eliminated me from participation in one of the most historic events in American history. The thrill of playing a part in such a scene would last a lifetime.

As I Knew Them

This book is reminiscent, not prophetic, and I claim no power to foresee who is to be President after March 4, 1929, but I do know that when Calvin Coolidge goes back to Northampton or to the farm in Vermont—to the place called Home —he will be on the way to his heart's desire.

"YOU DON'T LIVE IN THE WHITE HOUSE," SAID ROOSEVELT

If the reader will turn to another chapter and read again the talk I had with Roosevelt on the subject of life in the White House he will learn the truth about it. "You don't live there," said Roosevelt. "You are only Exhibit A to the country."

Many illustrations could be given by anyone familiar with Washington life. Let me give one.

When it was announced that President Coolidge had selected the Dakota Black Hills for his summer vacation, the cry went up throughout the country that he was going out there on a hunt for delegates—that he was to make an effort to repair the damage done to his political fortunes by his veto of the McNary-Haugen farm bill. Now, what was the truth? Within a week after his return from his Adirondack vacation in 1926, the President told me, while discussing vacation places, that he had made up his mind next year to try the Far West. He said that he had enjoyed the Adirondacks, but he wanted to get into unfamiliar territory—into entirely new surroundings. Of course he had neither farm legislation nor Presidential delegates then on his mind—just a desire to get to some place on vacation where life would be freer, simpler, less formal and official than had been possible at Swampscott or in the Adirondacks.

Yet months later, when it became public that he was going west, the wise men of politics instantly sought for a reason beyond the one simple reason that he really wanted to go there! The twelve-word message of August 2 is only another evidence that the hardest thing in the world to judge is the motive of another man. Seldom is it correctly guessed—particularly when a President is that man. Perhaps the Coolidge incident will hasten the time when the head of our government, whoever he may be, will be credited with an earnest purpose to do what he believes to be his duty or his real desire instead of being met with the suspicion that every move he makes is dictated by self interest.

There are more men in Washington doing the right thing at cost to themselves than there are men there doing the wrong thing at cost to the nation.

CHAPTER LXVII

THE "INABILITY" OF OUR PRESIDENTS

*Who Is To Determine That The Chief Executive Is Incapacitated?
—Only Eight Years Since Vice President Marshall Might Have
Taken Over The Presidency—Several Other Instances That Have
Led To Repeated But Unheeded Warnings—Wilson's Collapse Meant
A Bedside Government—The Timid Visit Of Senators To The White
House To See For Themselves.*

IT IS only a matter of eight years since there were many
people—some in high position—who honestly believed that
Vice President Marshall should declare President Wilson
physically unable to perform the duties of his office, and
assume the Presidency himself. The President's collapse on
his western tour, the paralysis that followed his return to the
White House, created a mild panic among the Cabinet officers.
There was a strong feeling that preparations should be made
in anticipation of a complete breakdown if not worse. Precedents were sought, but none could be found.

Was the President incapacitated enough for the Vice President to succeed him? Who was to guide the Executive branch
of government while the President was ill? Death speaks
for itself and creates its own vacancies, but "inability" is an
elastic term.

There was but one case at all comparable—that of Garfield,
who was shot in July, 1881, but did not die until September.
A period of unquestioned "inability" existed between the two
events. Had the shooting occurred during winter, with Congress in session, instead of in summer, the serious question
faced when Wilson broke down with Congress about to convene would have had to be faced in the Garfield case. Some
authorities insisted that Vice President Arthur succeeded automatically when Garfield fell mortally wounded. Others

thought the Vice President should decide when "inability" existed to an extent justifying action. The Garfield Cabinet and the whole country debated until death made further discussion unnecessary for that particular occasion—and then Congress calmly passed the question on undetermined.

THE WILSON BREAKDOWN

The same debating course was followed in the Wilson crisis. Fortunately Wilson in time regained sufficient strength to be outside the "inability" zone. Promptly he took the position that those who had considered the possibility of a successor to him were in a conspiracy "to oust" him from the Presidency, to use his own words. Secretary of State Lansing bore the brunt of his anger. But Lansing's activities settled nothing on the main question.

The one thing settled by the Lansing-Wilson correspondence is that for weeks the President knew nothing of the world outside of his sick room—not even that his Cabinet had met. Here is an extract from his letter to Lansing dated Feb. 7, 1920, showing how remote he was from the government, and yet how tenaciously he clung to Presidential rights.

> "Is it true, as I have been told, that during my illness you have frequently called the heads of the executive departments of the Government into conference? If it is, I feel it my duty to call your attention to considerations which I do not care to dwell upon until I learn from you yourself that this is the fact.
>
> Under our constitutional law and practice, as developed hitherto, no one but the President has the right to summon the heads of the executive departments into conference, and no one but the President and the Congress has the right to ask their view or the views of any one of them on any public question.
>
> I take this matter up with you because in the development of every constitutional system, custom and precedent are of the most serious consequence, and I think we will all agree in desiring not to lead in any wrong direction. I have therefore taken the liberty of writing you to ask this question."

As I Knew Them

Private Secretary Tumulty states in his book that Lansing called at his office a day or so after the Wilson collapse, and urged him to make public announcement of the President's inability. He refused. Lansing then called the Cabinet in special meeting "to consider the situation." Actually they had no "situation" to consider because they could get no facts about it. Vice President Marshall was anxious for sick-room news lest he be called upon when unprepared, but even he got none. Naturally newspaper attention was attracted, and Washington was full of rumor as to the possibilities—even that Lansing and Marshall held the same views. An emphatic statement by the Vice President settled the matter, in the sensible way characteristic of him, but until he spoke there was public feeling that he was likely to take action.

Suppose there had been no Vice President? There was none during the three years after Coolidge succeeded Harding, after Roosevelt succeeded McKinley, and after the death of Vice President Hendricks in 1885, and of Vice President Hobart in 1899.

Suppose Secretary of State Lansing, next in line, in case of a vacancy, had felt called upon to declare himself President? He went so far as to formally notify Marshall; he called the Cabinet in meeting. The Cabinet responded, demonstrating by their acquiescence how promptly the man at the foot of the table senses who sits at the head.

The next step in the same direction would have seemed a short one. Ambition has often led men in other nations to attempt that next step and one not so well justified. No weak man ever makes the attempt. The peril lies in a strong man with a stronger "cause."

A BEDSIDE GOVERNMENT OF THE COUNTRY

No jury of doctors at the time would have pronounced President Wilson capable of performing any serious duties of his office. Their diagnosis might easily have been used by a Vice President or Secretary of State to declare the "inability" of the President, and assume the place himself.

Despite the refusal of everyone in authority to act, and despite the considerate report of a committee of Senators as to the President's condition, it is a fact beyond dispute that President Wilson was physically incapacitated. There was complete collapse of the executive branch of government. Whether, as dependable report had it, Mrs. Wilson and Secretary Tumulty together or Mrs. Wilson and Dr. Grayson together ran the Executive department, or one or the other of them ran it alone, I do not know. If they did not, nobody did. For months, it was a bedside government, and as time wore on, the figures around the bedside lessened to an irreducible minimum.

Secretary of the Treasury Houston throws some light on the subject while detailing in his interesting book, "Eight Years in Wilson's Cabinet," how he learned of his promotion to that place. One Sunday in January, 1920, he received a telephone message that Mrs. Wilson wished him to call at the White House at 4:30 that afternoon. She greeted him with this remark, "You are wondering why I sent for you this afternoon. Of course, I did not ask you to come merely to drink tea. The President asked me to tell you he is anxious for you to accept the Secretaryship of the Treasury."

That settled, Mrs. Wilson said the President would like to have a suggestion as to who should succeed Houston as Secretary of Agriculture.

That settled, Mrs. Wilson "asked whether I had anybody in mind for Secretary of the Interior, Mr. Lane having resigned—in the press."

Further conferences that Secretary Houston had with Mrs. Wilson from time to time are not revealed in his book, except as they may be inferred from this closing paragraph in his letter of official farewell to President Wilson March 3, 1921: "I feel that I cannot close this note without an expression of indebtedness to Mrs. Wilson and of admiration for the part she has played and the judgment she has shown in dealing with important matters."

Thus, we get a glimpse—eight years later—into the White House in the last eighteen months of Wilson.

THAT TIMID VISIT OF SENATORS

Everyone will recall that Senatorial visit in December, 1919, to learn the truth about the President's condition. There was something of the hippodrome to their call at the White House, attended by two score reporters and almost as many camera men. The Senate had not authorized it. That august body was doubtful of its right to cross the White House threshold for purposes of inquiry—even an inquiry as to whether the President was incapacitated. It made no attempt. Rarely has it shown such restraint when the rights of the "coordinate branch" were involved.

The Senate Foreign Relations Committee, with Senator Lodge as Chairman, appointed Senators Hitchcock and Fall a committee "to lay before the President some papers relative to Mexican affairs and to confer with him regarding their disposition." What a pitiful subterfuge! Everybody wanted to know the President's condition. Surely some people with responsibility had a right to know. Yet nobody was permitted to know, and nowhere in our laws could there be found authority to know. The only way was by asking a conference about Mexico!

The Lansing cabinet meetings, the Marshall rumors, the White House barred to everyone, the unrevealing doctors' bulletins—all created uncertainty. Most uncertain was whether either House or Congress, or both in joint action, possessed the right or duty, formally, to inquire and determine whether a coordinate branch of government was capable of functioning or not.

Remember the Senators' timid overtures to Tumulty as to

whether they could or would be received? Remember the conferences between Mrs. Wilson and Dr. Grayson as to whether the President could stand it? Of course he could, they stoutly declared—after some hours of doubt.

The Senators saw—and graciously blinded themselves. They said hardly a word about Mexico, or anything else.

As Senator Fall, of New Mexico, left the President's bedside, he said:

"I shall pray for you, Mr. President."

"Pray don't, Senator," came back the quick rejoinder.

Senator Fall told waiting reporters the President seemed to be in excellent mental trim.

WHO IS TO DETERMINE WHEN AND HOW?

At a time of great panic, or partisan disputes, or differences with other nations;—it might be the duty (or the ambition)—of a Vice President or a Secretary of State to declare himself President.

Who is to determine when, and how? If the silence of the Constitution is deliberate, then its framers probably meant the initiative to be taken by the official upon whom responsibility falls. What power could have prevented Vice President Marshall from declaring himself President had he chosen to do so? Wilson certainly would have resisted. Congress also might have refused to recognize him if in session at the time, but such action would have meant chaos. If Congress were not in session, the new executive would have full swing until it reassembled.

A most serious weakness in our national structure is revealed—an inability through existing law, definitely and beyond question to establish under every situation that can be anticipated, and at all times, who is entitled to be recognized as the executive head of our nation. There are likely to be occasions in future when we cannot stand the strain of a collapsed executive department for so long a time as that of President Wilson's illness.

As a people we are so sure of ourselves, so certain that with us right will always prevail, that we ignore the fate of other nations as powerful in their day; we take no precaution to make the "man on horseback" impossible among us at crisis times. Our remissness gives point to a remark Roosevelt once made in private conversation; that our country may have to be "shot over" once more before it settles down to its ultimate destiny. He added that even the thought of such a possibility horrifies; we reject and scorn it as too remote for consideration, but if in years to come control of our government is ever to be in conflict just such uncertainty as exists governing election and succession to the Presidency is likely to be responsible for it.

WHAT THE CONSTITUTION SAYS

The Constitution speaks only in broad terms. It says:

> "In case of the removal of the President from office, or of his death, resignation or inability to discharge the powers and duties of said office, the same shall devolve on the Vice President; and the Congress may by law provide for the case of removal, death, resignation or inability both of the President and Vice President, declaring what officer shall then act as President, and such officer shall act accordingly until the disability be removed or a new President shall be elected."

Unfortunately, while Congress has enacted a "succession" law it has merely stated who after the Vice President shall succeed the President; it has deliberately failed to provide for the determination of "inability." That vital question is still in the air—where the makers of the Constitution left it.

Probably no man was more disturbed by the Wilson crisis than Secretary of the Treasury Houston. He was in the thick of its perplexities, and knew how closely we came to trouble then, how unwise it is not to clarify such situations before prejudice, passion and personal desires control them. I quote from his "Eight Years in Wilson's Cabinet" as follows:

> "The problem presented by the illness of the President is one for the handling of which machinery ought to be created. The Cabinet is in good position to pass upon the government's exigencies, perhaps in better position than any other body, but, for various reasons, it is not the body that should be charged with the final determination of the inability of a President to discharge his duties.
>
> "The Congress also is not the proper body. It might be of different political complexion from the President and there might be situations in which partisanship would enter.
>
> "It would seem that either a Commission should be set up composed possibly of Supreme Court justices, members of the Cabinet, and members of Congress, to sit as a jury and to determine the matter, or the determination might be left to the Supreme Court.
>
> "But whatever may be the best machinery, it is clear that some machinery should be set up."

A STUBBORN FACT YET TO BE FACED

Of the four causes of vacancy in the Presidency listed in the Constitution only two are definitely operative. Death, of course, is an obvious fact and the Vice President automatically succeeds; so would be removal by impeachment. But to whom would a President resign? Would he merely walk out of the White House, and notify the Vice President? Law provides for the resignation of every other officer except the President and Vice President. Of course, resignation is a remote contingency, but since it is mentioned, a way to resign ought to be definitely provided. I know that Vice President Fairbanks was anxious to leave Washington on account of his wife's health. He attributed her death to the exactions of her social duties; he would gladly have resigned if he had had any precedents.

Twice, in the past fifty years, the President's "inability" has been a stubborn fact; the Vice President in both cases blinded himself, and the country "muddled through." It "muddled through" five electoral count disputes, simply because they did not affect the results. Then came the Hayes-Tilden controversy, and a serious situation developed,—so serious that neither party dared attempt settlement in Congress.

Garfield's case was so hopeless from the start that I doubt whether a declaration of "inability" by Vice President Arthur would have been contested, but Wilson's resentment of Lansing's activities is proof that Vice President Marshall would have had to lay siege to the White House, had he assumed the Presidency.

No wonder that John T. Morgan, of Alabama, who for years ranked as one of the leading men of the Senate, wrote of the "inability" and the electoral count under the heading "Some Dangerous Questions."

CHAPTER LXVIII

"FIGHTING BOB" LA FOLLETTE

The Czar Of His State And Spokesman For More Than 4,000,000 Voters In The Nation—He Had Much To Give The Country, But He Failed Because He Would Not Do Team Work—Hiram Johnson In California Won And Holds His State As La Follette Held Wisconsin.

THE death of Robert Marion La Follette in 1924 closed the career of the only man except Theodore Roosevelt able to lead more than 4,000,000 voters from their party affiliations into support of his candidacy for the Presidency. Speaking in terms of proportion I suppose that the bolt of the Democratic faction headed by Breckinridge in 1860 was greater than that headed by either Roosevelt or La Follette. It certainly proved to be of more significance to the nation, for it insured Lincoln's election and that result led to a quick decision by the South to seek separation.

Roosevelt's 4,125,000 votes represented a little more than 30 per cent of the total cast in 1912, while La Follette's 4,-800,000 votes, because of the increase caused by woman suffrage, represented a little less than 15 per cent of the total in 1924. La Follette secured the 13 electoral votes of his own State of Wisconsin—against Roosevelt's 88 from seven States.

That more than 4,000,000 voters would give their ballots to any man despite their knowledge that they could not elect him is a tribute no one may dispute; the recipient must be accepted even by his severest critics as the spokesman for a great many people.

And La Follette was such a spokesman. When he entered the Senate in 1905, he was the acknowledged dictator of

Wisconsin politics. He had been five years Governor, had
utterly demolished the old Republican organization machine,
had freed the Badger State government of corporation control
and had enacted legislation so distinctly in the public interest
that no one has ever sought to repeal it. He took the Wisconsin State University at Madison out of the deep ruts of tradition and made it an institution commanding the respect of the
nation.

HAD TO WIN OVER PREJUDICE

Philetus Sawyer, Isaac Stephenson and John C. Spooner had
been the spokesmen in the Senate of the old Wisconsin régime,
and the appearance there of a man known to the political
world only as "Fighting Bob" was as comforting to the
Aldrich-Gorman bi-partisan crowd as a bull in a china shop.

Like "Pitchfork" Tillman, of South Carolina, La Follette
when he took his place in the Senate, found the bars up against
men of his "extreme" views; also like Tillman his early
speeches were made to crowded galleries but empty Senate
seats. The two Senators had a common experience, however,
in soon being accepted as men who had to be heeded. Even
those who rarely voted with them paid them the compliment
of attention. A Senator who never supported a La Follette
proposition told me once that no Senator was so thoroughly
prepared on the subjects he debated as the Wisconsin Senator.

I doubt that it ever deeply concerned La Follette whether
his colleagues listened to him or not; the Senate was to him
merely the platform on which he stood. His appeal was to
those beyond the two-party machine that even now holds the
Senate in its grip, though not so firmly as in years past. He
thrived on defiance. On several occasions he held the floor
of the Senate for several days while filibustering against legislation. Never in strong health, he was tempting fate in such
trials of endurance, but he liked heroic rôles, full of dramatic
intensity, and he did not fear the consequences.

As I Know Them

NEVER A COMPROMISER

La Follette was "Fighting Bob" when at 26 he defied the party machine in Dane County, Wisconsin, and won nomination and election as District Attorney; he was "Fighting Bob" when in 1884 he had himself elected to Congress against the same machine influence; and he was still "Fighting Bob" in his final days when he held his own national convention at Cleveland, Ohio, and had himself nominated for President on his own platform. Throughout his career he had no mood for compromise. Unlike Bryan, he never abandoned an issue. Whatever else may be charged against him, he was not an opportunist. He believed strongly—never timidly or for the moment.

Moreover and again unlike Bryan, he loved good books and he did not care for wealth. He sought knowledge and power, not riches. Every thought, every act, was devoted to his advancement in politics; he wanted power—always power —and always power for himself; never power for himself and others. His beadlike, deep-seated eyes, small beardless face, high forehead and high pompadour hair accentuated in the minds of those who watched him from the Senate galleries the traits he was known to possess. He seemed an actor playing a part, but in truth he was always in earnest.

HAD MUCH TO GIVE PUBLIC SERVICE

Of all the members of the Senate during La Follette's three terms, I doubt whether there was one who in steadfastness and courage of conviction, in personal integrity and in comprehension of governmental needs had more to give to public service than he. And the pity of it is that aside from the Seaman's law that bears his name, he is credited with so little. Why? Simply because he lived in and for his own ambitions; unless he could be commander of the ship he preferred to scuttle it rather than share with others the glory of bringing it to port. There were potentialities in La Follette that would have meant a great deal in directing government toward helpful policies for the people, but his passion for control, for a leadership that meant in fact dictatorship, stood in the way of accomplishment.

La Follette was the most self-centred man I ever met in politics. His lieutenants feared him and he distrusted them. Teamwork was impossible for him. He tolerated no equals. Every man who joined with him in Wisconsin was conscious of a watchful and suspicious eye upon his every move. All lived politically in dread of him, for his power to ruin was absolute and he used it as ruthlessly as a pirate of old. Bryan was self-centred, too, but to no such extent as La Follette; and he did not use his power to make men fear him. Bryan had multitudes of friends—"they would die for me," was his proud boast often and often repeated; but there were none that even in his own mind La Follette believed "would die for him."

Yet the voters of Wisconsin stood by him solidly through the nearly 30 years that he reigned as czar of their politics—while Governor and while Senator. Irvine Lenroot managed to be elected Senator in the great Harding sweep of 1920 though La Follette opposed him, but with that exception Wisconsin knew but one master in politics, and La Follette was the man.

WISCONSIN BETTER FOR THE LA FOLLETTE REIGN

Judging it from afar, it has been a well-governed State—no scandals have reached the public, while a persistent, intelligent effort has been made to bring the benefits of government to all. Every now and then we hear critics sound the praises of autocratic government—a government in which one man directs all. Wisconsin has been used as an illustration. Primaries and elections there have been only a formality, for whatever La Follette decreed was accepted at the polls.

As I Knew Them

The State was a little empire in the political world with La Follette as its emperor.

We may not like to acknowledge it, but Wisconsin is better for having its La Follette than New York with its Tammany, Illinois with its Democratic and Republican machines and Pennsylvania with its Quays, Penroses and Vares.

California is another State that has benefitted by leadership away from old moorings. There Hiram Johnson has been Czar since 1908 when he routed the Southern Pacific crowd from control of the State government. Conditions had become intolerable—a man of courage and independence was needed—and Johnson came to the front. The "interests" are more powerful in California than in Wisconsin, and Johnson has had a hard battle to hold the State. Nevertheless he has done so, electing himself Senator twice and always naming his own candidate for Governor. With all their mistakes, with all their self-centred ambitions, Johnson and La Follette, each in his own way, stand out as justified protests against influences that surely were in defiance of the public interest.

LA FOLLETTE'S ONE AMBITION

From the moment La Follette entered the Senate, he had but one purpose—to be President. He undertook to make a career at Washington that would be recognized by the country as entirely his own. His support of the Republican Presidents from Roosevelt to Coolidge was always perfunctory; he had no real interest in any of them. He was careful to allow nothing to go on record from him that would stand in the way of an attack upon their policies whenever he desired.

In all his speeches in the Senate you will seldom find a line indorsing any Administration policy. For twenty years he stood on the side-lines of politics awaiting his opportunity as hungrily as a fox watches a hen-coop. Like a flash he looked upon the overthrow of a Republican Congress in 1910 as a call to him to rally the Republican party to his standard and against

As I Knew Them

Taft in 1912. When he found that Progressives turned to Roosevelt as their leader, his vindictiveness led him to help Taft to secure control of the Chicago convention. Though nominally, later, in the campaign he supported Taft, he gave his State to Wilson on election day. I say "gave" because it was then literally in La Follette's power to give Wisconsin's vote to any candidate he really desired.

In another chapter I have written of La Follette's course at that time. So long as he could not persuade the Republican party to accept him as its leader, he was determined to have it remain under the control of the reactionaries. By contrast, he could thus build up an organization of his own. And after 1912 that was his one purpose and hope—a sick man engaged in a race with death to satisfy something more intense than ambition—a consuming passion to be President.

The last time I spoke with him was just before his convention met in Cleveland in 1924. Speaking of his campaign he said: "I don't care what the newspapers print in their editorials about me, if I can keep in their news columns. Give me a fair show on the news pages and they can damn me to their hearts' content in their editorials. Now that we have the radio and can reach people through it, I think newspaper influence in politics is steadily lessening."

553

Index

Index

Index

559

Index

Index

Index

Index

563

Index

Index

O

O'Brien, C. F., 288
Ochiltree, Thomas, 114
O'Dwyer, 4
Oglesby, Richard, 32
Ohio, political leaders, 32
Olcott, Charles S., 255
Olney, Richard, 223 *et seq.*
O'Neill, Bucky, 302
"On the Beach at Long Branch," 66
"Onward, Christian Soldiers," 410
Orlando, Vittorio, 504
"Outline of History, The," H. G. Wells, 271
Outlook, 327, 392, 395, 397
Owen, Robert, 71
Oyster Bay, Roosevelt at, 307, 312, 341, 342, 356, 379, 391, 407, 444

P

Page, Walter Hines, 285, 511
Paine, Albert Bigelow, 138
Paine, Augustus G., 193
Pali Peak, Hawaii, 213
Palisades Park Commission, 423
Panama Canal, 265, 296
Parades, Decoration Day, 51
  McClellan, 48
Paris, 504 *et seq.*
Parker, Alton B., 281, 282
  money issue, on, 206
  telegram, historic, 56, 206
Parker, George F., 206
Parker, John N., 409
Parsons, Herbert, 334, 359, 380
Patronage, Political, 102, 112, 122, 177, 483
Payne, H. C., 247
Payne, Sereno E., 32
Payne-Aldrich Tariff Bill, 347
  dislike of, 374
Peace Conference, 504 *et seq.*
  "Big Four," the, 506, 511
  League of Nations in the, 505
Peffer, W. A., 201
Pemberton, John Clifford, 75
Pendleton, George H., 80
Pennsylvania, political leaders, 32, 405
Penrose, Boies, 460 *et seq.,* 552

Perkins, George W., 23, 249, 305, 319, 321, 392, 393, 397, 400, 407, 428, 460 *et seq.*
  idealism of, 425
  influence, political, 421 *et seq.*
  Munsey, friendship with, 422
  public office, refusal of, 425
  service of, public, 423
Phelps, William Walter, 158
Philippines, 71, 73, 251, 253
  freedom of, 280
  independence of, 526
  purchase of, 279
Pinchot, Gifford, 306, 379
Platt, Orville H., 32
Platt, Thomas C., 14, 32, 70, 160, 179, 248, 271
  enemies, and his, 257
  political power of, 168 *et seq.*
  resignation of, 113
Plumb, Preston B., 33
Pluralities, 94, 453
Police Strike, Boston, 466, 529
"Political Education of Woodrow Wilson, The," James Kerney, 512
Politicians, politics and, 6 *et seq.*
  types of, 29 *et seq.*
Politics, Blaine's place in, 93
  "bloody shirt" era, 98
  business in, 262
  Decalogue in, the, 194
  factional, 81, 85, 99, 122
  "ifs" in, 463 *et seq.,* 531
  leaders, 85
  machine, 120, 168, 442, 549
  mistakes costly, 135
  money and, 19, 22 *et seq.*
  Mugwumps in, 126, 149, 388
  party problems, 427
  patronage in, 102, 110, 112, 177
  politicians, and, 6 *et seq.*
  types of men in, 33
  (*see also* Politicians)
Polk, James K., 232
Populist Party, 201
  Cleveland deal with, 202
  growth of, 206
Porter, Horace, 257
Portland, Maine, 53
Porto Rico, 71, 73, 251, 253, 257
Prendergast, William A., 405
Presidency, candidates, 466
  vacancy in the, 546

Index

Index

Index

568

Index

Index

Index